Anastasiia Kudlenko

Security Governance in Times of Complexity
The EU and Security Sector Reform in the Western Balkans, 1991–2013

With a foreword by Professor Elena Korosteleva

BALKAN POLITICS AND SOCIETY

Edited by Jelena Dzankic and Soeren Keil

2   *James Riding*
    The Geopolitics of Memory
    A Journey to Bosnia
    ISBN 978-3-8382-1311-8

3   *Ian Bancroft*
    Dragon's Teeth
    Tales from North Kosovo
    ISBN 978-3-8382-1364-4

4   *Viktoria Potapkina*
    Nation Building in Contested States
    Comparative Insights from Kosovo, Transnistria, and Northern Cyprus
    ISBN 978-3-8382-1381-1

5   *Soeren Keil, Bernhard Stahl (eds.)*
    A New Eastern Question? Great Powers and the Post-Yugoslav States
    ISBN 978-3-8382-1375-0

6   *Senada Zatagic*
    A Neglected Right
    Prospects for the Protection of the Right to Be Elected in Bosnia and Herzegovina
    ISBN 978-3-8382-1521-1

7   *Aarif Abraham*
    A Constitution of the People and How to Achieve It
    What Bosnia and Britain Can Learn From Each Other
    ISBN 978-3-8382-1516-7

8   *Giustina Selvelli*
    The Alphabet of Discord
    The Ideologization of Writing Systems on the Balkans since the Breakup of Multiethnic Empires
    ISBN 978-3-8382-1537-2

Anastasiia Kudlenko

SECURITY GOVERNANCE IN TIMES OF COMPLEXITY

The EU and Security Sector Reform in the Western Balkans, 1991–2013

With a foreword by Professor Elena Korosteleva

Bibliografische Information der Deutschen Nationalbibliothek

Die Deutsche Nationalbibliothek verzeichnet diese Publikation in der Deutschen Nationalbibliografie; detaillierte bibliografische Daten sind im Internet über http://dnb.d-nb.de abrufbar.

Bibliographic information published by the Deutsche Nationalbibliothek

Die Deutsche Nationalbibliothek lists this publication in the Deutsche Nationalbibliografie; detailed bibliographic data are available in the Internet at http://dnb.d-nb.de.

ISBN-13: 978-3-8382-1720-8
© *ibidem*-Verlag, Stuttgart 2023
Alle Rechte vorbehalten

Das Werk einschließlich aller seiner Teile ist urheberrechtlich geschützt. Jede Verwertung außerhalb der engen Grenzen des Urheberrechtsgesetzes ist ohne Zustimmung des Verlages unzulässig und strafbar. Dies gilt insbesondere für Vervielfältigungen, Übersetzungen, Mikroverfilmungen und elektronische Speicherformen sowie die Einspeicherung und Verarbeitung in elektronischen Systemen.

All rights reserved. No part of this publication may be reproduced, stored in or introduced into a retrieval system, or transmitted, in any form, or by any means (electronic, mechanical, photocopying, recording or otherwise) without the prior written permission of the publisher. Any person who does any unauthorized act in relation to this publication may be liable to criminal prosecution and civil claims for damages.

Printed in the EU

This book is dedicated to my family:
Olha, Yurii and Bohdan Kudlenko,
and Callum and Andriy Donnan

Table of Contents

Foreword 11

Acknowledgements 13

List of Abbreviations 15

Chapter 1 Introduction 21
    Security governance through the lens of complexity 23
    Analysing the transformation of regional and state security in the Western Balkans: RSCT meets SSR 26
    Research puzzle and methodology 31
    Structure of the book 33
    Contribution to knowledge 34

Chapter 2 Security Dynamics of the Western Balkans in 1991–2013 37
    Introduction 37
    Studying the security dynamics of RSCs 38
    The Balkan Regional Security Subcomplex 41
    The transformation of security dynamics in the Western Balkans from 1991 to 2013 47
        From regional conflict formation to a failed attempt at security regime (1991-1999) 47
    Becoming part of the European security community (1999-2013) 56
    Why the EU? The role of external actors in shaping security patterns of the Western Balkans 63
    Conclusion 70

Chapter 3 The EU and Regional Application of SSR in the Western Balkans 75
    Introduction 75
    Security sector reform: the parameters of analysis 76

    The EU as an actor of security sector reform 80

    The EU's impact on the regional dimension of SSR in
    the Western Balkans 89

        Setting the scene: before the reform was possible (1991-
        1995) 90

        SSR for stabilisation and peacebuilding (1995-1999) 92

        SSR as a tool for building (future) member states
        (1999-2013) 95

    Conclusion 107

Chapter 4 Security Sector Reform in Croatia 113

    Introduction 113

    Croatia as a regional frontrunner in security sector
    reform 114

    The EU and Croatia's security in 1991–1995 119

    The EU's impact on Croatia's SSR in 1995–1999 125

    The EU's impact on SSR in Croatia in 1999-2013 131

        Political level 133

        Organisational level 143

    Conclusion 160

Chapter 5 Security Sector Reform in Serbia 167

    Introduction 167

    Security sector reform in Serbia: overcoming the legacy
    of the regional aggressor 169

    The EU and Serbian security in 1991-1995 179

    The EU's impact on SSR in Serbia in 1995-1999 184

    The EU's impact on SSR in Serbia in 1999-2013 190

        Political level 193

        Organisational level 204

    Conclusion 221

Chapter 6 Security Sector Reform in Bosnia and Herzegovina **231**
    Introduction 231
    Security sector reform in BiH: from the shadows of war to the challenges of state-building 233
    The EU and BiH security in 1991-1995 248
    The EU's impact on SSR in BiH in 1995-1999 253
    The EU's impact on SSR in BiH in 1999-2013 258
        Political level 261
        Organisational level 268
        Conclusion 288

Chapter 7 Conclusion **297**
    Comparative analysis of the EU's involvement in SSR in Croatia, Serbia and BiH 297
    Changes in the character of security interdependence in the Western Balkans and the EU's SSR efforts in 1991-2013 316
    Changing security landscape in the Western Balkans and security governance in times of complexity 324

Bibliography **329**

Annex I **377**

Annex II **381**

Notes **393**

Index **395**

Foreword

The book examines the evolution processes of security reforms in the Western Balkans as a whole and three states of the region — namely, in Croatia, Bosnia and Serbia — through the lens of their co-relationship with the European Union and the impact of both entities have on each other's development. The undisputed novelty of this work is that it approaches this co-evolutionary relationship from a complexity-thinking and resilience perspectives, a relatively novel approach to understanding security governance in a VUCA-world of today — the world of vulnerability, uncertainty, complexity and ambiguity.

Notably, in a rather pioneering effort Dr Kudlenko tackles security reforms in the region as a process of co-adaptation and transformation, where both sides interactively learn from each other, in a myriad of complex ways, by focusing on the processes, mechanisms, and relations that enable a situated learning in a continuously changing environment. Consequently, this approach offers a more nuanced understanding of the emergent risks, capacities and agents involved that govern the complex relations between different-level stakeholders in the process of system transformations. To this end, the book is unrivalled in its contribution to knowledge, theoretically, conceptually, and methodologically. It takes our understanding of security and vulnerabilities to the whole new level — by rendering it a processual, emergent, and responsive vision, in search for more sustainable and effective modes of interaction in times of complexity.

A must read for all students of politics, European studies and complexity!

Elena Korosteleva
Professor of Politics and Global Sustainable Development
Director, IGSD
University of Warwick

Acknowledgements

This book started as a PhD project and became possible thanks to the support and assistance of many people and institutions. First of all, I am thankful to Canterbury Christ Church University for providing me with a generous scholarship to conduct the initial stages of this research and to the PhD programme in Politics and International Relations for creating a friendly and stimulating environment for my professional development.

I am indebted to my PhD thesis supervisors, Dr Soeren Keil and Professor Amelia Hadfield for their advice and constructive criticism, which allowed me to refine the quality of my work and sharpen my argument. Professor Hadfield has helped me to grasp the importance of a robust research design early in the process, while Dr Keil has not only advised me on empirical and theoretical questions, pertaining to the dissertation, but also supported me through challenges of my academic journey. I am also grateful to my colleagues in the Graduate School who were always ready to provide a helping hand in times of need. In particular, I would like to thank Amina M'lili and the late Simon Bransden.

I am grateful to the University of Kent and the GCRF COMPASS Project, which not only helped me choose the lens of complexity for developing my manuscript, but also provided financial assistance to release it in open access. Having moved from Kent to the Institute for Global and Sustainable Development at the University of Warwick, I was able to continue learning from Professor Elena Korosteleva, whom I would like to thank for all her priceless guidance and positive encouragement.

An important element of the book is the interviews, conducted with security sector experts from Bosnia, Croatia and Serbia. I cannot name anyone due to the requirements of anonymity, but I thank each and every person who took their time either to help me find the relevant interviewees or agreed to speak to me and share their views on security sector reform in the Western Balkans and the role of the EU in the process.

Finally, I would like to thank my family, who continue to support and encourage me throughout my academic career, no matter what turbulence they go through themselves. I am eternally grateful to my parents, Yurii and Olha Kudlenko, for instilling in me a thirst for knowledge and helping me pursue my passions. To my mum, Olha, I want to thank you for showing me the true meaning of resilience, and to my dad, Yurii, I am grateful for teaching me the importance of history, the subject he dedicated his professional life to. To my brother, Bohdan, I thank you for always having my back. And I could not thank enough my husband, Callum Donnan, and my son, Andriy, who have been with me every step of the way, patiently giving me the time and space to work on my manuscript. I dedicate this book to my family with love.

List of Abbreviations

ABiH	Army of Bosnia-Herzegovina
ACA	Anti-Corruption Agency
AFBiH	Armed Forces of Bosnia and Herzegovina
APL	Anti-Personnel Landmines programmes
BCP	border control point
BIA	security information agency
BHMAC	Bosnia Herzegovina Mine Action Centre
CAF	Croatian Armed Forces
CAFAO	Customs and Fiscal Assistance Office
CARDS	Community Assistance for Reconstruction Development and Stabilisation
CEE	Central and Eastern Europe
CFSP	Common Foreign and Security Policy
CPA	Civil Protection Authority
CROMAC	Croatian mine action centre
CSCE	Conference on Security and Co-operation in Europe
CSDP	Common Security and Defence Policy
CSO	civil society organisation
DCAF	The Geneva Centre for the Democratic Control of Armed Forces
DDR	disarmament, demobilization and reintegration
DIPR	Directorate for Police Restructuring Implementation
DOS	Democratic Opposition of Serbia
DPA	Dayton Peace Agreement
DPS	Democratic Party of Socialists
DS	Democratic Party
DSS	Democratic Party of Serbia
EAR	European Agency for Reconstruction
EC	European Community or European Commission
ECMM	European Community Monitoring Mission
EDA	European Defence Agency
EEC	European Economic Community
EIDHR	European Initiative for Democratisation and Human Rights
EPC	European Political Cooperation

ESDP	European Security and Defence Policy
ESS	European Security Strategy
EU	European Union
EUAM	European Union Administration of Mostar
EUMM	European Union Monitoring Mission
EUPM	European Union Police Mission
EUSR	EU Special Representative
FBiH	Federation of Bosnia and Herzegovina
FRY	Federal Republic of Yugoslavia
FYROM	Former Yugoslav Republic of Macedonia
GFAP	General Framework Agreement for Peace in Bosnia and Herzegovina
HDZ	Croatian Democratic Union
HDZ BiH	Croatian Democratic Union of BiH
HNS	Croatian People's Party
HSLS	Croatian Social Liberal Party
HV	Croatian Army
HVO	Croatian Defence Council
IBM	integrated border management
ICTY	International Criminal Tribunal for the former Yugoslavia
IEBL	inter-entity boundary line
IFOR	Implementation Force
IfS	Instrument for Stability
ILECU	International Law Enforcement Coordination Unit
IPA	Instrument for Pre-Accession
IPA MB	Instrument for Pre-Accession Multi-Beneficiary assistance
IPTF	International Police Task Force
ISPA	Instrument for Structural Policies for Pre-Accession
ITA	Indirect Taxation Authority
ITF	International Trust Fund for Demining and Mine Victims
JCDS	Joint Committee on Defence and Security
JHA	Justice and Home Affairs
JNA	Yugoslav People's Army
JSO	Special Operations Unit
KLA	Kosovo Liberation Army

LPA	local policing area
LTDP	long-term development plan
MAP	Membership Action Plan
MARRI	Migration, Asylum, Refugees Regional Initiative
MEPE	Multi-Ethnic Police Element
MHRR BiH	Ministry of Human Rights and Refugees of Bosnia and Herzegovina
MIPD	Multi-Annual Indicative Planning Documents
MoD	Ministry of Defence
MoI	Ministry of the Interior
MoS	Ministry of Security
MP	member of Parliament
MTT	Mobile Training Team
NATO	North Atlantic Treaty Organization
NSC	National Security Council
OECD	Organisation for Economic Co-operation and Development
OECD DAC	Development Assistance Committee of the Organisation for Economic Co-operation and Development's
OSCE	Organization for Security and Co-operation in Europe
PfP	Partnership for Peace Programme
PIC	Peace Implementation Council
PRC	Police Restructuring Commission
RA	Regional Approach
RCC	Regional Cooperation Council
RCF	regional conflict formation
RDB	Serbian Security Service
RSC	regional security complex
RSCT	Regional Security Complex Theory
SAA	Stabilisation and Association Agreement
SAF	Serbian Armed Forces
SAJ	Special Police Anti-Terrorism Unit
SALW	small arms and light weapons
SAM	Sanctions Assistance Missions
SAP	Stabilisation and Association Process
SAPARD	Special Accession Programme for Agriculture and Rural Development
SBDI	South Balkans Development Initiative

SBS	State Border Service
SCG	State Union of Serbia and Montenegro
SCMM	Standing Committee on Military Matters
SDA	Bosniak Party of Democratic Action
SDP	Social-Democratic Party
SDR	Strategic Defence Review
SDS BiH	Serbian Democratic Party of BiH
SECI	Southeast European Cooperative Initiative
SEE	South Eastern Europe
SEECP	South East European Co-Operation Process
SEEI	South East Europe Initiative
SEESAC	South Eastern and Eastern Europe Clearinghouse for the Control of Small Arms and Light Weapons
SFOR	Stabilisation Force
SFRY	Socialist Federal Republic of Yugoslavia
SIPA	State Information and Protection Agency/ State Investigation and Protection Agency
SNS	Serbian Progressive Party
SP	Stability Pact
SPS	Socialist Party of Serbia
SRP	Serbian Radical Party
SSR	security sector reform
SVK	army of Serbian Krajina
UN	United Nations
UNDP	United Nations Development Programme
UNHCR	United Nations High Commissioner for Refugees
UNMAC	United Nations Mine Action Centre
UNMIBH	UN Mission in BiH
UNMIK	UN Interim Administration Mission in Kosovo
UNPROFOR	United Nations Protection Force
UNPSG	United Nations civilian police support group
UNTAES	United Nations Transitional Administration for Eastern Slavonia, Baranja and Western Sirmium
UPFM	Unified Police Force of Mostar
USKOK	Office for the Prevention of Corruption and Organised Crime
VBA	Military Security Agency
VRS	army of the Republika Srpska

VS	army of the State Union of Serbia and Montenegro
VSO	Supreme Defence Council
VJ	army of the FRY
WEU	Western European Union
WEUDAM	Western European Union Demining Mission
WEUPOL	Western European Union Police Force
ZERP	ecological and fishing protection zone
ZNG	Croatian National Guard

Chapter 1
Introduction

The relationship between the European Union (EU) and the Western Balkans, which comprises Albania, Bosnia and Herzegovina (hereinafter Bosnia or BiH), Croatia[1], Kosovo[2], North Macedonia[3], Montenegro and Serbia, has not followed a linear path. From the failure of the "hour of Europe" and barely visible Regional Approach in the early and mid-1990s to the highly anticipated Stability Pact[4], closely followed by the Stabilisation and Association Process in the early 2000s, and the stalling of the accession process for the states of the region after 2013, when Croatia joined the bloc, there have been many ups and downs. By the second decade of the 2000s, the upward trajectory of the regional transformation has been interrupted as tensions between states continued to simmer and reforms started to unravel. In addition to being non-liner, this relationship was also shared: through its engagement with the region and by responding to the risks, emanating from it, the EU developed a new toolbox, including Common Foreign and Security Policy (CFSP) and Common Security and Defence Policy (CSDP), which has influenced its standing as a security actor not only on the regional, but also global levels.

This book studies *the co-evolution of the EU and the Western Balkans in the security sphere* by analysing the impact of the bloc on security sector reform (SSR) in the region and three of its states: Croatia, Bosnia, and Serbia. It covers the period from 1991, which marks the break-up of Yugoslavia, to 2013, the year when the first, and, at the time of writing, only state of the region became a member state of the EU. It has become customary for researchers to focus on either the break-up of Yugoslavia and the period of violence that ensued (Malcolm 1994; Glenny 1996; Ramet 2006) or study the region as a developing security community (Keil and Stahl 2013; Stojanovic Gajic and Ejdus 2018). This means that attempts at the analysis of the full scale of security transformation in the region are rare. By studying the security situation in the region during the wars of the 1990s and over a decade of post-conflict stabilization, that culminated in Croatia, the reform frontrunner, joining the EU, the book aims to improve the understanding of the region's shift from war and enmity to more amicable cooperation and peace in the studied period and the slowing down of reform processes in the region after 2013. While the analysis in the main body of the book focuses on the period from 1991 to 2013, the conclusion additionally highlights challenges, experienced by regional security systems in 2022.

The analysis provided here also challenges the prevalent critical view of the EU's role in the development of the Western Balkans. Since the European Community failed to prevent violence in the region due to the lack of suitable instruments and unity among its members in the 1990s, the EU's efforts to bring stability and peace to the region are normally presented as inadequate or failed (Bassuener 2021), of course, with a few exceptions (Peen Rodt and Wolff 2012; Juncos 2013). In contrast, this work steps away from the success—failure dichotomy, and instead draws the readers' attention to the processes of adaptation to change and learning through practice, undertaken by the EU while promoting SSR in the region. This is achieved on the basis of complexity thinking, which frames the work, in order to assess the suitability and adaptability of EU security governance to a VUCA-world (Burrows and Gnad 2017), i.e. a world of increasing vulnerability, uncertainty, complexity and ambiguity—the world of transformative change.

In the centre of analysis is *security sector reform (SSR)*, which encapsulates the complexity of EU security governance. Not only is it pursued by multiple EU agencies and institutions that do not always coordinate their actions and is financed through a plethora of financial instruments, but it has also been developing intermittently through practice, by trial and error. The EU started engaging with the reform long before it was formulated as a policy area, and the Western Balkans in many respects acted as a laboratory for fine-tuning its vision of the reform. By using complexity thinking, the focus is shifted from the preoccupation with the effectiveness of the EU's efforts (the angle prevalent in the study of the reform) to the processes of adaptation to change, iterative learning and transformation, experienced by the bloc and the regional actors. This approach also offers an opportunity, through its emphasis on relationality and non-linearity, to investigate the *complex security transformation* of one of the most turbulent regions in Europe and *the evolution of the EU as a unique international and security actor*. Finally, it will show how SSR transformed from *a tool of stabilization and crisis management into the instrument of EU member state-building*.

Security governance through the lens of complexity

Complexity thinking is a cross-disciplinary field of research that asserts the ubiquity of change, uncertainty and self-governance (Mitchell 2009; Cillliers 2001; Kavalski 2009, 2015). From the perspective of complexity thinking, all social (and natural) systems are open, non-linear, and emergent. They "emerge, and are maintained, as a result of the dynamic and non-linear interactions of their elements, based on the information available to them locally both as a result of their interaction with their environment and from the modulated feedback they receive from the other elements in the system" (de Coning 2018: 305). Openness of complex systems suggests that relationships between their elements are more important than the elements themselves (Cilliers 2001), while non-linearity demonstrates the unpredictability of change as an input cannot necessarily be causally linked to an output in a system with a myriad of interactions between elements (Korosteleva and Petrova 2021: 3). Emergence refers to a system's ability to adapt to change and "move out of phase with themselves and become other than what they were" (Dillon 2007 in Kavalski 2009: 534). In other words, open systems self-organise into forms that cannot be anticipated from the knowledge of their parts. They co-evolve with their environment in a never-ending process of adaptation in order to cope with constant change (de Coning 2018: 305).

According to complexity thinking, the transformation of the security dynamics of the Western Balkans can be seen as an adaptation to the changing world through interactions between different states of the region and multiple external actors, engaged in peace- and state-building processes. It is therefore not possible to identify a single factor or a definitive number of factors responsible for the region's move from war to peace. Yet this is not what this book is trying to do. Instead, it sets out to analyse how security relations between the EU and the Western Balkans changed throughout the studied period to understand how they shaped the transformation of the region and the bloc. To capture these interactions, it is suggested here to employ the lens of complex security governance.

Security governance has been developing since the late 1980s in at least four ways: as a general theory, as a theory networks, as a system of inter- and transnational regimes and as a heuristic device for reconceptualising the problem of security management to accommodate different patterns of interstate interaction, the growing number of non-state actors, expansion of security agenda and the rising importance of conflict management and resolution (Kirchner and Sperling 2007: 18). It is the latter application that is further developed in complexity thinking and in this work. Outside of complexity thinking, security governance is understood as the "coordinated management and regulation of issues by multiple and separate authorities, the interventions of both public and private actors ... formal and informal arrangements, in turn structured by discourse and norms, and purposefully directed toward particular policy outcomes" (Webber et al 2004: 4). The focus here is on control (management and regulation) and policy outcomes. When approached from the perspective of complexity, these aspects of security governance are reconsidered, while state/non-state actors, a wide security agenda, not restricted by military affairs but embracing "new" security threats, such as terrorism, formal/informal relations and the attention to discourse and norms are preserved. Based on Kavalski's (2009) summary of complexity in security studies, *complex security governance* can be defined as a process of dealing with security issues in the context of *uncertainty, cognitive challenges, complex risks,* and constant *adaptability* to changing environment.

The framework of complex security governance offers a new way of analysing how the EU as a complex security actor that is composed of multiple agencies, which apply diverse policy tools, attempts to influence security issues outside its borders. Unlike traditional approaches, preoccupied with problem-solving, *complex security governance* prioritises the focus on *processes, mechanisms and constructs* that enable adaptive learning in the complex and constantly changing environment. It questions rigid management and coordination of security, while recognising the importance of change.

The prevalence of uncertainty means unpredictability of the future. It demands from those employing security governance in the context of complexity to be flexible and ready for change. From this perspective, changes of EU policies towards the Western Balkans are seen not as a failure, but a necessity. In a similar vein, uncertainty and a complex mesh of relations that exist between and inside systems mean the impossibility of understanding global life or a regional security situation, that is studied here, in full, imposing cognitive constraints on policymakers as well as researchers. Thus, policymakers, whether inside a region or outside of it can have limited knowledge of a situation they are dealing with, insufficient data and/or inability to establish a cause behind it (Whitman 2005). The recognition of existing cognitive constraints points to the importance of a temporal dimension in the studies of complex security governance. That is why the analysis of the EU – Western Balkan relations takes into account the time of developments as well as the space, where they occurred.

The complexity of risks is also an important consideration in the process of security governance. Risks are not seen as something unusual from this perspective: they are an integral part of life, a part, which cannot be controlled as they emerge through the interaction of specific time and space contexts. It is another reason to pay attention to both temporality and spatiality when dealing with security governance. Finally, to cope with complex risks, complex systems need to constantly adapt to change, undergo constant transformations. Security governance's task is not to eradicate risks, which would be impossible, but to mitigate them, make them less disruptive (Kavalski 2009: 545). Complex security governance is therefore about constant transformation of all actors involved in the process and their co-evolution.

Security governance of complexity, when used as a heuristic device, as well as in its traditional reading, is pre-theoretical (Kirchner and Sperling 2007: 18). This means that to capture the evolution of the security situation in the Western Balkans and better understand the role of the EU in the process, there is a need to link the discussion to a theoretical framework that would be able to accommodate different levels of analysis (international, regional and state), deal with non-state and state actors, while taking into account a new security agenda, dealing with a variety of security risks and threats. Such a framework is provided by Regional Security Complex Theory (RSCT). The theory gives the language to talk about security interdependence and, simultaneously, provides tools to investigate the processes of formation, evolution and decline of regions in practice.

Analysing the transformation of regional and state security in the Western Balkans: RSCT meets SSR

The book argues that between 1991 and 2013 the character of security interdependence between the Western Balkan states changed from negative to positive, and that the EU was one of the key actors behind this change, while also evolving in the process. To explain the processes of transformation, which as was described above are of key importance for complex security governance, the work turns to RSCT as a comprehensive framework for analysing regional development from the security point of view. The theory was created to bridge the gap between the state and system levels of analysis, as neither of them could capture the complex nature of security (Buzan 2007: 159).

The central concept of RSCT is a regional security complex, which is defined as "a set of units whose major processes of securitisation[5], desecuritisation, or both are so interlinked that their security problems cannot reasonably be analysed or resolved apart from one another" (Buzan, Waever and de Wilde 1998: 201). Regions in RSCT are seen through the prism of security interdependence and geographical adjacency. To qualify as a regional security complex, simple proximity is not enough: the intensity of interdependence and network of relations between the units inside the region should be relatively stronger than the intensity of their relations with the outside world.

RSCT has been chosen for this study for four reasons. First, it has a relational character, which is of utmost importance for complexity thinking. While Buzan and Waever highlight the regional level as almost always operational and significant, they also differentiate other levels at which security relations can occur, namely: domestic, interregional and global (2003: 51). This work investigates three of the four levels. The domestic level, which studies the situation inside states, is applied to the case studies of Croatia, Serbia and Bosnia. The examination of local contexts is used to gauge the extent to which externally promoted security sector reforms were internalised and determine the influence of domestic developments on the security dynamic of the region. State-to-state relations between the Western Balkan countries in the security sector are analysed as part of the regional level of analysis, while interregional interactions are omitted from the analysis. Finally, the global level considers the impact of global actors engaged in the region, which, using the RSCT terminology, are represented by one superpower, the USA, and two great powers, Russia and the EU. Special attention is paid to the EU, although the roles of Russia and the USA are also assessed, the same as cooperation between the global actors. Two remaining great powers, Japan and China, are mostly omitted from the analysis due to the limited engagement with the region during the studied period. Interestingly enough, China's role grew considerably in the 2000s, outside of the studied period. Additionally, the role of Turkey in the region is also covered. Turkey is classified here as an insulator[6], not a global power. By choosing a theory which sees security as a relational phenomenon, the intention is to capture the interaction of all levels of analysis, without overestimating the role of any single one of them.

Second, RSCT offers a framework for studying the interrelation of external and internal factors in the development of security sectors. The Western Balkans is heavily dependent on external leverage, which since the start of the 21st century has been mostly associated with the EU, though in the early and mid-1990s was predominantly exercised by the USA and NATO. The recognition of the external impetus, however important, led to the establishment of certain bias in studies of the region, which overwhelmingly tend to treat it as a passive recipient of policies from the outside (Keil and Stahl 2014). RSCT manages to overcome this bias by emphasising the mutual character of security relations. According to RSCT, actors on all levels of the security hierarchy can influence each other. Thus, external impact coming from the global level can exacerbate rivalries existing on the regional level, while a domestic situation in a country can influence the external response to it (Buzan 2007: 183). Even more, the theory consistently directs the attention of researchers towards lower levels of analysis. There is little doubt in the significance of external push for the transformation of the security dynamics in the Western Balkans, yet this push should not be overemphasised. It is time the local context of the region was given more attention.

Combining RSCT with complexity thinking, it is important to highlight that the region as a whole, each of the three states, chosen as case studies, and the European Union are seen as open systems interacting with each other. The EU is studied here as a single actor rather than a collection of institutions and/or member states. The notion of the EU as a unitary actor on the international arena was first introduced by Sjøstedt (1977) and over the years developed by many other scholars, including Hill (1993), Ginsberg (1999) and Bretherton and Vogler (2005). There have also been attempts to study the engagement of the EU in foreign affairs from the point of view of its member states, whose number increased from 12 to 28[7] in the studied period, or through the constantly evolving infrastructure of its institutions (Wessels, Maurer and Mittag 2003; Juncos 2013). While recognising the evolution of the EU's foreign and security policies and the importance of individual member states in shaping the EU's response to the situation in the Western Balkans between 1991 and 2013, the EU is treated as a single actor since the focus here is on analysing the impact of the EU's SSR policy and not approaches of separate agencies. This approach serves a two-fold purpose. On the one hand, it offers an opportunity to study EU actorness in the security arena. On the other, it links the transformation of the security dynamics in the Western Balkans and emergence of an embryonic security community in the region to the process of European integration.

The third reason for choosing RSCT is linked with its vision of regions as dynamic constructs or as Buzan called them "action-reaction phenomena" (2007: 173). Regions or regional security complexes, according to the theory, are durable systems that are susceptible to change. As mentioned above, there is a tendency to focus on either side of the transformation of the Western Balkans: either describing the region as turbulent and made of weak and failed states (Rozen 2001) or hailing the successful leap towards stability and security (Kavalski 2008). This could be explained by limitations of approaches applied by researchers, which RSCT has the potential to overcome. It distinguishes three stages in the development of a security complex (four, including chaos), ranging from a *conflict formation* through *security regime* to *security community* (Buzan 2007: 180). These stages can also be seen as forms of security governance (Kirchner and Sperling 2007). Yet given the prevalence of interest in peacebuilding processes in the region, so far, more attention has been given to the emergence of security community there, while in this work two other forms of security governance are studied, too.

Finally, RSCT has been chosen due to its flexibility and the use of a thin, open analytical framework that allows "to catch security in its increasing variation—across levels, sectors, and diverse units" (Buzan 2007: 71). Although the theory differentiates between different levels of analysis and stages in the development of regional security complexes, it does not prescribe a rigid methodology necessary for the study of security issues. On the contrary, RSCT creates an opportunity for establishing theory-based scenarios, adjusted to the specifics of any region in the world (ibid.: 45), encouraging scholars to employ an inductive approach and giving them freedom to identify the unique factors explaining the development of separate RSCs and their main components. Here, security sector reform was chosen to examine the changes of security interdependence inside the Western Balkans, which can also be labelled as

Balkan subcomplex. *SSR that promotes effective management, transparency and accountability of security actors* reduces the focus of research to the transformation of security sectors.

Security sectors are at the core of different forms of security governance. They do not function in the same way, but their activity is equally important for the emergence and development of regional conflict formations (RCFs), security regimes and security communities. This is not to suggest that regions can be reduced to security relations alone, but to emphasise the fact that the latter determine the character of security interdependence. In RCFs, security institutions are often involved in fuelling hostilities between states and can even pose a direct threat to communities they are supposed to be protecting. Similarly, security structures could pose a latent threat by failing to protect borders or regulate economic activity (Hendrickson and Karkoszka 2002: 183). Security sectors in RCFs are also likely to be highly autonomous and carry disproportionately heavy political weight. The lack of transparency and accountability in the work of security forces means they cannot be trusted by security institutions from other states. They can be described as repressive, undemocratic, bloated and poorly structured (Short 2010: 11), or simply dysfunctional structures (Hänggi and Tanner 2005: 16). In security regimes, where war between members is still feared and prepared for, but considered unlikely, security institutions promote reciprocity. They keep member states accountable and contribute to the spread of a cooperative rather than competitive atmosphere inside regimes (Wallander, Haftendorn and Keohane 1999: 3). Here, security forces are governed more democratically and transparently than in RCFs and are under civilian control. The improvement, compared to RCFs, is considerable, but is still not as significant as in security communities. There, security sectors, as was noted by Adler and Barnett (1998), promote trust. They provide effective, accountable and legitimate security to citizens inside the community. It is not simply the security of states, they are responsible for, but also the security of individuals. Human security is at the heart of their work. Security forces in members of a security community, or more precisely in their mature types, enjoy the trust of the public and of other members of the community.

As can be seen, there are big differences in the functioning and governance of security sectors inside different RSCs, although nominally their role remains the same. It is argued here that tracing these changes can offer valuable insights into understanding the EU's security governance of threats and risks in the Western Balkans on the regional and state levels and how the bloc's engagement in the reform influenced its own position as a security actor. It can be objected, of course, that security sectors are meant to provide security to separate states and their citizens, not regions. The response to this objection can be found in the *relational character* of security as a concept. Security does not exist in a vacuum and a security sector of a state is likely to engage with the security sector of another state. The work of security sectors thus has importance on the domestic level as well as on regional and international levels (Hendrickson and Karkoszka 2002: 200; Ball 2010: 41). It should also be emphasised that security sectors are investigated in this work not as static structures, but as dynamic constructs which can transform and develop under the influence of both domestic and external actors, i.e. they are studied through the concept of security sector reform.

Research puzzle and methodology

The analysis that follows is guided by the question: *"How did the EU's engagement with SSR in the Western Balkans affect the security dynamics of the region and the bloc's evolution as a security actor?"* To find the answer, four additional questions are investigated:

- How did the security situation in the Western Balkan change between 1991 and 2013?
- What constitutes the EU's approach to SSR?
- How was this approach implemented in the Western Balkans on the regional level? And
- What factors explain discrepancies between the results, achieved by the EU in SSR in Croatia, Serbia and BiH?

It is argued here that the EU's governance of security risks and threats in the Western Balkans, that actualised through its engagement with SSR on regional and state levels, contributed to the shift of security dynamics of the region, from animosity to amity, while simultaneously strengthening the bloc's position as an international security actor. EU SSR efforts offered many learning opportunities to the bloc, yet produced varying results in the three case studies due to the presence of war legacy, varying degrees of state consolidation of individual Western Balkan states, proximity of the EU's membership promise and involvement of other external actors.

The objective of this research is three-fold: to analyse the transformation of the security situation in the Western Balkans between 1991 and 2013, to evaluate the role of the EU in the process by studying its SSR efforts and to explain differences in the security dynamics among individual Western Balkan states. To achieve these objectives, the book applies three research methods: process tracing, case study and comparative case studies. Process tracing is used to trace the evolution of the Western Balkans from a regional conflict formation to an emerging part of the European zone of peace or the EU/Europe security community. It also helps to understand the evolution of the EU's SSR approach and its application to the region. This method is a powerful "analytical tool for drawing descriptive and causal inferences from diagnostic pieces of evidence — often understood as part of a temporal sequence of events or phenomena" (Collier 2011: 824). It is used to examine the key events that took place in the Western Balkans in 1991-2013, such as the wars of Yugoslavia's dissolution, NATO's intervention, signing of the Dayton Agreement, the Kosovo conflict and launch of the Stabilisation and Association Process, and analyse their impact on the development of the security situation in the region. Additionally, this method ensures that temporal elements are taken into account alongside spatiality, underlined by RSCT.

The case study approach is applied to study the EU's impact on SSR in Croatia, Serbia and Bosnia. Relying on Gerring's definition of a case study as an intensive inquiry into "a single case for the purpose of understanding a larger class of cases" (2012), it is used to investigate the influence of the EU on security sector reforms in Croatia, Serbia and BiH to better understand the bloc's role in changes of the regional security situation. The three case studies represent states that used to be part of Yugoslavia, went through violent wars and stabilised under the influence of the international community. Nonetheless, the transformation of their security sectors is not identical, and the EU's SSR efforts achieved varying results. Each of the case studies includes the analysis of three elements of SSR – defence, police and border reforms, and traces two levels of the reform – political and organisational[8] – during three periods, identified with the help of RSCT. Such an approach ensures the possibility of using the comparative case study method in the conclusion of the book to compare the EU's SSR efforts in the three Western Balkan states and identify factors explaining the discrepancies in the results achieved. It follows the method of structured, focused comparison developed by Alexander George (1979; George and McKeown 1985; George and Bennet 2005). With the help of rich data and the in-depth analysis of the within-case variance of the EU's SSR policies that developed considerably over the studied period, the research is designed in a way that could be replicated to study the impact of the EU's security policies in many other contexts.

Data for the analysis was obtained from diverse primary and secondary sources, including official documents, contemporary accounts of Yugoslav wars, scholarly articles, monographs as well as 25 elite interviews[9], conducted in the region in 2016 and 2021.

Structure of the book

The book consists of seven chapters. Chapter 2 provides a brief overview of the key concepts of RSCT, before delving into the discussion of changes in the security situation in the Western Balkans between 1991 and 2013. It finishes with the analysis of the role of the EU in the process, compared to other international security actors. Chapter 3 analyses SSR concept as understood and developed by the EU. It provides a comprehensive summary of the EU's SSR framework and argues that it has mainly been developed through practice. Having defined the EU's approach to SSR, the chapter examines its implementation in the Western Balkans on the regional level, identifying the goals and results it achieved by 2013.

Chapters 4, 5 and 6 study the application of the EU's SSR framework in Croatia, Serbia and Bosnia respectively. SSR in each state and the impact of the EU on it are explored within three periods: 1991-1995, 1995-1999 and 1999-2013. While some observations are made about the similarities and differences of the EU approach to the three countries, the comparison of case studies is reserved for the final chapter.

The concluding chapter serves three purposes. First, it compares the EU's SSR policies in Croatia, Serbia and BiH, by analysing differences and similarities in the EU approaches to the three countries and the results they achieved. Second, it summarises findings on the EU's use of SSR to bring peace to the Western Balkans and its role in changing the character of security interdependence in the region. Finally, it looks at how the EU's engagement with the reform in the region is emblematic of the EU's evolution as a security actor and how it can be used to improve our understanding of EU security governance in times of complexity.

Contribution to knowledge

This book intends to contribute to the creation of new knowledge theoretically, conceptually, and empirically. On the *theoretical level*, it contributes to the emerging discussion of adaptive governance in the complex world (Chandler 2018). Despite discussions on the complexity of security governance gaining clout on the global level (Kavalski 2009, 2015), they are still rare on the EU level. This gap is addressed by applying complexity thinking to Reginal Security Complex Theory, used in the book to trace the complex security relationship between the EU and the Western Balkans (both on the regional and state levels). Relying on this lens, it offers new theoretical insights on determining the boundaries of regional security (sub)complexes (Cilliers 2001) and identifying temporality as an additional component for understanding the transformation of security dynamics, alongside RSCT's territoriality (Kavalski 2009).

INTRODUCTION 35

Conceptually, this work develops security sector reform beyond its traditional understanding as a tool of peace- and state-building (Jackson 2011) by connecting it to the process of EU member state-building (Keil and Arkan 2015). It highlights how the understanding of the reform has changed, with the EU shifting focus to using SSR not only to prepare the Western Balkan states for membership in the bloc, i.e. a tool of member state-building, but also to encourage the regional players take ownership of their security development, adapting SSR as a mechanism of resilience building. Resilience as self-governance forms an integral part of complexity and is often linked to the level of an individual or community (Korosteleva 2020). It can also be studied through the prism of institutions, in this case — security institutions, linked to "defining functions" of the state (Rose 1976). Security institutions, through their nature and ability to absorb external shocks, are shown here to contribute to the adaptive capacity of societal systems (Joseph 2018: 13).

Finally, *empirically*, a long view is taken on the transformation of regional and state security in the Western Balkans from 1991 to 2013, on the one hand, and the evolution of the EU as a security actor, on the other.

---

1   It has become customary to leave Croatia out since it joined the bloc in 2013. However, as the focus of the study is on the period from 1991-2013, it is considered here as a Western Balkan state.
2   This designation is without prejudice to positions on status and is in line with UNSCR 1244 and the ICJ Opinion on the Kosovo Declaration of Independence.
3   Throughout most of the studied period, North Macedonia was known as the Former Yugoslav Republic of Macedonia (FYROM). In the work, both titles are used.
4   The Stability Pact was initiated by the Germany's EU Presidency yet was not owned by the EU. For more on the initiative, see Chapter 2.
5   The concept of securitisation, developed by the Copenhagen School, denotes the process of making something a security issue. For more, see Bourne (2014: 52-57).
6   An insulator, according to RSCT, refers to "a location occupied by one or more entities where larger regional security dynamics stand back-to-back" (Buzan and Waever 2003: 41).
7   Going down to 27 as the result of the UK's departure.
8   The meaning of each is explained in Chapter 3.
9   Interviewees included high-ranking local security personnel, experts from NGOs with experience in SSR and representatives of the EU, NATO and OSCE

working on SSR in Croatia, Serbia and BiH. Due to the sensitivity of the topic, all interviews were anonymised. In 2016, interviews were conducted in states of the region, while in 2021, due to COVID-19, online.

Chapter 2
Security Dynamics of the Western Balkans in 1991–2013

Introduction

This chapter introduces key concepts of Regional Security Complex Theory (RSCT) and applies them to the case of the Western Balkans. Thanks to complex security governance, two innovations are introduced to the theory: concerning the understanding of boundaries of regional security complexes (RSC) and the inclusion of temporality alongside territoriality, emphasised by RSCT.

The Western Balkans is defined as a subcomplex within the European regional security complex (RSC) and its development is studied throughout the book through three periods. The analysis of the first two periods, i.e. 1991–1995 and 1995–1999, shows the region to be governed by predominantly negative patterns of security interdependence, except for several post-conflict years, when the international community focused on its stabilisation. Here, the focus is on the impact of the wars of Yugoslavia's dissolution on the regional security situation and an attempt by external actors to change negative security relations after the end of fighting with a number of regional policies, which are understood as an attempt to transform a regional conflict formation (RCF) into a security regime. The transformation, supported *inter alia* by the Dayton Peace Accords (DPA) and the EU's Regional Approach, did not take hold, and the incipient security regime disintegrated with the outbreak of the war in Kosovo. By contrast, the period from 1999 to 2013 is presented as the time of predominantly positive security dynamics in the Western Balkans, the time when the subcomplex becomes more stable and secure and develops the characteristics of an embryonic security community. This security community, however, is not self-sustaining, but a fragment of the European RSC. The Stability Pact[10] (SP) and Stabilisation and Association Process (SAP) are to be given here special attention to show how the EU's policies towards the Western Balkans have become more proactive and comprehensive.

As mentioned before, the book recognizes the importance of external factors in the transformation of the Western Balkans and aims to improve the understanding of the EU's role in the process. These issues are discussed in the final part of the chapter. Here, the discussion focuses on the USA, NATO and the EU as the key players in the area, and on the UN, OSCE, Russia and Turkey as actors playing supplementary roles. This section also clarifies why the EU is currently the most important actor in the region and why neither NATO nor the US qualify for this role, despite leading the external effort in the Western Balkans for most of the 1990s. It is also argued that the Western Balkans is exceptionally well-placed to study the credentials of the EU as a security actor. This is not only because the EU developed a set of security tools in response to the Balkan conflicts of the 1990s, but also because it tested the application of many of them for the first time in the Western Balkan states.

Studying the security dynamics of RSCs

According to RSCT, each security complex has a distinctive indigenous security dynamic, which is formed under the influence of distributions of power and relations of amity and enmity inside the region. Having introduced the patterns of amity and enmity, RSCT has gained an important advantage over other approaches, also trying to explain security in the regional context, but doing so only on the basis of polarity[11]. The patterns of amity and enmity, representing two extremes of the interdependence spectrum, with neutrality and indifference in-between, can give a clearer idea of the relational patterns observed between different states or units of the region, and even more, between different regions and different levels of analysis (Buzan 2007: 160). This is because patterns of amity and enmity are more durable, or "stickier" and more easily traceable than fluid and abstract movement of the distribution of power (ibid.). The character of interdependence, which can be positive, i.e. reflected in friendship and shared interests, or negative, represented through fear and rivalry, is usually determined by a mixture of factors, such as history, culture, religion, ideology or legacy of wars as well as many others (Buzan and Waever 2003: 48). Here, it is studied on the example of security sector reform.

It is important to stress that defining regions based on patterns of amity and enmity does not make them imagined or purely discursive constructs. Security complexes are real, socially constructed regions, which comprise a set of units (usually states) linked by patterns of polarity and interdependence, located in geographical proximity to each other. Most threats tend to travel faster over short distances, that is why adjacent states often find themselves interlocked in nodes of security interactions with their neighbours (Buzan and Waever 2003: 45). If these interactions have a durable nature and security interdependence between neighbouring states is mutual, they can then form a security complex.

Despite emphasising the importance of geographical proximity, RSCT can also account for external influences on security complexes, which can transcend borders and distances. This power is only accessible to global actors, which, thanks to their capabilities and the anarchic nature of the international system, are not restrained by territoriality and can interfere in security relations of any region in the world, regardless of its location. The USA and Russia, for example, representing a superpower and great power respectively, can influence the security dynamics of the Western Balkans, without being inside of the region. Their impact is exercised through the mechanism of penetration. Furthermore, geography is not equally influential across all security sectors: it is most potent in political, military, societal and environmental areas and least obvious when it comes to dealing, for example, with economic issues (Buzan and Waever 2003: 45). These caveats notwithstanding, the issue of territoriality remains one of the central ideas in the theory. On the one hand, it binds together the security dynamics of units, allowing for the inclusion into the analysis of non-state actors, such as the EU, and states whose sovereignty is either contested or dependent on external support, e.g., Kosovo and BiH in the Western Balkans. On the other, it gives a certain order to the map of the world by dividing it into mutually exclusive complexes with distinctive security interdependences.

From the point of view of complexity, the division of the world into mutually exclusive regions is problematic, given that all complex systems are open. Yet, it is only so if boundaries of regions or RSCs are considered to be rigid or set in stone, which they are not. As discussed above, RSCs are durable but dynamic: they change, transform, and evolve, and these changes often concern boundaries. Complexity thinking offers a new understanding of boundaries: they are no longer seen as constraining, as separating one thing from another, e.g., one region from another, but as uniting elements that are closely interconnected by a network of relations, as bringing together components of a system, or in the case of the Western Balkans, states of the region. Following Cilliers (2001), a boundary is understood as "something that constitutes that which is bounded" and "something enabling rather than confining".

Another innovation introduced here into the reading of RSCT from complexity thinking concerns temporality. The relations of interdependence between members of the same RSC do not simply occur on a certain territory, they also have a temporal dimension. This dimension, however, is missing from the theoretical observations, developed by Buzan and colleagues or at least not explicitly acknowledged. According to complex security governance, territoriality cannot be divorced from temporality, which Kavalski (2009) captures with the concept of "timescapes". In what follows, both elements of these timescapes are analysed to get a better understanding of the changes in the regional security dynamics and the role of the EU in the process. That is why key events, such as the signing of the Dayton Peace Agreement or the war in Kosovo are given special attention.

To understand these changes, the book turns to the typology of RSCs on the basis of their position on the spectrum of amity and enmity[12], dividing them into regional conflict formations, security regimes and security communities[13]. Regional conflict formations represent regional complexes dominated by conflict and war, which can also be inclusive of singular occurrences of amity among units of the complex. Security regimes can be described as regions, whose members cooperate between each other on security-related issues to avoid war and confrontation by attempts to mute the security dilemma on the basis of their actions and assumptions about the actions of others (Buzan 2007: 180). Security community is an amity-based regional complex, in which relations between members are cooperative and friendly to such an extent that no unit of the complex fears or prepares for war. This typology is well-positioned for the analysis of transformations in security situations of RSCs and units inside them. By placing RSCs on the spectrum of security interdependence, it offers a framework for the study of changes in their security dynamics. It is especially useful for researching regions, whose security dynamics changed significantly either from the negative pole of enmity to the positive pole of amity, or vice versa. That is why this is the typology applied in this book to explain the transformation of the security situation in the Western Balkans. It is argued here that between 1991 and 2013 the Western Balkans, under the influence of the international community, transformed from a region with overwhelmingly negative patterns of interdependence to an emerging part of the EU/Europe security community.

Overall, RSCT offers a comprehensive framework for analysing regional security, which apart from distinguishing regions or regional security complexes, also pays attention to other levels of analysis.

The Balkan Regional Security Subcomplex

In their seminal work "Regions and Powers", Buzan and Waever (2003) used the Balkans as an example of a regional security subcomplex. Like an RSC, a subcomplex represents a group of units, whose security situations are closely interconnected, yet in contrast to an RSC, a subcomplex forms a part of a larger complex, outside the context of which it cannot be understood (ibid.: 378). This section will demonstrate that the security dynamics of the Western Balkan states are highly interdependent, while the region is also connected to the EU, thus qualifying as a subcomplex inside the European RSC.

The analysis of the Balkan subcomplex is provided here through the exploration of its essential structure, which, the same as in the case of a fully-fledged RSC, includes a boundary, anarchic structure, and patterns of polarity and enmity/amity. It should be noted that the complexity of the region's development is not always easy to capture through the application of theoretical provisions and that is why the investigation of the Western Balkans offered in this work should not be considered as the only possible interpretation of RSCT's approach to the region. Another note of caution should be added about the used terminology. The book, following Buzan, uses the term "Balkan subcomplex", although it argues that the boundary of the subcomplex from 1991 to 2013 mostly coincided with the territory now referred to as the Western Balkans, while the borders of the region fluctuated and were often blurred. It is believed here that there is no need to use another term for the subcomplex, because, first, its borders are susceptible to change, and second, the preservation of the original term ensures the continuity of research.

Defining the boundary makes a logical starting point for the analysis of any RSC or regional security subcomplex, yet in the case of the Balkan subcomplex it is not a straightforward task. One of the main reasons for this is the absence of agreement on what constitutes the Balkans as such. The region has varying definitions not only from the cultural and historical points of view, but also in terms of geography (Todorova 1997: 161). Traditionally the Balkans is said to comprise Albania, Bosnia and Herzegovina, Bulgaria, Croatia, Kosovo, North Macedonia, Montenegro, Romania, Serbia and Slovenia[14]. Greece and Turkey (at least the European part of the latter) are often mentioned, too. The list, however, is not fixed, and the negative connotation of the term "Balkan" prompts states of the region to seek other labels for self-identification (Koneska 2007).

With the beginning of the wars of Yugoslavia's dissolution in 1991[15], violence was predicted to spread around the whole Balkan Peninsula. In the early 1990s it became popular to depict the Balkans as an inherently unstable territory, different from Europe, and characterised by "ancient hatreds and age-old animosities" (Gledhill and King 2010: 245). The accounts, such as the one produced by Robert Kaplan in "Balkan Ghosts" explained the Yugoslav wars of the 1990s "as a product of the social enmities of a "time-capsule world", a land in which communities have "raged [and] spilled blood" for centuries" (Kaplan 2005 quoted in Gledhill and King 2010: 245). The ominous predictions about all the Balkan states plunging into ethnic violence, however, did not come true. The violence, conflicts and political upheavals were mainly concentrated in what is now known as the Western Balkans, although they did affect the broader region. Nonetheless, this effect was not strong enough to turn all the Balkan countries into a separate regional conflict formation.

The Balkans, not only in the 1990s, but already after World War II, represented a heterogeneous group (Todorova 1997: 140). Failure to recognise this heterogeneity is one of the possible explanations for entrenching the view on the Balkans as a backward region, suffering from endemic violence.[16] During the first half of the 20th century, the Balkans functioned within three political frameworks, divided by "the Cold-War line" (ibid: 162). Greece, having escaped the Soviet Union's communist sweep, together with Turkey aligned themselves with the Western powers; Bulgaria and Romania, although the latter to a lesser extent, were included into the orbit of the USSR's influence as members of the Eastern Block, while Yugoslavia and Albania pursued a neutral path, which in Albania's case took the form of isolationism. The division of the region was not necessarily conspicuous because the security interdependences during the Cold War were overlaid by the superpower rivalry. Countries in the Eastern Bloc had their security dynamics subordinated to that of the Soviet Union, while the rest of Europe's security relations was overlaid by the United States. Like other non-aligned countries, Yugoslavia and Albania, which chose the path of neutrality in 1948 and 1961 respectively, despite having communist governments, still had their security dynamics overlaid as their major security concerns were defined externally.

When the Cold War ended, and the overlay was lifted, there was a big temptation in policy circles and academia to lump all Balkan states together into one region (Lampe 2006: 266-267). Such scenario would not be at all impossible because the states emerging from overlay are seen likely to develop different patterns of security interdependence to those they displayed before overlay was imposed (Buzan and Waever 2003: 63-64). Had the wars of the Yugoslavia's dissolution had an overpowering effect on the wider region, spilling violence outside Yugoslav states, the Balkan subcomplex could have developed into the Balkan RSC, separate from the European security community. The domestic polices of the Balkan states and approaches towards the region by the international community, however, have prevented this from happening.

Greece, an EU member since 1981 and NATO member since 1952, became firmly integrated into the EU/Europe security community; Bulgaria, Romania and Slovenia joined Central and Eastern Europe (CEE), as part of the European RSC, whose security dynamics were structured by and subordinated to the process of European integration; while Albania, Bosnia and Herzegovina, Croatia, North Macedonia, Kosovo, Montenegro and Serbia emerged as a separate subcomplex, yet still within the European RSC. Turkey continued assuming the role of an insulator—a state, situated between RSCs, where security dynamics of the EU/Europe, post-Soviet RSC and Middle East met back-to-back (ibid.: 41). While it is tempting to try to determine the exact moment of emergence of this differentiation between the Balkan states, such an endeavour runs the risk of simplifying and distorting the reality for the purpose of making the theory and practice match perfectly. The trajectory of security development of the Balkan states split along four routes defined above under the impact of a plethora of factors, among which: the speed, intensity and quality of reforms, different economic and political starting points, wars of Yugoslavia's dissolution, inconsistency, and poor coordination of approaches among the external actors, especially the USA and the EU (Papadimitriou 2001: 72). The combination of these factors caused the fluctuation of the boundary of the Balkan security subcomplex, which remained blurred throughout the 1990s.

While there is no space here to analyse the post-Cold War development of all the Balkan states in detail[17], it is important to explain why only Albania and the post-Yugoslav states, apart from Slovenia, formed a separate subcomplex and how their security dynamics became inherently connected to the European RSC. But first a few words should be said about Slovenia[18], Bulgaria and

Romania, which are approached here as members of "the eastern circle" of the European RSC, i.e. separately from the Balkan subcomplex (Buzan and Waever 2003: 364). The main reason for this is that starting from the early 1990s these states, together with the CEE countries, embarked on the journey of reforms with the ultimate goal of joining the EU. While the goal was getting closer to certain candidates and moving away from others, depending on their performance, it always remained real. The dependence on the EU became the central factor, defining political, economic and security situations in these states. All of them had security problems, concerning minorities, state borders or other historical and ethnic issues, yet these problems were subordinated to the process of the European integration. Bulgaria, Romania and Slovenia were sporadically included into numerous regional initiatives, organised under the aegis of the USA, the EU and NATO, which could potentially link security dynamics to other Balkan states, but none of these initiatives was strong enough to unify all Balkan states into a single security region.[19] In a similar manner, Turkey and Greece took part in some of the regional schemes[20] and tried to assist in managing and resolving the Balkan conflicts of the 1990s, but neither state was sufficiently closely involved to become part of the Balkan subcomplex. Their interest in the region, underpinned by ethnic and historic ties, was not enough to interlink their security dynamics with the conflict-affected region.

The security situation in Albania and all post-Yugoslav states, save Slovenia, was substantially different to that of other Balkan states mentioned above. Since the early 1990s it was defined by a dense network of conflicts (both existing and potential) and policies of stabilisation, pursued by the international community under the leadership of the USA. Unlike in CEE, the issues of minorities and state borders were heavily securitised. At the end of the 1990s, stabilisation efforts were strengthened by the integration policies of the EU. When the states of the region were offered the membership perspective, first through the Stabilisation and Association Process and later by the 2003 EU Summit in Thessaloniki, their security dynamics became inherently linked to the EU. Albania, the only non-Yugoslav member of the Balkan subcomplex, found itself included into this regional formation as a result of at least three factors: continuing political instability in the country, poor economic performance and persisting problems with neighbouring states over the status and rights of the Albanian minorities. The security patterns in the Balkan subcomplex, which from 1991 to 1995 were predominantly dictated by enmity, shifted slightly towards the pole of amity with the DPA and Regional Approach coming into force in 1995 and 1996 respectively. It is argued below that these initiatives were trying to transform the Balkan conflict formation into the security regime, which after failing in 1998-1999 gave way to an embryonic type of security community, linked to the European RSC. While this transformation is analysed in the next two sections, the current section will be completed by examining the remaining parts of the essential structure of the Balkan subcomplex — its anarchic structure and patterns of polarity.

As former Yugoslav states were gaining independence, the composition of the region and distribution of power remained largely the same. If before 1991 Bosnia, Croatia, North Macedonia[21], Montenegro, Kosovo, Slovenia, and Serbia were interconnected as parts of the Socialist Federal Republic of Yugoslavia, after 1991 all of them, apart from Slovenia, but with the addition of Albania became closely interlinked through conflict and conflict networks, which are described below. Although two states of the region have their sovereignty partially limited[22], none of them is fully subordinated to a third party, which means the anarchic structure of the subcomplex is still in place. The subcomplex has two poles: one in Serbia and one in Albania. Serbia's security situation is most closely linked to BiH, Croatia, Montenegro, and Kosovo, while Albania's security dynamics are interdependent with those of North Macedonia, Kosovo and Serbia. It is important to mention that neither of these poles can be the centre of the region as the overall pattern of security in the Western Balkans is decided in the EU. The patterns of enmity and amity in the subcomplex varied greatly in the studied period and the analysis, presented in the following two sub-sections, aims to scrutinise the processes behind these variations.

The transformation of security dynamics in the Western Balkans from 1991 to 2013

From regional conflict formation to a failed attempt at security regime (1991-1999)

While the signs of Yugoslavia's demise were discernible already at the end of the 1980s, it was the events of 1991-1992 which signalled the emergence of an RCF on the Balkan Peninsula. The outbreak of war in Slovenia and Croatia in June 1991 and then in Bosnia in March 1992 brought violence, instability and enmity to the (post)Yugoslav space, and evoked fears about the destabilisation of the Balkans as a whole (Daalder 1996: 45). These fears notwithstanding, the conflict and violence were contained on the territory of the post-Yugoslav states and Albania. Albania and all former Yugoslav states, apart from Slovenia, thus constitute constant members of the Balkan subcomplex, which between 1991 and 1995 represented an RCF. Other Balkan states, e.g. Romania and Bulgaria, joined the formation occasionally as a result of domestic development and policies pursued by the external actors present in the region. Yugoslavia and Albania, having experienced "parallel fates as political systems bound mainly by national militaries, command economies, and political economies" during the Cold War (Pugh, Cooper and Goodhand 2004: 147), found their security situations interdependent and interlinked even when the Cold War rivalries stopped. Although Albania did not experience direct violence at the beginning of the 1990s, it still emerged as one of the poles of the Balkan subcomplex thanks to a whole range of connections with the post-Yugoslav space, which are explored further on the example of economic, military, political and social networks. What is more, as a country "pushed to a much smaller size than its 'ethnic' span" (Buzan and Waever 2003: 385), it was also linked to Yugoslavia through the prospect of conflict[23], which was realised at the end of the 1990s in Kosovo.

The conflicts in the Western Balkans, born of the political crises, dire economic conditions and specific historical experiences[24], grew increasingly violent to a great extent due to the inadequacy of the international community's response. The wars of Yugoslavia's dissolution[25] broke out at the end of the Cold War, at the time when stability, which for decades had been produced by the rivalry of two blocs, disappeared from Europe (Glaurdic 2011: 9). The disintegration of the Eastern Bloc made major powers wary of any further changes with the potential to destabilise the international system. That is why the initial response to the Yugoslav crisis of the 1990s was to try and preserve the unity of the federation. The proliferation of the "ancient hatred" argument as an explanation of the Yugoslav wars in the media and certain academic circles[26] provided external actors with a convenient reason for non-intervention. As a result, when the break-up of Yugoslavia became imminent, the international community found itself unprepared to deal with its consequences. One of the first to react was the European Community (EC): its bid to manage the conflict was announced in June 1991 by Jacques Poos, the Chair of the EC Foreign Affairs Council and Foreign Minister of Luxembourg, in his "hour of Europe speech" (Riding 1991). This endeavour of the EC was supported by the USA, which was looking forward to reducing its engagement in European security (Baker and DeFrank 1995: 636-637). The wars of Yugoslavia's dissolution, however, showed the impossibility of the task: the EC, transformed into the European Union (EU) under the Treaty of Maastricht in 1993, lacked the appropriate instruments, an effective foreign and security policy, unity among its key members, and, most importantly, military power to stabilise the turbulent region. While Germany, France, the UK and other EU member states made sizeable contributions to managing the conflict through the UN and NATO, the EU failed to provide a coherent and unified response as a single actor.

Consequently, in the first half of the 1990s, the USA emerged as the most important international actor in the Yugoslav wars: not only did it lead NATO operations and bombing campaigns, but also coordinated the negotiations, which resulted in the Dayton Peace Accords, bringing the Bosnian war to an end in 1995. Having reluctantly assumed the leadership role, the USA put an end to the strategy of containment, pursued by the international community in the Balkans since 1991. Before 1995 the external players, although present in the region, were not deeply involved in the conflicts, but focused mainly on containing them within the borders of former Yugoslavia. This meant that the security situation in the Balkan subcomplex between 1991 and 1995 was predominantly internally driven (Buzan and Waever 2003: 383). Yet, even at the time of international disengagement, the subcomplex was not entirely isolated. There were two main threads connecting it with a wider world, namely, the expectations of the local actors and a range of networks, which united the Western Balkan states into an RCF. Many of the local actors interpreted, and in certain cases, misinterpreted messages from foreign governments and international organisations as signs of support, which, on the one hand, made the warring parties less likely to look for compromises, and, on the other, did not allow the external players to disengage from the wars in the Balkans completely. Croatia's expectations, for example, were with Germany, and through it, with the EU and NATO, Serbia's—with Russia, while Bosniaks counted on the support of the USA (ibid.). While these expectations were formed because of complex processes[27], the complexity of networks, piercing through the Western Balkan states and uniting them into an RCF, was much greater. That is why these networks merit special attention.

RCFs are characterised by a complex nature of conflicts, which are so closely interconnected with each other that they cannot be easily untangled. The intricacy of relations between members of an RCF were explained by Armstrong and Rubin (2002) through the concept of networks, which form the basis of conflict formations. It is argued here that the Balkan subcomplex in 1991-1995 represented an RCF because of the proliferation of conflicts and violence, supported by a series of networks, which not only tied the region together but also connected it to the European RSC. Following the work of Pugh, Cooper and Goodhand (2004), four main types of networks are distinguished in the Balkan subcomplex, which can be defined as economic, military, political and social. Before analysing these networks, it should be reiterated that it is not possible to draw distinct lines between them, which can be explained by the already mentioned high interconnectivity of relations in an RCF, which represents an open and complex system.

Political networks in the Western Balkans can be observed on the example of the major local players involved in the Balkan conflicts of the 1990s. The war in Croatia was fought not simply between Croatia and Belgrade, it was also a war between the Croatian government and Croatian Serb rebels, backed and supported by the Yugoslav People's Army (JNA) and Serb paramilitaries, mostly based in Krajina and eastern and western Slavonia. The situation in BiH was even more complicated: the fighting between three major ethnic groups — Bosnian Serbs, Bosnian Croats and Bosniaks, also referred to as Muslims — was aggravated by the involvement of Serbia (from 1992 part of the Federal Republic of Yugoslavia (FRY)) and Croatia. Furthermore, these wars were fought not just by governments and national armies, but also by mercenaries, criminal syndicates, and war entrepreneurs, hence a connection with economic and military networks. Monopoly on violence was lost by the states, embroiled in conflicts, making security relations overly complicated. Another political network started emerging between Kosovo, through Kosovo Liberation Army (KLA), Serbia (together with Montenegro as the other part of the FRY), Albania and later North Macedonia, at that point known as the Former Yugoslav Republic of Macedonia (FYROM). In contrast to other political networks in the region, it did not emerge at the time of open warfare yet was actively influenced by the events in the neighbouring states. In addition, political networks between the Western Balkan states were developing through connections between political parties and movements. For example, the Croatian Democratic Union of Bosnia and Herzegovina (HDZ BiH) was closely linked to the Croatian Democratic Union (HDZ), and the National Liberation Army of Macedonia (UÇK) was in close association with the Kosovo Liberation Army (UÇK). It is symbolic that the names of these parties and movements were abbreviated in the same way, underlying the connection between countries.

Economic and military networks in the Balkan subcomplex in 1991-1995 were closely linked to political ones, but also to each other. Their interconnectivity, in fact, was so high that they can only be analysed together. The link between poor economic conditions and violence, however, has not always been recognised, but was for a long time disregarded. As noted by Strazzari and Coticchia (2012: 149), "caught in an obsessive attention to identity dynamics, clashes of civilisations and ethnic wars, most commentators overlooked the fact that the flaring up of violence in the Balkans was preceded by a decade of economic crisis". Caused by the weakness of states and demands for reform as well as debt repayment from foreign creditors and Western governments, a sharp economic decline in the Western Balkan states had three main implications for the development of the Balkan subcomplex.

First, shadow economies and clandestine economic activities financed the warring parties, including the governments of states, which often formed criminal networks themselves or provided them with protection. The Albanian regime, for example, invested in cigarette smuggling and networks, connecting Greek, Montenegrin, and Italian players (Strazzari and Coticchia 2012: 150). In many cases, illicit schemes were run by representatives of security services and army officials (Bechev 2011: 37), which later had a bearing on the importance of security sector reform for the region. Second, cross-border criminal syndicates provided the public with bare necessities and sources of income at the time when states were too weak to handle social and economic spheres (Strazzari and Coticchia 2012: 151-152). Having penetrated everyday life, organised crime remains one of many unresolved problems of the Western Balkans even today.[28] Third, war economies ensured an uninterrupted supply of weapons to the region after the imposition of the EU and UN arms embargoes on the Yugoslav republics in 1991 (ibid.: 150). In the mid-1990s the arms smuggling began in Kosovo. Many weapons were brought into Kosovo after they had been looted from the army depots in Albania (Bechev 2011: 37). Instead of suppressing transnational criminal activities, the arms and later economic embargo and international sanctions created a favourable environment for their proliferation.

Transborder linkages also left a big impact on civilian populations, which can be seen on the example of social networks. The Western Balkan conflicts made hundreds of thousands flee their homes and seek refuge abroad, in many cases in neighbouring states, but also in Western Europe and North America. Large numbers of refugees from Bosnia, for example, came to Serbia and Croatia, while Kosovo Albanians were forced to relocate to Macedonia and Albania. Bosnia, in this respect, suffered the most: between 1992 and 1995 2.2 million people fled their homes, which accounts for more than 50% of the country's pre-war population (MHRR BiH 2005: 45). 1.2 million out of these 2.2 million sought refuge abroad, while the rest were internally displaced (ibid.). Furthermore, the wars contributed to the spread of human trafficking, which did not stop with the end of fighting. The criminal channels were widely used to traffic women for work in the sex industry in the West and provided refugees from both inside and outside the Balkans with entry points to the EU (Bechev 2011: 38). Another dimension was introduced to social networks through diasporas. Not only did they provide financial help and sanctuary to those fleeing war (Pugh, Cooper and Goodhand 2004: 35), but they also played a key role in political and military matters in their homeland. Thus, diaspora Croats were involved in state-building processes during the first Tudjman government through special government offices (Winland 2008: 83-84) and even took part in direct combat as part of the Croatian Armed Forces (Lukic 2008: 193-194).

As can be seen, the proliferation of political, economic, military, and social networks in the Balkan subcomplex had a two-fold effect. On the one hand, it brought the region together, although its members were often in conflict with each other. On the other, it linked the Western Balkans to the European RSC. Shared security concerns, politics, informal economies, and interconnected societies united the former Yugoslavia (minus Slovenia) and Albania into a regional conflict formation with predominantly negative security dynamics. It should be emphasised that the networks, which originated in the Western Balkans, unlike conflicts in 1991-1995, and later in 1998-1999, were not contained in or around the territory of ex-Yugoslavia (Bechev 2011: 35). Instead, they spread to other Balkan states, such as Bulgaria and Romania, and even further to the EU, e.g. Italy and Austria, and beyond, e.g. Switzerland. War economies and criminal networks connected the Western Balkans to the rest of Europe and the world, not allowing the region to be sealed off. The fact that these networks spread beyond the borders of the

Western Balkans, however, does not mean that there is a need to redefine the Balkan subcomplex to incorporate all the states affected by them. The boundaries of the subcomplex still more or less coincided with the boundaries of the Western Balkans because this is where the conflicts took place and networks were the densest.

After the wars in Croatia and BiH stopped, the region started to slowly stabilise. Most Western Balkan states reinstated the state monopoly on violence[29], cutting ties with paramilitary and irregular forces (Kaldor 2012: 57), and thus bringing an end to some of the political and military networks. Many other networks, e.g. those built around clandestine economy, remained active, yet went further underground, or became dormant, to be reinvigorated by regional players during the Kosovo conflict.[30] The stop of direct large-scale violence, however, signalled to the international community that the regional conflict formation in the Balkans could be disentangled and brought closer to the amity pole of security interdependence.

Starting from 1995 the strategy of containment gave way to external intervention with a regional twist. Yet, at that point there was still no agreement as to what constituted the region and therefore numerous externally driven regional initiatives were aimed at various South-East European states. Moreover, regional security was still predominantly seen as separate from the rest of Europe. The situation changed in 1999-2000, when the EU started emerging as the leading actor in the region and the Western Balkans became formally recognized as a coherent region. It was also at this time that the region's security was linked to the broader European security. Before that happened, however, the international community tried to pacify the subcomplex by pressuring and nudging its members to build reciprocal security relations, normally found inside a security regime.

To initiate change, the international community, still led by the USA, used negotiation and imposition. The processes were carried out through a plethora of initiatives, which singled out regional cooperation as an important condition for the restoration of peace and normalisation of relations between regional actors as well as with the outside world. While regional interdependence of predominantly negative character, which defined the Western Balkans as a conflict formation between 1991 and 1995, resulted mostly from domestic factors, the states of the region started moving away from conflict and towards emerging security regime under the influence of external powers. The first attempt to employ a regional approach to the post Yugoslav space was made by the UN in 1992. By pressuring Albania, Bulgaria, Romania and Macedonia to implement economic sanctions against rump Yugoslavia, the UN introduced the element of multilateralism into its relations with the regional actors (Bechev 2011: 43). Yet, it was not until 1995-1996 that regional approaches became a norm for the external actors looking to resolve the Balkan conflicts. The Dayton Accords, Sub-Regional Arms Control Agreement, Regional Approach and Southeast European Cooperative Initiative (SECI) promoted regional cooperation as a key element for the stabilisation of the area.

The Dayton Accords[31], whose primary purpose was to stop the war in BiH gained importance regionally and not only in BiH thanks to the involvement of Croatia and FR Yugoslavia in the negotiation process and because "regional stability in and around former Yugoslavia" was identified as one of its goals (GFAP 1995, Article V, Annex 1B). The signing of the peace agreement was made possible by the efforts of the US government and military commitment of NATO. Representatives of Clinton's administration present on the ground and NATO's air strikes on Serb positions provided a powerful impetus for change. The negotiations, held at the Wright-Patterson Air Force Base on the outskirts of Dayton, Ohio, in November 1995, involved representatives from France, Germany, Italy, Russia, the United Kingdom, USA and the EU, and were headed by Richard Holbrook, the then US assistant secretary of state for European and Canadian affairs.[32]

Among the DPA provisions, hard security was given a priority, which is exemplified by the inclusion of military aspects of the peace settlement into the first annex (GFAP 1995). The Agreement also included proposals for arms control and confidence-building measures to diminish the risk of future conflicts, improve security relations between former adversaries and therefore promote reciprocity in the Balkans (McCausland 1997: 19). Thus, in June 1996, the FRY, Croatia and BiH signed the Sub-Regional Arms Control Agreement[33], known as Florence Agreement and provided for by Article IV, Annex 1A of the DPA, committing to reduce their weapons according to a 5-2-2 ratio, based on their respective populations and the FRY's armament holdings (Boese 1999). As the agreement was negotiated between the parties under the external pressure[34], it contained elements of both arms control and disarmament (McCausland 1997: 21). Although, it involved only three regional players, it is believed to have improved cooperation, transparency and predictability of security relations in South-Eastern Europe (SEE) (OSCE 2016).

The Regional Approach (RA) was launched by the EU in 1996 to supplement the Dayton Agreement and OSCE peace-building efforts (Papadimitriou 2001: 74). It was designed as a framework for political stabilisation and economic recovery of the Western Balkans. The RA offered these countries assistance under the PHARE[35] and Obnova[36] programmes, autonomous trade preferences and Co-Operation and Association Agreements (Watanabe 2010: 131). It identified good neighbourliness and economic integration at the regional level as preconditions for accessing the EU policies (Bechev 2011: 45-46). The SECI was another strategy for the stabilisation of the region yet created by the USA. While having a broader geographical outreach than the Regional Approach (in additional to the Western Balkan states (apart from FRY), it covered other SEE states—Bulgaria, Greece, Hungary, Moldova, Romania, Slovenia and Turkey), it was considerably limited in scope. The SECI's primary focus was to facilitate regional cooperation through combating trans-border crime and promoting infrastructure development (Watanabe 2010: 131-132).

While there were other regional initiatives, some of which—locally driven like the South East European Co-Operation Process (SEECP)[37], it was the DPA, Florence Agreement, Regional Approach and to a lesser extent SECI that gained the most prominence. Through levers of conditionality and direct imposition they promoted the principles of regional cooperation, good neighbourliness, transparency and reciprocity, which could have turned the region into a security regime, had they been accepted and adopted by all regional players. There were, however, three main reasons why the security regime did not take root in the Western Balkans. First, the legacy of wars that displaced millions of people, caused thousands of deaths and ethnically cleansed many parts of the region remained mostly unaddressed[38], making the emergence of reciprocity and trust between former adversaries extremely complicated. Second, the lack of agreement and coordination among external actors as to what constituted the Balkan region and how to approach it, reduced the effectiveness of the regional initiatives they were introducing. Third, in the immediate post-war period, the international community continued treating the Balkans as an area, different from the rest of Europe, whose stability could be achieved without long-term commitment. As a result, peace in the Western Balkans turned out to be short-lived, while the pole of amity remained distant. Although the externally led regional initiatives of 1995-1999 did not establish a security regime in the Balkan subcomplex, they prepared the ground for the next stage of security transformation that started with the Kosovo conflict. The next section explains how in 1999-2000 the process of Euro-Atlantic integration substituted the policies of containment and intervention of the early and mid-1990s respectively and what impact it had on the security dynamics of the Balkan subcomplex.

Becoming part of the European security community (1999-2013)

After a short period of peace, violence returned to the Western Balkans with the war in Kosovo, which lasted from February 1998 to June 1999[39]. The conflict served as a turning point for the security evolution of the region. Instead of setting the Balkan subcomplex on the downward spiral back to the regional conflict formation, it offered the states of the region an opportunity to join the EU/Europe security community, which materialised thanks to the combination of external and internal factors.

In terms of external factors, the strategy of integration, chosen by the EU and NATO, was of key importance. This work offers three explanations for its development. First, Kosovo exposed limits of reactive and selective responses to the crises in the Balkans (Vucetic 2001: 116). Prior to 1999, it was widely believed that the region could be stabilised with the help of humanitarian aid and a plethora of externally-led initiatives, promising regional actors benefits for cooperation in various spheres, ranging from trade to security. These measures, often hastily arranged and poorly coordinated, were mainly concerned with tackling the consequences of previous conflicts, without offering any long-term strategy for the development of the region. The fact that external actors could not agree on what constituted the region did not help matters either. The eruption of violence in Kosovo in 1998 and its escalation in 1999, which required another NATO intervention, highlighted limitations of the existing approaches to the Balkans and called for their urgent rethinking (Bechev 2006: 34).

Second, the Kosovo crisis reiterated the interdependence of the Western Balkan states and emphasised the fragility of peace, established in the region (Bechev 2011:49). When Serbian forces launched operations aimed at the ethnic cleansing of the Albanian population in Kosovo in the spring of 1999 (Zakosek 2008: 592), it was not only Kosovo which suffered from these actions. The influx of refugees into neighbouring countries, mainly Albania and FYROM, placed their economies under huge pressure and in the case of the latter ignited inter-ethnic tensions (Bechev 2011:49). Moreover, regional trade and economy also sustained losses, because of the damages endured by Serbia, an important regional centre, as a consequence of NATO's operation *Allied Force*.

Third, the re-emergence of conflict in the Western Balkans at the end of the 1990s provided a forceful push for the inclusion of the region into the EU's area of responsibility. The geographical proximity of the region to the EU member states (Kavalski 2008: 77), media coverage of the Kosovo war in Western media (Buzan and Waever 2003: 387) and complex transnational nature of the consequences of the conflict, in particular in terms of refugee flows and networks of organised crime (Watanabe 2010: 145), were among the key reasons for the emergence of the Western Balkans as a part of Europe, part of "us", the area, which Euro-Atlantic powers could not allow to descend into violence and cruelty (Buzan and Waever

2003: 387). By acknowledging the European identity of the region, after almost a decade of uncertainty and attempts to depict its problems and crises as foreign and non-European, the international community signalled that the future of the Western Balkans was not only linked to the European zone of peace, but also belonged there. After the fighting in Kosovo was stopped with the help of NATO, the EU started assuming a more active role in the region. Although slowly and cautiously, the EU became more open to the idea of formally including all Balkan states, and not just Bulgaria and Romania, into its realm. The model of integration, which had been used to stabilise Europe after World War II, was once again chosen as an instrument for peace, reconciliation and a guarantee of human and minority rights (Solana 2000). It should be noted here that the EU's intentions were not as much an altruistic endeavour as an attempt to protect itself and its members from the instability and conflict, spilling over from the turbulent region.

The integration of the Western Balkans into the European security community became a possibility also thanks to some domestic changes. Of special importance were regime changes in Croatia and Serbia—the two largest states of the region. The death of Franjo Tudjman in 1999 and electoral defeat of Slobodan Milosevic in 2000 brought in new governments, which were open to reforms and more responsive to the demands for regional cooperation, coming from outside. By the end of 2000, all Western Balkan states expressed their commitment to the European integration (Vucetic 2001: 111), further strengthening the role of the EU in it.

The first step towards the inclusion of the Balkan subcomplex into the European security community was made with the Stability Pact (SP) for SEE. Initiated by the German Presidency of the EU Council in the summer of 1999, the SP was a multilateral initiative, supported by a wide coalition of international financial institutions, such as the World Bank and European Investment Bank, international organisations, including OSCE, Council of Europe and NATO, and governments of many states, e.g. Japan, Russia, the USA, Canada as well EU member states (Busek and Kuehne 2010: 11). Overall, it represented a long-term proactive approach to conflict prevention (Watanabe 2010: 135), based on the combination of integration policy and cooperation at the SEE level (Bechev 2006: 34). Regional cooperation was in fact singled out as one of the key prerequisites for drawing the region closer to the perspective of full integration into the Euro-Atlantic structures (Busek and Kuehne 2010: 12). While being only one of the many broad goals of the policy, which among others included establishing lasting stability, encouraging democratisation, preserving multinational and multiethnic diversity, improving economic cooperation and combating organised crime in SEE (ibid.: 12-13), regional cooperation was presented by the Stability Pact as "both a recipe for interdependent growth and a generator of much-needed political stability" (Bechev 2006: 34). In essence, the SP was an attempt on behalf of the international community to establish a regional security framework, which would foster amicable relations among the SEE states as well as between the latter and the outside world. It was also an expression of its commitment "to the idea(l) of one Europe" (Vucetic 2001: 112).

While having considerable advantages over many previous approaches to the Balkans, mainly in terms of offering a coordinated long-term policy with the prospect of eventual integration into the EU structures, the Stability Pact also had several deficiencies, which prevented it from fully realising its security community-building potential.[40] These deficiencies can be grouped into three main categories pertaining to finances, actors, and goals. First, the SP was handicapped by the limited resources at its disposal, which were disproportionate to the grand objectives the scheme promised to achieve. Having no budget of its own, the SP was dependent on funds from its donors, notably the EU, its member states and international financial institutions, whose capacity and desire to assist varied greatly (Bechev 2011: 53). Second, the SP targeted all South-Eastern European states, bundling together the Western Balkan states with Bulgaria and Romania, and inviting more advanced Hungary, Slovenia and Turkey to participate as non-beneficiaries. It is no wonder that there was a rather weak feeling of belonging to the stabilisation process in SEE (Vucetic 2001:28). The ambiguity over the ownership of the initiative — placed under the umbrella of the OSCE, but in many respects led by the EU and perceived as an

EU instrument by the regional actors—raised further questions regarding its value. Third, the broad goals outlined in the Stability Pact, largely remained abstract and distant, due to a lack of clarity as to the ways in which they could be achieved.

The Stabilisation and Association Process (SAP), launched by the European Commission in May 1999 as a supplement to the SP, was able to avoid the deficiencies described above. As the initiative, funded and coordinated solely by the EU, and aimed at the Western Balkan states only, the SAP became the centrepiece of the EU's policy towards the region already by 2001 (EC 2002: 9). With the SAP, the EU gave the Western Balkan countries the promise of "the fullest possible integration ... into the political and economic mainstream of Europe" (EC 2003: 2) and the blueprint for reforms in the form of Stabilisation and Association Agreements (SAA). The SAP was designed as a simultaneously bilateral and regional approach: it seeks to create links between individual Western Balkan countries and the EU as well as to encourage regional cooperation between the countries themselves and with their neighbours in the region (EC 2002: 11). It is through the combination of these bilateral and regional relations that the EU has been drawing the Balkan subcomplex into the sphere of its influence and making it part of the European security community. Apart from the SP, which in 2008 was substituted with the regionally owned Regional Cooperation Council (RCC), and the SAP, the EU has been using a variety of other instruments to encourage regionalisation within the Western Balkans and the region's integration into the EU. Among these: the Community Assistance for Reconstruction Development and Stabilisation (CARDS) programme, which gave way to the Instrument for Pre-Accession (IPA) in 2007, the EU-Western Balkan summits, and an array of cooperation agreements and economic assistance programmes (Bechev 2011: 57-58).

As the arsenal of the EU tools for the Western Balkan states grew and possibility of a large-scale violence in the region diminished, the EU came to occupy centre stage in the affairs of the Balkan subcomplex. NATO continues to play an important role in the region through the Partnership for Peace Programme (PfP), Membership Action Plan (MAP), South East Europe Initiative (SEEI) as well as through the physical presence of its troops on the ground, e.g. in Kosovo, but no longer leads the efforts of the international community to stabilise the Western Balkans and to set the region on the path to peace. This role has been taken over by the EU after it launched the SAP and extended the membership perspective to all Western Balkan states at the Thessaloniki summit of 2003. That said, the impact of NATO and the US on the security situation in the Western Balkans should not be underestimated: these actors were instrumental for stopping the bloodshed in the region in 1995 and 1999. It was only through their efforts that the wars in Bosnia and Kosovo were stopped. Their subsequent engagement with the countries of the region contributed and keeps contributing to the strengthening of their political, economic and security situations.

While recognising the significance of NATO and the US in the Western Balkans, this work, however, does not evaluate their roles in the process of extending European security community to the said region at length, especially as this was done elsewhere.[41] Although it is now widely acknowledged that the EU is the leading actor in the Balkan subcomplex (Bechev 2011: 57, Watanabe 2010), there are still considerable lacunae in the research literature on the subject, especially regarding the EU's influence on the security situation of the region.[42] This work attempts to remedy this deficiency by examining the EU's role in security sector reform (SSR). This involvement is seen as an example of the EU's attempt to change prevalent patterns of security interdependence in the region from negative to positive, which can shed light on the ways through which the elites of the Western Balkan states have been socialised to align their domestic and foreign policies with those of the EU.

Socialisation is a means used by external powers to promote peace and establish initial stages of security communities. It is a complex process through which norms, rules and values are transferred between international actors and are internalised as patterns of domestic policy-making and foreign policy-formation (Kavalski 2008: 65). In the Western Balkans, the EU came to exercise its socialising powers through bilateral and regional initiatives. These initiatives are meant to strengthen the statehood of local actors and make peaceful relations a norm in the region (ibid.: 95). The interconnection between two levels of the EU's interaction with the Western Balkans—levels of states and the region—is both strong and complex. While each state is required to engage in regional cooperation and build good neighbourly relations to progress with the integration into the EU, the EU evaluates every state's success on the individual basis. In many respects, amicable relations between Western Balkan states develop because of changes in domestic policies, which are often, but not exclusively, promoted by the EU through bilateral contractual relations, e.g. expressed in SAAs. On the one hand, considering the fragility of states in the region, the EU's policies are aimed at building their capacity and improving the efficiency and efficacy of their institutions (security sector reform is an example of this approach). Such activities are sometimes interpreted as an effort at member state-building (Keil and Arkan 2015). The recent history of conflict in the region, on the other hand, prompts the EU to also focus on fostering the introduction and maintenance of peaceful foreign policy practices among regional members (Kavalski 2008: 95). The combination of these two approaches has initiated the emergence of *security community in the Western Balkans, which forms the extension of the European zone of peace*, i.e. it is not a separate security community but a part of the European one. Since the recipients of the EU's policies tend to be mainly state elites, in the final period researched here, the Western Balkans represented an elite or *embryonic form of security community*. Such a security community is based not on a common identity, but on elite cooperation (ibid.: 80-81).

According to Deutsch (et al 1957), who first investigated security communities extensively, their success depends on three essential conditions. The EU's policies in the Western Balkans can be shown to foster their emergence, which, in turn, proves that there is potential for the embryonic security community in the region to evolve further. The conditions in question are: the compatibility of main values among politically relevant strata, political responsiveness and mutual predictability of behaviour. The compatibility of the main values is pursued by the EU through its insistence through the SAP on the adoption by all the Western Balkan countries of "the values and models on which [the EU] is founded" (Council of the

EU 2000: 54). The regional decision-makers commit to these values, which include social, economic and political rights and liberties, by adopting the EU's *acquis* and choosing to follow the norms of peaceful interaction between each other. Political responsiveness is achieved by reforms aimed at improving the effectiveness and efficiency of state institutions, which, while carried out by domestic actors, are often initiated from outside. One of the tasks of these reforms is to bring the states that introduce them to compatible standards. SSR, as already mentioned, gains special importance in post-conflict environments and is one of the key reforms contributing to the development of the security community in the Western Balkans. Mutual predictability of behaviour is closely linked to the condition of responsiveness: it develops as a result of strengthening state institutions and presupposes that state elites display similar patterns of behaviour.

It can be concluded that between 1999 and 2013, the security situation in the Western Balkans has been steadily improving and this change has been consistently guided by the external effort. The next and final section will evaluate the role of the most active members of the international community in the evolution of the security dynamics in the region and explain why the EU is best placed to assist it on the way to peace, stability and prosperity.

Why the EU? The role of external actors in shaping security patterns of the Western Balkans

The analysis, presented in the current chapter, has shown that the security situation in the Western Balkans between 1991 and 2013 was shaped under the influence of internal and external factors. It has also demonstrated that the change of prevalent patterns in regional security relations has been guided by the international community. The turn from "ethnic strife, conflict and competition to cooperative engagement" (Bechev 2012: 72) was fostered by the USA/NATO and the EU, with the help of other external actors, among which the UN, OSCE, Russia and Turkey deserve a special mention. The transformation from a regional conflict formation, through a failed attempt at security regime, to part of the

EU/Europe security community became possible thanks to a plethora of largely externally driven regional initiatives, approached as peace-building projects (Solioz and Stubbs 2012: 23). Some of these initiatives, such as the Regional Approach, Stability Pact and Stabilisation and Association Process, were designed to bring the Balkan states closer to the Euro-Atlantic institutions, and gradually to integrate the former into the latter. Because of the geographical proximity, exposure to the complex threats emanating from the region, the need to repair a reputational damage sustained with the failure of its early efforts to stop violence and the USA's attention increasingly being directed to other parts of the world, at the end of the 1990s the EU emerged as the leading actor in the Western Balkans. Since then, it has been working towards making the region part of the European security community through the combination of regional and bilateral tools. The growing connection between the Balkan subcomplex and European RSC has prompted researchers to speak of it as "a microcosm of this larger whole rather than some separate 'other'" (Cottey 2012: 66).

Alongside its stabilisation and accession policies and financial instruments mentioned above, the EU has been exerting its socialising powers on the Western Balkans through its European Security and Defence Policy (ESDP), now Common Security and Defence Policy (CSDP). It is symbolic that the region, which prompted the EU to develop the ESDP in the first place[43], provided favourable grounds for testing this policy through military and civilian operations (Howorth 2007: 55-56). In January 2003, the EU took over the police and rule of law operation in BiH from the UN, staying there for almost ten years; in March of the same year, it deployed EUFOR *Concordia*, its first ever military mission, to North Macedonia, and in December another police mission—EUPOL *Proxima*, also there. Since 2004 the EU has overseen keeping peace in BiH, having substituted NATO's stabilisation force SFOR with EUFOR *Althea*, and from 2008 it assumed responsibility for the rule of law reform in Kosovo with EULEX.[44]

As can be seen, the EU has been learning through practice to guide the transformation of the Western Balkans from the area, affected by the legacy of war, to a part of the conflict-free community.⁴⁵ At the beginning of the 1990s, however, the bloc could not rise to the challenge as it "lacked the cohesion, determination and instruments to bring the crisis under control" (Lehne 2004: 111). The USA, who originally wanted to stay out of the Yugoslav conflicts and saw them as a European problem, had no choice but assume the leadership role in the international effort to stop the violence and stabilise the region. The US-led NATO interventions ended the wars in Bosnia in 1995 and in Kosovo in 1999. It is also important that peace negotiations between the warring parties of the Bosnian war took place at a US Air Force base in Dayton, Ohio (ibid.), which gave the name to the peace accords. Although the US acted mainly through NATO, it also invested in regional schemes outside the NATO framework such as the already mentioned SECI and South Balkans Development Initiative (SBDI). Still, these initiatives had a limited focus (restricted to several spheres such as infrastructure and energy) and lacked inclusivity. The SECI, for instance, excluded rump Yugoslavia, which consisted of Serbia and Montenegro, while Croatia opted for an observer status in the scheme, and SBDI covered only three states — Albania, Bulgaria and FYROM (Bechev 2011: 44-45). NATO's arsenal for the Balkans, which includes both generalised programmes like PfP and more specialised mechanisms like SEEI, allows the alliance to preserve its significance in the region.

Like the EU, the US and NATO have been fostering the good neighbourly relations between the SEE states and transmitting their values into the practices of regional actors. PfP, for example, required commitment to the "protection and promotion of fundamental freedoms and human rights, and safeguarding of freedom, justice and peace through democracy" (NATO 1994). These actors therefore have also been exercising their socialising powers in SEE, yet their capacity to promote change of the security interdependence is seen here as less powerful than that of the EU for at least three reasons.

First, none of NATO and USA's instruments target or have been specifically devised for the Western Balkans as a region. While the term "Western Balkans" is a construct of the EU-speak, it covers the countries, which are intrinsically linked to each other through the networks of potential or real conflict. Considering the region's legacy of war, it is argued here that it is essential for the region to receive a tailored approach, which aims to prevent any future outbreaks of violence and works as a roadmap for reforms. The SAP is an example of such an approach. Of course, it can be objected that the regional aspects of the SAP, are not nearly as effective as the bilateral contractual relations with the Western Balkan states or that members of the region do not necessarily share the feeling of belonging to it. These objections, however, miss the point. The EU's regional approach is not competing with its bilateral agreements, nor does it aim to create a separate Western Balkan region. The SAP offers the regional actors place in the EU and prepares them for the integration into its structures, while helping them with solving problems of poor cooperation and conflicts of the past.

Second, the EU is the only international actor which offers the Western Balkan states a comprehensive programme for development. The SAAs, concluded with the states of the region, identify a range of political, economic and security objectives, as well as encourage regional cooperation. NATO, although no longer exclusively preoccupied with traditional hard security issues, still predominantly focuses on the security sphere, while the US supports reforms in separate sectors. The two latter actors are therefore in a somewhat disadvantaged position compared to the EU when it comes to the areas of domestic and foreign policy of the Western Balkan countries they can influence.

Third, the USA's impact on the Western Balkans is subdued by its status as an extra-regional actor. The region is connected to the EU geographically and politically. The EU can exercise its powers in the region not only as a global power, but also as the centre of the European RSC to which the Balkan subcomplex is attached. The USA, on the other hand, can exert its influence on the region as a superpower, which can transcend borders and distance, but being outside the region its impact is not comprehensive. What concerns NATO, while it has a stake in European security, its ability to shape security policies of actors diminishes if the latter do not seek accession to the organisation. With the memory of the 1990s conflicts and their resolution still fresh, many of the regional actors continue to look to NATO for security, yet not all of them consider pursuing its membership. For example, Serbia, the biggest state of the region, does not aspire to join NATO, having proclaimed military neutrality in 2008. Hence, the EU is better placed for guiding the security transformation of the Western Balkans than the US or NATO, although the latter two continue to matter.

In the studied period, the security situation in the Western Balkans was also influenced by the UN, the OSCE, Russia and Turkey. Their importance, however, was not nearly as notable as that of the US, NATO or the EU. It was widely believed at the end of the 1990s that the UN would become a leading security actor in the world (Carlsson 1992), which could foster a global security community (Rochester 1993), yet the Yugoslav crises revealed it did not have the potency to perform this role. The UN, similarly to other members of the international community, was rather slow and reluctant to intervene in the conflicts. In 1991 it brokered a cease-fire in Croatia but was unable to foster a permanent settlement of the conflict (Daalder 1996: 60). In 1992 it deployed the United Nations Protection Force (UNPROFOR) to supervise the cease-fire in the country, which only contributed to the status quo. UNPROFOR's mandate in BiH was considerably broader, but still lacked efficiency, as it focused largely on humanitarian relief, and not peace enforcement (ibid.).[46] The creation of UN safe areas during the Bosnian war did not improve the UN's standing either: the fall of Srebrenica, the massacre of Bosniaks by Serb forces in July 1993 and the attack on the marketplace in Sarajevo in 1994 showed that it did not have the capacity or resources to manage the conflicts (Pugh, Cooper and Goodhand 2004: 149). The ability of the UN to act quickly and forcefully was stifled by the consensus-based decision-making processes of its Security Council.[47] The UN's poor performance in the region was one of the main triggers for NATO's engagement in the conflict. Having failed at leading the international effort, the UN assumed a supplementary role to NATO and later the EU (Kavalski 1998: 100), which it has been performing through international missions, such as the law enforcement mission in Bosnia and the UN Interim Administration Mission in Kosovo (UNMIK).

The OSCE, similarly to the UN, was supposed to play a greater role in the Balkans but proved unable to do so. Having declared "a new era of democracy, peace, and unity" at its Paris summit in November 1990 (OSCE), it found itself unprepared to provide a solution to escalating conflicts in the Balkans only a year later. Like the UN, its ability to act was constrained by the decision-making procedures, demanding consensus. Even a special "consensus-minus one" policy, introduced in response to the Yugoslav wars, did not allow the OSCE to act decisively and bring order to the Western Balkans (Daalder 1996: 60). As a result, it resolved to influence the region through monitoring missions and overseeing of initiatives, set up by other actors, such as was the case with the Stability Pact or SECI. Its role, therefore, was also supplementary.

Two remaining external actors, which influenced the security situation of the Western Balkans between 1991 and 2013 represent states, and not international organisations. The actors in question are Russia (a global player according to RSCT) and Turkey (an insulator). Russia became involved in the post-Yugoslav conflicts thanks to its close links to Serbia (Headly 2007). As Serbia's long-time ally, it assumed the role of a mediator between this Balkan state and the international community. The mediation effort, however, was not always productive and often had the air of contradiction to the policies pursued by the Western actors. In 1994 and 1995 Russia opposed NATO's bombing of Bosnian Serbs, arguing for the continuation of peace talks, and in 1999 was objecting to the air strikes against the rump FR Yugoslavia (Norris 2005: 13-15). Russia obstructed the work of the six-nation Contact Group, which also included France, Italy, Germany, the US and the UK, and was set up to provide a response to the Yugoslav crises.[48] In 1999, when the war in Kosovo escalated, it tried to persuade other members of the group that the conflict was an internal matter of Serbia.[49] Russia's actions therefore contributed, although indirectly, to Serbia's aggression: seeing the support from its Slavic partner, Serbia was less likely to yield to the demands of NATO and the UN. Not all the Russian efforts, however, were obstructive. The Yeltsin administration's mediation played an important role (alongside NATO's intervention) in persuading Serbia to withdraw forces from Kosovo. The Russian troops also participated in peacekeeping operations in

Bosnia as part of NATO's Implementation Force (IFOR), later turned into SFOR (although under a special US command rather than NATO's) and in Kosovo. In the latter Russia provided the largest non-NATO contingent, which stood at around 1,500 troops (Nikitin 2004). In general, Russia showed it was still important for the security of the region but did not necessarily act as a partner of other external actors.

Finally, Turkey was brought into the Yugoslav crises through its historical ties with the region, going back to the Ottoman Empire. Its involvement in the conflicts was mainly motivated by the concern over "the breakdown of regional order and stability" (Sayari 2000: 176), which was perceived as a threat to its own security. Despite emphasising the importance of the post-Yugoslav area for regional security, Turkey tried to minimise its involvement in the conflicts (Buzan and Waever 2003: 393). In fact, most of its contribution into improving the situation in the region was made through participation in multilateral initiatives, led by the USA, NATO, the UN or the EU. For example, in BiH Turkey supported military intervention by NATO, was part of the UN peacekeeping force and partner to the USA in providing military training to the new armed forces of the Federation of Bosnia and Herzegovina, one of the two entities making up BiH after Dayton (Sayari 2000: 177-178). In addition to various multilateral initiatives, Turkey was also working on developing bilateral relations with individual states of the region, e.g. Albania and FYROM. While Turkey's engagement with the regional actors was important, the country neither had the capacity to play a more active role, nor was willing to do so. From the point of view of RSCT, the relative restrain exercised by Turkey in the Western Balkans can be explained through its position as an insulator — a state situated between different security complexes. In the case of Turkey these are the European RSC, post-Soviet RSC and Middle Eastern RSC. Although Turkey keeps challenging this status through activities in neighbouring regions, its inability to significantly change the regional balance of power proves it still is an insulator.[50]

It should also be noted that external actors, involved in the Balkan subcomplex in 1991-2013, often engaged in cooperative activities. For example, NATO and the EU closely cooperated with the OSCE on the work of the Sanctions Assistance Missions that monitored the implementation of the UN sanctions against post-Yugoslav states. While the following chapters analyse the engagement of the EU with other members of the international community to promote SSR in the Western Balkans, the role of the international cooperation in the Yugoslav crises is discussed elsewhere.[51]

Conclusion

In 1991-2013, the Balkan subcomplex largely coincided with the area now defined as the Western Balkans, although its outer boundaries remained blurred, especially, in the early 1990s. Here, however, based on complexity thinking, boundaries are seen as an enabling factor for identifying Western Balkans as a distinct region, rather than a demarcation line, separating it from the rest of Europe and the world. During the studied period, the subcomplex developed two poles — one in Serbia and the other in Albania. Yet the security situation of the region is not decided in either of them. It emanates from the core of the European regional security complex, to which the Balkan subcomplex is attached geographically, politically, and economically. The place of the Balkan subcomplex in Europe has not always been a given. The EU and other external actors were reluctant to engage with the war-ridden area and pursued the policies of containment from 1991 to 1995. At this time, the subcomplex presented a case of regional conflict formation, i.e. a region, whose security situation is defined through a combination of closely interlinked conflicts, which cannot be easily untangled. Interestingly enough, the networks connecting the Western Balkan states were also responsible for bringing the region closer to the EU as they exposed the latter to many transnational threats, such as trafficking of drugs and persons, organised crime and illegal migration. Despite the strengthening connection of the Western Balkans to the EU, it was the USA and NATO that ended the period of containment by intervening to stop the war in BiH in 1995. The EU lacked the appropriate instruments, a developed security policy, military might as well as unity among its key members to stabilise the region.

Starting from 1995-1996, under the influence of externally driven initiatives such as the Dayton Accords and Regional Approach, the Western Balkans became more stable and achieved short-term peace. Although the international community used negotiation and imposition to introduce the subcomplex to the principles of regional cooperation, good neighbourliness and reciprocity, its members did not stop considering war as a preferable means of settling disputes. The RCF therefore failed to transform into a security regime. It was the Kosovo conflict of 1998-1999 that brought about change. While it was again the efforts of the USA and NATO which ended the war, the EU claimed responsibility for the stabilisation and development of the region afterwards. The bloc emerged as the leading security community-building actor, which used its socialising powers to foster amicable relations among the Western Balkan states. Since 1999 the EU's arsenal of instruments for the Western Balkans has been continuously growing and now includes a number of regional and bilateral tools, which are aimed at strengthening the statehood of local actors and making peaceful regional relations a norm. It was therefore not just the Western Balkans that went through a considerable transformation, but also the EU as it developed its security and foreign policy portfolio. For this reason, it is essential to look at the EU—Western Balkan relations through the prism of temporality and space, recognising the limitations existing at each point in time and paying attention to processes that led to the emergence of new capabilities and capacities on both sides of the relationship.

Moreover, bilateral and regional initiatives, pursued by the EU, should not be considered contradictory or competing, but complementing one another. Through bilateral agreements with individual Western Balkan states the EU attempts to make their institutions more effective and efficient and their state elites more open to the idea of cooperation. These initiatives foster congruence between the Western Balkan states and the EU, as well as among the regional actors, and make the extension of the European zone of peace to the region possible. Taking these considerations into account, it can be said that tracing the development of the bilateral relation between the EU and Western Balkan states, especially in the sphere of security, can provide important insights into understanding the mechanisms of security-community building. In this work this is done on the example of the EU's impact on security sector reforms in BiH, Croatia and Serbia. In conclusion, it should also be added that the USA and NATO continue influencing the security dynamics of the Western Balkans, but no longer lead the effort of the international community in the region.

Having established the leading role of the EU in shaping the security situation inside the Balkan subcomplex, Chapter 3 considers the EU's engagement with the SSR concept in theory and practice. It demonstrates that SSR is one of the best tools for both scrutinising the evolution of the security situation in the Western Balkans and assessing the impact of the EU on the process.

---

10   The Stability Pact was initiated by the Germany's EU Presidency yet was not owned by the EU. For more details, see section three of this chapter.
11   Attempts to analyse regional security on the basis of the concept of polarity can be found in Cantori and Spiegel (1970) and Ayoob (1986).
12   For other typologies, see Buzan and Waever (2003).
13   Each of these types are also studied in standalone theories, which can complement RSCT. For regional conflict formations, see Lake and Morgan (1997), Ayoob (1995), Kanet (1998), Raimo Vayrynen (1984) and Andrea Armstrong and Barnett R. Rubin (2002, 2005), security regimes – Jervis (1982) and international regimes more broadly – Hasenclever, Mayer, and Rittberger (1997). For security communities, see Deutsch et al (1957), Adler (1998), Adler and Barnett (1998).
14   Not all the states listed have been in existence as sovereign actors throughout the researched period. Six of them, namely Slovenia, Croatia, Bosnia and Herzegovina, Serbia, Montenegro and North Macedonia, used to be republics of the Socialist Federal Republic of Yugoslavia (SFRY). Kosovo was also a part of the SFRY, however, as an autonomous province (until 1991), and not a republic. Even today the sovereignty of BiH and Kosovo remains limited – in the case of Bosnia by the Office of the High Representative, and in the case of Kosovo by the non-recognition of its status. For the detailed overview of SFRY's disintegration, see Ramet (2006).
15   There are different views on the beginning of the dissolution of Yugoslavia. While it is possible to trace the collapse of the country to the breakup of the last Communist party congress in January 1990 (Lampe 2006) or a series of localised conflicts taking place in different parts of the federation in 1990-1991 (Ramet 2006), this research starts with 1991, which saw the declaration of independence from Yugoslavia by two of its republics, namely Croatia and Slovenia, and the outbreak of large-scale violence in the region.
16   For more on violence and the Balkans, see Gledhill and King (2010), and Pridham and Gallagher (2000).
17   For more on the development of the Balkan states after the Cold War, see Lampe (2006), Radeljic (2013), Gallagher (2003) and Bideleux and Jeffries (2007).

18 Despite being part of the SFRY and going through a short period of war, Slovenia did not become part of the Balkan RCF. Instead, it joined the CEE frontrunners of the European enlargement process. It is notable that the EU started referring to the country as part of CEE early on, too (EC 1997). For more on Slovenia's post-Yugoslav development, see Radeljic (2013: 3-5) and Papadimitrou (2001: 74-76).
19 Under the influence of external pressure and internal developments, Slovenia, Bulgaria and Romania can sometimes be included into the Balkan subcomplex, hence, the observation about the blurred nature of the boundaries of the subcomplex. However, for the purposes of this research and ease of analysis the Balkan subcomplex is understood to coincide with the Western Balkans.
20 For example, Turkey was one of the participating non-beneficiary states in the Stability Pact, and both Tukey and Greece were included into the Southeast European Cooperative Initiative.
21 While in SFRY, North Macedonia was known as Macedonia or Socialist Republic Macedonia. After the dissolution of Yugoslavia and until 2019, it was known as the former Yugoslav Republic of Macedonia (FYROM).
22 These states, as already mentioned, are BiH, where the international community exercises power through the Office of the High Representative, and Kosovo, whose independence, proclaimed in 2008, is not yet recognised fully and which therefore remains under the UN Interim Administration Mission.
23 In 1996-1997, Albania experienced civil unrest and minor violence due to the country's bad economic performance and collapse of several financial pyramid schemes. Despite fears, the turmoil did not turn into civil war. For more details, see Jarvis (2000) and Elbasani (2004).
24 For the discussion on causes of the break-up of Yugoslavia, see Daalder (1996).
25 A comprehensive overview of the break-up of Yugoslavia can be found in Glenny (1996), Posen (1993), Malcolm (1994) and Ramet (2006).
26 For example, see Larrabee (1990). For the counter argument, see Gagnon (2004).
27 The role of external actors in the demise of Yugoslavia and connections between Balkan states and members of the international community are analysed in Brenner (1992), Lucarelli (2000), Ullman (1996) and Glaurdic (2011).
28 On the problem of organised crime in the Western Balkan, see Glenny (2009) and Benedek et al (2010), UNODC (2020).
29 In BiH, despite the existence of two armies at the end of the war, state security was provided by NATO's IFOR and later SFOR. For more details, see Chapter 6.
30 For in-depth studies of separate networks originating in the Balkans, see Lindstrom (2004), Pugh (2007) and Bojicic Dzelilovic and Kostovicova (2013).
31 For more on the DPA, see Chapter 6.
32 The process of negotiating the DPA and events leading up to it are analysed in Holbrook (1999).
33 For further analysis of the initiative, see Boese (1999).
34 Negotiations were conducted by the OSCE that also oversees the implementation, but other external actors influenced the Agreement by supporting the DPA.
35 PHARE is a pre-accession financial instrument of the EU for cooperation with CEE countries, which was extended to South-Eastern Europe.
36 The OBNOVA programme was the main channel of EU's assistance to the Western Balkan states until it was integrated into CARDS in 2001.

37 For a detailed analysis of regional initiatives in South Eastern Europe, see Cottey (2012: 60-64) and Bechev (2011: 43-49).
38 Although the International Criminal Tribunal for the former Yugoslavia was established in 1993, it did not achieve much in the region in the 1990s, in absence of substantial support from the international community and will to cooperate among the post-Yugoslav players. For the ICTY's role in SSR, see Chapters 4-6.
39 The Kosovo war is analysed in detail in Judah (2002), Cottey (2009), Mertus (1999) and Bieber and Daskalovski (2003).
40 For the detailed discussion of the Stability Pact as a security community-building institution, see Vucetic (2001).
41 For example, see Bjola (2001), Fluri (2003) and Yalnazov (2000), Mulchinok (2017).
42 The role of the EU as a security actor in the Balkans has been in the centre of attention of many works, e.g. an important contribution into this subject was made by Kavalski (2008), yet the processes and mechanism used by the EU to extend its zone of peace to the region remain largely understudied.
43 The Kosovo crisis is widely recognised to be one of the triggers behind the ESDP. For the discussion of other drivers, see Howorth (2007: 57).
44 An overview of CSDP missions in the Western Balkans can be found in Merlingen (2013), Usanmaz (2018).
45 While the EU has strengthened its position as a security actor, its power in terms of military security is still far behind the USA and NATO. For the specifics of the EU as a security provider see Kirchner (2011).
46 For a detailed account of the UNPROFOR mandates in Former Yugoslavia, see UN (1996).
47 Not much has changed in the UN's ability to act since that time as is revealed by Russia's full-scale invasion of Ukraine in 2022.
48 The Contact Group was convened as an informal forum for coordination of diplomatic strategies and crisis management in the Balkans in 1994. It brought together major European powers, the US and Russia to deal with the Balkan conflicts, especially in Bosnia and Kosovo. For more on its role, see Schwegmann (2000).
49 Kosovo had been an autonomous province within Serbia, then part of Yugoslavia, since 1974. In 1990, its autonomous status was revoked by Serbian President Slobodan Milosevic, which gave an impetus to the radicalisation of the Kosovo Liberation Army that started as a peaceful resistance movement of Kosovar Albanians (Bhaumik, Gang, and Yun 2006).
50 Turkey's role as an insulator is discussed in Buzan and Waever (2003: 391-395), also see Barinha (2014).
51 For example, see Caruso (2007).

Chapter 3
The EU and Regional Application of SSR in the Western Balkans

Introduction

Security sector reform (SSR) is widely recognized as an important tool of conflict prevention, peace-building, development, and even democratisation and state-building (Churruca Muguruza 2008; Gross 2013; Bailes 2010). The EU has been actively engaged in the conceptualisation and implementation of the reform since the 1990s. The current chapter discusses what constitutes the EU's approach to SSR and how it has been applied to the Western Balkan region. The discussion is divided into three sections. Section one introduces the concept and explains how and why it is studied in the book. Section two studies the EU as an actor of SSR and shows that the reform occupies an important place within a wide range of EU policies. Following Spence (2010: 93), it is argued that as part national, part transnational policy area, security sector reform provides a favourable context for regional application and "epitomises European integration". It also demonstrates that the EU has been engaged in SSR-related activities for a long period of time, although without necessarily labelling them as such. SSR, due to its comprehensive nature, is approached by the EU not as a simple mechanical exercise aimed at reducing the number of troops or controlling military spending in third countries, but as a vehicle for transferring EU norms and values. It will therefore be argued that security sector reform is intrinsically linked to the development of amicable security relations and the process of security community-building.

The final section of Chapter 3 evaluates the implementation of SSR strategies by the EU in the Western Balkans on the regional level. It looks at how the EU has been engaging with the security sectors of the region, what goals it has been pursuing and what it has achieved by 2013.

Security sector reform: the parameters of analysis

SSR emerged as a key component of development and security assistance, and to a lesser extent an element of democracy promotion in the end of the 1990s[52] (Hänggi 2004: 1). The United Kingdom became the first state to pursue and promote the SSR agenda on the international level. Soon this initiative was undertaken by a plethora of other states (e.g., the Netherlands, Germany and France), non-governmental organisations (e.g., the Geneva Centre for the Democratic Control of Armed Forces (DCAF) and the Bonn International Centre for Conversion), and intergovernmental actors (the Development Assistance Committee (DAC) of the Organisation for Economic Cooperation and Development (OECD), the EU and UN). The latter category played a major role in conceptualizing SSR by developing its definitions, explicating its principles, and analysing the applicability of the concept to various contexts. Academic enquiry has followed policy work shortly: security sector reform is investigated as part of civil-military relations (Edmonds 1988; Barany 1991; Schnabel and Ehrhart 2006), police studies (Marenin 2005; Neild 2001; Perito 2009) and development research (Brzoska 2003; Chanaa 2002). Despite all the attention, the concept does not have a single, universally accepted definition and is therefore open to interpretation.

This work uses the definition, provided by Heiner Hänggi, who understands security sector reform as all polices, programmes and activities, which are "aimed at the effective and efficient provision of state and human security within a framework of democratic governance" (2009: 337). As a tool, SSR[53] can be utilised by both domestic and external actors who seek to improve the provision of safety, security and justice inside a state or region (Meharg and Arnusch 2010: 3). Normally, four defining characteristics are differentiated in the concept: a comprehensive (or holistic) nature, its emphasis on good governance, focus on human security and context-dependent character.

SSR is seen as a comprehensive concept due to at least four reasons: it is based on the broad view of security; it brings together a set of reforms, which were previously pursued in isolation from each other, e.g. reforms of the police, army, intelligence services and judicial systems; it incorporates not only security bodies, but also institutions and organs, responsible for their control and oversight; and it recognises non-statutory security forces, such as guerrilla armies and private security companies, as part of the security sector (Hänggi 2009: 342).

The second key feature of SSR is connected with the recognition of the concept as a governance issue (Ball 1998: 5). SSR cannot be considered complete without covering elements of the public sector, which manage and oversee security policies and practices of a state. This is because good governance, which can be defined as "the effective, equitable, responsive, transparent, and accountable management of public affairs and resources" (USAID, USDD and USDS 2009: 4), and the rule of law are widely seen to be of crucial importance for the work of security sectors. It is important to highlight here that SSR is not a neutral, value-free concept, but a normative notion: it mainly seeks to improve the governance of the security sector in accordance with democratic principles (Meharg and Arnush 2010: 7), which prompts some researchers, including the author, to consider democratic governance a component of security sector reform. Hence, a growing tendency in scholarly literature and policy circles to connect SSR with the processes of democratisation and democracy promotion (Chanaa 2002: 28; Edmunds 2007: 27; Hänggi 2009: 337). The focus on human security is another element adding normative value to SSR. The human security agenda, or rather its broad variant, maintains that security of an individual holds significance for national, regional and international security and argues that people's security and safety cannot be provided through military means alone (Ball 2010: 32). SSR subscribes to this view and sets out to improve the security of individuals as well as states, while attempting to have an impact on all aspects of human development, including economic, environmental, food and societal security (Hänggi 2003:6). This approach to human security, however, reflects an ideal vision of SSR, which is largely confined to theoretical discussions and is yet to see practical implementation.

The fourth and final feature of SSR, considered here, is its context-dependent character. It is widely accepted that there is no universal model of SSR and that the success of SSR efforts highly depends on the attention to domestic environments and promotion of local ownership of the reform (Hänggi and Tanner 2005: 17; Hendrickson and Karkoszka 2002: 176; Stalvant 2011: 17). While most frequently SSR is associated with post-conflict environments, it is also employed in developing, post-authoritarian contexts as well as developed states. It is not normally imlemented in the context of conflict, but even there it can be attempted.[54] Finally, sometimes several contexts overlap, as can be seen on the example of the Western Balkan states, which adds further complexity to the study of the reform.

As already mentioned, following the broad definition of security, the security sector is not limited to security institutions, but also includes security management and oversight actors. In can be defined as "those organisations that apply and manage coercive force for collective purposes" (Edmunds 2007: 25). In each country the list of such organisations will be different yet will include institutions from the following categories: core security actors, security management and oversight bodies, non-statutory security forces[55] and non-statutory civil society groups.[56] To maintain the analysis manageable, the book investigates the impact of the EU on reforms of the army, police, border control services, civil management and oversight bodies in Croatia, Serbia and BiH. This choice is determined by three main factors. First, there are currently very few examples of states undertaking a reform of the security sector in its entirety, although a holistic approach to SSR is highly commended (Hendrickson and Karkoszka 2002: 197). Exceptional cases like Sierra Leone only prove the existence of a large gap between the conceptualisation and implementation of SSR, because even there a reform does not include all the elements of the security sector as promoted by major SSR actors.[57] The focus on several components of SSR is therefore justifiable. Second, the disparate composition of security sectors in different countries may jeopardise the cohesion of research. This book analyses the EU's involvement in the reforms of several core security actors (army, police and border services) and security management and oversight bodies (parliamentary and governmental actors, and civil society) because they can be found in all three Western Balkan countries, selected for this research. This way the investigation remains cohesive and consistent. Third, the choice of the security and oversight bodies is also dictated by the history of the region. There, core security actors and security control and oversight institutions, were directly involved in permeating violence. Their reform has been prioritised by both local and external actors, which is why they can provide valuable data for the analysis. Overall, the *EU's engagement with security sector reform in the region is approached as an exercise of complex security governance* that is affected by uncertainty, cognitive challenge, complex risks and the need for constant adaptability to avoid vulnerability.

To investigate how chosen elements of the security sector in the Western Balkan states have been reformed under the influence of the EU, a two-tier framework of analysis is applied, which is based on the defining characteristics of SSR and its key objectives. As mentioned above, SSR does not follow a set model and is unique for each country. Yet, regardless of the context in which it is applied, there are two objectives SSR pursues everywhere: to develop a professional, effective and efficient security sector for both a state and its citizens and to ensure there are operational control and oversight mechanisms in the security sector in place (Hänggi 2004: 5). Both objectives will be studied below in the context of the Western Balkans: the first one through the organisational level and the second — through the political level of analysis.[58] The organisational level will examine changes within security sectors of the chosen Western Balkan states, while the political one will focus on the governance of their security sectors and the ways they fit into the broader political context.[59] Particular aspects of each level are to be defined below, when the EU approach to SSR is analysed. It should also be noted that in post-conflict environments the objectives of SSR are supplemented with the goal to deal with the legacy of war (Hänggi 2004: 5). Therefore, considering the recent history of the Western Balkans, both levels of analysis will pay special attention to the post-conflict contexts.

Finally, a few words should be said about the applicability of SSR to the context of RCFs. Although security sector reform is not typically pursued during wars, the analysis of security sectors in the Western Balkans[60] during the RCF phase is still provided. This is important for two reasons: to understand whether elements of SSR are possible in separate units of an RCF and to identify the starting position of security reforms in the region. If the first point could shed light on factors contributing to changes of security dynamics in RCFs, the second sets the parameters of the challenge facing local actors and the EU when attempting SSR in the Western Balkans. As SSR focuses on the provision of effective and efficient state and human security within a framework of good governance, it is seen as a vehicle for promoting amicable relations between regional actors and therefore a means of moving regions along the spectrum of security interdependence from a pole of enmity to the pole of amity.

The EU as an actor of security sector reform

The role of the EU as an SSR actor has been widely acknowledged in scholarly and policy literature (Churruca Maguruza 2008; Dursun-Ozkanca and Vandemoortele 2012). There is even a view that the EU in itself represents a project of SSR as it was "built on broad transformation of national government including security and defence structures" (Ekengren 2010: 101). While the latter view is considered here rather far-fetched, it is still possible to see the EU as well-placed for promoting SSR around the world with the potential for changing security interdependence between states.

Today, the EU approaches SSR as a key element of conflict-prevention, peace-building, democratisation, sustainable development and state-building (EC 2015: 2). Its SSR-related activities are aimed at the bodies that provide security to citizens, as well as at the institutions in charge of management and oversight of such bodies. In other words, the EU subscribes to a broad vision of SSR, which "goes beyond the notion of effectiveness of individual services ... and instead focuses on the overall functioning of the security system as part of a governance reform policy and strategy of the public sector" (EC 2006: 3). SSR is a versatile instrument, which "sits at the centre of Europe's foreign, security and development policies" (Spence 2010: 93).

The first applications of SSR took place in the context of the post-communist transition of Central and Eastern Europe (CEE) in the 1990s, which until today, alongside Sierra Leone and South Africa, remains one of the most successful cases of SSR (Dursun-Ozkanca and Vandemoortele 2012: 143). While many of the international efforts to improve the security situation in CEE came from NATO, the EU also obtained experience in the reform through engagement with the states of the region. Thus, the EU helped them improve border security as part of the Schengen system of movement control and was the leading external contributor to the reform of judiciary (Bailes 2010: 75).

The EU started engaging in SSR more proactively and systematically with the introduction of the Common Foreign and Security Policy (CFSP) by the Treaty of Maastricht in 1993 and its key element, the European Security and Defence Policy (ESDP), now Common Security and Defence Policy (CSDP), established at the Cologne Council in 1999, partly in response to the war in Kosovo. Since the early 2000s, ESDP/CSDP has been providing the EU with a convenient foreign-security policy platform for the promotion of SSR (Faleg 2012: 171). SSR, as part of the "security-good governance-development paradigm" (ibid.), fit effortlessly into the framework of CSDP, designed to tackle new challenges to European security. It quickly became incorporated into a number of the EU's missions and operations, deployed around the world to establish secure environments, based on the rule of law and respect for human rights. While only a handful of CSDP missions can be formally identified as SSR missions, e.g. EU SSR Guinea-Bissau and EUSEC RD Congo, various aspects of security sector reform became part of the mandate of almost 30 other missions (Jayasundara-Smits and Schirch 2016: 2). Rule of law missions in Iraq and Georgia, police missions in BiH, Macedonia and Palestinian Territories, and the civilian security sector mission in Ukraine are just a few examples.

It is important to note here that when the EU first launched these missions, it did not have a well-defined concept of SSR. The concept was developed and refined through practice, which, as already stated, spread through foreign, security and development policies. Today the EU is the most important development donor in the world, providing almost half of all the aid to developing countries (Law 2007a: 10). Starting from the 1990s it accepted the fact that its development aid could not be successful, unless coupled with efforts to improve the functioning and management of security systems of countries undergoing transitions and post-conflict transformations. Within the EU's development framework, SSR has been approached as a component of good governance and part of a wider public-sector reform (Hänggi and Tanner 2005: 31). As mentioned in the Commission's Communication "Governance and Development", SSR is an instrument, which should be used "to create safe security environments and to keep the security sector permanently subject to the same governance norms as other parts of the public sector and military forces under the political control of a civilian authority" (EC 2003a: 8). Before the Council adopted the EU Concept for ESDP support to SSR in October 2005 and the Commission released "A Concept for European Community Support for SSR" in May 2006, it was the EU policy documents on development that contained "the most elaborate conceptualisation" of SSR (Hänggi and Tanner 2005: 32).

The EU's concept of SSR has undergone significant alterations and considerably matured over the years. Partly because the concept was still under development, partly because the EU was a new actor in security in the 1990s, the initial experience of the EU with SSR was timid and erratic. Thus, in CEE the EU advocated more professional police and border control authorities as well as the introduction of civilian oversight over these services, yet it neither had an overarching view for the development of the security sectors in the states of the region, nor a unified vision as to what those sectors stood for. Even in the Western Balkans, the first attempts of the EU to engage with SSR were limited. For instance, the working group on Security and Defence issues of the SP, initiated by the EU, defined SSR as "right-sizing, re-orientation, reform, and capacity-building of national defence forces" (Gourlay 2008: 82). In other words, SSR was equated with defence reform. With time, the EU came to embrace SSR as a holistic approach, which could be applied not only to police forces, intelligence and army, but also management and oversight bodies, justice institutions and non-statutory forces (ibid.).

SSR was not simply developing alongside the EU's security toolbox but was among the main factors behind its evolution. As Faleg put it, SSR is one of the policy innovations, which contributed to "the EU's commitment as a security provider" (2012: 162). By not restricting the security sector to traditional military spheres, where the EU could not and still cannot compete with NATO[61], SSR allowed the EU to engage in projects of peace-building and stabilisation in many regions of the world. As part national, part transnational policy, SSR is applied by the EU as a tool of integration to bring the security sectors of neighbouring states, linked by common security problems and challenges, to shared standards, consistent with democratic norms and principles. While SSR does not dictate the number of troops or size of security budgets, it ensures that security systems function effectively and are governed democratically. The expectation is that the states and regions undertaking SSR, under the guidance of the EU, will "move in similar direction in the streamlining of security thinking into broad sectors of public administration, civil society and business" to meet threats of cross-border crime, terrorism, failing states and disasters (Ekengren 2010: 116).

While using SSR to respond to complex risks, the EU has been cultivating friendly regional relations, helping states choose cooperation over competition and peace over war. In this respect, SSR "epitomizes European integration" (Spence 2010: 93) as it is used as a tool of externalising the EU's internal success as the security community (Ekengren 2010: 103). By harmonizing the work of security systems in the third states SSR leads to regional integration and the emergence of amicable security relations. What is more, the application of SSR is meant to help the EU to reduce differences between EU and non-EU countries, making sure all adhere to the same principles when it comes to the work and management of security services. In a world where the line between internal and external security is blurred, this is especially important. However, it is essential to understand that the EU's SSR-related activities have not always had the potential to change the security dynamics of regions and be utilised as an instrument of security community-building. As will be demonstrated through the case study of the Western Balkan states, at first the application of SSR efforts, led by the EU in the region, was limited, much like the EU's approach to the region in general. Yet by engaging in SSR and expanding its understanding of the reform, the EU has been learning through practice. Thus, it can be claimed that through continuous learning and adaptation to the changing context, the EU became an active and credible actor in the field.

The EU's policy framework on SSR was formed in 2005 and 2006 with the release of the already mentioned concepts by the Council and Commission as well as the Draft Council Conclusions on a combined vision on SSR. It was further refined with two communications from the Commission: Roadmap for the development of an EU-wide strategy on SSR (EC 2015) and Elements for an EU-wide strategic framework to support security sector reform (EC 2016). These documents were the product of decades of work on the reform of the bloc and its member states. This work can be divided into two main strands: practice in SSR-related activities and involvement in the development of the concept in cooperation with third actors. The Commission's concept states that SSR "has been an integral part of EU integration, enlargement and external assistance for many years. Through Community instruments, the EU has supported reform processes in partner countries and regions in different parts of the world under a wide range of policy areas" (EC 2006: 3). Indeed, over the years the EU contributed to different aspects of SSR through a variety of activities, in particular through its missions, including those performed by the Western European Union (WEU)[62]. For instance, in 1987-1988, the WEU was involved in mine-clearing operations during the Iran-Iraq war and in 1994-1996 provided police support to the EU administration of Mostar in Bosnia (Eekelen 2008: 117). After CSDP came into effect in 2003, SSR elements have become incorporated into many of its missions (Churruca Muguruza 2008: 90). The Western Balkans has been and remains one of the key geographical areas of the EU's support for SSR (ibid.: 96). Since 2003 six CSDP missions were deployed to the region confirming that the Western Balkans not only provided the inspiration for the creation of CSDP, but also gave the EU an opportunity to test it in practice (Juncos 2013).

The start of the EU's involvement in the conceptualisation of SSR, like its practical engagement with the policy, dates to the beginning of the 1990s. Since then, the EU has been actively cooperating with the OSCE, NATO, the Council of Europe and the Organisation for Economic Co-operation and Development's (OECD) Development Assistance Committee (DAC) to develop norms and best practices of SSR (Law and Myshlovska 2008: 10). While some of this cooperation was explicitly aimed at the formulation of the SSR agenda, other projects referred to a broader context of post-Cold War security relations, which pertained to SSR indirectly. The OSCE's Code of Conduct on Politico-Military Relations, adopted in 1994, is an example of the latter category. The EU was one of the main contributors to the Code, which called for the democratic control of all security forces (ibid.) and contained many commitments regarding such areas as arms control, confidence-building, conflict prevention and crisis management (Hänggi and Tanner 2005: 22).

It is notable that the European Commission and EU member states were among the contributors to the OECD DAC's SSR documents, which later not only provided the basis for the EU's concepts of SSR, but also became key points of reference for all SSR practitioners (Law and Myshlovska 2008: 11). Until today the guidelines on "Security System Reform and Governance" (2004) and "Handbook on Security System Reform" (2008), produced by the OECD DAC with the assistance of various actors, including the EU, remain the most influential documents in the sphere of SSR. The EU has also cooperated with non-governmental actors to develop its own approach to SSR. For example, the work, done by the Geneva Centre for the Democratic Control of Armed Forces (DCAF) on SSR, had an impact on the formulation of the Concept for ESDP support to the reform (Faleg 2012: 176).

As an actor of SSR, the EU has at least three comparative advantages over other actors engaged in the field. First, it has a broad variety of foreign-policy instruments at its disposal, ranging from diplomacy to civil and military missions, for the advancement of SSR (Churruca Muguruza 2008: 75). These instruments can provide short-, medium- and long-term assistance to all sorts of contexts, whether developed, developing or post-conflict. Second, the EU is the largest contributor of the development aid in the world with a global outreach and access to considerable financial resources. While SSR is part of the development agenda, the EU, is well-positioned for its promotion. Third, as a *sui generis* actor, the EU is committed to the advancement of SSR on both state and regional levels. Regional aspects of SSR are perceived as highly promising among SSR practitioners, scholars and policy-makers (Ekengren and Simons 2010: 3). A regional approach is seen as a possibility to make SSR efforts more effective and shape them in ways "that could also contribute to a change of individual states' security and defence priorities by efforts including other partners in the region" (ibid.). The EU has not simply emphasised the importance of a regional dimension to SSR in its strategic documents, but also has been pursuing its implementation in practice. The Stabilisation and Association Process (1999), Cotonou Agreement (2000), European Neighbourhood Policy (2004) and the EU Strategy for Africa (2005) are all examples of regional policies, which include provisions on SSR (Jayasunara-Smits and Schirch 2016: 4).

The EU, therefore, has considerable experience in SSR and several advantages over other actors in the field. This work, however, does not claim that the EU's engagement with security sector reform has been flawless. There are, of course, some problems impeding the progress. First, there are serious discrepancies between the commitments on paper and the results on the ground. While in its concepts the EU promotes a comprehensive idea of SSR, in practice, it does not always use a holistic approach[63]. Secondly, there is a problem of coordination between all the EU actors, involved in SSR. The reform is attempted not only by the Council and European Commission, but also individual member states, whose governments do not necessarily coordinate their actions with the EU policies. Third, during the studied period the EU lacked a unified policy framework on SSR, which meant its SSR-related activities and policies were not always used "in a coherent, coordinated and complementary way" (EC 2015: 2). With the adoption of the EU-wide framework on SSR in the summer of 2016, it made a step in the right direction, but the consequences of this step remain outside the scope of this study.

The key documents on SSR that are of relevance to the study include the above-mentioned Council and Commission programmes, released in 2005 and 2006. While offering different readings on the reform, which reflect their respective fields of expertise, these concepts also share some similarities, including: using the OECD definition of SSR, emphasising human security, recognising the importance of regional dimension and advocating complementarity of the Council and Commission's SSR-related efforts. In the Commission's interpretation, SSR "means transforming the security system, which includes all [security sector] actors, their roles, responsibilities and actions, working together to manage and operate the system in a manner that is consistent with democratic norms and sound principles of good governance, and thus contributing to a well-functioning security framework" (EC 2006: 6). In a similar manner, the Council contends that SSR contributes to "an accountable, effective and efficient security system, operating under civilian control consistent with democratic norms and principles of good governance, transparency and the rule of law, and acting according to international standards and respecting human rights, which can be a force for peace and stability, fostering democracy and promoting local and regional stability" (Council of the EU 2005: 4).

Both documents underline that the visions of SSR contained in them are deliberately broad to provide for complementarity between SSR activities, undertaken by the EU (Council of the EU 2005: 6; EC 2006: 4). Neither of the concepts on its own reflects the EU-wide SSR strategy, which means they can only be considered to represent the EU's SSR framework together. While this complementarity is important, it could not compensate for the absence of a single EU policy on SSR. The Draft Council Conclusions on a Policy Framework for Security Sector Reform (2006) presented an interim solution to this problem by reiterating key provisions from the Council and Commission concepts. Nonetheless, it did not provide an overarching guidance for the EU's engagement in SSR, partly due to its provisional nature, partly due to the lack of detail on its three pages. Consequently, both the Council and Commission continued approaching SSR on the basis of their respective strategies until the release of an EU-wide SSR concept in 2016.

Since this work studies the EU-wide impact on SSR in the Western Balkans, the author developed an inventory, which could capture SSR efforts of both the Council and the Commission. This is provided in Annex I and is based on the Council and Commission's Concepts for SSR, using the modified model of Hänggi and Tanner (2005: 100-104). The latter is a detailed, yet not complete, list of activities related to the promotion of security sector governance, designed to help scholars and policy-makers assess how the EU and other international actors perform in SSR. The model, presented in Annex I is adjusted to the context of the Western Balkans. It incorporates two levels of analysis that were introduced earlier. This is the political level that ensures countries, undergoing SSR, have operational control and oversight mechanisms of their security systems and organisational level that studies SSR efforts aimed at building a professional security sector.[64] Considering the focus of this work, the activities of the organisational level concern the defence sector, police and border control services, while the inventory is applied to analyse the impact of the EU on SSR in Croatia, Serbia and Bosnia.

Summing up, it is possible to say that the EU remains one of the leading SSR actors in the world. Security sector reform is incorporated into numerous EU policies, designed to prevent conflicts, manage crises and contribute to sustainable peace, state-building and development (EC 2015: 2). Because of its versatility and unique position in security, governance and development frameworks, SSR can serve as a "key to understanding the potential of the EU's role as an international actor", help assess claims about its approach to international relations as being unique and contribute to the discussion about the EU's ability to transfer its norms and values to other countries and regions of the world (Spence 2010: 93). Since the early 2000s, the EU's SSR-related activities have been used as a security-community building tool. Prior to that, however, the EU's attempts to strengthen security sectors outside its territory were inconsistent and sporadic, as well as lacking in power to be the main force behind the transformation of negative security dynamics, such as found in the Western Balkans, when the region represented an RCF. The final part of the chapter analyses the application of the reform in the region in detail, following the periodisation, introduced in Chapter 2.

The EU's impact on the regional dimension of SSR in the Western Balkans

Paraphrasing Hänggi and Tanner, the Western Balkans can be identified as one of the most exciting laboratories of externally assisted security sector reform in the world (2005: 43). As a result of the conflicts of the 1990s, many of the countries of the region lost the domestic monopoly over their security sectors and were unable to disentangle the networks of conflict that turned them into an RCF without external help. Over time, the international community that had to intervene to stop the bloodshed singled out SSR not only as an instrument for restoring peace in the region and normalising life there, but also as a "fundamental building block of democratic transition" (DCAF 2006: 5). The EU was among the first to recognise SSR as an explicit reform agenda for the Western Balkans. If in the 1990s it was tackling SSR-related activities timidly, hoping that regional security sectors would reform eventually, mostly as a by-product of political and economic conditionality, from the early 2000s SSR was identified as an important policy area, which had to be pursued openly and comprehensively to bring about results (ibid.). The EU was also at the forefront of the international effort to advocate the regional approach to SSR. This section looks at how this approach was pursued by the EU in the Western Balkans between 1991 and 2013. To ensure consistency, it follows the periodisation introduced in Chapter 2, which defined the region as a regional conflict formation in 1991-1995, failed security regime in 1995-1999 and emerging security community since 1999.

Setting the scene: before the reform was possible (1991-1995)

The analysis of the first period differs from the two that follow, and this is because the EU did not pursue SSR in the Western Balkans on the regional level from 1991 to 1995.[65] Apart from being utterly unprepared to take on the task of SSR on the regional scale at this time, the EU was unable to engage with the reform due to the impossibility to conduct SSR during the time of open warfare. While there is a variety of contexts, where security sector reform can be applied, the conflict environment can very rarely accommodate the reform. Even though the armed conflict did not affect all the Western Balkan countries at the beginning of the 1990s, the region was united by the prospect of conflict into a regional conflict formation, making the international community and the EU pursue the policy of regional containment, not reforms. Moreover, at this point the EU did not yet see the Western Balkans as a coherent region. Nonetheless, the period of 1991-1995 is still included into this study as it is crucial for understanding the full extent of the evolution undergone by the EU on the way to becoming a leading SSR actor in the Western Balkans.

After initial hesitation, in the early 1990s the EU started actively searching for ways of containing and managing conflicts engulfing the Balkan subcomplex. Most of its activities at this period could be grouped under the headings of diplomatic effort and humanitarian assistance. At first the EU's shuttle diplomacy in Former Yugoslavia was handled by a troika of Foreign Ministers, but from the autumn of 1991 it became the task of a special envoy. The position from 1991 to 1995 was held, at different periods, by three high-profile politicians: Lord Carrington, David Owen (both former British Foreign Secretaries) and the former Swedish Prime Minister Carl Bildt. While each of the envoys had their own approach to the task entrusted to them by the EU, none of them managed to find a workable solution to the crises. Without any clear common strategy to guide them, they found themselves responding to events on the ground in an *ad hoc* manner. The slowness of the Brussels bureaucracy led many to accuse the EU of "contributing to the processes of Yugoslav disintegration" (Gordon, Sasse and Sebastian 2008: 9).

The failures of the EU's peace-making process, which were studied in detail elsewhere[66], can be explained through the lack of ability and willingness to act. CFSP, which was introduced in the Maastricht Treaty, became fully ratified only in 1993, i.e. after the start of conflicts in the former Yugoslavia (ibid.: 8). In the absence of a common working framework, individual member states disagreed not only on the plan of action, but also on the nature of the problem (Peen Rodt and Wolff 2012: 140). For instance, France, an old ally of Serbia, was in favour of preserving Yugoslavia intact, but Germany, itself only recently unified, was supporting the recognition of Croatia and Slovenia's independence. While some states favoured an intervention, whether through the UN or WEU, others preferred to stand back. In general, at the beginning of the 1990s the EU did not have a political will or capacity to act as a single actor.

Regarding humanitarian aid, from early stages of the conflict the EU's assistance was aimed at satisfying basic social needs, such as food, water and medicine (Bojicic-Dzelilovic, Kostovicova and Randazzo 2016: 5). This type of assistance, directed by the European Humanitarian Office, which cooperated closely with the Red Cross, United Nations High Commissioner for Refugees (UNHCR), UNICEF and the World Food Programme, played an important role in offering relief to refugees and displaced persons (ibid.). Another channel for the EU's impact was the efforts of its individual member states. Many of them contributed forces to the UNPROFOR peacekeeping missions at first in Croatia and later in Bosnia, while Germany, the UK and France were also members of the Contact group, set up to negotiate peace between the warring parties. All these efforts notwithstanding, the EU could not stop the bloodshed in Bosnia in 1995, leaving it to the USA and NATO to bring the conflict to an end with the Dayton Peace Agreement (DPA).

It is important to re-iterate that not all the Western Balkan countries went through war at this period. Albania and FYROM managed to stay peaceful, although remained connected to the more turbulent parts of the region, via a variety of networks, discussed in the previous chapter. Even in these countries, however, the EU did not engage in SSR. Its approach was quite patchy and inconsistent at best: a non-preferential trade and cooperation agreement with Albania was concluded in 1992, the same year the country became eligible for financial support under PHARE, but FYROM had to wait till December 1995 for the establishment of diplomatic relations with the Union[67]. Such lukewarm attitude is understandable as most of the EU's attention in the region at the beginning of the 1990s was aimed at managing territorial conflicts between states and ethnic groups (Bechev 2011: 108). This conflict management was reactive, *ad hoc* and ineffective.

SSR for stabilisation and peacebuilding (1995-1999)

Despite all the shortfalls and failures, the Balkan wars of the early 1990s provided the EU with a steep learning curve. Following the signing of the DPA, the bloc assumed a more active role in providing security to states of the region (Watanabe 2010: 130). In Bosnia, alongside economic assistance, it took on tasks of policing and administration support. In Albania, it was the EU's intervention which prevented the crisis, caused by the collapse of pyramid saving schemes in 1997, from disintegrating into a prolonged conflict. Within the framework of the WEU, EU states also arranged a demining mission in Croatia. Even more importantly, since 1996 the EU started looking for ways to influence security systems of the Balkan states on the regional level. Traditionally, the studies of the EU's SSR-related activities in the Western Balkans, go back to 1999-early 2000s, but rarely earlier[68]. Here, scholars look at the SAP and the Stability Pact as the first platforms through which the EU promoted SSR regionally. The fact that SSR as a concept was formulated at the end of the 1990s is an important factor perpetuating this approach. The current work sees this vision as flawed: mainly because it fails to recognise SSR-related issues promoted by the EU through the Regional Approach. Of course, the RA had its limitations. It was often said to lack "substance and concrete measures of support" (Uvalic 2003: 105). With a broad and ambitious objective, which can be summed up as "the successful implementation of the Dayton/Paris peace agreements and the creation of the area of political stability and economic prosperity, also by fostering the process of political and economic reforms and the respect of human and minority rights and democratic principles" (EC 1996:1), it offered modest rewards under the PHARE and Obnova programmes. For example, Croatia and the FRY received a little over 218 million Euro in 1996-1999 (Uvalic 2003: 105).

Nonetheless, the RA deserves attention because it contained first regionally-aimed requirements from the EU on reforms of security sectors for the Western Balkan states. These requirements mainly concerned the police, border services, judiciary and, in the case of Bosnia, Croatia and the FRY, cooperation with the International Criminal Tribunal for the former Yugoslavia (ICTY). The initiative also promoted regional cooperation on security issues, thus trying not only to stabilise the Balkan subcomplex, but also cultivate reciprocal relationships between its members and help it move away from the negative pole of security interdependence. The RA demonstrated the willingness of the EU to tackle elements of SSR, even before it had formally formulated its vision on the reform. Furthermore, it indicated the issues, the EU's SSR support would prioritise in the future.

The Regional Approach was the first initiative, which recognised that the Western Balkan countries formed a distinctive group, different from both CEE and other South-East European states. Based on the Royaumount Process, the RA aimed to promote stability and good-neighbourliness between BiH, Croatia, the FRY — all subject to obligations under the peace agreements — as well as Albania and FYROM (EC 1998: 1). It was launched on 26 February 1996 but obtained financial mechanisms and a framework of conditionality later (Gordon, Sasse and Sebastian 2008: 11). Thus, the Obnova programme, which became the EU's main financial tool for the Western Balkans, was introduced in July 1996, and political and economic conditions for the RA were established by the Council on 29 April 1997 (ibid.). The conditions were divided into two categories: general, i.e. applying to all the countries covered by the RA, and specific. The former, among others, included democratic reforms, respect for human rights, return of refugees, economic reforms and regional cooperation (EC 1997a: 2). The latter were mainly designed to help three post-conflict states of the region to become more stable and secure and were linked to their compliance with Dayton and Erdut Agreements[69]. BiH, for example, was required to establish common institutions, while Croatia — to dissolve Herceg-Bosna structures and assist BiH in ensuring the effective functioning of the United Police Force of Mostar (EC 1998a: 4).

SSR-related requirements were included into both categories of conditionality and were applied to each Western Balkan country, whether affected by war or not. A strong emphasis was placed on policing, representation of minorities and fight against organised crime. For instance, in 1998 BiH was encouraged to put more effort into building independent judiciary and multi-ethnic police, FYROM was praised for achievements in the sphere of rule of law but berated for insufficient progress in the law enforcement reform and minority representation in security forces, while Albania was asked to become more active in fighting fraud and corruption (EC 1998b: 2-6). Additionally, the RA contained first and that is why rudimentary EU requirements for good governance of the security sectors in the Western Balkans (ibid.). It should be noted that Croatia and the FRY were least committed to the reform agenda, promoted by the EU. In fact, the efficiency of the Regional Approach suffered considerably because of these countries' ambivalence and sometimes even hostility towards externally induced reforms[70]. Moreover, the RA did not gain noticeable recognition among other members of the international community, e.g. NATO and the USA, that were engaged in promoting the stabilisation of the post-Yugoslav space, too but could not agree on what countries to cover under their policies. Poor coordination of efforts among external members in the post-conflict period can be seen as one of the reasons for the failure of the security regime in the Western Balkans and pacification of regional relations.

While recognising the existence of SSR-related elements in the RA, it is important not to over-exaggerate their significance. References to issues, which are now included under the umbrella of SSR, were scattered around documents on the Regional Approach, without any clear indication that they could be considered part of the same package. This circumstance, combined with the lack of domestic and external support for the initiative, led to many wasted opportunities in the Western Balkans at the time when the needs

SECURITY DYNAMICS OF THE WESTERN BALKANS   95

for SSR were immense. Most states of the region were embarking on post-authoritarian and post-conflict transitions and were struggling with adjusting their security sectors, which in some cases, had been directly involved in violence and conflict, to new circumstances (Dowling 2008: 174). The security systems of the Western Balkans states tended to be "fragmented, underdeveloped (although some sectors, typically the armed forces, [were] over-developed for peaceful conditions), over-politicized and structured along ethnic lines" (Caparini 2006: 9). The presence of non-state actors, such as guerrilla movements and paramilitary organisations, as well as low levels of civilian expertise within governments and parliaments on the issues of security, added further challenges to SSR in the region (Hänggi and Tanner 2005: 46-47). The EU's regional response to the SSR needs of the Western Balkan states in in the post-conflict period were therefore disproportionate and underdeveloped. It is hardly surprising, as the EU was still ill-equipped to deal with security issues outside its borders: CFSP was still weak and CSDP was not yet introduced. The EU was also continuing to pursue a reactive policy towards the region, while not yet considering it a future member of the European zone of peace.

SSR as a tool for building (future) member states (1999-2013)

The Kosovo war, as was outlined earlier, provided a powerful impetus for the change of the EU policies towards the Western Balkans. While the fighting in the region was once again stopped through the American and NATO intervention, it was predominantly the task of the EU to stabilise and normalise relations among the Western Balkan states afterwards. To achieve this ambitious task, the EU opted for a proactive approach and a combination of civilian and military instruments, "available under the CFSP umbrella alongside enlargement instruments specially tailored to address the legacy of armed conflicts" (Bojicic-Dzelilovic, Kostovicova and Randazzo 2016: 4). With the launch of the Stabilisation and Association Process (SAP), the EU committed itself to assisting the region's transformation from violence and instability to peace, while the Thessaloniki European Council in 2003 confirmed that the Western Balkans' future was in the bloc (Butt 2004: 7). Over time, six CSDP missions were deployed to countries of the region[71] and generous donations were made available for their reconstruction first through the CARDS programme, which substituted PHARE and Obnova in 2000, and then through the Instrument for Pre-Accession Assistance (IPA) that replaced CARDS in January 2007. Assistance to the region was also offered through both more specialised instruments, such as the Instrument for Structural Policies for Pre-Accession (ISPA) or Special Accession Programme for Agriculture and Rural Development (SAPARD), and more general financing tools such as the European Initiative for Democratisation and Human Rights (EIDHR).

At this period the EU has come to acknowledge openly and explicitly the importance of security sector reform for the reconstruction, stabilisation and Europeanisation of the region. It was no longer hoped that security sectors would become effective and efficient by themselves after reforms of other sectors were completed. This shift in approaching SSR in the Western Balkans can be best summed up with an excerpt from the Food for Thought Paper, prepared for the EU Presidency Seminar on SSR in the Western Balkans, held in Vienna in February 2006. This document stated that

> "democratic change within, and modernisation of, security sector institutions [would] not necessarily come as an intrinsic by-product of political and economic reforms promoted through the process of EU integration. On the contrary, good governance of the security sector must be explicitly identified as a key component of the reform agenda. Failure to address security sector reform issues as an integral part of the overall democratisation and development process would risk impeding or even derailing the EU's regional stability objectives and the enlargement efforts in the Western Balkans" (DCAF 2006: 5).

After 1999, SSR became a vehicle for the transfer of EU norms and values to the Western Balkans. Through the reform, the bloc tried to help states of the region to improve internal and external security by demanding their security sectors to adhere to the principles of good governance, human rights, the rule of law and transparency. The Western Balkans offered the EU exceptionally favourable ground for the application of its comprehensive SSR policy.

Even more, the region provided the bloc with several opportunities to hone its approach to the reform. In 2006, for example, two consecutive EU Presidencies held two high-profile events on SSR in the Western Balkans: on 13-14 February, a seminar "Security Sector Reform in the Western Balkans" was organised by the Austrian Presidency in cooperation with DCAF and the EU institute for Security Studies, and in December, a conference "Enhancing security sector governance though security sector reform in the Western Balkans — the role of the European Union" was held in Zagreb by the Finnish Presidency and DCAF. These events were organised not only to address the most urgent SSR needs in the Western Balkans, but also to discuss the future of the EU as an actor of SSR and determine the most effective ways of translating the newly agreed SSR agenda into operational actions under the Council and Commission frameworks (Law and Myshlovska 2006: 13).

There were two main channels through which the EU attempted promoting SSR in the Western Balkans on the regional level at this period: the Stability Pact (SP) for South Eastern Europe and the SAP. Two initiatives were different in terms of ownership, outreach, approach and weight, attached to them both by the EU and the Western Balkan countries themselves. Although initially the SAP was presented as a supplement to the SP, within only a few years, it assumed primacy in the EU toolbox for the region, pushing the Stability Pact, which in 2008 was replaced by the Regional Cooperation Council, into the background. Despite the policy's influence waning fast and the EU being only one stakeholder among many, the Stability Pact played an important role in raising the profile of security sector reform in South-Eastern Europe in general and in the Western Balkans in particular. Established with an aim to transform the governance dynamics in the region (Bojicic-Dzelilovic, Kostovicova and Randazzo 2016: 6), the SP operated on the basis of three working tables, each presenting sectors "considered vital for the success of conflict prevention and peace-building" (Watanabe 2010: 139). Working Table I focused on democratisation and human rights, Working Table II was dedicated to economic reconstruction, development and cooperation, and Working Table III dealt with security issues, which were divided among two sub-tables: one on military security and the other on justice and home affairs (JHA). Security sector reform was seen as a "cross-sub-table issue", cutting across both hard and soft security (Hänggi and Tanner 2005: 50).

Within the SP, the lead on military issues was taken by NATO, while the EU assumed leadership in JHA. The latter emerged as an important tool for post-conflict reconstruction. Criminal networks, which emerged and proliferated during the conflicts in the 1990s, survived in the post-Yugoslav space even after the fighting ceased. By using the grey zones, characterised by "blurred responsibilities for the rule of law, transparent borders, displaced persons, unreturned refugees and populations living in dire social and economic conditions without tangible prospects", these networks created fertile ground for the resurgence of past conflicts (Delevic 2007: 82). Moreover, they also spilled over to the EU countries, thus posing a tangible threat to the European security community, its norms and values. It was therefore of the utmost importance for the EU to encourage the Western Balkan countries to fight organised crime and adhere to European standards in JHA. The Stability Pact offered a useful platform to pursue these goals in a broader regional context, which while being superior to the previous attempts of the international community to stabilise the Balkans, was still in many ways deficient. One of the biggest deficiencies of the Pact, that from certain perspectives could also be its advantage, was its broad membership. SEE states, covered by the policy, did not represent a homogeneous group: the inclusion of Moldova, Bulgaria and Romania alongside the Western Balkan states made it very difficult for the EU, as well as other donors involved in the scheme, to engage with all the participating states equally, implement projects with universal appeal for every participant or achieve meaningful regional cooperation between all of them, especially in such a sensitive area as security. That is why, many of the regional initiatives launched under the framework of the Stability Pact, with time started focusing on the Western Balkans only (Bechev 2011: 123). The Migration, Asylum, Refugees Regional Initiative (MARRI), formed in 2003, is an example of such an initiative. With the mandate to promote closer regional cooperation and common, comprehensive and harmonized approach in areas of migration, asylum, border control, visa regime, integration and return of refugees and displaced persons, MARRI has been working to ensure the development and stability of the Western Balkans (MARRI 2022). While under regional ownership, the initiative has benefited from close cooperation with the EU and its member states.

The prioritisation of JHA issues within the SP allowed the EU to become engaged in SSR more deeply. The launch of the SAP, however, was even more important for the development of the EU's SSR agenda and its application in the Western Balkans. While the Stability Pact emphasised the idea of regional cooperation as a prerequisite of achieving safe, secure and prosperous SEE (Watanabe 2010: 138), the SAP linked the stabilisation of the Western Balkans to the process of integration into the EU. SSR thus became one of the requirements for the countries of the region's accession to the European Union. Without creating any new conditionality for the region, the reform of the security sector emerged as part of a broader agenda, introduced by the SAP (Pöysäri 2007: 34).

The SAP took on the task of "regional stabilisation through more proactive peace-building policies" that took into account the specifics of the post-conflict situation in the Western Balkans (Gordon, Sasse and Sebastian 2008: 10). It expressed the EU commitment to the economic and structural development of the region by offering financial and technical aid, and most importantly, eventual accession to the bloc in exchange for the adoption of principles of the rule of law, democratisation, free markets, building stable institutions and regional cooperation (Bojicic-Dzelilovic, Kostovicova and Randazzo 2016: 5). Through the SAP, the political elites of the Western Balkans are obliged to subscribe to the values, shared by the EU states, which would enable them to develop compatible norms and principles among each other, thus switching from the competitive and aggressive behaviour to cooperation. Therefore, the SAP has been developing the compatibility of main values held by the elites inside the region and working on fulfilling one of the essential conditions for the development of a security community, identified by Deutsch. SSR was used by the EU as an important tool of security governance in this process. With the introduction of the SAP, it received a new application: in addition to being a tool of post-conflict stabilisation, peace-building, democratisation and sustainable development, it also became an instrument of EU integration and state-building or, to be more precise, member state-building. By emphasising capacity-building and efficiency of the security sector in the equal manner as the need for transparency, democratic and civilian oversight and accountability, the EU has been attempting to build self-sufficient, resilient states in the region, whose security systems would function according to the same principles and standards as security systems in EU member states. These actions can be interpreted as attempts to achieve political responsiveness and mutual predictability of behaviour in the Western Balkans — two other conditions of the security community.

SSR in the Western Balkans can therefore be seen as a steppingstone towards functioning statehood, regional cooperation and European integration. Aligning the security systems in the region with the EU standards is meant to bring it fully into the European zone of peace, where war and conflict are matters of the past. The SAP does not try to cultivate a separate Western Balkan identity, but rather works on Europeanising the Western Balkans and making it part of the EU/Europe security community. However, the full integration of the region into the European security community did not take place by 2013. Although a future in the EU was recognised as a goal by the ruling elites in all Western Balkan states, many of them struggled to deliver the reforms, including in the security sector, to fulfil the EU conditionality. Moreover, cooperation between the states was guided by desire to comply with EU demands, rather than trust. That is why the Western Balkan *security community* is still *embryonic* and is an extension of the European zone of peace.

Although created as a policy for the region as a whole with an explicit focus on regional cooperation, the SAP has a distinct bilateral component. After all, each Western Balkan state is assessed on individual merit before it can progress within the Process. Bilateral relations find reflection in Stabilisation and Association Agreements (SAA), and negotiations leading to the signing of these agreements, agreed with each country separately. SSR issues feature prominently in annual country reports that monitor progress in the sphere of the rule of law, democratic control of the armed forces, effective border management, anti-corruption measures and offer recommendations for further legal and institutional changes (Caparini 2006: 13). The level of the EU's involvement in SSR and issues it prioritises differ from country to country, which is why it is important to complement regional analysis of the SAP with the study of the EU's relations with individual Western Balkan states. While this is done in Chapters 4-6, the remainder of this chapter analyses the aspects of SSR, which the EU has been promoting through the SAP on the regional level. These aspects involve both soft and hard security issues.

The area of soft security has been emphasised within the framework of the SAP since its early days. The break-up of Yugoslavia created new states and around 5,000 km of new borders, which prompted the EU to make border security in the Western Balkans the first official priority for its CARDS programme (Hänggi and Tanner 2005: 51). Furthermore, to establish effective border security in the region, the EU worked closely with other external actors. Thus, the EU's approach for several years was embedded into the multilateral Ohrid Border Process. Launched at the 2003 Ohrid Regional Conference on Border Security and Management by the EU, NATO, the OSCE and Stability Pact, it acted as "a common platform for border security and management" in the Western Balkans (Cascone 2008: 154). The Process, apart from identifying goals for border security of the region, also divided tasks between the organisations leading it (ibid.) The EU was leading the effort on the Integrated Border Management (IBM) for the Western Balkans (Caparini 2006: 17-18). The key objective of the IBM was to establish open but controlled and secure borders, and to improve the stabilization of the region through reinforcing the rule of law, institutional capacity and regional cooperation (IBM Guidelines 2007: 17). Even after 2007, when the Ohrid Process was successfully completed, the EU continued supporting the implementation of the IBM for the Western Balkans, and in certain cases started introducing regional states to the IBM strategy, used inside the bloc (EC 2008: 12).[72] In 2008-2010, border reforms in the region were subordinated to the process of visa liberalisation. The introduction of visa-free regime for citizens of FYROM, Montenegro and Serbia in December 2009 (EC 2009) and for Albania and Bosnia and Herzegovina in November 2010 (EC 2010) were important achievements in this respect.[73]

Police reform is another area of soft security in the Western Balkans the EU has been supporting on the regional level. Since the launch of the SAP, trans-border approach to the sphere of policing has been consistently highlighted by the EU as instrumental for addressing security challenges facing the region, such as terrorism and organised crime (EC 2006b: 18). As a result, the Western Balkans benefited from a number of projects aimed at improving regional police co-operation and capacities under both CARDS and IPA. In 2001, regional CARDS project provided the basis for effective law enforcement cooperation between the Western Balkan states by developing the capacity of the Interpol National Central Bureaux (NCBs). Between 2001 and 2006 CARDS guided the development of international law enforcement coordination units, assisted Western Balkan states with the establishment of working connections between NCBs and remote access units at border crossings, and funded comprehensive assessment reports in JHA as well as an inventory of JHA assistance provided to each of the Western Balkan states by the EU and other donors (ibid.: 14). With time, the EU started paying more attention to coordination of efforts with other external actors present in the region to avoid duplication and repeating mistakes of the past. Other aspects of police reform, which benefited from the CARDS funds regionally included, but were not limited to training schemes (e.g. the 2002 Justice and Police Training Scheme for high and medium level decision-makers in the SAP countries), data-processing and information exchange projects (e.g. in 2006 the EU was engaged in implementing a monitoring instruments project to establish guidelines on collecting and interpreting police and judicial statistics), and assessments of corruption and crime in the Western Balkans (e.g. the 2006 CARDS project) (ibid.: 14-17). With the adoption of the Stockholm Programme "An open and secure Europe serving and protecting the citizens" in December 2009, the EU invited Western Balkan states to subscribe to the EU-wide framework for police and judicial cooperation, thus showing once again that the future of the region was in the bloc (EC 2011: 16).

Under IPA, regional dimensions of SSR have been approached through Multi-Beneficiary programmes. While the bulk of the EU assistance is provided to the Western Balkan countries through national programmes, IPA allocates around 10% of its funds to regional projects. For instance, in the period from 2007 to 2009, 401.4 million EUR was spent on multi-beneficiary aid (EC 2007: 4), and in 2011-2013 this assistance reached 521 million EUR (EC 2011: 14). Although IPA covers the Western Balkans, Turkey and Iceland, it is the Western Balkan countries which benefit from multi-lateral programmes the most. This is because of the significance, attached to regional cooperation for the achievement of political stability, security and economic prosperity in the region at the EU-Western Balkan summits in Zagreb (2000), Thessaloniki (2003) and Salzburg (2006) (EC 2006b: 10). All programme documents on IPA Multi-beneficiary assistance highlight the importance of constructive regional cooperation between the Western Balkan states and recognise it "as a qualifying indicator of the countries' readiness to integrate into the EU" (ibid.).

Justice and Home Affairs sector under IPA Multi-Beneficiary Assistance received around 4.6% of the instrument's budget between 2007 and 2013: in 2007-2010 the EU spent 28.5 million EUR on these reforms and in 2011-2013 the spending reached 24 million EUR (EC 2011: 15). In the Western Balkans, the IPA funds were regularly spent on regional judicial, police and prosecutor cooperation. The Multi-Beneficiary Multi-Annual Indicative Planning Documents (MIPD) 2007-2009, 2009-2011 and 2011-2013 identified support for regional cooperation between law enforcement agencies and judicial authorities in the Western Balkans as essential instruments for fighting organised crime and terrorism (EC 2007: 13-14; EC 2011: 16-17). Multi-beneficiary support in JHA was envisaged to "facilitate networking as well as the sharing of best practices and lessons learned in the region" (EC 2006b: 19). As a direct result of such support, countries of the region acquired International Law Enforcement Coordination Units (ILECU) and significantly improved cooperation in prosecution and investigation matters not only between each other but also with international actors. The ILECUs, set up under the IPA Multi-Beneficiary ILECUs I project that lasted from September 2008 till December 2012, are bodies that provide contact points and harmonise cooperation between both national actors, involved in the sphere of the rule of law, such as Ministries of Interior, Ministries of Finance and the Prosecutors, and international law enforcement agencies, such as Europol or Interpol (EC 2011: 17). These units contributed to the development of well-functioning information and intelligence management environment in the region. Under the DET ILECUs II[74] project (February 2010–January 2013), the EU allocated funds for improving police cooperation in the Western Balkans in the matters of illicit drug trafficking, financial crime and terrorism prevention (ibid.).

The Instrument for Pre-Accession Multi-Beneficiary (IPA MB) programmes on JHA also focused on facilitating prosecutors' networks (e.g. IPA 2010 MB project "Fight against organised crime and corruption: Strengthening the Prosecutors"), improving regional capacities for dealing with war crimes (e.g. IPA 2013 MB project "Strengthening Regional News Exchange from the International War Crimes Tribunal for the Former Yugoslavia (ICTY), the International Court of Justice (ICJ) and the International Criminal Court (ICC)"), fighting cybercrime (e.g. IPA 2010 MB project "Regional Cooperation in Criminal Justice: Strengthening capacities in the fight against cybercrime – CyberCrime@IPA") and creating opportunities for enhancing the combat and prevention of organised crime (e.g. IPA 2012 MB project "Witness Protection in the Fight against Organised Crime and Corruption (WINPRO II)") (EC 2013: 6-7). What is more, the IPA MB assistance financed many actions in the sphere of disaster risk management, which also falls into the category of security sector reform. With the help of such projects as the Disaster Risk Reduction initiative, the EU has been promoting regional response to natural disasters to ensure Western Balkan states could cope with these trans-border issues in a more resilient way (EC 2007: 15).

In the sphere of hard security, the EU also made an impact. In the Western Balkans, unlike in any other region, the EU does not shy away from engaging in the defence and military dimensions of

SSR (Hänggi and Tanner 2005: 52). Although defence reform has traditionally been NATO's domain, the EU has come to appreciate the significance of the sphere in the region for itself. The European Commission's reports referred to the progress in military reforms early on (Dowling 2008: 175-176), while annual stabilisation and association reports place a strong emphasis on the democratic governance of the defence sectors of the Western Balkan states (Hänggi and Tanner 2005: 52). According to these reports, the countries of the region are required to strengthen civilian and democratic control over their armed forces, demilitarise their borders, reduce military spending and ensure that procurement procedures in the defence sectors follow EU public procurement legislation. The EU's impact on the defence sectors in the region can also be felt through its two military operations — CONCORDIA in FYROM and ALTHEA in BiH — launched under the framework of CSDP. In contrast to JHA, however, the EU's engagement with defence matters in the Western Balkans on the regional level, has been much more subtle and indirect. It has also been predominantly carried out on a bilateral basis. This can be partly explained by the EU's inexperience in the sphere.

The EU's assistance to regional cooperation in the Western Balkans in general and hard security cooperation in particular has been increasingly provided through RCC, which since 2008 worked as the successor of the Stability Pact. With security cooperation being one of this regionally-owned organisation's priority areas, the EU has had many opportunities to support the development of regional networks. As already stated, the majority of the EU aid in this sphere is indirect: it comes through the provision of expert help for events organised by one of the initiatives in the domain of security cooperation (e.g. EU officials and SSR experts often participate in sessions held at the Centre for Security Cooperation RACVIAC or act as observers for South Eastern and Eastern Europe Clearinghouse for the Control of Small Arms and Light Weapons (SEESAC)), through the funding of RCC's work (the EU provided around a third of the running costs of the RCC's Secretariat for the first three years of its existence and continues co-funding its work at the time of writing (EC 2010a: 3)) or contribution into the development of RCC's strategy (e.g. Strategy and Work Programme 2011-2013, adopted by RCC in 2010 was prepared with the help of the EU (EC 2013: 3)). It should be noted that while the EU attempts a comprehensive approach to SSR in the Western Balkans, which covers both military and non-military aspects (Hänggi and Tanner 2005: 53), in the sphere of hard security its approach differs considerably from the approach to the area of soft security. These differences are linked to the focus and outreach of the EU assistance. On the one hand, the EU promotes defence and intelligence reforms in individual Western Balkan states (as evidenced in the stabilisation and association reports). On the other, it engages in security cooperation projects, supported by the RCC, in a broader context of SEE, which goes beyond the Western Balkans, which again shows how blurry boundaries can be in complex systems. What is more, the EU pays considerable attention to coordinating its efforts in defence matters with those of NATO.

As can be seen, the EU has made substantial investment into various SSR-related projects in the Western Balkans on the regional level since 1999-2000. Having evolved as an international and security actor to an extent thanks to the events in the region, it developed a regional approach to the Western Balkans, which interlinks the processes of regional cooperation and European integration. By promoting regional cooperation in the sphere of SSR, the EU encourages new patterns of behaviour in the Western Balkan states and brings them closer to the standards of the European security community, which rejects the idea of states being self-sufficient. Of course, the number of projects launched or supported by the EU is not an indicator of their effectiveness. An in-depth study of the results achieved in each and all of the EU initiatives in the sphere is needed before one can assess how successful the EU has been in its endeavours. While such study is beyond the scope and focus of the current project, the empirical evidence analysed here suggests that between 1999 and 2013, the EU used SSR for facilitating amicable relation between Western Balkan states through exposing their security sectors to values and norms, found inside the bloc, demanding better effectiveness from their border systems, police and armies and emphasising the importance of regional cooperation.

Work, conducted by the EU in the regional SSR at this period, brought Western Balkan countries closer not only to each other, but also to the Euro-Atlantic security standards. Thus, contributing to the development of compatible values among state elites, political responsiveness and mutually predictable behaviour that are normally found inside security communities.

Conclusion

Security sector reform is a process of a comprehensive nature, that places emphasis on good governance, human security and contexts, in which it is implemented. The EU has been engaged in the promotion of SSR around the world since the 1990s. In its toolbox, SSR has been applied as an element of conflict-prevention, peace-building, democratisation, sustainable development, state-building and member state-building. It is a versatile instrument that combines elements of foreign, security and development policies to transform the overall functioning of deficient security systems. In the Western Balkans, SSR has been used as a tool of integration and cultivating friendly neighbourly relations between previously warring parties. Security community-building-potential of SSR has not always been discernible but emerged thanks to many years of trial and error. The basis of the EU's SSR policy framework was formulated in 2005 and 2006 with the release of the Council's "EU Concept for ESDP support to Security Sector Reform (SSR)" and Commission's "Concept for European Community Support for Security Sector Reform". The documents were informed by the practical work of the bloc and contributions of the Commission and individual member states into the discussions of SSR with third actors, involved in the reform's conceptualisation.

As an actor of *sui generis* nature and the world's largest donor, which has a variety of foreign policy tools at its disposal, the EU is uniquely positioned for the promotion of SSR on state and regional levels. Its vision of SSR, apart from the already-mentioned concepts, is also formulated in the Draft Council Conclusions on a Policy Framework for Security Sector Reform (2006) and two Commission Communications—Roadmap for the development of an EU-wide SSR strategy (EC 2015) and Elements for an EU-wide strategic framework to support security sector reform (EC 2016). According to these documents, SSR is defined as a multi-sector and long-term process, which is aimed at achieving accountable, effective and efficient security systems that operate under civilian control and are consistent with the principles of good governance, transparency and the rule of law.

Having prompted the EU to develop and test its security and defence policy, the Western Balkans created favourable ground for the application and evolution of the bloc's SSR vision, too. If in the early 1990s the region turned into a regional conflict formation, after the end of conflicts, it became one of the most exciting laboratories of externally assisted security sector reform in the world (Hänggi and Tanner 2005: 43). The EU was among the first actors to approach SSR in the Western Balkans on the regional level, although in 1991-1995, it was not able to engage with the reform but mainly dealt with crisis management through diplomatic effort and humanitarian assistance. The diplomacy of the USA and Contact Group, backed up by NATO intervention, created an opportunity for change in 1995. The EU, having launched the Regional Approach, defined the Western Balkans as a distinctive region and communicated its first requirements for regional SSR. These requirements mainly concerned the work of the police, border services, judiciary and in the case of Bosnia, Croatia and Serbia, cooperation with the ICTY. Additionally, the EU formulated demands for good governance of regional security sectors. Although the initiative promoted regional cooperation and good neighbourliness, it did not gain enough domestic or external support to foster reciprocity between regional players and turn the RCF into security regime. SSR in the RA was approached timidly and sporadically: requirements to fight corruption and organised crime or reform the police were disjointed and scattered around the RA documentation, instead of being presented as part of a coherent reform agenda. This is not surprising, however, as that the bloc had no single programme document on the reform at the time and was only at the start of its learning journey. In general, the EU's response to SSR needs in the Western Balkans in 1995-1999 was underdeveloped.

The region was still seen as a separate area, foreign to the European security community.

The Kosovo conflict changed this perception and persuaded the EU to abandon its *ad hoc* approaches in favour of proactive policies. With the introduction of the SP and SAP, SSR came to be acknowledged as an essential element for the stabilisation and Europeanisation of the region. When the Western Balkans received the promise of membership, the reform of security sector, in addition to being used as an instrument of peace-building, crisis management and democratisation, became a tool of member-state building. To make security sectors of the region transparent, accountable and democratically governed, or in other words compatible with the principles and standards practiced in its own member states, the EU sponsored several high-profile events on the topic of SSR in Western Balkan states and launched a series of SSR-related regional projects. Most of these projects tackle SSR-related issues without labelling them as such. Yet, in their objectives and envisaged results they are aligned with the bloc's SSR vision.

It is therefore possible to conclude that in 1999-2013, SSR was used by the EU to change the character of security interdependence in the Western Balkans from negative to positive as a security community-building tool. In 2013, the region was still far away from a "we-feeling", described by Deutsch, but it was much more stable and secure than it was even a decade ago. The EU's SSR-related projects were mostly executed in the top-down manner, which means the security community that emerged in the region was elite-driven. It was also an extension of the EU/Europe security community and not a separate formation. Moreover, it should not be forgotten that the analysis of the EU's engagement with SSR on the regional level in the Western Balkans demonstrates a steep learning curve for the bloc as a security provider in the context of constant change, crisis, and growing vulnerabilities.

While the regional dimension of SSR is significant, it is important to understand that it can only amplify the work done on the state level. This is partly connected with the sensitivity of the security sphere, and partly with the way the EU has been managing its relations with the Western Balkan states. To understand the full extent of the EU's impact on the security situation in the Western Balkans, it is therefore necessary to analyse the bloc's engagement with SSR on the state level. Croatia, Serbia and Bosnia, as countries at different stages of integration into the EU, are used for this analysis in the next three chapters.

---

52   While the term "security sector reform" was introduced in the late 1990s, the origin of the concept can be traced back to the 1950s-1960s. For the history of the concept, see Chanaa (2002).
53   SSR is only one of the terms, others include "security system reform", "justice and security sector reform" and "security sector transformation". For a more detailed explanation of differences in terminology, see Meharg and Arnusch (2010) and Hänggi and Tanner (2005).
54   For example, the case of Ukraine after 2014.
55   In his definition, non-statutory security forces are part of the security sector only if they apply coercive force for collective, and not private purposes.
56   According to Edmunds, the security sector does not include justice and law enforcement institutions, yet the justice sector is still considered significant for SSR.
57   For slightly broader definitions of the security sector with lists of institutions they include, see OECD (2007) and UNDP (2002).
58   The political level of SSR is sometimes divided into the first and second generations. This differentiation is omitted from this research. For further discussion, see Edmunds (2007; 28-33).
59   The organisational and political levels of analysis come from the three-tiered framework, developed by Edmunds (2007). The third level in Edmund's system is the international level, which refers to the role played by external actors in domestic SSR. The international level is not only closely inter-connected with the remaining two levels, it can also incorporate them. This is because external SSR efforts can be aimed at transforming the way security sectors work (organisational level of analysis) and are governed (political level of analysis). Since the current work investigates the role of the EU in SSR of the Western Balkans, it can be said it conducts research on the international level of analysis. For more details, see Edmunds (2007: 27-44).
60   On the state level, when analysing SSR in Croatia, Bosnia and Serbia.
61   For the discussion of the role of the EU as an actor of international affairs which combines civilian and military capabilities, see Manners (2002).
62   The WEU was a forum for consultation and dialogue on security and defence in Europe in 1948-2011, which provided the framework for the creation of a European defence policy, for details see EEAS (2016).
63   See the discussion of the EU's impact on SSR in Croatia, Serbia and Bosnia in Chapters 4-6.
64   The corresponding categories in the original version of the model are labelled as governance and efficiency and effectiveness dimensions.
65   Attempts at SSR on a state level at this time were also limited. For the only example of the EU's involvement with the organisational level of the reform before 1995, see Chapter 6.

66 See, for example, Edwards (1996), Gnesotto (1994), Kintis (1997) and Woodward (1995).
67 This was due to a dispute with Greece over the name that FYROM wanted to assume. For more, see Floudas (1996).
68 For example, see Edmunds (2007) and Caparini (2006).
69 Erdut Agreement was signed on 12 November 1995 between the government of Croatia and local authorities of Eastern Slavonia, Baranja and Western Sirmium to end the Croatian war.
70 See Chapter 4 and 5 for details.
71 The first civilian mission, EUPM BiH, was deployed to Bosnia and Herzegovina from 2003 to 2012, while the first military mission, CONCORDIA, was launched and completed in FYROM in 2003. Two more missions worked in FYROM: EUPOL Proxima — a civilian police training mission from 2003 to 2005 and EUPAT — a short police advisory team operated from the end of 2005 till June 2006. At the moment of writing, there are two active missions in the region: EUFOR Althea — a peace-enforcement mission in BiH, launched in December 2004, and EULEX Kosovo — a rule of law mission, launched in 2008. For details, see EEAS (2022).
72 For details of the IBM concept for the Western Balkans see sections on border reform in Chapters 4-6.
73 The impact of the process on border reforms in Serbia and BiH is analysed in Chapters 5 and 6. Croatia did not participate, as it had already been on the positive list.
74 Drugs — Economic Crime — Terrorism/Prevention and ILECUs II.

Chapter 4
Security Sector Reform in Croatia

Introduction

The security sector in Croatia is a product of the country's war of independence (1991-1995) and nearly a decade of President Franjo Tudjman's semi-authoritarian rule[75]. Each branch of the sector was built from scratch in the context of the Homeland War[76], and was initially engaged in countering an external threat and the process of state-building (Donais 2005: 227). With the end of the war, the focus shifted to the protection of the regime, established by Tudjman and the nationalist Croatian Democratic Union (HDZ), which meant that rare attempts at SSR in 1995-1999 were sporadic and half-hearted. The political changes of 1999-2000, brought about by the death of Tudjman, defeat of the HDZ in parliamentary and presidential elections as well as the fall of Milosevic's regime in neighbouring Serbia, created an opportunity for transforming Croatia into a democratic state and respected member of the Euro-Atlantic community. Security sector reform emerged as an important indicator of the country's transformation. With the help of external actors, which not only set the normative and technical criteria for the reform, but also increased its salience and urgency (Edmunds 2007: 191), Croatia made considerable progress towards making its security sector efficient, effective and democratically governed.

This chapter aims to assess the role of the European Union in this process. It starts with an overview of the results achieved by the Croatian government in the sphere of SSR between 1991 and 2013 and continues with the analysis of the EU's contribution to the reform. To ensure consistency, SSR in this as well as two chapters that follow is studied within the framework of three periods that correspond to the time when the Western Balkans presented a regional conflict formation (1991-1995), unrealized security regime (1995-1999) and embryonic security community (1999-2013). Whenever possible, organisational and political levels of the reform are differentiated[77], and attention is paid to both internal and external factors influencing SSR. Finally, regional dimension of the reform is emphasised, yet observations regarding similarities or differences between responses to EU requirements on behalf of Croatia, Serbia and BiH, as well as the evaluation of SSR as a tool of the EU's complex security governance are reserved for the concluding chapter of the book.

Croatia as a regional frontrunner in security sector reform

The violent disengagement of Croatia from the Socialist Federal Republic of Yugoslavia (SFRY) left a lasting impact on the organisation and management of its security sector. Having proclaimed independence in June 1991, Croatia found itself fighting an internal conflict with the breakaway region of Krajina and deterring military attacks of the JNA (Jovic 2006: 85). In 1993-1994 the country also got involved in the Bosnian war, supporting the secessionist Croat Republic of Herceg-Bosna (ibid.). Even more, after regaining control over Western Slavonia and the Krajina region with Operations *Flash* and *Storm* in 1995, that helped to change the regional balance of power, the Croatian Army fought alongside the Army of BiH against the Bosnian Serbs[78] (Goldstein 1999: 252-255). The first few years of the country's existence were therefore spent in continuous conflict,[79] which is typical for an element of a regional conflict formation (RCF). The entire Croatian security sector was built for fighting the war, which meant there was no clear division of roles between different security actors. With an aim "to place the maximum number of men under arms to fend off Serb aggressors", Tudjman and the HDZ government did not pay much attention to the issues of professionalism or governance when it came to the security sector (Dowling 2008: 188). Initially, the Ministry of the Interior (MoI) was the only institution with legitimacy to use force and therefore defend the country.[80] In April 1991, understanding that the war was imminent, the Croatian parliament passed statutory changes to set up the Croatian National Guard (ZNG) as part of the police force (Ivkovic 2015: 98). Although legally within the structure of the MoI, the ZNG was at the same time put under the command of the Ministry of Defence (MoD) to carry out military duties (Knezovic and Stanicic 2011: 11). When Croatia passed the Defence Act in September 1991, the ZNG became incorporated into the Croatian Army (HV) (Vukadin, Borovec and Ljubin Golub 2013: 32). These changes notwithstanding, the Croatian police force continued to play an active role in the defence of the country until the end of 1992. Moreover, even after its war-fighting role started subsiding, the police remained at least partially militarised until 1995 (Edmunds 2007: 126).

The absence of clear dividing lines between key security institutions in Croatia in 1991-1995 was not surprising, given that powers of the executive, legislature and judiciary were not defined either. In such circumstances, it was easy for President Tudjman to exert unlimited power over all state institutions, including in the security sector. The closeness of Tudjman to the security sector provided the latter with a high degree of "nationalist legitimacy in Croatian society" (Edmunds 2007: 54). Security bodies were not simply seen as the defenders of the Croatian people, but also as the architects of the Croatian state itself (ibid.). Thanks to its role in the war, the heroic halo would be attached to the whole security sector, but with a strong emphasis on the army, for a long time.

With the parliament unable to provide oversight, the president, as the Commander-in-Chief, personally responsible for promoting the officer corps, and the HDZ penetrating all levels of army and the police, the security sector was highly politicised and overwhelmingly unprofessional. In addition, the speed with which the police (40,000 in June 1991) and army (200, 000 at the end of 1991) grew had negative effects on the quality of training of security personnel (Edmunds 2007: 123). It would be unfair, however, to see the period of 1991-1995 in a purely negative light. Given the circumstances in which the security sector was formed (i.e. during early stages of the state-building process, with ongoing conflicts on several fronts, the EU and UN arms embargoes in place and minimal continuity with the Yugoslav security institutions), its development is remarkable. The Defence Act and Law on Internal Affairs outlined the legal basis for the democratic practices of the country's army and police respectively already in 1991 (ibid.: 55-56). Croatia's border security system was also established in 1991 as part of the MoI and was one of the few examples of a non-militarised border service in the region (Tanner 2011: 73). Of course, there was a big difference between the conceptualisation of security issues and their practical implementation, yet the fact that Croatia was trying to preserve at least a façade of democracy deserves mentioning.

When in January 1992 the UN-initiated ceasefire came into force, Croatia's security sector started moving towards clearer delineation of roles between its key components. The HV gained enough potency to take over military tasks, while the police could shift their focus to public policing. Starting from 1993, discussions on democratic policing became common in the government and broader society. These discussions rarely went beyond rhetoric, but in some cases, they led to important changes, especially on the organisational level. In 1993, the introduction of twenty administrative regions made the police less centralised (Edmunds 2007: 135). In 1994, the set-up of the Internal Affairs Office and the Office of Report Analysis and Development within the MoI emphasised the professionalization of the service (Ivkovic 2004: 188). Whilst important, these innovations had a limited effect on the work of the police because the code of silence and corruption that spread among all levels of the force in the absence of proper civilian and parliamentary oversight, were not easy to uproot. The army, on the other hand, did not experience even minor reforms at this period. With one-third of the territory still occupied and Croatian troops being engaged in the Bosnian war, the HV remained a highly centralised and politicised force, heavy on manpower and light on professionalism. In short, the period of 1991-1995 was the time when Croatia built the security sector from scratch. Security bodies that were built lacked transparency, accountability and civilian control. With close links to the regime, they suffered from politicisation and absence of clear-cut roles. Overall, the Croatian security sector at this time displayed characteristic features of a security apparatus compatible with a regional conflict formation. SSR efforts were extremely limited and noticeable only in the sphere of policing.

The period from the end of 1995 to 1999, changed the situation only slightly: police reform intensified on both organisational and political level, but when it came to the army, which was renamed the Armed Forces of the Republic of Croatia (OSRH) in 1996, the reform was almost synonymous with downsizing. After the war ended in 1995[81], the attention of the security sector started shifting from territorial defence to the protection of the regime. Tudjman and the HDZ government continued exerting unprecedented levels of control over security institutions, especially the army, and manipulating their heroic image to advance the regime's interests (Dowling 2008: 188).

In 1995, the OSRH was downsized to 100, 000 troops but was still too large for Croatia. By 1999, the number of troops was reduced further by 40,000, while their structure and high military budgets remained almost intact. The regime preferred to keep a large military force as a physical embodiment of the strength of the Croatian state (Edmunds 2007, 128). Except for several small-scale training programmes, supported by individual states, such as the USA, the UK and Germany, the army was mainly closed to external influence (Wheaton 2000). The nationalist strategy, pursued by Tudjman led Croatia to "unofficial isolation" in the second half of the 1990s and strained relations with the EU, NATO and the ICTY[82] (Jovic 2006: 86-89). These tensions were also manipulated by the regime to justify the need for a strong army.

Nonetheless, police reform saw some progress during this period. Occupying a less prominent role in the country's mythology, to a great extent, due to the spread of corruption, the service was more open to the prospect of change. The major focus in the mid-1990s was on depoliticisation, demilitarisation, professionalisation, demystification and downsizing (Ivkovic 2015: 98). The Criminal Code and Criminal Procedure Code were adopted in 1996 and 1997 respectively to help the police adjust to the new political and social conditions. The service also benefited from external assistance: from 1996 to 1998, the UN Transitional Administration for Eastern Slavonia, Baranja and Western Sirmium (UNTAES) worked on a transitional police force in the Danube region. In 1998, it was succeeded by the UN civilian police support group (UNPSG), which mainly dealt with monitoring tasks, and in 1998-2000 the OSCE became the main external actor involved in the country's police reform (Mobekk 2005: 160-161). The semi-authoritarian nature of Tudjman's regime, however, did not allow a deep reform. At the end of the 1990s, the police still lacked professionalism and specialisation. As "general practitioners", police officers could carry out duties to protect public order one day and to ensure security of borders the other (Ivkovic 2004: 190). The border service, although non-militarised, had neither enough staff, nor a specialised training programme. Thus, the Croatian security sector in the second half of 1990s underwent only minor transformation, with limited effects on the size of the key security actors and slight democratisation of police practices. The inward-looking leadership of the country was not interested in building reciprocal relations with its neighbours, rendering the international community's efforts at promoting a security regime in the region futile.

2000 marked the beginning of a new era in the country's history as well as SSR. Having redirected its foreign policy towards the West, the new Croatian government opened itself to external conditionality. By making transformation of the security sector one of the conditions for membership, NATO and the EU gave a real impetus to SSR in Croatia. This impetus was much needed, given that the first post-Tudjman years brought little change. There were, of course, some initial attempts to reform the security sector, but they rarely went beyond constitutional amendments (which reduced the presidential powers and strengthened legislature) and new legislation (e.g. the 2000 Police Law, the 2002 National Security Strategy, Defence Strategy, Defence Act and Law on Service in the Armed Forces) (Caparini 2006: 31). More legislative acts followed shortly, for example, the Strategic Defence Review (2005), Long Term Development Plan for the Croatian Armed Forces (2006), the Border Protection Act (2004), Development Strategy of the Border Police of the Republic of Croatia (2005) and the Ministry of the Interior Programme Guidelines for the period 2004—2007 (Ivkovic 2015: 99-100).

These and some other documents prepared the background for the depoliticisation and modernisation of the army, restructuring and specialisation of police services, professionalisation of the border police, removing war criminals from the system, as well as increasing transparency and improving the oversight of the security sector as a whole. The pace of these reforms was uneven (with police reform going faster due to the work done previously) and depended largely on the pressure coming from outside. NATO, which accepted Croatia's second PfP application in 2000, provided inspiration and guidance for defence reform (Donais 2005: 227), while the EU was instrumental for improving border security and galvanizing changes in the police. This was also the time when Croatia embraced (under external pressure) regional cooperation: for the first time since 1991, it started engaging with Serbia, Bosnia and other Western Balkan countries.

By 2013, Croatia built a modern army, standing at 18, 600 strong (Howorth 2014: 77) and capable of participating in NATO[83] and EU operations, achieved a professional and well-equipped border service and the slimmed-down police, consisting of 20, 700 officers (Vukadin, Borovec and Ljubin Golub 2013: 37) as well as satisfied all major requirements of the ICTY. On the surface, the country's security sector is professional and democratically governed, yet a closer look discloses some problems: there are still discrepancies between legislation[84] and its implementation in practice, lack of civilian expertise on security issues, persisting issues of corruption and poor accountability. SSR therefore cannot be considered fully complete in the country. Nonetheless, Croatia achieved the biggest progress in the area among all Western Balkan states. The next section will analyse the role of the EU in the process.

The EU and Croatia's security in 1991–1995

With the start of hostilities in Slovenia and Croatia in 1991, which marked the beginning of the SFRY's disintegration, the EU, then still the European Community (EC), found itself at the forefront of the international effort to contain violence in the region. Despite a variety of instruments, deployed by the EC, which *inter alia* included Troika visits, a peace conference, arms embargo, economic and trade sanctions, a monitoring mission and Arbitration Commission, the European intervention failed. Starting from January 1992, other external actors, namely the USA and NATO, took over the leadership role in the Balkans. The EC had to step back as it was not ready for the crisis in the region in the early 1990s: in the absence of military strength and a working foreign policy, it had to rely on predominantly diplomatic tools, set up in the rigid framework of the European Political Cooperation (EPC). The EPC, which was substituted by the CFSP after Maastricht, was characterised by slow pace and consensual nature of decision making (Caruso 2007: 12). Apart from inadequate preparation, the EC also demonstrated a lack of unity. Germany's unilateral decision to recognise the independence of Croatia exposed this deficiency and proved the fragility of European diplomacy. Having failed to make a difference in the region initially, the EC/EU did not withdraw from the area entirely but continued looking for ways of influence. There were at least three reasons why the region remained of importance for the EC/EU. First, the war and continuing instability in the Western Balkans exposed EU member states to the problem of refugees and asylum seekers. Between 1991 and 1995, around 200, 000 Croatian Serbs left the country, and because of operations *Flash* and *Storm*, this number grew by further 190, 000 (PACE 1999). While not all of these ended up in the EC/EU, the pressure on the bloc, especially considering refugee flows from other Western Balkan states, particularly Bosnia, kept mounting. Second, with Austria nearing the accession, the EU was about to share its external border with a turbulent region. It was therefore in its interest to pacify the Western Balkans. Third, Germany's decision to recognise the independence of Croatia and Slovenia, forced the European Community to play a more active role in the regional affairs.

In Croatia, in 1991-1995, the EU did not engage in SSR directly but influenced the country's security situation through the European Community Monitoring Mission (ECMM), Arbitration Commission and arms embargo. This work would later have an impact on the bloc's role in Croatia's SSR. The ECMM was established by the Brioni Agreement on 7 July 1991 as a monitoring mission to observe the withdrawal of the Yugoslav Army from Slovenia (Landry 1999: 2). Already on 29 July 1991, the mission's mandate was extended to include Croatia, the situation in which was deteriorating daily (Caruso 2007: 22). Organised by the EC/EU, the ECMM received backing from the OSCE, which could not summon enough support for sending its own observer mission to the region (Blockmans 2007: 129). The tasks, performed by the ECMM monitors, which were dressed in white and had EC logos on their clothes and vehicles, expanded quickly. If at first the EC teams monitored the implementation of ceasefires and the withdrawal of troops, as of 1992 they were actively engaged in preventive diplomacy and confidence-building activities (Landry 1999: 3). Thus, the ECMM set up hot lines between the warring parties, conducted mediation tasks, assisted with the exchange of prisoners and protected minorities (ibid.). With the deployment of UNPROFOR, it also became responsible for monitoring the so called "pink zones", i.e. areas in Croatia, controlled by the JNA and populated by Serbs, but outside the UN jurisdiction (Caruso 2007: 22). At the end of 1992, after the no-fly zone was declared above Bosnia, the ECMM was asked to observe the military air traffic at Croatian airports (MDNL 2007).

Most importantly, the ECMM was responsible for collecting information about the security situation in Croatia. Daily reports were sent out not only to Brussels and individual EU member states, but also to the OSCE, UN, Council of Europe and other agencies (Caruso 2007: 22). The intelligence from the mission was important for understanding the situation on the ground.[85] With headquarters in Zagreb and several coordination centres around the country, the ECMM was the key source of information on the Croatian war. In the context of the EU's role in Croatia's SSR, the ECMM's value was two-fold: first, it provided the EU with direct access to information on security in the country and second, it offered the bloc some flexibility. Having a diplomatic monitoring mission in Croatia during the conflict allowed the EU to access actors and areas inaccessible to others. The information collected by the ECMM was not used for SSR efforts immediately, but it gave the EU a unique perspective on the country, whose semi-authoritarian regime would soon lead it to the international isolation. Moreover, many of the former ECMM staff would later return to work on different externally-funded projects of SSR, especially in the sphere of border security and police.[86] The flexibility and adaptability of the mission allowed the EU to expand its mandate and get involved in practical tasks in defence and policing (e.g. monitoring airfields and patrolling areas with minority populations) without resorting to formal reviews of memorandums of understanding, which made the work of the ECMM possible.

These positive features notwithstanding, the ECMM had a limited effect in Croatia and other countries where it was deployed[87]. As a preventive mission with a small budget, it did not have a real leverage to improve the security situation on the ground. It is understandable therefore that its role was later overshadowed by the UN and NATO (Landry 1999: 1). Despite being an EU-level mission, until 2000 it was predominantly used as an instrument of member states. Its work was guided by the EU Presidency, which not only decided on its main tasks, but was also responsible for the budget allocation that was later reimbursed by individual member states (Blockmans 2007: 131). This changed in 2000, when the ECMM was transformed into the EUMM and firmly put into the framework of the CFSP. From the point complex security governance, however, the ECMM's work in 1991-1995 should not be dismissed. As will be shown below, the EU started providing substantial influence on SSR in Croatia in the early 2000s. These endeavours to transform the functioning and governance of Croatia's security sector were not entirely new: they were based on the work conducted by the EU in the country during the 1990s. The ECMM was one of the first EU efforts to shape Croatia's security environment. The information, gathered by the mission in 1991-1995, provided the EU with first-hand knowledge on security challenges and needs in Croatia. The ongoing conflict made it impossible for the EU to apply this knowledge instantly, yet it laid the foundation for its future SSR work.

Another early EU effort to influence Croatia's security situation is linked to the work of the Arbitration Commission on Yugoslavia, known as the Badinter Commission, after its chairman Robert Badinter. The Badinter Commission was established on 27 August 1991 by the EC as part of the Conference on Yugoslavia to arbitrate between Yugoslavian authorities on the issues pertaining to the country's fragmentation (Radan 2000). In the Croatian case, the Commission's decisions were not always followed: the country's independence was recognized by the EC under Germany's pressure even though the Badinter Commission concluded that Croatia did not fully implement all necessary provisions to protect its minorities. Nonetheless, some of the rulings were crucial for the establishment of the country. One of such rulings, released on 11 January 1992 as Opinion No 3, was on the topic of border delimitation.[88] In Opinion No 3, the Badinter Commission was asked to determine whether internal boundaries between Yugoslav republics could be regarded as international borders. It delivered an affirmative answer. The SFRY's internal borders were to become frontiers protected by international law on the basis of the principles of respect for the territorial status quo and *uti possidetis* "upon the recognition of statehood of a seceding federal unit" (ibid.). It is worth mentioning that the principle of *uti possidetis*, which proclaims respect for borders existing at the moment of independence, was first used in Latin America on decolonisation issues, and later applied in Africa (Pellet 1992: 180). Its application in the Balkans was a way to exercise control by the EC in the circumstances of escalating violence. By choosing to recognise internal borders between Yugoslav republics as international boundaries, the EC/EU, and the international community after it, separated territoriality from ethnicity and, as a result, denied statehood to the autonomous territories of Kosovo and Vojvodina, the same as the self-proclaimed Serbian Krajina in Croatia and Croatian Herzeg-Bosna in BiH (Blockmans 2007: 147).

The Badinter Commission's opinion on borders decided the shape of Croatia as well as confirmed its eligibility for the international personality as a state. This decision is of profound importance for the country's SSR and understanding the role of the EU in it. The EU as a convener of the Arbitration Commission set the criteria for determining the country's international borders and therefore its existence as such. It is important to understand, however, that Opinion No 3 had some limitations. It neither solved Croatia's border disputes with other countries nor made borders unchangeable. The EC distanced itself from border disputes in the Western Balkans by adopting a joint EPC Statement on 31 December 1991, which stipulated that recognition by the European Community and its Members States should not be seen as an acceptance "of the position of any of the republics concerning the territory which is a subject of a dispute between two or more republics" (quoted in Blockmans 2007: 145). Although the Commission forbade states to acquire territory by force, it allowed modification of frontiers by agreement (Pellet 1992: 180). Consequently, Croatia found itself engaged in a number of border disputes, some of which threatened to jeopardise its EU membership at a later stage.[89]

The third and final area of the EU activities in Croatia in the first half of the 1990s, which is important from the point of SSR, relates to the arms embargoes, imposed on Yugoslavia. It is often forgotten that the first embargo on armaments and military equipment applicable to the whole of Yugoslavia was adopted by the EC on 5 July 1991. This embargo, which fell under the jurisdiction of member states, was enforced by the EC/EU and upheld on Croatia until November 2000. Apart from this, the EC/EU also supported the arms embargo, established by the United Nations Security Council on 25 September in Resolution 713. To assist the UN with the implementation of its Resolution, the EU cooperated with the OSCE and NATO. For example, it contributed naval forces through the WEU to monitor the costal lines of former Yugoslav republics in 1992 (Caruso 2007: 17).

The imposition of the arms embargo on the Yugoslav republics in 1991 was one of the key factors causing the surge in organised crime and war economies in the Western Balkans, leading the area to develop into a regional conflict formation between 1991 and 1995. These sanctions also unintentionally led to the spread of illegal practices in the security sectors in the region. Forced to create its security forces from scratch in the hostile environment of Serb-led aggression, Croatia was badly hit by the arms embargoes, imposed by the EC/EU and UN. To obtain armaments, the state and security elites colluded with regional warlords and sought access to Western black-markets. The illicit channels for obtaining weapons were coordinated on the highest levels. Gojko Susak, who headed the MoD between 1991 and 1998, was personally responsible for finding arms for the HV abroad and bringing them to Croatia (Lukic 2008: 198). He was also behind the rise to prominence of diaspora officers and the creation of parallel chains of command in the army. The latter allowed Tudjman to send troops to Bosnia without a formal order from himself or the approval from the Parliament (ibid.).

It would be wrong to assume that these negative effects resulted from the EU-initiated arms embargo alone. Arguably, the UN embargo had a bigger impact on the situation in the former Yugoslavia and in Croatia as it was supported by a bigger number of actors. The EU arms embargo and its efforts to assist the UN, however, were among the factors, contributing to the spread of illicit practices in the Croatian security sector and organised crime firming up its grip over the country. This side of the arms control efforts is easy to ignore, but important to acknowledge to understand the complexity of Croatia's security situation in the early 1990s and the power of unintended consequences in complex security governance.

To conclude, it is possible to say that although in 1991-1995 the EU was not directly involved in SSR in Croatia, partly because of the extremely limited nature of reform efforts in the country during this period, partly because it was preoccupied with a bigger task of handling Yugoslavia's dissolution and lacked the appropriate instruments, it still managed to influence Croatia's security situation. The ECMM provided the EU with first-hand information on developments in the country and an opportunity to monitor (sometimes mediate) the interaction between warring parties; the Badinter Commission determined the major shape of independent Croatia through its opinion on borders and the arms embargo unintentionally contributed to the criminalisation of the security services in the country. At this period, the EU was not in the position to dictate the development of the country's security sector, nor could it do so after the war. Nonetheless, 1995-1999 saw the EU's first attempts to tackle SSR-related issues in Croatia.

The EU's impact on Croatia's SSR in 1995-1999

After the Croatian war ended in 1995, the EU switched its focus to the stabilisation of the country and bringing it back to normality. To achieve these goals, it continued some of the earlier efforts, like the ECMM and extension of its arms embargo, as well as introduced new channels of influence. In the context of SSR, of special importance were the EU's de-mining activities and its attempts to bring changes to Croatia's security sector through the Regional Approach.

In 1995-1999, the ECMM in Croatia was mainly preoccupied with monitoring the implementation of the Dayton Peace Agreement[90] and the Erdut Agreement[91]. In 1997, the mission moved its headquarters from Zagreb to Sarajevo as the situation in BiH was less stable and required bigger international presence and attention. The EU arms embargo remained in place even after the adoption of the UN Security Council Resolution 1021 of 22 November 1995, which lifted the UN restrictions (Blockmans 2007: 153). The bloc's decision was motivated by a desire to ensure safety of international personnel present in Croatia, but also in BiH and Serbia. Since 1998 the equipment that could be used for internal repression or terrorism was embargoed as well (SIPRI 2012). Through these activities, the EU contributed to the arms control in Croatia, trying to reduce the number of weapons available, and thus promoting the pacification and stabilisation of the country. Nonetheless, the illegal channels for arms acquisitions did not disappear, and clandestine structures continued their work. Yet the absence of open warfare and therefore urgency to obtain weapons led criminal networks to reduce the intensity of their activities.

These are the circumstances in which the EU undertook first steps to reform the army, police and border security in Croatia. In the sphere of defence, the EU first and foremost tried to deal with the immediate legacy of conflict. On the one hand, it meant reducing the threat to local citizens, emanating from the remnants of war and encouraging returns of refugees and displaced persons, thus — the engagement in de-mining activities, on the other, ensuring that the country's defence system functioned in compliance with international standards, hence — criticism of the state's influence over the defence sector and emphasis on the need for the system's overhaul.

The EU started contributing to Croatia's mine clearing action in 1998. It was the year, when Croatia ratified the Convention on the Prohibition of the Use, Stockpiling, Production and Transfer of Anti-Personnel Mines and on their Destruction, known as the Ottawa Convention, confirming its determination to eliminate a post-conflict landmine threat (EC 2010b: 5). It was estimated that around 103, 000 mines and other unexploded military supplies were spread around the country after the end of the Homeland War (ibid.). On 9 November 1998, the European Council requested that the WEU "implement actions consisting of coordination, supervision and training of mine clearance specialists and mine clearance instructions in Croatia" (Novota et al 2009: 14). The Western European Union Demining Mission (WEUDAM) became operational in May 1999. Between 1998 and 1999, the EU spent 1.5 million EUR on the mine action in Croatia. It was a way to help the country to remove one of the biggest obstacles preventing its citizens from returning to normal life as well as contributing to solving an economic, ecological, infrastructure and safety problem (EC 2010b; EC 2010: 5). While creating a safer environment for the people of Croatia, the EU-sponsored mine action also raised the level of professionalism of the Croatian defence sector. Over time, the army personnel developed high levels of expertise in de-mining and dealing with explosive remnants of the war. This expertise Croatia was later able to offer to other countries recovering from conflict through the framework of NATO or EU external action, even before joining the bloc in 2013. Furthermore, when the EU granted funds for scientific research into mine action to the Croatian mine action centre (CROMAC), it contributed into the development of the civilian expertise on the subject.

Additionally, the EU tried to deal with the post-conflict legacy within the context of Croatian defence reform through the Regional Approach, which contained a series of references to SSR. In the context of the defence sector, the RA emphasised cooperation with the ICTY, which was also important for the political level of the reform. The EU saw cooperation with the tribunal as essential for the country's stabilisation. Although the Parliament of Croatia adopted the Constitutional Law for Cooperation with the ICTY on 19 April 1996, which recognised the court's jurisdiction over the war crimes committed in the former Yugoslavia, the country's authorities showed limited interest in assisting the tribunal with the indictment of Croatian and Bosnian Croat war criminals (Pavlakovic 2008: 451). Instead, the Tudjman regime obstructed the tribunal's work, especially in relation to the 1995 operations *Storm* and *Flash* that became an integral element of the myth of the sanctity of the Homeland War (ibid.). The EU used RA reports to criticise poor cooperation of the Croatian government with the ICTY and expressed dissatisfaction with contradictions existing between commitments on paper and in reality (EC 1997a: 10; EC 1998: 11). The only achievement commended by the EU in this area was Croatia's agreement to extradite several Bosnian Croats, indicted by the ICTY in 1997 (EC 1998: 11). Despite having many grievances about Croatia's obstructions of the ICTY's work, the EU did not use coercion to change the country's behaviour. It did, however, keep the suspension of PHARE, enacted in August 1995, in place.

EU efforts to influence police and border reforms in Croatia through the RA were similarly limited. In the sphere of policing, the EU focused predominantly on raising professionalism of the police staff and eliminating non-transparent and criminal practices from their work, mainly in reference to refugee returns. Thus, the police were regularly criticised for creating bureaucratic obstacles for Serb returnees, while offering privileged treatment to Croat refugees and displaced persons. The criticism was equally directed at regular police and Transitional Police Force within the UNTAES region (EC 1997a: 8). Like in mine-clearing action, EU efforts were meant to normalise life in the country and lessen the burden on its member states. In contrast to de-mining, however, the EU's rhetoric was not supported with finances: at the time, the Union quite gladly let the UN, working through the UNPSG, and the OSCE lead the reform of the police. The EU's emphasis on this sphere increased manifold with the launch of the SAP.

In border reform, the EU's emphasis was on restoring and establishing border controls and crossings between Croatia and its immediate neighbours. Specifically, the EU actively supported Croatia in (re)opening border control points (BCPs) with different parts of BiH according to international standards, which posed a big challenge not only because of the length of the border between the two states, but also due to problems of post-conflict reconciliation. The Croat Republic of Herceg-Bosna, though formally disbanded in 1996, continued its activities in some of Bosnia's cantons even in 1998, while relations with the Republika Sprska (RS)[92] remained tense. Most of EU efforts in this area were guided by the DPA, which imposed obligations on Croatia regarding the establishment of the customs border and agreements with the RS (GFAP 1995). In the immediate post-conflict phase, there was visible imbalance between the sides: while Croatian citizens enjoyed free travel through the RS, Serbs (including Bosnian Serbs) were required visas to enter Croatia and were subject to restrictive customs regimes (EC 1998: 11). From the second half of 1998, these imbalances became less pronounced: visas were no longer required from holders of new BiH passports and less strict customs regulations were introduced on border crossings between Croatia and the RS. The EU also tried to harmonise relations between Croatia and BiH regarding access to the Port of Ploce. The latter, although located on the territory of Croatia, was of strategic importance for BiH. The EU hailed as an achievement the initialling of the 1998 agreement granting transit rights and free unrestricted use of the port to BiH (EC 1998c: 11). The Agreement did not have any legal effect, however, because Croatia refused to ratify it. In border reform, similarly to the reform of the police, the EU settled for a supporting role to other international actors. For instance, in March 1998, the European Commission sent a Customs Assistance Mission to Croatia, where it assisted the OSCE in Eastern Slavonia, Baranja and Western Slavonia with confidence-building and monitoring activities (ibid.). This supporting position was reconsidered in the early 2000s.

Apart from aiding different areas of Croatia's security sector, the EU attempted to influence the political level of the reform, mainly through criticising the HDZ's pervasive regime and the country's lack of cooperation with the ICTY. Namely, the EU expressed dissatisfaction with the lack of separation of powers in Croatia and continuous influence of the HDZ over the command structures of army and the police (EC 1998c: 8). The strained relations between the EU and the Croatian government at this period and the limited leverage the bloc had over the country, meant that this criticism did not result in any real change in the way Croatia was run and exercised control over its key security institutions.

In brief, the EU's SSR efforts in Croatia between 1995 and 1999 were directed at stabilisation and pacification of the country. While lacking an overarching strategy, they were meant to normalise Croatia and bring its defence, police and border services closer to international standards. The EU did not try to lead in any of the security sector areas, but merely supported timid national endeavours or assisted other international actors. Nonetheless, it is important to acknowledge that the bloc attempted to influence SSR in the country even prior to the establishment of its security and defence policy, and before the concept of SSR was codified. While at that stage the CFSP was only a few years old, the basic character of the EU's involvement in security sector reform of Croatia in 1995-1999 is not surprising. One should not forget that the undemocratic context of the Croatian political system and Tudjman's semi-authoritarian regime at the time did not create favourable conditions for SSR either (Edmunds 2007: 193). The EU-Croatia relationship took a downturn in 1997 when the EU started promoting the Regional Approach. The RA, its conditionality (including on SSR), and even the concept of the Western Balkans were met with hostility in Croatia as the regime saw them as an attempt to create a neo-Yugoslavia. To show its opposition to the RA, Tudjman's government even amended the Constitution by adding an article that prohibited Croatia's participation in any association that could lead to the recreation of Yugoslavia (Jovic 2006: 86). Although technically Croatia remained part of the RA, in practice it did little to satisfy its conditionality, which severely restricted the efficiency of the EU's efforts in the sphere of SSR. Croatia's hostility towards the outside world and regional cooperation contributed to the failure of the security regime, promoted in the Balkans by the international community in the postwar period. Despite existing limitations, EU activities to reform the Croatian army, police and border services between 1995 and 1999, prepared a foundation for a more active engagement of the bloc in Croatian SSR with the launch of the Stabilisation and Association Process for the Western Balkans.

The EU's impact on SSR in Croatia in 1999-2013

When the SAP was revealed in June 1999, Croatia barely showed interest in the initiative. It was only after Tudjman's death in December 1999 and the establishment of a new coalition government at the start of 2000 that the country became more open to the idea of European integration (Tull 2003: 138-139). Croatia confirmed its commitment to the process by initialling the Stabilisation and Association Agreement in May 2001, the negotiations on which started in the autumn of 2000. From this moment forward, it started moving swiftly, though not without obstacles, towards the EU membership. On 29 October 2001, the SAA was signed, in February 2003 the formal application for EU membership was submitted and in June 2004, the country was confirmed as a candidate state (Edmunds 2007: 200). The SAA entered into force in February 2005 and the membership negotiations officially launched in October 2005, after the initial suspension over poor cooperation with the ICTY in March the same year.

The reorientation of Croatia's foreign policy and evolution of the country's relations with the EU had a three-fold effect on security sector reform. First, SSR was placed in a wider context of democratisation and Europeanisation processes. The EU, as an actor of SSR, was concerned not simply with bringing the security sector of the country in line with the principles of good governance and rule of law, but also with adjusting it to EU-specific requirements, which would enable Croatia to become a functioning member state. SSR, therefore, became a tool of member state-building and security community-building. Hence, the focus on strengthening cooperation between Croatian security institutions and EU security agencies (e.g. European Police Office (Europol)), adoption of the EU *acquis* and pre-accession involvement of Croatian security personnel in the development of EU security-related initiatives (e.g. battle groups and CSDP missions). Second, SSR received unprecedented levels of attention due to its connection with the process of Euro-Atlantic integration. Croatia's achievements in police, border and even defence reforms were meticulously tracked by the EU in annual progress reports, with new goals and benchmarks set out periodically. As noted by Edmunds (2007: 200), thanks to EU and NATO conditionality, "the Croatian security sector has found itself, almost by accident, at the vanguard of an integrationist process whose implications are far wider than defence and security issues narrowly defined". Third, by pursuing SSR within the SAP framework, the EU strengthened the regional dimension of the reform. While in the SAP each Western Balkan country is assessed on the merit of its individual successes, regional cooperation is identified as one of the policy's key priorities. In the sphere of security, this focus is particularly strong. As a result, SSR in Croatia is linked to SSR efforts in the region.

While there was no single programme for SSR in Croatia promoted by the EU, references to the reform occupied a prominent place in the SAP. SAAs, adjusted to the specific requirements of each Western Balkan state, contained political and economic objectives to be met to bring the region in line with EU standards, including in the sphere of security. In Croatia's SAA the information relevant for SSR was included in Articles 75-80, dedicated to JHA, as well as dispersed around more general provisions, for instance, concerning political dialogue with the EU (Art. 7-10) or regional cooperation (Art. 11-14) (SAA 2005). With the start of accession talks in October 2005, the EU began tracing progress in the country's SSR and setting benchmarks for the reforms of police, border services and, to a lesser extent, army through the political component of the Copenhagen criteria, Chapter 24 on Justice, Freedom and Security, which in the context of this work is analysed through provisions relevant to the spheres of policing and border security, and Chapter 31 that focuses its attention on CSDP and some broader aspects of EU security policies.[93] The political criteria, that require an accession country to achieve "stability of institutions guaranteeing democracy, the rule of law, human rights and respect for and protection of minorities" (EC 2016a) are important for promoting the political level of SSR, i.e. the level that ensures civilian, parliamentary and public control over the security sector. Chapters 24 and 31, on the other hand, provided guidance for transforming the functioning of the police, border control services and army, or in other words, the organisational level of SSR.

Additionally, in 1999-2013, the EU promoted change in the work of Croatia's security sector with the help of financial instruments, such as CARDS National Programme 2001-2004, CARDS Regional programme 2001-2006, PHARE National Programme 2005-2006 and IPA 2007-2013 (Novota et al 2009: 28-38). Through CARDS, the EU supported the modernisation of security institutions and systems as well as worked towards introducing Croatia to key European values, such as respect for the rule of law and human rights. Regional CARDS was used to promote good neighbourly relations between the Western Balkan states and improve cooperation between their security services. Under PHARE, funds were spent on strengthening institutions and human capacity for speeding up not only the harmonisation of the Croatian legislation with the EU *acquis*, but also the practical application of the EU norms. The Instrument for Pre-Accession Assistance, which replaced a series of the EU financial tools for candidate states and potential candidates in 2007, was similarly used for providing organisational support to the country's security sector through allocations to training and technical assistance.

As can be seen, compared to the previous two periods, the EU's SSR toolbox expanded considerably since 1999. But what effect did this have on the execution of security sector reform in Croatia? To answer this question, two key objectives of SSR are analysed: the objective of ensuring operational control and oversight over the security sector, i.e. the political level of the reform, and the objective of developing professional and effective security actors, i.e. the organisational level.

Political level

The EU's contribution to the political level of SSR in Croatia can be divided into three areas: *management and oversight of the security sector, cooperation with the ICTY and regional cooperation*. All these spheres became more receptive to the EU's influence after the death of Tudjman and the change of government in the country. When the Social Democrat-led coalition introduced constitutional changes in November 2000 and March 2001[94], the power of the president significantly decreased, and the power of the legislature increased (Dowling 2008: 188). As a result, the regulation of the security sector became more balanced: with the president losing a substantial part of the authority, the government and parliament acquired new responsibilities in the sphere of security (Knezovic and Mahecic 2012: 79). The EU was largely satisfied with the new parliamentary system established in Croatia after 2000, which contrasted sharply with regular criticism of the poor separation of powers in the country in the mid-1990s. In the sphere of security, the updated Constitution allocated specific, though sometimes overlapping roles to the parliament, government and president of the republic. The Croatian parliament monitors the implementation of national security policy and development of the military through its supervision powers over the government and public administration offices (ibid.). It also decides on the matters of war and peace and adopts the Strategy of National Security and the Strategy of Defence (Knezovic and Stanicic 2011: 27). The president is the Commander in Chief of the Croatian Armed Forces and therefore has final authority over the army during war, while the government controls budget, planning and personnel issues of the defence sector in the time of peace (ibid.: 29). In many cases, defence decisions cannot be enacted unless they are approved by both the president and prime minister: this arrangement was introduced to avoid a situation where a single actor had too much authority over the army (Knezovis and Mahecic 2012: 81).

While the EU did not have direct input into the amendment of the Croatian Constitution, it used changes introduced in the post-Tudjman period to assist Croatia on the way to democratisation and European integration. In the sphere of security, this meant support for the establishment and reform of governmental bodies, responsible for the civilian oversight of the sector, demanding adjustment of legislation on the security expenditure or legal advice to parliamentary bodies dealing with security issues. Thus, the EU contributed to the institution-building processes in the MoI by financing the development of a national border management information system and the architecture, necessary for its implementation (EC 2002b: 10) and assisted with the restructuring of the MoD and

General Staff in view of ESDP/CSDP activities (EC 2007a: 5). Apart from engaging with the traditional ministerial bodies, involved in security, the EU also monitored the work of other relevant ministries. For instance, to help with the reform of the border service and ensure its alignment with the EU legislation and Schengen *acquis*, the EU followed the development of the Ministry of Finance (in particular, the Customs Administration), the Ministry of Agriculture, Forestry and Water management, the Ministry of Health and Social Welfare and the State Inspectorate (EC 2006c: 6). The civilian oversight of the security sector in Croatia was also strengthened thanks to EU demands for accountability in the public procurement. Not only general procurement legislation was changed in Croatia to fit in with the EU requirements, but specific legal acts were adopted for the security sector as well. In 2012, for example, the Croatian Government approved the Regulation on public procurement for security and defence purposes to comply with relevant EU legislation[95] (GRC 2012).

In general, however, direct action aimed at the improvement of the civilian, parliamentary and public oversight of the security sector in Croatia was rare on the EU's part[96]. In most cases, the EU contributed to this area through broader activities, designed to enhance the overall transparency of the state administration. Specifically, the EU's continuous emphasis on the work of the Office for the Prevention of Corruption and Organised Crime (USKOK)[97], and Office of the Ombudsman, helped to make Croatian security bodies more transparent and accountable. For instance, the Commission's progress reports often focused on cooperation of the USKOK with the police (EC 2005: 94, EC 2006d: 56, EC 2009a:10). In a similar way, Croatian parliamentary committees dealing with security issues, namely Committee for Internal Policy and National Security, Committee for Foreign Affairs, Committee for Finance and Budget and the Council for Civilian Oversight of Security and Intelligence Agencies, benefited from the EU's support through generalised projects, not specific to the security sector. The twinning project "Support to the Parliament of Croatia for the Preparation for EU Accession", funded under the IPA 2007, would be an example of such an initiative. The project contributed to strengthening the institutional framework and administrative capacities of the Parliament, by training not only MPs but also staff working in the committees.

Despite minor criticisms, the European Commission expressed its general satisfaction with the level of civilian and parliamentary control of the army already in 2005 (EC 2005: 13). A year later, in 2006, it also commended the level of external supervision over the police, provided by the parliamentary committees, NGOs and by the public (EC 2006c: 10). Nominally, Croatia has had civilian and parliamentary control of the security sector in place since independence, as it was enshrined in the country's 1990 Constitution (Lukic 2008: 205-206). While this control was not exercised in practice in the 1990s, its sheer presence allowed Croatia to speed up the implementation of the political level of the security reform after the regime change. A strong constitutional base[98], updated in the early 2000s to strengthen the country's democratic standing, was one of the reasons for a rather limited level of interest, displayed by the EU in the oversight of the Croatian security sector. Apart from several mentions in progress reports and a few studies, commissioned by the EU bodies[99], the EU left the issue to be tackled within the NATO accession process. Most of the EU influence on the development of parliamentary and civilian control of the security sector in Croatia therefore had an indirect nature. A similar situation could be observed in public control. The EU supported public scrutiny over the security sector by investing into the development of independent media and civil society more generally, for example, through such projects as the IPA-financed "Civil Society Facility – Enhancing the capacities of the civil society sector for the monitoring of implementation of the EU *acquis*", or by promoting access to public information. The adoption and implementation of the Freedom of Information Act, Data Secrecy Act as well as the constitutional changes in 2010[100], were a direct response to EU conditionality. Additionally, in the final stages of the accession process, the EU engaged directly with the CSOs working in the security sphere, by inviting them to participate in discussions of Chapters 23, 24 and 31. While it is difficult to evaluate to what extent such activities by the EU had an impact on the security sector, it is without a doubt that they contributed to the improvement of the transparency and accountability of the state apparatus as a whole, influencing security bodies almost unintentionally. Thus, unlike in the early 1990s, unintended consequences of EU security governance in the region were of positive character.

The second area through which the EU influenced the political level of SSR in Croatia was the *cooperation with the ICTY*[101]. With the launch of the SAP, full cooperation with this *ad hoc* UN tribunal, set up in 1993 to contribute to the restoration and maintenance of international peace (Kerr 2014: 103), was identified as one of the key political conditions for Croatia's integration into the EU (Obradovic-Wochnik 2013: 94). The work of the tribunal had a direct link to SSR in the country. This is because large numbers of security personnel, including those of the highest rank, were embroiled in war crimes. Furthermore, the indictments, coming from The Hague, faced opposition movements from the army, intelligence and the police, showing the lack of democratisation and professionalization of Croatia's core security actors. Ensuring effective cooperation with the ICTY was therefore of utmost importance for the transformation of the country's security sector and achieving a break with the past.

As mentioned above, in the 1990s, the tribunal was vilified as a biased, anti-Croatian institution that tried to present the defenders of Croatia's independence as war criminals (Pavlakovic 2008: 453). As the result of Tudjman's anti-ICTY stance and regime-sponsored propaganda, the new coalition government that came to power in 2000 found it hard to approach the task of cooperation with the tribunal effectively. Headed by Ivica Racan and comprising of representatives of the Social-Democratic Party (SDP), Croatian People's Party (HNS) and Croatian Social Liberal Party (HSLS), the government announced its readiness to fulfil commitments before the ICTY already in April 2000 (ibid.). Yet nearly a year later in February 2001, the Racan's cabinet faced its first major crisis when veteran organisations, right-wing parties and even elements of the Catholic Church organised mass protests against the possible extradition to The Hague of General Mirko Norac (ibid.: 454). Although Racan managed to keep the premiership and resolved the situation by convincing the ICTY that the Croatian judiciary could handle the case of Norac, accused of war crimes in Gospic and Medak, he failed to obtain popular support for cooperation with The Hague. Even the second Racan cabinet, formed without HSLS in July 2002, was ineffective in this area. Its biggest ICTY-related challenge occurred in September 2002, when it received an indictment for Janko Bobetko, Chief of Staff of the Croatian Army during the Medak Pocket operation that led to the killing of Serb civilians in 1991 (Edmunds 2007: 203).

The Bobetko case presented a predicament for Racan for two main reasons. On the one hand, he was faced with growing resentment at home since Bobetko was a highly respected war hero and the most senior military person in Croatia, who fought not only in the Homeland War, but also in World War II (Jovic 2006: 96). On the other, the EU was starting to doubt Croatia's commitment to the processes of democratisation and European integration. The failure of Racan's government in summer 2001 to apprehend General Ante Gotovina, another national hero, who was in charge of Operation *Storm* as the Commander of the Split Military District (ibid.), was an important factor feeding these doubts. The ICTY's lack of enforcement powers encouraged other external actors to exert pressure on Croatia in connection with the Bobetko case, to avoid the repetition of the situation with Gotovina (Obradovic-Wochnik 2013: 94). The EU, having made progress within the SAP conditional on cooperation with the ICTY, warned Croatia that its refusal to serve Bobetko's indictment could jeopardise its prospects for membership (Pavlakovic 2008: 457). To make matters worse, the UK and Netherlands refused to ratify the SAA, signed in October 2001, until the Bobetko case was resolved (Jovic 2006: 97). The Racan's government, although initially standing by Bobetko, had to agree to arrest and extradite him to The Hague. This agreement, however, materialised only after it had lost the appeals against the extradition both at the Croatian Supreme Court and the ICTY (Pavlakovic 2008: 457). Bobetko died in Zagreb in May 2003, without ever making it to The Hague, but the Gotovina case remained an important obstacle on Croatia's way to the EU (and NATO) for several more years (Jovic 2006: 97).

In late 2003, it fell to the HDZ, which had returned to power under the leadership of Ivo Sanader, to handle the Gotovina case. Sanader confirmed his government's commitment to the course of the European integration in general and cooperation with the ICTY in particular (Pavlakovic 2008: 461). While being in a stronger position than his predecessor thanks to the fact that the new opposition, now led by the SDP, was in favour of the said cooperation, Sanader still could not resolve the issue quickly. To a great extent, this could be explained by the persistently strong anti-ICTY sentiment in the Croatian society[102], which placed the government in a precarious position and made it balance between the international pressure and local discontent. While performing this balancing act, Sanader tried to shift the blame for unpopular decisions onto the international community and especially the EU. Instead of educating the public and promoting the idea that the ICTY's work was aimed at achieving reconciliation and strengthening peace, Sanader presented cooperation with the tribunal as something required to gain access to the EU. As a result, the popular support for the European integration was waning, with the numbers opposing the EU membership more than doubling between the middle of 2004 (20 per cent) and the middle of 2005 (48 per cent) (Franc and Medjugorac 2013). Euroscepticism, largely inspired by the EU's ICTY conditionality, as well as poor understanding of the bloc, remained high until the end of the accession process.[103]

Nonetheless, the EU played a key role in resolving the Gotovina crisis. By suspending membership talks that had to start with Croatia in March 2005, the bloc forced Sanader to step up efforts to locate the fugitive general by developing and implementing a special Action Plan and accepting the help of European intelligence agencies, aimed at identifying and disrupting networks of Gotovina's support, especially in the security sector (Jovic 2006: 100). The ease with which the general escaped captivity in 2001, when the indictment was issued, and problems experienced by the government with locating him since were widely seen at the time as a sign of unreformed and corrupt security apparatus (ibid.). New efforts allowed the Chief Prosecutor of the ICTY Carla Del Ponte to declare that Croatia was fully cooperating with the tribunal in

October 2005, which consequently led to the official start of the EU membership negotiations with the country that same month (Edmunds 2007: 206). Gotovina was arrested in Spain in December 2005 and convicted in The Hague in 2011. Although the conviction was overturned by the Appeals Judgement in November 2012, the Gotovina case still demonstrates the importance of EU pressure for establishing a working relationship between Croatian elites and the tribunal (Kerr 2014: 109).

By refusing to ratify the SAA over the Bobetko case and postponing negotiations over Gotovina, the EU made a sizeable contribution into changing attitudes and behaviours among the political leadership of the country (Obradovic-Wochnik 2013: 98; Edmunds 2007: 206). Although begrudgingly and with varying degrees of reluctance, Croatian elites accepted that cooperation with the ICTY was a necessity. This change did not automatically find a reflection in wider society, which preserved a largely negative view of the tribunal (Obradovic-Wochnik 2013: 98). This could be partly explained by the vilification of the ICTY, perpetuated by the media (Vukusic 2014: 161), and partly by the sanctity of the Homeland War and its key figures in the country's nationalist mythology, promoted and supported by certain political parties, e.g. the HDZ, and influential interest groups. Of course, the EU was not the only external actor that had an impact in this sphere: e.g. in 2002, the USA suspended financial aid to Croatia's judicial reform (Jovic 2006: 97) and NATO warned the country that its unwillingness to apprehend Bobetko put its membership bid under threat (Edmunds 2007: 204). Yet while others engaged with the issue sporadically, the EU continued monitoring Croatia-ICTY relations consistently. After the arrest of Gotovina, who was the last Croatian high-profile fugitive, the Commission's key concerns in relation to ICTY matters were linked to ensuring security guarantees to witnesses and informants (EC 2006d: 13-14) and providing the tribunal with access to the military documents, relating to cases of generals Gotovina, Cermac and Markac[104], all of whom were accused of crimes against Serb civilians during and after Operation *Storm* (EC 2008a: 16; EC 2009a: 16).

In short, by assisting the ICTY with the prosecution of war crimes committed by members of the Croatian Armed Forces and police, the EU left an impact on both the country's state apparatus and SSR. Compelling Croatia's leadership to cooperate with the ICTY contributed to making the entire Croatian security sector more professional, transparent and democratic. Although, the EU's ICTY-related pressures led to attitudinal changes only on the elite level, they were not insignificant. On the contrary, the emphasis of the EU on cooperation with the tribunal can be seen as one of the factors behind behavioural changes of political leaders in Croatia but also in BiH and Serbia, and therefore behind the emergence of the elite security community in the region.

Regional cooperation is the third and final area where the EU's influence on the political level of Croatian SSR was felt the most. As already discussed, the SAP is not simply a bilateral policy but also a regional one, as it puts a strong emphasis on cooperation between the Western Balkan states. The EU's commitment to strengthening regional ties in the Western Balkans was reflected not only in the SAAs, but also financial instruments, supporting the post-conflict development and democratic transition of the region, e.g. regional CARDS programmes and Multi-Beneficiary assistance under IPA (EC 2002a: 6). In the sphere of security, the EU continuously promoted regional cooperation starting from 1995, which was described at length in the previous chapter. To avoid duplication of what was already discussed, this section highlights the requirements for the regional dimension of SSR, directed specifically at Croatia. In a similar manner, regional conditions for SSR will be analysed in reference to Serbia and BiH.

The regional focus in the context of Croatia's SSR in 1999-2013 was most visible in the spheres of police cooperation, dealing with the legacy of war and border management. With the start of membership negotiations with Croatia in 2005, the EU started emphasising the importance of cross-border cooperation between the police and border services of Croatia and its neighbours, especially those belonging to the Western Balkans region, but not only. For instance, the EU welcomed the conclusion and implementation of agreements on police cooperation with Serbia, BiH, but also Hungary,

Germany and Poland (EC 2008a: 17; EC 2009a: 58; EC 2010c: 57). Such agreements were meant to contribute to capacity-building processes and development of professional police networks. Thanks to the agreement with Serbia, for example, the Croatian government was able to identify and arrest a suspect in the killing of a prominent Croatian journalist in October 2008 (EC 2009a: 58). Cooperation was specifically encouraged to prevent illegal migration and combat organised crime. Already in 2005, the collaboration between Croatian and Serb-Montenegrin police agencies on the prevention of illegal migration and smuggling was seen by the EU as a success story (EC 2005: 31). In November 2008, Croatia signed a Memorandum of Understanding with Albania, Bosnia, FYROM, Montenegro and Serbia to establish a system for the exchange of statistical data on illegal migration and participate in regional early warning system (EC 2009a: 56). Nearly two years later, in October 2010 Croatia concluded another agreement with the same Western Balkan neighbours to set up a regional office on fighting organised crime (EC 2010c: 57). Regional cooperation on matters relating to war crimes was highlighted by the EU not only to improve relations with the ICTY, but also promote collaboration on domestic war trials. Finally, cooperation around border security in Croatia was promoted through joint training sessions, common actions and information exchanges to prevent and combat cross-border crime (EC 2005: 91). Additionally, the EU closely monitored border disputes between Croatia and its neighbours, particularly those with Serbia, BiH, Montenegro and Slovenia[105]. It should also be mentioned that the EU saw military cooperation between Croatia and other Western Balkan states as beneficial (EC 2010c: 17), yet this matter did not receive as much of the bloc's attention as regional relations in policing and border security.

In brief, the regional aspect of SSR in Croatia was promoted by the EU as part of the regional element of the SAP, incorporated into the political criterion of the membership negotiations. By encouraging Croatia to cooperate with other Western Balkan states and wider neighbourhood in the sphere of security, but predominantly police and border matters, the EU worked towards improving the good governance and professionalism of the country's security sector (EC 2008: 19-20) as well as harmonising security relationships between former adversaries. All three areas, discussed above — management and oversight of the security sector, cooperation with the ICTY and regional dimension of SSR — were fostered by the EU to assist Croatia with ensuring political control over the security sector and improvement of its democratic and good governance. While aimed at similar objectives, EU activities in these fields were not pursued as a single SSR policy, rather they were part of a much broader process of European integration. Whether the EU could have had a bigger impact on the political level of the reform, had it had a comprehensive strategy in place, remains an open question. Nonetheless, it is possible to say, that even without such a strategy, the EU helped Croatia to adjust the practices of the actors, involved in the oversight of the security sector, to democratic norms and principles.

Organisational level

The absence of an overall SSR strategy did not stop the EU from influencing the reform on the organisational level either. In contrast to the previous period, the EU showed more interest in the sphere of *defence*. If previously, it was only the mine clearing action and cooperation with the ICTY (in terms of removing compromised personnel from the army) that attracted the EU's attention, in 1999-2013 the sphere of the bloc's involvement in Croatia's defence matters expanded considerably. The EU provided the military with policy advice, training opportunities as well as technical aid and post-conflict assistance. Nonetheless, the driving force behind defence reform in the country was NATO. Though the first three post-Tudjman years left the military largely unchanged due to political games and power struggle between the SDP and HSLS (Lukic 2008: 202), Croatia started moving towards NATO already in 2000, when it joined its Partnership for Peace (PfP) Programme (Baric 2006: 2). In May 2002, only a few months after the parliament hastily approved the first National Security Strategy and Defence Strategy, Croatia entered the Membership Action Plan (MAP). Under the MAP, the country started reassessing its military capabilities and defence budget, and gradually adjusted them to NATO planning requirements (ibid.). Since 2002, NATO played a key role in determining priorities and long-term plans of the Croatian Armed Forces (CAF). For instance, its officials were closely consulted during the preparation of the Strategic Defence Review (SDR) in 2005 and Long-Term Development plan (LTDP) of the CAF in 2006 (Pietz 2006: 36). Relying on NATO's assistance, Croatia downsized its active military personnel, modernized the army and turned it into a flexible, interoperable force. In recognition of these reform efforts, NATO accepted Croatia as a member at the Strasbourg/Kehl Summit in April 2009 (Knezovic and Stanicic 2011: 49). In certain aspects, the EU benefited from NATO's assistance, too. For instance, Croatia's contributions for the EU Battlegroups and ESDP/CSDP missions were possible thanks to the training and equipment provided through NATO (Pietz 2006: 37). Overall, the EU and NATO's SSR-related activities in Croatia complemented each other.

Having started assisting Croatia with de-mining in 1998, the EU increased its level of post-conflict support exponentially when the country started moving towards membership in the bloc. Even more, with time, it chose to allocate funds for de-mining programmes directly to Croatia. Between 2001 and 2005, de-mining projects financed by the EU were administered by the International Trust Fund for Demining and Mine Victims (ITF), located in Slovenia (EC 2010b: 9). This could be explained by inadequate level of local expertise in the area[106], high levels of corruption in Croatia and the lack of trust to local institutions on the EU's part. Since 2006, the Croatian Mine Action Centre (CROMAC) gained enough experience to be deemed capable of administering EU funds that were coming first under the framework of CARDS, and then under IPA. The total contribution to mine clearing action through CARDS 2002, 2003, 2004 and Cross-Border programmes that were conducted between 2001 and 2008 amounted to just over 13 million EUR[107] (ibid.: 10). IPA provided around 6.2 million EUR between 2009 and 2013[108] (CROMAC n.d.). The EU-funded projects, coordinated by CROMAC, often received additional funds from the Croatian state budget, though the bloc on average covered 70-80 % of the expenses (ibid.). As before, the EU provided grants for mine clearance activities to support the return of refugees and internally displaced persons, enhance economic and social conditions in war-affected areas, speed up reconstruction of infrastructure and improve the overall security situation in the country.

Even when membership negotiations were nearing to a close, the EU continued supporting Croatia in its efforts to remove the mine threat. In 2013, the country secured 3.3 million EUR for de-mining, while still having 637 square km of its territory classified as Suspected Hazardous Area (APMBC 2013). Thanks to the continuous EU support, a big part of the Croatian territory has become safer. Moreover, Croatia developed valuable expertise in de-mining, which its military personnel as well as civilian actors could share with the UN, NATO and the EU via CSDP missions. The EU's contribution therefore had an important impact on the capacity-building of Croatia's defence sector, helping its staff to develop knowledge and skills that could be applied to post-conflict environments inside and outside the country.

The EU also provided Croatia with policy and legal advice on defence reform. While NATO was guiding the country strategically and helped it devise such important documents as the above-mentioned SDR and LTDP, the EU focused on less comprehensive, yet still important, issues. The arms control was one of them. In 2002, Croatia subscribed to the EU Code of Conduct on Arms Exports (EC 2006d: 63) and with the start of membership negotiations in 2005 started aligning the national legislation as well as institutional practices to EU standards regarding the non-proliferation of weapons of mass destruction (WMD) (EC 2007a: 4). The EU's emphasis on the issue of small arms and light weapons (SALW) has also been instrumental for the development and implementation of the National Strategy and Action Plan for the Control of Small Arms and Light Weapons (ibid.). The EC closely monitored Croatia's progress in joining non-proliferation and arms control regimes, such as the International Atomic Energy Agency, the Preparatory Commission for the Comprehensive Nuclear-Test-Ban Treaty Organisation and the Proliferation Security Initiative (ibid.). While the Union regularly expressed concern over a discrepancy between the commitments to arms control, undertaken by the Croatian government legally, and its performance on the matter, it did not exercise much pressure to change the situation (EC 2006d: 63). In general, the EU's aim was to ensure that Croatia adhered to the same principles as its member states.

With the help of EU funds and through the United Nations Development Programme's (UNDP) administration, Croatia worked to raise public awareness of the threat posed by SALW possession (SEESAC 2010). In 2010-2012, the EU supported the UNDP-coordinated "Fewer Weapons, Fewer Tragedies" campaign, that was part of the EU regional project "SEESAC[109] arms control in the Western Balkans" (GRC 2012a: 339). In fact, in the sphere of SALW, it was often UNDP that administered projects, at least partially funded by the bloc (ibid.). Along with the policy, post-conflict and technical aid, the EU supported defence reform in Croatia through training assistance. While a lot of Croatia's military personnel benefited from NATO exchange programmes (Pietz 2006: 36), the EU invested resources in preparing Croatia to be part of its own security infrastructure, particularly CSDP and the Battlegroups. Croatia declared its "willingness to support, participate in, and contribute to" ESDP/CSDP early in the negotiation process (EC 2005: 106). To prepare relevant personnel, the EU responded with training and administrative capacity-building activities for Croatian officials working in the MoD and General Staff (EC 2007a: 5; EC 2010c: 65). It also offered support with upgrading IT infrastructure and arranging study visits to Brussels for defence staff (EC 2007a: 6). To prove its commitment to CSDP, Croatia started sending its personnel to both military and civilian missions before becoming an EU member state, which was an important form of knowledge exchange, too. Thus, Croatia contributed a 15-member reconnaissance team to the EU's military operation in Chad and the Central African Republic (EUFOR *TCHAD/RCA*); several representatives of the CAF were also sent to participate in EU NAVFOR *Somalia – ATALANTA* operation off the Somali coast and were involved in providing logistical support to EUFOR *Althea* in Bosnia (EC 2009a: 66; GRC 2012a: 335). Participation in the EU operations not only provided the army with an opportunity to gain valuable experience in conflict and crisis management, but also allowed it to share the expertise it had received through the EU's (and NATO's) assistance for SSR. This expertise mainly lay in the areas of mine clearance, reconciliation, transitional justice and SSR itself (EC 2007a: 6). As a small country, Croatia made "a relatively limited but not insignificant contribution to EU's ESDP capacities" (ibid.: 7).

In a similar manner, Croatia was involved in the development of the EU Battlegroup concept. For the first time, it participated in the Nordic Battlegroup that was on stand-by from January to June 2011 (GRC 2012a: 336). Here, Croatia mainly contributed equipment and medical teams. The following year, it joined the Battlegroup led by Germany on a much bigger scale, which required nearly 250 Croatian soldiers to undergo specialised training (ibid.). Involvement with the EU Battlegroups contributed to further professionalisation and modernisation of the CAF.

As can be seen, the EU considerably expanded its efforts to assist Croatia's defence reform after 1999. If in the previous period, it was mainly preoccupied with de-mining and promoting cooperation with the ICTY, in 1999-2013, its area of engagement grew to include policy and legal advice and training activities, mostly linked to its own security infrastructure. The focus was on preparing Croatia for challenges of the future membership in the bloc, which means defence reform was used by the EU as a member state-building tool. Although major changes in the military sphere occurred under the influence of NATO, which accepted Croatia as its member in 2009, the EU is still widely recognised as an important contributor to the country's defence reform (Pietz 2006: 38; Knezovic and Stanicic 2011: 32-33).

In policing, the EU played even a bigger role. This is because *police reform*, just like the reform of border services, is covered under the umbrella of Justice and Home Affairs (JHA), one of the priority areas within the SAP and throughout the accession process. With immediate post-conflict problems having been addressed by the UN agencies and OSCE, the EU chose to focus on assisting Croatia with developing a "professional, reliable and efficient police organisation" that was properly equipped to implement the EU rules and principles (EC 2005: 91). In the European Commission's view, poor law enforcement was posing a threat for the socio-economic development in a state, undermining respect for human rights and provision of human security (EC 2004: 14). To make the Croatian police an effective, modern and democratic service, the EU focused on legislative alignment, capacity building and technical support. Special attention was paid to developing policing capabilities for tackling organised crime and corruption that were widespread not only in the Croatian society in general but also in the police. As Croatia progressed in the negotiation process, the EU requirements grew more detailed and specific, but initially the bloc focused on technical aspects and human resources development.

Thus, the first EU projects directed at policing in the post-Tudjman Croatia were financed under CARDS 2002 and 2003 and aimed at developing an effective Central Intelligence System. The system was to strengthen the capacity of the MoI and General Police Directorate to tackle transnational organised crime, money laundering, trafficking in human beings, drugs and weapons, and illegal migration (EC 2002b: 9). Early on, the EU also supported the set-up of specialised crime analysis units in each of Croatia's twenty police districts and provided advice on developing training programmes for police officials and IT specialists working in them (EC 2003b: 18). These efforts established a foundation for the development of intelligence-led policing in Croatia, which from 2008-2009 allowed for a more efficient prosecution of criminal offences in corruption and organised crime (Vukadin, Borovec and Ljubin Golub 2013: 44).

When Croatia introduced its present administrative territorial division, that breaks the country into twenty counties and the capital city of Zagreb, in 1997, the Ministry of Interior was among the first state institutions to be reorganised (Ivkovic 2004: 186). As a result, the police were given a three-tier system: with the MoI and the General Police Directorate on top, twenty police administrations in the middle and 175 police stations at the bottom (ibid.: 187). While, on the one hand, this reorganisation meant that the Croatian police became decentralised and therefore more independent from the centre, on the other—it created a disconnected system of law enforcement agencies. With the start of the membership negotiations in October 20005, the EU quickly identified this latter issue as an obstacle on the way to achieving a well-integrated and professional police organisation. An internal network that could link the headquarters of the General Police Directorate with twenty police districts and 175 police stations was required from the government as a matter of priority (EC 2005: 93; EC 2006d: 56). These changes of infrastructure were needed to strengthen the administrative capacity of the country's police: transparent procedures, effective channels of communication and modern equipment were necessary to enhance the information exchange and inter-agency cooperation inside a three-tier system (EC 2005: 95). Another way of strengthening administrative capacity, singled out by the EU, was through improving the staffing and training policies, implemented by the MoI.

Although the Croatian government proclaimed professionalization of police as an objective in the mid-1990s, the country's law enforcement still lacked a well-defined Human Resources policy and working training system nearly a decade later (Ivkovic 2004: 182-183). Even more, the process of European integration added another dimension to police reform requiring police officials to familiarise themselves with EU-specific standards and best practices, especially those referring to the free movement of people, goods and services and police cooperation (EC 2002a: 49). Through such projects as PHARE 2005 "Strengthening Human Resources Management, Education and Training at the Ministry of the Interior — Police Academy" and "Preparation for the implementation of the Schengen *Acquis*", the EU contributed to enhancing the professional capacity of the country's police service. Similarly, a project on community policing, implemented by the MoI in 2002 with EU support, helped to transform an outdated, repressive police system into a citizen-oriented public service (EC 2005a: 1). It was later recognised as one of the success stories of the EU's engagement with Croatia's police reform (MWH Consortium 2008: 21).

While the work of Croatia's police was for a long time determined by the historic context of war and collapse of Yugoslavia, it is not surprising that professionalization of the service was taking a long time. Nonetheless, the dedication of the post-Tudjman era governments to the course of European integration and preliminary work conducted by internal and external actors on policing practices in the second half of the 1990s allowed Croatia's police reform to progress relatively fast, especially compared to other states in the region. That is why soon after the introduction of IPA in 2007, the EU supplemented its assistance for the development of general professional policing capacity in Croatia with specialised support to prepare the national law enforcement for tackling a range of specific contemporary threats such as cybercrime, terrorism or corruption. Many of the IPA-funded projects combined technical support with a training element. The IPA 2009 project on "Capacity Building in the Field of Fight against Sexual Exploitation and Sexual Abuse of Children, and on Police Assistance to Vulnerable Crime Victims", that ran from 2011 till early 2013, is an example of such initiatives. Under this project, the Croatian police were introduced to best practices in investigating sexual exploitation and abuse of children and other vulnerable victims, as well as provided with cutting-edge IT equipment for criminal investigations on mobile devices and computers (MoI RC 2011: 8). An earlier IPA 2007 project "Strengthening Capacities of Ministry of the Interior to combat Narcotic Drugs Trafficking and Drug Abuse" was implemented between February 2010 and July 2011. Through Twinning and supply components, it contributed to strengthening the ability of the Croatian MoI to supress organised production and resale of drugs.

The overarching theme for these two initiatives as well as for an overwhelming majority of EU-funded projects in the sphere of policing implemented in Croatia from the early 2000s was the fight against organised crime. Lack of progress in tackling organised crime in the country and the Western Balkans more broadly was seen by the EU as a major source of concern (Strazzari and Coticchia 2012: 155). Trafficking in drugs and persons, money laundering, corruption and other criminal activities were perceived not only as factors preventing the emergence of effective states in the region, but also as a direct threat to the area of freedom, security and justice inside the bloc (ibid.). To improve the situation, the EU provided the Croatian police with specialised training and technical support through projects like the above-mentioned IPA 2007 and 2009, as well as CARDS 2004 "Combating Trafficking in Firearms,

Ammunition and Explosives", IPA 2008 "Strengthening Capacities of the MoI for Crime Prevention" and IPA 2009 "Supply of IT Equipment for Police Stations" (MUPRH 2017). It also exposed the police to the EU best practices in the field, e.g. through developing links with the EU's law enforcement agency Europol. The Croatian Parliament ratified the operational agreement with the agency in June 2006 and set up a Europol section within the Department for International Police Cooperation shortly after (EC 2006d: 55; EC 2007c: 53). This allowed the government to post a Liaison Officer to Europol headquarters in February 2008 (EC 2008a: 59).

Given the transnational nature of organised crime, to further strengthen the capacity of the Croatian police, the EU promoted interagency cooperation and regional initiatives. For example, training on human trafficking were organised not only for Croatian police officers, but also representatives of the social welfare system, health care, tourism and civil society organisations (EC 2009a: 58), while the Croatian Ministry of Interior was involved in the realisation of numerous regional projects such as Regional CARDS 2004 "Strengthening Capacities of the Police in Fight Against Organised Crime in the Southeast Europe" and Regional IPA 2010 "Strengthening capacities in the fight against cybercrime" (MUPRH 2017). By complementing national programmes with regional efforts, the EU was trying to break up criminal networks that spread through the Western Balkans in the 1990s and engender trust among states of the region. To further demonstrate the country's commitment to regional cooperation in the sphere of policing and the rule of law, Croatia participated in several CSDP missions in neighbouring countries. For instance, it provided logistical support to the EUPM in BiH and contributed police personnel to EULEX in Kosovo[110] (GRC 2012a: 335). Participation in civilian CSDP missions, just like in military operations, was also a valuable opportunity for knowledge exchange. It is important to note that even after Croatia became a member state of the EU in July 2013, Brussels continued investing in strengthening the country's capacity to tackle organised crime. Several projects were implemented in Croatia after accession to the bloc, e.g. "Strengthening Capacities of Ministry of Interior to Combat Cybercrime" under IPA 2011, and "Enhancing administrative and operative capacities of the National Police Office for Suppression of Corruption and Organized Crime" IPA 2012 (MUPRH 2017).

Finally, while preparing to join the EU, Croatia received policy and legislation advice from the bloc. As a result, it had to revise key legislation on policing, e.g. the Criminal Code, the Police Act and the Secrecy Act (EC 2007c: 53) and sign cooperation agreements with EU agencies, e.g. the Europol and Eurojust, and EU member states, e.g. with France and Austria (EC 2008a: 59). Moreover, Croatia had to set up several new policing bodies, such as the National Police Office for the Fight Against Corruption and Organised Crime.

Overall, the EU's engagement with police reform in Croatia was aimed at creating an effective institutional and legislative framework that could be compatible with demands of a modern, democratic state that could become a fully functional EU member. The EU tracked the development of administrative capacity of the Croatian police, its legislative and regulatory framework, as well as invested into its education system and infrastructure (EC 2002a: 49). It did so to make the three-tier police system of the country accountable, professional, and most importantly sensitive to the EU-specific requirements. The reform therefore was guided by the process of European integration and used as a tool of member state-building. As it had a regional dimension, it was also used for harmonising relations with other Western Balkan and SEE states, promoting cooperation and good neighbourliness. The link between police work and JHA raised the profile of police reform in Croatia considerably. The same thing happened with *border reform*.

The EU placed a strong emphasis on reorganisation of Croatia's border police soon after the country's government announced its commitment to the process of European integration (Trauner 2011: 71). Already in 2002, the European Commission stated there was a need for Croatia "to establish greater security at international borders that will diminish cross border crime and illegal migration, and at the same time facilitate cross border movement of people by developing and implementing asylum and migration policies" (EC 2002a: 54). Border security was of utmost importance for Croatia due to the unusual length of its external borders and unresolved border issues with some of its neighbours, including Serbia and Bosnia. For a small country with the population of around 4.5 million (World Bank n.d.), controlling and safeguarding the state border of 3, 332 km, with 950 km of sea border and a large number of border lines drawn over difficult terrain (MoF and MoI RC 2010: 5), was quite a challenge. Border disputes and post-conflict tensions in the region did not make the task any easier. As Croatia was moving closer to becoming an EU member, the salience of border reform kept growing. The EU was adamant to ensure that Croatia was ready to secure the external borders of the bloc (which were to coincide with the borders of the country in 2013) and was able to "assume greater responsibility" in preventing illegal migration before it was granted the membership (Trauner 2011: 104).

In comparison to military and police reforms, the EU's engagement with *border reform* represented the most comprehensive effort. When the first CARDS project "Integrated Border Management: Border Police" was launched in Croatia in 2002, it resulted not only in creating the strategic basis for the development of the Croatian border police, but also outlining the framework for future EU projects in the sphere (EC 2006e: 6). The project, implemented by twinning partners from Germany and Slovenia in 2002-2003, involved a detailed assessment of the Croatian border police to determine its needs in "legislation, general organisation and human resources, technical equipment and IT structure, as well as training and education" (ibid.). It should be noted that it was not the first external attempt to assess the state of Croatia's border security: the EU project followed closely the Stability Pact initiative "National Action Plan for the Republic of Croatia with a View of Development and Long-Lasting Stabilisation of the Areas Pertaining to Asylum, Migration and State Border Surveillance" that finished in 2002 (MoF and MoI RC 2010: 7). To a certain extent, the EU disregarded the work conducted within the previous project, which led to the repetition of activities and inefficient use of funds (Trauner 2011: 72). Nonetheless, the first CARDS project still had important implications: it defined the structure and personnel concept for the newly created Border Police Directorate within the General Police

Directorate (EC 2006e: 2) and, as already mentioned, laid the foundation for several strategic documents on the topic of border security. The Border Police Development Strategy was drafted first, which opened the way for the development of the National Strategy for Integrated Border Management (IBM), produced in the framework of the CARDS 2001 Project "Integrated Border Management—Interagency Cooperation", completed in 2004-2005 (MoF and MoI RC 2010: 7).

In recognition of interconnectivity between border management issues facing Croatia and the rest of the Western Balkans, the EU insisted that the country developed and implemented a comprehensive IBM strategy, aligned with the Integrated Border Management guidelines formulated for the region in 2004 within the Ohrid Process. Using these guidelines as a foundation, the Croatian IBM strategy, released in 2005, established mid- and long-term goals for enhancing cooperation within national border services, as well as improving interagency and international cooperation of all agencies involved in managing the national borders (MoI RC 2010: 3). The agencies in question included the Ministry of Interior—Border Police Directorate, the Ministry of Finance—Customs Directorate, the Ministry of Agriculture—Veterinary Directorate and Directorate for Food Safety and Phytosanitary policy, the Ministry of Health—Directorate for Sanitary Inspection and State Inspectorate (ibid.: 8). For the EU, the IBM was not simply about ensuring an effective border control, but also about trade facilitation and cross-border cooperation (Trauner 2007: 8). Additionally, in other Western Balkan states, but not in Croatia, it was about the demilitarisation of borders. The IBM was envisaged as a tool for combatting all types of cross-border crime, such as illegal migration, terrorism, human trafficking and drug smuggling, on the one hand, and for promoting "legitimate cross-border activities, such as tourism, trade and trans-border cooperation", on the other (ibid.). To assist Croatia with the implementation of the IBM strategy, the EU allocated substantial funds through CARDS, PHARE and IPA to introduce modern equipment into the country's border surveillance and control as well as customs surveillance system, build a National Border Management Information system (EC 2004: 15), develop working

IT structures and install databases in numerous state border agencies (MoF and MoI RC 2010: 8-9). For instance, the EU allocated nearly 10 million EUR for the development of the National Border Management Information system (NBMIS) through projects within CARDS 2002, CARDS 2003 and IPA 2007 that were implemented between 2005 and 2012 (MUPRH 2017).

As can be seen from these early attempts, the EU tried to assist Croatia with designing a border security system that would be well-coordinated on national and regional levels. Neither police nor army reform were receiving the same level of attention from the bloc. This was because the EU was rather inexperienced when it came to reforming these sectors. And in many respects, it was learning by doing. Border security, however, was already a familiar topic for the Union from the time of the fifth enlargement, when the CEE countries had to adjust their visa, asylum and migration policies to gain EU membership. Of course, the Western Balkans was different, as it required the EU to address the post-conflict legacy of the region. Overall, however, it was easier for the EU to approach border reform because of its previous experience. Compared to other states in the region, Croatia was in a much stronger position to respond to the EU requirements: its borders were never controlled by the military and it started the reorganisation of the border system even before the negotiation process with the EU was launched. Despite this position of relative strength, the Commission was regularly dissatisfied with the progress of border reform in the country. It often criticised staff shortages, limitations in training, inappropriate infrastructure and lack of equipment at headquarters and numerous BCPs (EC 2005: 91; EC 2008a: 58; EC 2010c: 56). The Croatian government was struggling to find the necessary funds for strengthening the control of and surveillance over the country's long land and sea borders and bringing border security in line with the EU requirements. The Croatian case was not helped by the fact that the EU's comprehensive approach to border security kept evolving and becoming more demanding. For instance, as a result of a peer review mission to Croatia in 2010 and 2011, it became evident that the country's National IBM Strategy needed further adjustment to comply with the EU IBM concept, which was different to the one applied to the Western Balkans (MoI RC 2010: 3). The EU's concept was closely connected with the creation of the borderless Schengen zone, while the IBM concept in the Western Balkans was an integral ingredient of SSR aimed at establishing a working system of well-coordinated national and regional agencies, involved in border management (Marenin 2010: 18-19). To bridge the gap between the two and help Croatia move closer to the EU standards, more funds were directed to the country through such projects as IPA 2010 "Support to the alignment of the Croatian IBM Concept with EU IBM Concept" (MUPRH 2017).

The Croatian border agencies and bodies responsible for their oversight have also benefited from the EU training assistance. Aside from practical assistance with basic and specialised training, for example, for the border police in using new equipment to perform border surveillance and checks according with the international standards (MoF and MoI RC: 10; EC 2008a: 56), the EU also had an impact on the development of training strategies for the country's key border agencies. For instance, within the PHARE 2006 project "Blue Border Surveillance", implemented in 2008-2010, Croatia drafted the Maritime Police Development Strategy that defined "the organisation and training of the maritime police" (MoI RC 2010: 5). Under the EU's influence, the MoI also developed educational manuals in the field of asylum and refugee work (EC 2009a: 56). Even more, the professionalism of Croatia's border security staff as well as their number kept growing thanks to the continuous monitoring by the EU.

Having facilitated the adoption of the Border Police Development Strategy and National Strategy for IBM, the EU started steering Croatia towards implementing the Schengen *acquis*. The Border Police Development Strategy was, in fact, the first document to clearly define the reform guidelines for the Croatian border police from the point of view of EU accession (Trauner 2011: 74). Croatia was required not only to considerably update its IT systems and equipment used for the provision of border security, design a working financial plan for the reorganisation of the border police into a modern and independent service within the structure of the general police, but also to ensure the legislative alignment with the *acquis*.

This latter process progressed at a moderate pace, to prepare Croatia properly for taking the responsibility for the protection of the external EU borders (EC 2012: 13). In early 2007, Croatia adopted the Schengen Action Plan that offered the overview of activities the government had to complete until 2012 (Trauner 2011: 75). To give Croatia impetus to start implementing this action plan, the PHARE 2005 project "Preparation for the Implementation of the Schengen *Acquis*" was implemented in 2007-2009 (MoI RC 2010: 5).

From the point of view of the EU, border security in Croatia was not possible to reach until the country developed effective asylum, migration and visa policies that were aligned both with the bloc's standards and respective policies of other Western Balkan states. This meant that the EU carefully traced the evolution of national legislation on asylum and migration (often requiring amendments and revisions of laws to eliminate discrepancies between the Croatian approach and its own vision[111]), paid close attention to the improvement of reception and accommodation facilities for asylum seekers in the country and provided assistance for Croatia's participation in the Dublin and EURODAC regulations[112] that were at the heart of the EU asylum system (Trauner 2011: 86-95). While Croatia was predominantly viewed as a transit country for asylum seekers and irregular migrants, its status as a country of destination was becoming clearer, the closer it approached the EU (EC 2008a: 56). In terms of visa policies, Croatia had to fulfil numerous obligations, too, although it did not need to go through the visa liberalisation process like the rest of the region[113]. This is because it was never placed on the negative list[114] and its citizens could freely travel to the EU. Nonetheless, it still had to align its national visa policy with the EU's positive and negative lists, adjust its travel documents and visa forms to the *acquis* requirements and pursue favourable visa regimes with the Western Balkan neighbours (EC 2010c: 55). Thus, the EU was instrumental in achieving a visa-free travel between Croatia and Serbia as well as BiH (Trauner 2011: 83). Although, Serbia and BiH were for a while on the EU's negative list, Croatia was encouraged to allow travel of these countries' citizens to its territory without visas as a way of improving cooperation and resolving tensions in the region. The EU's approach to border reform in the region was therefore another way for promoting amicable relations and positive security interdependence between regional players.

Arguably, one of the biggest challenges in the sphere of border security for Croatia was the issue of border delineation. Since gaining independence, Croatia had border demarcation issues with several of its neighbours, including Slovenia, Serbia, Montenegro and Bosnia. The EU was reluctant to get involved in these disputes, preferring to treat them as bilateral issues, separating them from the process of European integration. The sensitive nature of the disputes and the fact that they involved EU member states did not allow the bloc to avoid dealing with the problem entirely. A border dispute with Slovenia is a case in point. While Croatia had several border-related issues to settle with Slovenia, it was the drawing of the maritime border that proved to be most publicised and challenging to settle. The two countries could not agree where to draw a sea demarcation line in the Piran Bay. While Croatia insisted on dividing the Northern Adriatic in the middle, thus splitting it between itself and Italy, leaving Slovenia without access to international waters, Slovenia argued for the creation of a corridor between the Croatian and Italian zones (Trauner 2011: 79). Croatia's intention to create an ecological and fishing protection zone (ZERP), that would prohibit foreign exploitation of the Croatian part of the Adriatic Sea, made the issue even more heated. When in 2008 ZERP came into effect, despite earlier commitments to suspend it for EU member states (EC 2008a: 16), Slovenia and Italy blocked any further negotiation progress for Croatia. It took the mediation of the Council of the EU to resolve the issue temporarily, by convincing Croatia to fulfil its earlier obligation regarding putting a break on ZERP for EU countries (Trauner 2011: 80). Nonetheless, Slovenia kept threatening to derail Croatia's accession talks unless a viable solution of the maritime border dispute was found (Lang 2012: 13). These threats only stopped when both countries signed an agreement on 9 November 2009 to settle the dispute via international arbitration (ibid.). The EU, that had to supervise the progress, was relieved to decouple this argument from the accession process. When Croatia joined the bloc on 1 July 2013, the first hearing of the arbitration tribunal had still not happened, though the procedural meeting had been held in April 2012[115] (EC 2012a: 9). It is sometimes argued that the EU lost an opportunity to contribute to settling the dispute before finishing the negotiations. This argument is somewhat flawed, however, as the bloc does not have special *acquis* on border delineation, which is why candidate countries are encouraged to reach agreement either bilaterally or through international arbitration (Trauner 2011: 78).

The EU had a similarly limited effect on the border disputes with Serbia and BiH. Serbia had disagreements with Croatia regarding the border demarcation around two islands near the town of Vukovar and at the Danube river (EC 2006d: 17-18), which the Commission monitored through progress reports without offering a lot of assistance for their resolution. In the case of BiH, the biggest problems related to the Croatian Port of Ploce that had strategic significance for Bosnian economy and the Bosnian town of Neum, which separates the southernmost part of Croatia, including Dubrovnik, from the rest of the country (Lang 2012: 13). As explained above, the EU was eager for Croatia to solve these disputes with BiH soon after the signing of the DPA, yet, like in the case with Slovenia, it preferred to treat the issues as bilateral and not link them to the accession talks. Nonetheless, the bloc did not stand completely aside. In fact, it played a key role in getting Croatia and BiH to sign agreements on border management on 19 June 2013. These agreements obliged the countries to implement the EU standards for border controls, customs and transit traffic as well as defined the rules for using the port of Ploce and the Neum corridor by both sides (EC 2013a). While this was only a temporary solution, which would need to be reviewed in the future, it would not have been possible without the EU guidance (ibid.).

In short, Croatia's border security in 1999-2013 underwent significant changes thanks to the impact of the EU. The latter contributed to the reorganisation of the border police, modernisation of the equipment and IT systems used at border crossing points, rise of professional standards, changes of national legislation, development of closer ties between a range of state agencies involved in border management through the IBM concept, and reaching at least temporary solutions of border disputes between Croatia and its neighbours. Attempting a comprehensive approach to border reform, the EU not only placed it in the regional IBM framework, applicable to the rest of the Western Balkans, but also closely coordinated its efforts with other conveners of Ohrid Process, within which the concept was devised.

Conclusion

It should be reiterated that Croatia went through a colossal transformation between 1991 and 2013: from a country fighting for its independence to a member state of the European Union. The evolution of Croatia's security sector within the same period is equally impressive. Created practically from scratch in the flames of war, the country's security bodies can currently be seen as largely professional, modern and democratically governed. Of course, some problems persist, e.g. discrepancies between legislation and practice or lack of civilian expertise on security issues have not been eradicated, yet the progress achieved in the transformation of the security sector over the studied period is undeniable. SSR in Croatia had a slow start: after the end of the war in 1995, police and border control services underwent minor reorganisation, while army structures remained mainly unreformed. The only visible change in the defence sector was the reduction of the number of troops. It was only after the death of Tudjman in 1999 and the emergence of new pro-European coalition government, that SSR truly gained prominence. Under the influence of external actors, it was quickly identified as one of the major indicators of the country's transformation on the way to democracy and Euro-Atlantic institutions. The EU, who by that time mostly recovered from the failure of "the hour of Europe", made SSR part of the European integration process. The Croatian case illustrates the evolution of the bloc as a security actor particularly well. The EU has come a long way from an observer and peripheral actor, which in 1991-1995 was side-lined by other external actors and influenced Croatia's security situation through the ECMM, arms embargo and Badinter Arbitration Commission to an agent of SSR in the early 2000s. Relying on the foundation, laid in 1995-1999 through technical assistance, humanitarian work and the Regional Approach that were meant to stabilise and pacify the country, the EU started actively promoting the reforms of police, border services and to a lesser extent the army, when it became clear that Croatia's future lay in the bloc.

The EU's first attempts to transform the work and management of Croatia's security sector were timid and sporadic. De-mining activities, assistance with restoring border controls and resolving visa issues with the neighbouring states can hardly be defined as a comprehensive approach to SSR. When assessing the EU's early activity in this sphere, however, one needs to take into account the complexity of a broader context. In the post-war country under the semi-authoritarian regime, where the EU's failure to manage the conflict was still vividly remembered and any external attempt to promote regional cooperation was perceived as a step towards the reconstruction of Yugoslavia, the chances of any significant influence on such a sensitive sphere as security were slim. Moreover, it should not be forgotten that at that point the EU was still lacking a working security and defence policy or a clearly defined concept of SSR. Nonetheless, it still tried to promote good neighbourly relations and reciprocity through SSR-related activities. With the launch of the SAP, that almost coincided with the change of government and foreign policy direction in Croatia, the situation changed dramatically. The EU became an active promoter of different aspects of SSR, paying attention to both political and organisational levels of the reform. Having provided a detailed overview of its engagement in the defence, police and border reforms in Croatia between 1991 and 2013, five observations can be made about the EU as an actor of SSR in the country.

First, *the EU has become more confident in promoting SSR with time*. Choosing to tackle technical issues at the start, it slowly moved on to providing legal and policy advice on generic and specialised security issues as well as offering training activities to Croatian security personnel. While it demonstrated varying levels of interest in defence, police and border reforms, giving preference to the latter two and settling for a supporting role to NATO in the defence sector, it did not leave any of them without attention.

Second, despite subscribing to the idea of the comprehensive SSR in theory, *the EU approached the reform in Croatia in a manner that cannot be described as well-defined or coordinated.* Among the three aspects of SSR studied in this chapter, only border reform was more or less comprehensive: it started with a careful assessment of needs and challenges facing the actors involved in border management, and included a range of technical, strategic and policy elements. What is more, it was also aligned with the EU's approaches to other Western Balkan states.

Third, *the EU was reluctant to use negative conditionality or coercion while facilitating SSR and touch upon sensitive issues relating to it.* Croatia's accession talks were threatened twice[116]: first time over the issue of poor cooperation with the ICTY and second time over the maritime border dispute with Slovenia, by that time an EU member state. In both cases, the EU persuaded the Croatian elites to find a solution, though not necessarily a permanent one. It was not common for the EU to resort to punitive measures to achieve desired changes in the work of the Croatian security sector. This was partly because the Croatian government was mostly willing to cooperate, partly because the sphere of security remained an intergovernmental, rather than a supranational policy, in the EU.

Fourth, *by promoting SSR, the EU was working not simply towards improving the security situation in Croatia, but also towards preparing the country for the membership in the bloc,* for joining the European security community. By investing resources in creating a professional police service in Croatia, developing a modern and aligned with the EU principles and standards border management system and democratically-governed armed forces, the EU was attempting to build an effective member state. That is why, on many occasions, the priorities in SSR, e.g. tackling organised crime in police reform or developing and implementing the IBM strategy in border reform, were defined according to the concerns of the EU, not Croatia's needs. The latter were not fully ignored, e.g. the de-mining assistance that has been provided by the EU since the late 1990s was a direct response to the needs of the post-conflict country. Yet, the general EU's approach to the reforms of police, army and border services was dictated by demands of the European integration process. SSR was therefore used a tool of member state-building and a vehicle for sharing with Croatia values and norms found inside the EU.

Fifth, *SSR in Croatia, as promoted by the EU, had a clear regional dimension*. The EU attempted to improve Croatia's relations with its Western Balkan neighbours both bilaterally and regionally. Croatian soldiers were encouraged to join the CSDP missions in Kosovo and BiH, while police officers, border and customs officials took part in joint trainings with their colleagues from Serbia, FYROM or Montenegro. This cooperation was not based on mutual trust but guided by the elites that shared the vision for the future of the region as part of the European Union.

---

75   While there is no agreement in the literature on the nature of the Croatian regime during the rule of Tudjman, in this book it is described as semi-authoritarian. This is because Croatia in the 1990s, with regular elections and state apparatus keeping the semblance of democracy, cannot be considered conventionally authoritarian. For further discussion, see Ottaway (2003: 109-130).
76   This term is used to refer to the Croatian war of 1991-1995, without any normative judgement.
77   Due to the rudimentary character of SSR in Croatia, as well as Serbia and BiH, in the 1990s, and the EU's limited engagement with the reform during the first two periods, a detailed analysis of political and organisational levels of the reform is not always possible.
78   For the discussion of Croatia's contribution to changing the regional balance of power in 1995 and its role in the final stages of the Bosnian war, see Ramet (2002: 230-232), Stoessinger (2001: 229-232).
79   For the history of Croatia's emergence as an independent state and the role of war in the process, see Tanner (2010).
80   In the SFRY, the military was organised on the federal level, while the police forces were managed by the federal republics.
81   In 1995, two military-police operations, Flash and Storm, defeated the remaining Serb troops on the territory of Croatia. However, the full territorial integrity of the country was achieved only in 1998 with the peaceful reintegration of Eastern Slavonia. For more, see Gagnon (2004: 131-177).
82   Croatia's application to join NATO's PfP submitted in 1997 was rejected due to persisting semi-authoritarian tendencies in the army. Moreover, the EU's Regional Approach was met with hostility in the country, the same as the ICTY's work.
83   The country joined the Membership Action plan in 2002 and became the member of NATO in 2009.
84   In addition to the legal acts mentioned above, during the studied period Croatia also released the Law on the Police Activities and Rights (2009), Law on Police (2011) Defence Strategy (2013) and Defence Law (2013).
85   Interview of the author with a security expert in Croatia in September 2016.

86   Interviews conducted by the author with a former ECMM diplomat in Sarajevo and a security expert in Zagreb in September 2016.
87   In the 1990s ECMM established regional centres in BiH, Albania, Bulgaria and Hungary, in the early 2000s it also came to FYROM, Serbia, Kosovo and Montenegro.
88   For the texts of Opinions 1-10, see (CoY AC 1992).
89   See the final section of this chapter.
90   See discussion in Chapter 6.
91   The Erdut Agreement, officially the Basic Agreement on the Region of Eastern Slavonia, Baranja and Western Sirmium, was signed on 12 November 1995 to peacefully end the war in Croatia by establishing transitional arrangements for integrating Serb-held territories into Croatia's constitutional and legal order. For details, see Erdut Agreement (1995).
92   The DPA divided Bosnia into two entities: The Federation of Bosnia and Herzegovina and Republika Srpska that retained considerable autonomy from the common state, see Chapter 6.
93   From the point of SSR, Chapter 23 on Judiciary and Fundamental rights is also important. Yet it is omitted from this analysis as the current work studies SSR on the example of the defence sector, the police and border services.
94   See the consolidated text of the Constitution of the Republic of Croatia (2001).
95   Namely, Directive 2009/81/EC of the European Parliament and of the Council of 13 July 2009 on the coordination of procedures for the award of certain works contracts, supply contracts and service contracts by contracting authorities or entities in the fields of defence and security and amending Directives 2004/17/EC and 2004/18/EC.
96   Interview, conducted by the author with a security expert in Zagreb in September 2016.
97   A department of the State Attorney's Office set up to investigate and prosecute corruption.
98   The Constitution of Croatia states that the Constitution and the law shall regulate the organization of defence, command, administration and democratic control over the armed forces of the Republic (Art. 7), and that the realization of the civil control over the armed forces and the security services is within the competences of the Parliament of the Republic (Art 80) (Closa Montero 2007: 5).
99   For example, see Bilandzic (2006).
100 See Constitution of the Republic of Croatia (2010).
101 The work of the ICTY influenced the organisational level of SSR in Croatia, too, for instance, by contributing to the democratisation and professionalization of the country's army and police through the removal of war criminals from thei ranks. However, the role of the tribunal goes beyond the organisational level of the reform, which is acknowledged in the part of the book that follows.
102 For instance, according to a survey published in the Croatian daily Jutarnji list in March 2005, 54.5 per cent of respondents were against the extradition of Gotovina to The Hague, while 84.8 per cent said they would not report him to the police if they met him (Edmunds 2007: 205).
103 Croatia's EU accession referendum held in January 2012 attracted only 43.5 per cent of voters, 66 per cent out of which voted for joining the EU and 33 – against it (Franc and Medjugorac 2013).
104 Out of 161 persons, indicted by the ICTY by 2013, only five (not including Bobetko) have been Croatians. These were: Rahim Ademi, Mirko Norac, Ivan

Cermak, Mladlen Markac and Ante Gotovina. Cermak was acquitted, while Gotovina and Markac had their convictions overturned (Kerr 2014: 109).
105 A closer look at some of these disputes is provided below in the section on border reform.
106 CROMAC was established in 1998 but needed time to build its capacities.
107 Nearly 6 million EUR was administered through ITF (EC 2010b: 10).
108 The funds allocated under IPA 2009-2013 were spent on projects that lasted up till 2015 and in total equalled over EUR 9 million (CROMAC n.d.).
109 The SEESAC—South Eastern and Eastern Europe Clearinghouse for the Control of Small Arms and Light Weapons—is an initiative established in 2002 and given the mandate by the UNDP and Regional Cooperation Council. Its goal is to "strengthen the capacities of national and regional stakeholders to control and reduce the proliferation and misuse of small arms and light weapons" in SEE region (SEESAC n.d.).
110 Croatian police officers also took part in EU crisis management missions further afield, e.g. in the EUPOL Afghanistan.
111 For example, the Asylum Act was adopted in 2004 and amended several times afterwards on the EU's requests.
112 The Dublin Regulation determines what EU member state is responsible for the examination of an asylum application, while the EURODAC Regulation establishes an EU asylum fingerprint database (EC 2017).
113 See Chapters 5 and 6 for Serbia and Bosnia's experiences.
114 The negative list includes countries whose nationals must hold a visa when crossing the external borders of the EU, while the positive list covers the countries whose nationals are exempt from the visa requirement.
115 For details of the dispute after 2013, see Ilic (2017) and Morgan (2017).
116 In terms of demands for security sector reform.

Chapter 5
Security Sector Reform in Serbia

Introduction

Security sector reform (SSR) in Serbia can be described as a highly inconsistent and politically charged affair. In the studied period, it encountered many obstacles, three of which deserve a special mention. First, the country's SSR suffered over the unresolved issue of statehood (Ejdus 2010: 9). Between 1991 and 2013, Serbia existed in four different configurations: until April 1992 within the SFRY, in 1992-2003 within the Federal Republic of Yugoslavia (FRY), in 2003-2006 as part of the State Union of Serbia and Montenegro (SCG), and from 2006 as an independent state. This means that until 2006, Belgrade did not have full control over the security sector, having to share security responsibilities with Podgorica. The unilateral declaration of independence by Kosovo in 2008 created further uncertainty around Serbia's statehood, placing another burden on the country's security sector.

The second factor that presented a major obstacle to Serbia's security sector reform in the studied period is the country's image as an aggressor. Having engaged in four armed conflicts in the 1990s,[117] Serbia has been treated with suspicion by its neighbours and the international community alike. This led to prolonged isolation of the country and heightened tensions over its reluctance to cooperate with the ICTY. Although during the wars of Yugoslavia's dissolution atrocities were committed by all sides[118], the scale of crimes and violence perpetuated by the Serbian side in Croatia, BiH and Kosovo far exceeded those committed by its adversaries (Gow and Zverzhanovski 2013: 126). As a result, the legacy of war left a lasting imprint on Serbia's security sector. The continuing unwillingness of the Serbian elites to cooperate with the ICTY after the ousting of Milosevic further complicated the already difficult process of SSR. While Croatia, albeit reluctantly, shared security files with the tribunal and worked together with European intelligence agencies to transfer its war criminals to The Hague, Serbia was unable to locate Ratko Mladic, the Bosnian Serb military commander during the Bosnian war, and Radovan Karadzic, the former Bosnian Serb leader, for 16 and 13 years respectively (Pond 2013: 11). Since elements of the security sector were implicated not only in committing war crimes in the 1990s, but also in harbouring fugitives from the ICTY in the early 2000s, SSR in Serbia was significantly affected by the country's war crimes legacy.

The third obstacle to transforming Serbia's security sector has been linked to the country's slowness in committing to the path of democratisation and Euro-Atlantic integration. Partly because of the internal power struggle between the two strongest actors — the Democratic Party (DS) and Democratic Party of Serbia (DSS) — inside the Democratic Opposition of Serbia (DOS) that came to power in the immediate post-Milosevic period, partly because of strained relations with the international community, SSR in Serbia was delayed (Ejdus 2010: 9-10). By the time the infighting stopped, and EU membership became tangible[119], valuable time, that could have been spent on reforming the country's security sector, damaged by years of war and semi-authoritarianism, had been wasted. This becomes even more evident if one looks at the progress achieved in Croatia at the same time. Having rejected semi-authoritarianism at nearly the same time as Serbia, Croatia committed to the path of Euro-Atlantic integration much sooner and managed to transform its security sector into an effective player, equally respected by European and American partners.

The current chapter analyses the impact of the EU on Serbian security sector reform. Following the structure used for the case study of Croatia, it starts with an overview of SSR in the country in 1991-2013 and continues with the investigation of the EU's contribution to the reform during the same period. Before starting the analysis, it should be mentioned that although Serbia used to be part of larger entities in the studied period, this work studies SSR only in the republic itself, leaving out Montenegro and Kosovo[120], as the process of the reform took different forms there and therefore requires separate studies.

Security sector reform in Serbia: overcoming the legacy of the regional aggressor

It has become customary to examine security sector reform in Serbia starting from 2000, after the ousting of Milosevic. While the pace and depth of the reform intensified in the post- Milosevic period, it is still important to analyse the security situation in the 1990s, to understand what preceded this development. Serbia's security sector had its beginnings in the security apparatus of the SFRY. Unlike Croatia who had to build an army from scratch in the midst of conflict, Serbia had a strong military almost instantly. When Yugoslav republics started announcing their independence, the Yugoslav People's Army (JNA), *de facto* became a Serbian army (Popovic et al 2011: 14). Yet together with infrastructure, equipment and a large percentage of personnel, Serbia also inherited the JNA's strong traditions of autonomy and allegiance to communism (Edmunds 2007: 153). In the SFRY, through its close ties with the Communist Party, honed by Tito, the army acted as a pillar of the socialist system (Popovic et al 2011: 14), which meant that Milosevic had to reform it before using it by his own regime. The task was not simple, for the military was a federal institution, over which Milosevic, as the president of Serbia, had no direct control. Nonetheless, by using the combination of formal and informal tools, the JNA slowly transformed into the nationalist regime's ally. With the creation of the FRY in 1992[121], Belgrade found it easier to control the federal politics in general and military affairs in particular, since the Montenegrin government and the ruling Democratic Party of Socialists (DPS), consisted of Milosevic's close associates from the Yugoslav League of Communists (Hadzi-Vidanovic and Djuric 2007: 16) and the Montenegrin presidency, then held by Momir Bulatovic, also a Milosevic sympathiser, was nearly powerless (Bieber 2003:17).

To further strengthen his grip over the army, Milosevic turned to the process of Serbianisation. With many soldiers and officers leaving due to the SFRY disintegration, the number of Serbs in the JNA was rising substantially. Moreover, in the JNA, the officer corps, at least at the junior and middle level, was predominantly Serbian, making it easier for Milosevic to ensure that armed forces supported the Serbian side first in Croatia and later in Bosnia (Gow and Zverzhanovski 2013: 28). The Serbianisation was galvanised when the JNA split into three armies: the army of the FRY (VJ), the army of the Republika Srpska (VRS) in Bosnia, and the army of Serbian Krajina (SVK), the Serb breakaway state in Croatia (ibid.). The division of the JNA was part of the strategy to distance Serbia from wars in the region (Edmunds 2007: 153). While the VRS with 67, 000 soldiers kept fighting in BiH, Milosevic could tell the international community that the VJ had nothing to do with the conflict (ibid.). The reality, however, was different: Belgrade continued supporting the VRS with personnel, weapons and intelligence until the end of the Bosnian war (Gow 2003: 59-60), and even paid its officers' wages until 2002 (Gow and Zverzhanovski 2013: 124). The VJ, that was 135,000 strong after the separation from the VRS and SVK (Edmunds 2007: 153), went through several purges in 1992 and 1993 that led to the dismissal and retirement of many in the officer corps, leaving only nine generals from the JNA in place in 1993 (Gow and Zverzhanovski 2013: 29). These purges were targeting non-Serb personnel with an aim to build a loyal and trustworthy Serbian security sector (ibid.).

In fact, most endeavours to reform the army in 1991-1995 pursued this goal, even the elements compatible with the concept of SSR. For example, decommunisation, completed in 1993, did not result in depoliticisation of the armed forces but conditioned them to be more receptive to the nationalist ideology, promoted by Milosevic's Socialist Party of Serbia (SPS) (Gow and Zverzhanovski 2013: 37). Similarly, the process of civilianisation of the MoD that started in 1992 "was nothing more than a front" (Gow and Zverzhanovski 2013: 57). There was no democratic control over the VJ either. Without any formal strategy, the functioning of the VJ was regulated by the 1992 FRY Constitution, which obliged the army to defend the "sovereignty, territory, independence and constitutional order" of the country (Art 133). The inclusion of the provision on constitutional order created a pretext for using the army in internal conflicts (Popovic et al 2011: 15). Moreover, the Constitution introduced the Supreme Defence Council (VSO), that looked like a democratic tool but was manipulated by Milosevic to exercise control over the VJ.

The VSO, that was composed of the federal, Serbian and Montenegrin presidents, had a poorly defined decision-making process and lacked accountability (Edmunds 2007: 86). Such ambiguities allowed Milosevic, even as the President of Serbia, to use the VJ to his own advantage. In addition, his regime benefited from establishing alternative chains of command in the army (ibid.).

Nonetheless, until 1997-1998 Milosevic did not fully trust the army. Instead, he turned his attention to the police that as a republican institution was much easier to control. Under a new Law on Internal Affairs (1991), the police were centralised and organised as a section of the Ministry of Interior (Edmunds 2007: 156). The Serbian MoI held operational control also over the autonomous provinces of Vojvodina and Kosovo that had lost their policing powers (ibid.). By offering police officers higher salaries, better equipment and training, Milosevic was building a loyal force. Militarisation of the police was therefore the next logical step. The police gradually received a military appearance (Popovic et al 2011: 16), military equipment and military education (Weber 2001: 44). The Police Academy, established in 1993, with military subjects, military-style uniforms and military training followed the model of the Belgrade Military Academy (Bakic and Gajic 2006: 11). In 1995, an 18-level military ranking system made the police even more like the army (Trivunovic 2004: 243). Police officers were regularly given rotating shifts in war zones in Croatia and BiH (Rose 2011: 41).

In 1993, there were 80,000 police officers in Serbia, yet even that was not enough (Rose 2011: 41). Additionally, Belgrade established several specialised police forces and developed extensive links with paramilitary units as well as networks of organised crime. For instance, in 1992 the Serbian Security Service (RDB) and Special Police Anti-Terrorism Unit (SAJ) were centralised and placed under the MoI control (ibid.: 40). By financing paramilitary groups, such as the Serbian Chetnik Movement and Serbian Guard, Milosevic not only strengthened his position at home but also gained an instrument for fighting wars in Croatia and BiH (Edmunds 2007: 154-155). As can be seen, changes in the police work in 1991-1995 were regressive and completely devoid of principles promoted by SSR.

Border security in the FRY was ensured by the federal-level army and navy, while the Serbian MoI was also involved in controlling certain border crossing points (BCPs) (Bakic and Gajic 2006: 23). In the circumstances of war and international sanctions, many border officials were involved in the state-sanctioned smuggling of arms and various commodities (Andreas 2005: 342). Overall, in 1991–1995, the army, police and border services were bent to serve the nationalist regime to support its war activities in neighbouring states. The politicisation and criminalisation of key security bodies in Serbia at the start of the 1990s were typical of a unit, forming part of a regional conflict formation[122]. Yet Serbia, then part of the FRY, was not an ordinary unit of the Balkan subcomplex, but one of its poles, as discussed in Chapter 2. As such, its policies had a direct bearing on the security situation in Bosnia, Croatia, Montenegro and Kosovo, and left a significant imprint on other units of the subcomplex. It should be reiterated that the prevalent environment of this period was that of war: after suffering a defeat in Slovenia, the JNA became openly involved in military action in Croatia and BiH. Although after the introduction of the international sanctions, Milosevic suspended formal ties with the Serb leaders in the two countries, he continued providing them with financial and military aid covertly (Hadzi-Vidanovic and Djuric 2007: 5). The war dominated not only Serbia's regional discourse, but also its domestic policies. It was skilfully used by the regime to suppress opposition and gave prominence to ultra-nationalist leaders, such as Vojislav Seselj[123], leader of the Serbian Radical Party (SRP) (Ostojic 2014: 25). The divisions between Serbian opposition parties and support of the nationalist ideology among many of them are two main reasons that for a long time made Milosevic the only legitimate interlocutor in the eyes of the international community (ibid.).

After the wars in Croatia and BiH ended, Milosevic briefly toyed with the role of peace-maker to improve his relations with the international community (Popovic et al 2011: 7). While keeping the semblance of democracy, he used the security sector to consolidate his power, which meant that there was not much room for SSR in 1995-1999 either. With no more external conflicts to fight, the country's security apparatus had to be reduced in size. The reduction was achieved mainly by disbanding various paramilitary groups (Edmunds 2007: 155) as well as cuts and purges in the army (Ramet 2002: 341). Still, such actions did not bring substantial results, as in 1999, the army was nearly 110, 000 strong. In 1996, the VSO released the "Model of the Yugoslav Army", that promised to transform the VJ into "a modern ... organisation" (Sikavica 2001). The plan was not fully implemented and only led to a reduction of regiments (Gow and Zverzhanovski 2013: 74). Having become the president of the FRY in 1997, with a weak MoD and practically non-functioning VSO (ibid.: 42), Milosevic brought the army under his full control by the end of 1998, right in time for the Kosovo conflict.

Nonetheless, the police kept their position of prominence. The process of militarisation continued as it was a way of sidestepping the Dayton-induced arms control measures (Edmunds 2007: 156). As the international community monitored any changes in the levels of armament of the VJ, Belgrade kept investing in the military training and equipment for the police. During the Kosovo conflict around 40, 000 regular police (ibid.: 183) and 50, 000 special police forces and army troops were involved in fighting (Ramet 2002: 319), confirming the importance of the force for Milosevic. The failure of the Rambouillet peace plan and plight of hundreds of thousands of Albanian civilians[124] prompted NATO to start a 78-day bombing campaign in March 1999 (Edmunds 2007: 157). Launched without the UN approval, Operation *Allied Force* initially targeted Serbian forces in Kosovo, but quickly expanded to include strategic targets in the FRY (Ramet 2002: 327). In such circumstances[125], SSR was among the last things on the mind of the Belgrade elites. The situation with border security was not any better: borders were still militarised and the reinstatement of a weapons embargo against Serbia in 1998 by the UN as well as introduction of additional sanctions by the EU in 1998-1999 (Ramet 2002: 318) meant that a large proportion of border guards continued engaging in illegal activities.

In short, in 1995-1999 Serbia's security sector saw minimal changes, with the country slipping further into illiberalism, and only keeping up the appearance of democracy. The main difference from the previous period was in the inward-looking trajectory, pursued by the security actors, as they were now directed by the regime to focus on the internal situation in the country. War stopped dominating Serbia's security landscape for only a few years and returned in 1998 with the violence in Kosovo. By initiating a campaign of ethnic cleansing against Kosovo Albanians, Serbia rejected the principles of reciprocity, regional cooperation, good neighbourliness and transparency, promoted by the Dayton Accords, Regional Approach, Sub-Regional Arms Control Agreement and other external initiatives. The security regime that started emerging in the Western Balkans after 1995, did not take hold because of Belgrade's inability to stick to the peaceful path. Croatia and Bosnia did not fall back to violence, however, and the sub-region started moving towards the European security community as the result of domestic political changes (as demonstrated by the fall of Tudjman and Milosevic) and change in the EU's approach to the Western Balkans in 1999, seen in the support for the Stability Plan and launch of the SAP. Yet, in 1995-1999, Serbia, overwhelmingly perceived by the international community as an aggressor and pariah state (Mladenov 2014), was still isolated. The FRY's security sector did not receive any substantial external support. On the contrary, it suffered from the NATO bombing that significantly damaged the country's security infrastructure[126] and the UN and EU sanctions that nearly led the country to economic collapse (Hadzi-Vidanovic and Djuric 2007: 17).

The end of the Kosovo conflict in 1999 and electoral defeat of Milosevic in October 2000 offered an opportunity for change. In the Serbian security sector, however, this opportunity was not seized immediately due to at least three reasons. First, Serbia remained part of the FRY, and any attempt to reform federal institutions that included the army and border security was challenged by the Montenegrin ambivalence and sometimes outright hostility[127]. Even after the FRY was transformed into the State Union of Serbia and Montenegro in 2003, the task of conducting SSR remained difficult. Montenegro continued to ignore or sabotage shared policies in anticipation of the referendum of independence, set by the Union's constitutional Charter for 2006 (Dowling 2008: 183). Second, the non-violent transfer of power in 2000 was achieved through negotiation with the security sector leadership, which prevented a clean break with the past. Because Vojislav Kostunica, the new FRY President, struck a deal with the then Chief of Staff Nebojsa Pavkovic and Zoran Djindjic, the future Prime Minister of Serbia, made an agreement with Ulemek Lukovic, commander of the Special Operations Unit (JSO), the old Milosevic cadre remained in place, hindering the prospect of a quick SSR (Ejdus 2010: 10). Third, SSR was postponed, due to a continuing power struggle between two strongest members of the DOS coalition. While Kostunica's DSS and Djindjic's DS were arguing over spheres of influence, the country's security sector continued to stagnate.

The first post-Milosevic years achieved very little in terms of transforming the military. It was not until 2003 that the army started seeing substantial changes. Boris Tadic, the new Minister of Defence, released a ten-point plan of reform to create a modern armed force under strict civilian control (Gow and Zverzhanovski 2013: 61). On his orders, in May 2003 the previously independent General Staff was subordinated to the civilian control of the MoD, transferring to the latter its responsibilities for the personnel, education and procurement (ibid.: 62). Cooperation with the ICTY was also improving, but slowly. Even when cooperation with The Hague was included into the DPA and the FRY signed a Memorandum of Understanding with the tribunal in 1996, the ICTY remained highly unpopular in the country (Ostojic 2014: 58). The Law on Cooperation with the ICTY was passed only in April 2002, introducing a regulatory framework into Belgrade's relationship with The Hague. Nonetheless, the legacy of war crimes remained a sensitive issue in Serbia. The country's leadership continued to resist ICTY demands, while its security sector was involved in harbouring The Hague indictees, including Mladic and Karadzic. It was the pressure of the USA and the EU, which linked the issue to the progress with PfP and EU membership respectively, that brought about the emergence of a more cooperative stance in Serbia starting from 2005-2006 (Gow and Zverzhanovski 2013: 142). Still, the relationship remained strained and was slow to bring results: Milosevic, arrested in 2001, died in 2006 before the completion of his trial; Karadzic, arrested in 2008, was sentenced to forty years in prison in March 2016 on accounts of genocide, war crimes and crimes against humanity (ICTY 2016), while Mladic, caught in 2011, was sentenced to life imprisonment after being convicted of genocide, war crimes and crimes against humanity only in 2017 (ICTY 2017). Consequently, SSR in the country suffered as the key security agencies struggled to deal with the legacy of war that tainted their ranks.

Except for the adoption of several minor strategic documents, not much was achieved in the defence reform by 2006, when the SCG peacefully dissolved. The Strategic Defence Review (SDR), adopted in June 2006 based on the 2004 National Defence Strategy, outlined the vision for the Serbian Armed Forces (SAF) and promised to create a lean, modern force until 2015 (Watkins 2010: 9). While the SDR adoption was an important milestone, defence reform in Serbia, as before, was led more by a difficult economic situation than by strategic documents (Kusovac 2002). It is no wonder therefore that downsizing the army emerged as one of the key priorities. First attempts in this area were implemented through a UK-funded PRISMA initiative and via the Defence Reform Fund, launched in 2004 (Edmunds 2007: 168). Eventually, the SAF shrank to 28,150 in 2013 (World Bank 2016). Additionally, Serbia's mandatory military service was phased out by 2010 (Gow and Zverzhanovski 2013: 79, 82).

Unlike in Croatia, NATO played a limited role in defence reform in Serbia. Treated with hostility over its bombing campaign in 1999, NATO provided mainly technical assistance for modernisation of the army through the PfP programme, which Serbia joined in 2006. Any closer cooperation and the question of membership became unfeasible with Serbia releasing a declaration of military neutrality in December 2007 (Popovic et al 2011: 35). Adopted in anticipation of Kosovo's independence, this vague and underdeveloped resolution, significantly slowed down the course of Serbia's defence reform. In the absence of NATO's leadership, the EU had to become more active in the reform. Thus, several strategic documents on defence, such as the Law on Defence, Law on Armed Forces, National Security Strategy and a new Defence Strategy, all released in 2009, were developed under the EU's guidance (Milic 2014: 21; Ejdus 2010: 19). These documents reiterated Serbia's commitment to the rule of law, transparency and democratic civilian control. Their value, however, was undermined by the fact that they were adopted without a systematic plan and full harmonisation with the constitution (Ejdus 2010: 19).

A lack of comprehensive approach was evident in police reform, too. Prime Minister Djindjic, who was believed to have co-opted police leaders to support the peaceful transfer of power, approached the reform selectively (Rose 2011: 44). Driven by budget needs, he prioritised areas that could improve the country's economic situation. The fight against organised crime was among the first issues tackled. In 2002, the parliament adopted a new Criminal Procedure Law and Law on Organised Crime that set up a series of new bodies, including a special prosecutor's office and a new police unit for combating organised crime (ibid.: 45). Efforts were also made to make secret services, notorious for their links with organised crime in the 1990s, more accountable and transparent. The 2002 Law on Security Information Agency, for example, transformed the RDB into a security information agency (BIA), separated it from the MoI and put it under the government control (Watkins 2010: 10). The assassination of Djindjic on 12 March 2003 highlighted both the importance of work started, and the shallowness of results achieved. Operation *Sabre* launched by the government in the aftermath revealed complex and deep connections between organised crime and security sector (Popovic et al 2011: 30). Scores of police officers and military personnel were investigated and indicted for links with organised crime, while the JSO, implicated in the murder, was disbanded (Edmunds 2007: 95; Caparini 2006: 18-39).

An impetus for the reform was given by the Law on Police (2005) that emphasised demilitarisation, depoliticization and professionalisation of the service (Milic 2012: 2). As the result, military ranks were abolished (Popovic et al 2011: 31) and political influence on appointments and promotion in the police was reduced (Ejdus 2010: 14). The separation of the police from the MoI and requirement for the Chief of Police to be civilian further improved the service. Other notable changes included the reduction of personnel, that in 2006 dropped to 26, 527 of uniformed officers and 42, 720 MoI employees (Rose 2011: 73), reform of police education, provided by the Academy of Criminalisation and Police Studies from

2006 (ACPS 2022), and strengthening of civilian and democratic oversight. The latter, not without problems, is provided through several new and reformed bodies, such as the parliamentary Defence and Security Committee that also oversees defence matters and the Internal Affairs Sector of the MoI (MoI RS n.d.). The 2011 Law on Police and 2013 Law on Private security provide evidence that Serbia's police reform was not finished in 2005-2006.

It is important to note that the reform of police attracted a more active participation of external actors than defence reform. The OSCE, supported by the EU, assisted with the development of the Multi-Ethnic Police Element (MEPE) and community policing after the insurgency of ethnic Albanians in South Serbia in 2000-2001 (Bakic and Gajic 2006: 3-6). The first reform programmes in the sphere of policing, the so-called Monk and Slater reports, were prepared by the OSCE and Council of Europe, and not by the government (Trivunovic 2004: 245-246). Still, while help provided by external donors was useful, it failed to shape the reform because it followed a project-based, rather than comprehensive approach (Watkins 2010: 11). With time, police reform has become one of the key areas of negotiation in Serbia's membership talks with the EU (Popovic et al 2011: 36).

Border reform in Serbia was externally driven, too. After plans to set up a Border Police Service in 2000-2001 by the Federal MoI fell through due to Montenegro's ambivalence, the first strategic documents on transferring border security from the military to the police were released with the assistance of the OSCE, DCAF, the Stability Pact and the EU's European Agency for Reconstruction (EAR) (Bakic and Gajic 2006: 23-24). Moreover, following the Ohrid Process, Serbia committed to implementing the Integrated Border Management, developed by the EU to promote legitimate cross-border activities and eradicate illegal ones (Watkins 2010: 11). The Border Police directorate assumed control over the first border posts along the Hungarian border in October 2005, finalising the transfer in December 2006 (Rose 2011: 98). Yet, the demilitarisation of borders was only completed in 2008, with the adoption of the Law on Protection of the State Border (ibid.: 70).

Overall, by 2013 SSR in Serbia had some important achievements: most legal provisions regulating the work of security bodies were harmonised with international standards; the rule of law, transparency and accountability were recognised as key values in the sector; the police and army were put under democratic and civilian control, and border security was demilitarised. The progress is considerable, especially looking at the starting point in the 1990s, when Milosevic used the security sector to fight wars in the neighbourhood, oppress opposition and increase his grip over the country. In 2013, Serbia was no longer a pariah state, but a member of the developing security community in the Western Balkans, attached to the EU core.

Nonetheless, SSR in Serbia has not been smooth. Due to the unresolved issue of statehood, the legacy of four wars, continuous power struggle between political elites, the Kosovo problem and strained relations with external actors, SSR posed many challenges for the Serbian government. Thus, with the institutional framework for democratic governance of the security sector largely in place, there have been problems with practical implementation of their tasks, while many legal acts, such as the Law on Defence and Law on Police required amendments. Moreover, only border reform went through a comprehensive reform, led by an IBM strategy. Military and police reforms, on the other hand, were approached selectively, responding to the requirements of the market and external actors, meaning that in 2013 SSR in the country was far from complete. The remainder of the chapter looks at SSR in Serbia in more detail but from the point of the EU's impact.

The EU and Serbian security in 1991-1995

With Serbia providing support to its para-states in Croatia and Bosnia in 1991-1995[128], the EU's engagement with the country had a predominantly punitive character[129]. In the absence of SSR-related activities on the EU's part, it is still important to analyse the engagement of the bloc in Serbian security during this period for at least three reasons. First, to ensure consistency of the research that distinguishes three main periods within the 1991-2013 timeframe both on regional and national levels of analysis. Second, to appreciate the evolution of the EU as an actor of SSR, and third, to better understand the scale of transition the Serbian security sector underwent in the studied period. While SSR rarely starts from a blank sheet, it is crucial to look at the past to fully comprehend the factors that enabled and/or hindered the change of behaviours, norms and values of key security actors in the country (Gow and Zverzhanovski 2013: 22). This section differentiates three main ways through which the EU affected the security situation in Serbia as part of the SFRY/FRY in 1991-1995, namely: the introduction of independent EU sanctions against Yugoslavia, support for the implementation of the UN sanctions and work of the Arbitration Commission.

On 5 July 1991, the EC and its member states imposed an embargo on armaments and military equipment applicable to the whole of Yugoslavia and called on other international actors to follow suit (EPC 1991). The USA joined the EC embargo on 8 July, the OSCE on 4 September 1991, while the UN Security adopted resolution 713 on 25 September 1991 (Blockmans 2007: 114). Instead of stopping or at least limiting Serb aggression, the arms embargoes set the balance of military power in Serbia's favour (Lopez 2000: 74). Having kept the majority of the JNA assets, Serbia was least affected by these punitive measures. The EC/EU left a much stronger impact on Serbia through its economic sanctions. Frustrated with the Yugoslav republics' failure to uphold a series of ceasefires and accept a peace plan presented at the Conference on Yugoslavia at The Hague in October 1991, the EC unilaterally suspended the trade concessions provided for by the 1980 Cooperation Agreement between the European Economic Community (EEC) and the SFRY on 11 November 1991 (Council of the EU 1991). The Agreement became inactive on 26 May 1992 (Blockmans 2007: 119). Additionally, the EC suspended the generalised System of Preferences benefits, PHARE assistance, food aid and financial cooperation (Ginsberg 2001: 66). On 2 December 1991, backdating the decision to 15 November 1991, the EC restored trade concessions and financial aid to all Yugoslav republics, but Serbia and Montenegro[130] (Council of the EU 1991a). In May 1992, to punish the FRY for its offensives against Bosnia, the EC imposed a trade embargo on the country. These actions, while isolating Serbia and Montenegro and hurting the state economically, contributed to the consolidation of the Milosevic regime. They also significantly dampened the relationship between Belgrade and Brussels, giving Milosevic pretext to portray the EC as an untrustworthy and biased mediator (Ginsberg 2001: 77).

At the time, sanctions were one of the few tools used by the EC/EU that was yielding results. Serbia was acting as a pariah state (Mladenov 2014) by providing covert help to Bosnian and Croatian Serbs and relying on illicit networks, closely linked with organised crime, to finance the Milosevic regime. The EU therefore needed a way to demonstrate such behaviour would not be tolerated. After several failed attempts at stopping Yugoslavia's disintegration through diplomatic measures, it turned to economic instruments as means of influencing the warring parties. With the first sanctions launched before the emergence of the CFSP, the EC showed remarkable level of cooperation, considering that the arms embargo was the competence of its member states (Blockmans 2007: 117). Later, when the violence erupted in Kosovo, the EU would resort to sanctions again, which can be interpreted as a sign of it believing in their effectiveness. The choice can also be explained by the lack of alternatives in the EU's foreign policy toolkit. After all, CSDP would only be developed in the aftermath of the Kosovo conflict.

Apart from implementing its autonomous sanctions, the EC/EU also supported the UN sanction regime. The UN Security Council imposed comprehensive sanctions on the FRY in resolution 757 on 30 May 1992. This document provided the foundation for all later sanctions that were extended to *inter alia* target Yugoslav assets abroad and limit its goods transshipments (Lopez 2000: 74). To assist the UN with the monitoring and enforcement of the regime, the EU worked through the Sanctions Assistance Missions (SAMs) and the WEU operations. The SAMs were set up by the OSCE in seven Eastern and South-East European states in 1992 and 1993 and relied heavily on EU contributions. The European officers worked together with Americans and Canadians at border posts throughout the region, feeding back information to the SAM

Communication Centre in Brussels, financed and partly staffed by the EU (Caruso 2007: 88). In July 1992, the WEU[131] embarked on an operation in the Adriatic to supervise the implementation of the UN arms embargo against the former Yugoslavia (WEU 2000: 15). NATO conducted its own operation in the area, until in June 1993 it was decided to combine these efforts with the WEU for Operation *Sharp Guard* (ibid.). Both the SAMs and WEU actions, as well as the UN sanctions, were terminated after the signing of the Dayton Agreement (ibid.). The EU arms embargo, however, remained in place.

Although the primary goals of sanctions, implemented by the EU in the early 1990s were to stop violence, persuade Milosevic to exert pressure on Bosnian Serbs[132] and uphold human rights (Portela 2005: 98), they unintentionally led to the criminalisation of the FRY. The EU and UN sanctions were therefore part of the enabling environment[133] for criminalisation that manifested itself in state-sponsored organised crime, flourishing underground economy, society-wide tolerance of smuggling and regional clandestine networks, typical of regional conflict formations (Andreas 2005: 336-337). The security sector, due to its closeness to the Milosevic regime, played a special role in institutionalising organised crime in the country. Military leaders were engaged in smuggling oil to Serbia and Montenegro, and arms to Croatian and Bosnian Serbs, while the state security apparatus and MoI oversaw and coordinated the state-sponsored embargo-busting system (ibid.: 342). Although it is difficult to measure to what extent the criminalisation of the FRY was enabled by the international sanctions in general and the EU contribution in particular, the unintended link between comprehensive sanctions and criminalisation of the state cannot be denied (ibid.: 337-338).

Finally, the EC/EU influenced the trajectory of Serbia's development via the work of the Arbitration Commission on Yugoslavia. For the purposes of this study, Opinions 2 and 3 of the Commission are of most importance as they have shaped Serbia (initially, within the FRY) and consequently its security sector[134]. When the Serbian population in Croatia and BiH was not granted the right of self-determination under international law in Opinion 2[135], Milosevic's aspirations for a Greater Serbia suffered a blow. Primarily, however, this decision meant that Serbian para-states in Croatia and Bosnia could not be given international recognition. Opinion 3, which is analysed in detail in the previous chapter, cemented this view by admitting that only former internal boundaries that were used between SFRY republics for administrative purposes could be regarded as international borders (Blockmans 2007: 146). To prevent escalation of violence and deter warring parties from redrawing borders by force, the EU used a principle of boundary delimitation as the principal tool for determining not only the shape of new territorial entities[136] but also their international personality as states (Craven 1996: 390). As a result, Kosovo and Vojvodina remained parts of Serbia and did not get a chance to become independent. It should be noted, however, that Serbia and Montenegro decided to remain together due to the workings of the Milosevic regime, rather than under EU pressure[137]. The latter would be crucial for the emergence of the SCG in a decade's time. In short, the Arbitration Commission's work effected Serbia's international standing, its personality as a state and the position of its external borders; it also contributed to deepening the anti-EU sentiment in the country. Although formally an independent body, it was convened by the EC, which meant Serbia's dissatisfaction with the decisions of the Commission turned into dissatisfaction with the EC's mediation effort (ibid.).

Overall, the EU-Serbia relations in the early 1990s were strained. While remaining committed to peaceful solution of the Balkan conflicts, the EU gave preference to punitive measures in its relations with Belgrade. These measures, having no military backing, while weakening the FRY's economy, did not stop violence in the region and to a certain extent aggravated the situation. The arms embargo against all Yugoslav republics, gave Serbia, in charge of the JNA, a military advantage, while support to the UN comprehensive sanctions aggravated criminalisation of the state and its security sector. The Badinter Commission prepared a legal framework that regulated the dissolution of Yugoslavia (Craven 1996: 335), further alienating Milosevic. These negative dynamics, propped up by Belgrade's distrust of Brussels, did not allow the latter to have a tangible effect on Serbia's security sector. The ending of Croatia's war and cessation of hostilities in BiH in 1995 offered the EU new opportunities of influence, or so it at first seemed.

The EU's impact on SSR in Serbia in 1995-1999

In 1995-1996, Milosevic appeared to be embracing the role of regional peace-maker. Having enforced a comprehensive set of UN sanctions[138] against the Bosnian Serbs in August 1994 (Lopez 2000: 75) and signed the Dayton Peace Agreement (DPA) on behalf of the FRY and the Republika Srpska in December 1995, he was portraying himself as a guarantor of peace in the region (Ostojic 2014: 27). His intentions seemed genuine when the FRY, together with BiH and Croatia, concluded the Sub-Regional Arms Control Agreement, provided for by Article IV, Annex 1B of the DPA, on 14 June 1996. To reward this behaviour, the UN formally ended its sanctions on the FRY on 2 October 1996 (Associated Press 1996), and the EU granted it with autonomous trade preferences in 1997 (Papadimitriou 2001: 74). Still, the reciprocity and regional cooperation, brought to the Western Balkans through a combination of negotiation and external imposition did not take hold. In early 1998, as the situation in Kosovo was flaring up, Serbia[139] chose to resort to violence, abandoning the peaceful path and tilting security balance in the region towards the negative pole of interdependence again. The fragile security regime in the Western Balkans started crumbling due to the actions of a single member, which according to the theory of regimes was not that uncommon (Jervis 1982: 359). Although violence was contained in Serbia and Kosovo, it had reverberations throughout the Western Balkans: Albania and FYROM were flooded with refugees[140], tensions in BiH were running high (ICG 1999), while Croatia and Montenegro, as well as the region more widely, suffered economically from the damage to trade routes and plummeting investor confidence (IMF 1999).

It was envisaged that from 1996 the EU-FRY relations would be mostly regulated through the Regional Approach that was introduced to support the implementation of the DPA and promote regional cooperation. Given Serbia's response to the Kosovo

Liberation Army's (KLA) rebellion, which was interpreted as disregard for the fundamental principles of democracy and human rights, the EU froze nearly all contractual relationships with the FRY in 1998 (EC 1998a: 2; Papadimitrou 2001: 76). It is noteworthy that from this time forward, the EU started making a distinction between Serbia and Montenegro, commending the latter for its commitment to democratic reform and reprimanding the former for the open conflict in Kosovo (EC 1998b: 4). In the circumstances of the Kosovo war, the RA was ignored by Serbia/the FRY. Nonetheless, the EU continued using RA documentation to monitor the situation in the country and highlight policy issues that required improvement, including in the security sector. Specifically, the EU focused on cooperation with the ICTY, police practices, regional cooperation and the issue of state power, which had importance for the political level of SSR.

In terms of the ICTY, the European Commission criticised the FRY for failing to bring known indicted war criminals to The Hague and influence the RS to fulfil its Dayton obligations (EC 1997a: 15). The only exception was the transfer of one Croat serving in the Bosnian Serb army (ibid.). By reiterating the idea that extradition of indictees would violate the FRY constitution, Yugoslav officials advocated war trials at home (EC 1998: 18). The EU, like other members of the international community at the time (Stojanovic 2009: 82), did not go beyond criticism and was unable to make the FRY change its stance.

Regional cooperation was promoted by the EU as a means of stabilising the Western Balkans and achieving return to normality. From the point of view of SSR, the EU's preoccupation with normalising border relations deserves special attention. Thus, the EU reacted favourably to the news of the FRY making progress on restoring border traffic and BCPs with Croatia as part of a broader package of inter-state cooperation (EC 1997a: 15; EC 1998: 18). The deterioration of relations with Albania over the Kosovo issue and mutual accusations about the violation of air space and border areas, on the other hand, were met with concern (EC 1998b: 18). As with the issues of the ICTY cooperation and police violence, however, the EU limited itself to mildly indignant remarks, without offering any credible solution to the problems.

Finally, by shedding light on the FRY's lack of respect for democratic principles, the EU touched upon some issues of relevance for the political level of SSR. Although the security sector was not mentioned directly in the RA reports when they discussed a widening gap between the FRY and Serbia's legislation and their practical implementation, these documents should not be ignored as they demonstrate the bloc's commitment to helping the Western Balkans get closer to international and European standards of democratic governance, which is of utmost importance for SSR. Specifically, Serbia was criticised for poor government accountability and absence of effective separation of powers (EC 1997a: 12). The imbalance between federal and republican competences, with Serbia considerably overpowering Montenegro, was perceived as a constraint for the democratic development of the country (EC 1998b: 13). Later, when Serbia, first as part of the SCG and since 2006 on its own, started pursuing the European membership, the EU would emphasise the need for a democratic and civilian oversight of the security sector more explicitly.

As can be seen, the Regional Approach had only indirect significance for Serbia's SSR. Given little interest in the initiative in the FRY, it was mainly used as a monitoring tool by the EU, and not as a reform instrument. Although, the monitoring process via the RA could not provide the EU with the same amount of information as it received from the ECMM missions in Croatia and BiH, it was still an important way of demonstrating the bloc's interest in stabilising the FRY and the region as a whole. It was also the first attempt on behalf of the EU to set conditions and standards for the FRY that touched upon aspects of the security sector's work and management. The Kosovo war precluded the Union from developing this conditionality further and prompted it to bring back the policy of sanctions.

In 1998-2000, the EU imposed a series of autonomous sanctions against the FRY that included an arms embargo, travel restrictions, an oil embargo and a range of financial restrictions[141]. The first three categories had special significance for the FRY's security sector and therefore require further analysis. It is important to acknowledge that the EU sanctions followed mostly from the decisions of the Contact Group on Yugoslavia and were independent from the UN Security Council. Frustrated with Russia's slow decision-making within the group and hesitation in the UN, the EU members of the Contact Group decided to act through the CFSP (Buchet de Neuilly 2008: 3). The decisions were reached relatively fast due to a vague language that remained open to interpretation[142]. The degree of unity demonstrated by the EU member states in responding to the Kosovo conflict was still notable. Here, the CFSP that was not around during the start of conflicts in Croatia and BiH, was put to use rather quickly. Another point to make is that the objectives of the EU sanctions changed over time (de Vries 2002: 90). In the spring of 1998, they were aimed at prompting the FRY to stop the oppression of the Albanian population in Kosovo. Towards the end of the year the goal was to persuade Milosevic to negotiate a political solution to the war (ibid.). Finally, the EU ramped up the severity of its restrictive measures to oust the Milosevic regime to make such a solution possible (ibid.). Additionally, the sanctions were aimed at bringing peace and lasting stability to the region (Council of the EU 1999).

The EU sanctions were not comprehensive, but aimed at various sectors, including the security sectors of the FRY and Serbia. The arms embargo was targeting them most directly. While the UN embargo was suspended in November 1995 and lifted in October 1996, the EU with the 1996 Common Position 96/184/CFSP kept its own restrictions on arms, munitions and military equipment against the FRY, BiH and Croatia in place (Council of the EU 1996). When the situation in Kosovo deteriorated, there was no need for the introduction of a new arms embargo[143]: on 19 March 1998, the EU simply reaffirmed its embargo from 1996 with Common Position 98/240/CFSP and supplemented it with the prohibition on export to the FRY of equipment that could be used for internal repression or terrorism (Council of the EU 1998). While it is problematic to assess the effectiveness of the EU arms embargo, the same as its sanctions on the FRY over Kosovo more generally, as they were implemented alongside the UN sanctions (de Vries 2002: 88), it is still possible to make some observations about their effect on the country's security sector.

Under the 1996 Sub-Regional Arms Control Agreement, the FRY was required to reduce holdings in five categories of traditional armaments to approximately 75 per cent of its 1996 levels (OSCE 2014: 2). Although, it was a substantial reduction in its military power, the FRY kept the highest number of arms in the region. The introduction of the EU arms embargo in 1998 therefore could not disadvantage the country too much. It did, however, put the Kosovo side in a precarious position as it was subject to the sanctions, too[144]. Additionally, Milosevic was not that worried about the arms embargoes because he could rely on illicit networks, tried and tested during the wars in Croatia and BiH and because for years he had been investing in militarising the police (Ramet 2002: 318-19, 339). Taking this into consideration, perhaps the biggest result of the EU arms embargo and its sanction regime more generally, was exacerbation of the anti-EU sentiment among the Serbian state and security elites. The travel restrictions[145] which *inter alia* introduced a visa ban on the FRY and Serbian representatives with clear security responsibilities, implicated in repressive action in Kosovo, is especially well placed for demonstrating this effect.

Initially, by adopting Common Position 98/240/CFSP on 19 March 1998, the EU identified only ten high-profile security officials from the FRY for non-admission in the territories of its member states. The document stipulated, however, that the list would be extended to other officials if they refused to respect demands of the international community. After releasing a second list with the names of persons who acted against the independent media in December 1998[146], the EU took around six months to formulate the position that imposed visa restrictions on Milosevic, his family, all ministers and senior officials of the FRY and Serbian governments as well as leaders of the military, police and security services (Council of the EU 1999a). By identifying the security sector leadership as a separate group, the EU recognised its strong link with the Belgrade regime. It also made itself widely unpopular among the security top brass. In 2000, more police and army personnel were added to the list, which grew to nearly 800 names[147] (Blockmans

2007: 159-160). After the removal of Milosevic from office in October and parliamentary elections in December 2000, the list of visa restrictions was significantly reduced to include Milosevic himself, his family members and several persons indicted by the ICTY, among the latter—Dragoljub Ojdanic, Former Minister of Defence and Vlajko Stojilkovic, Former Minister of the Interior (Council of the EU 2001). The travel restrictions inconvenienced high-ranking security personnel from the FRY and Serbia by preventing them from travelling freely to the EU, yet there is not enough evidence to suggest they were effective in making the persons they targeted change their behaviour (Blockmans 2007:170).

The usefulness of the oil embargo raised questions, too. Introduced by Council Regulation (EC) 900/1999, which became effective on 1 May 1999, it banned the sale, supply and export of petroleum and petroleum products to all parts of the FRY[148], primarily to deprive the VJ of means to conduct military operations and repressive action in Kosovo (de Vries 2002: 95). It is widely believed that the imposition of the oil embargo by the EU provided substantial support to NATO's bombing campaign and was among the factors that convinced Milosevic to withdraw from Kosovo (Hoist 2000; de Vries 2002: 95; Blockmans 2007: 170). On the other hand, some critics argue that the continuation of the oil embargo after the end of the military intervention contributed to further criminalisation of the economy as the regime profited from smuggling gasoline and other petroleum products (Hoist 2000; Blockmans 2007: 170). This "second round of oil embargo", launched on 4 October 1999, eased petroleum restrictions for Kosovo and Montenegro, reflecting the EU's determination to bring about the change of regime in Belgrade and its commitment to achieving regional peace and stability (Council of the EU 1999e; Portela 2005: 110). It was partially suspended in March 2000 and fully lifted in October 2000, following the electoral defeat of Milosevic (de Vries 2002: 96).

To sum up, despite initial optimism over Milosevic's role as a guarantor of peace in the region, the EU did not engage in SSR in Serbia in 1995-1999 directly. It attempted to set conditions for certain aspects of the security sector via the Regional Approach, but with Serbia opting for a military solution to the conflict in Kosovo that threw the region back to the negative pole of security interdependence, was unable to convince Belgrade to cooperate. As a result, the RA provisions on cooperation with the ICTY, policing, border security and requirements for effective separation of powers remained ignored by the Milosevic regime. With violence returning to the Western Balkans, the EU was quick to utilise the CSFP to reinstate sanctions against the FRY and Serbia. The security sector was mostly targeted through the arms embargo, travel restrictions and oil embargo. Although these restrictive measures had mixed results, they contributed to the weakening of the Milosevic regime by isolating Serbia, even from its FRY partner, Montenegro. They also unintentionally led to the aggravation of the anti-EU sentiments among the Serbian security leadership. These feelings of unease and distrust of the EU would continue in the post-Milosevic era, making the task of SSR even more challenging.

The EU's impact on SSR in Serbia in 1999-2013

Although the ousting of Milosevic created a favourable environment for Serbia's transformation, the reform processes in the FRY were not smooth. Relations with the EU remained strained due to virtually non-existent cooperation with the ICTY, a highly fragmented domestic political scene, the unresolved Kosovo question and uncertain future of the Yugoslav federation itself (Edmunds 2007: 216). In such circumstances, security sector reform did not receive as much attention from the EU as it deserved. Nonetheless, as Serbia worked on improving its relationship with the bloc, the EU started promoting the SSR agenda more forcefully.

The framework for the EU's engagement with Serbia's SSR, just like in Croatia, was provided by the Stabilisation and Association Process. The SAP signalled the end of an era of sanctions and start of the process of European integration (Pippan 2004: 220). The normalisation of political situation in Serbia was seen by the EU as crucial not just for the recovery of the country, but also for bringing lasting peace to the Western Balkans.[149] Unlike Croatia, Serbia was unable to progress quickly towards signing the Stabilisation and Association Agreement, although the FRY expressed commitment to the SAP already in November 2000 at the Zagreb Summit (Tocci 2007: 90). The growing disagreement between Montenegro and Serbia was among the factors holding back the FRY. To avoid the resurgence of violence and discourage other independence movements in the Western Balkans, the EU employed the diplomacy of the High Representative for the CFSP, Javier Solana, to convince Podgorica and Belgrade to stay together (Caruso 2007: 80). On the promise of a more favourable road to EU membership (Noutcheva 2012: 70), on 14 March 2002, the leaders of Serbia, Montenegro and the FRY signed the "Belgrade Agreement"[150] which transformed the federal Yugoslavia into a union of semi-independent states with shared defence and foreign policies, but separate economic systems (Caruso 2007: 80). Having received a positive outcome on the Feasibility Study for accession (EC 2005b), the State Union began negotiations on the SAA in November 2005, but already in May 2006 the EU suspended them over insufficient cooperation with the ICTY (EC 2006f: 4-5). Shortly after this decision, Montenegro voted for independence in the referendum.

Following improvements in Belgrade's relations with The Hague, the SAA talks were resumed in June 2007. Serbia signed the SAA with the EU on 29 April 2008, applied for EU membership on 22 December 2009 and received the candidate status on 1 March 2012 (EC 2016b). The SAA entered into force in September 2013, while the European Council approved the accession negotiation framework for Serbia in December 2013 (ibid.). A nearly five-year gap between the signing and implementation of the SAA can be explained by Serbia's reluctance to ensure full cooperation with the ICTY and complication of relations with Kosovo that unilaterally declared independence in February 2008. The door to membership was only opened when Serbia arrested and transferred to The Hague two remaining ICTY fugitives, Ratko Mladic and Goran Hadzic in 2011, and when it showed commitment to the EU-facilitated dialogue with Pristina, signing the "First agreement of principles governing the normalisation of relations" in April 2013. Except for an armed insurgency in South Serbia in 2001 and the 2003 assassination of Prime Minister Djindjic, the security situation in Serbia after 1999 was largely stable. A peaceful split of the SCG in May

2006 and Belgrade's preference for legal and diplomatic measures to contest Kosovo's declaration of independence[151] confirmed that the Serbian elites saw the country's future defined by peace and cooperation rather than war and confrontation. Security sector reform was one of the tools that prompted this realisation.

The EU's role in Serbia's SSR in 2000-2013 has been described as compartmentalised and inconsistent[152], but at the same time pragmatic, transformative[153] and constantly evolving[154]. This variance of opinion can be partially explained by the lack of a single, EU-facilitated, SSR programme for Serbia. Like in Croatia, in Serbia EU requirements for SSR need to be distilled from a variety of sources, such as the SAA and accession negotiations. The SAA touches upon elements of defence, police and border reforms in Articles 80-87 that are united under Title VII "Justice, Freedom and Security" as well as in more general sections under Title II "Political Dialogue" (Art. 10-13) and Title III "Regional Cooperation" (14-17) (SAA 2013). Before the SAA was enforced, however, demands for change in the work and management of Serbia's security sector could be derived from the European Partnership, adopted in 2004 and updated in 2006 and 2008, that defined short- and medium-term reform priorities for the country. The European Commission's annual progress reports scrutinised changes in the Serbian security sector through sections on political criteria and European standards in Justice, Freedom and Security[155]. From 2011, when the Commission released its Opinion on Serbia's application for EU membership, benchmarks for SSR were included into the political criteria, which apart from the stability of institutions, required Serbia to commit to regional cooperation and comply with the ICTY requirements, and Chapters 23, 24 and 31. As the focus here is only on the army, police and border services, Chapter 23 is left out from the analysis.

By framing SSR in Serbia through the SAP, the EU offered financial assistance to the country in general and its security sector in particular through the CARDS National Programme 2001-2006, CARDS Regional Programme 2001-2006 and IPA in 2007-2013[156]. Within CARDS, projects on JHA and IBM had direct significance for SSR, while IPA offered SSR support through projects within the sub-components of Political Requirements and European Standards, as well as the component of Cross-border Cooperation. Through all these instruments the EU pursued a broad range of goals in SSR that *inter alia* included the achievement of civilian control over Serbia's security sector, democratisation and depoliticisation of the army and the police, tackling the legacy of war, attainment of effective and efficient border controls and strengthening of security cooperation on the regional level. In short, the SSR activities attempted by the EU between 2000 and 2013 were targeting both political and organisational levels of the reform.

Political level

Like Croatia, Serbia experienced the EU's impact on the political level of SSR in three areas: *oversight of the security sector, cooperation with the ICTY* and *regional cooperation*. The constitutional and legal uncertainty surrounding the FRY and SCG prompted the bloc to also pay attention to the questions of *state consolidation*, which introduced another dimension to the reform in Serbia. Thus, the EU emphasised the question of separation of power, not just between the legislative, executive and judicial branches but also between the federal/State-Union and republican level. In the security sector, shared competences in defence and border security were of particular concern for the EU (EC 2005c: 52). The disintegration of the SCG in May 2006 removed this extra layer and allowed the Union to refocus its attention in Serbia on the same issues that it prioritised throughout the Western Balkans (EC 2008b: 3). Nonetheless, in 2008, the Kosovo issue brought the state-consolidation agenda back into spotlight.

The *oversight of the security sector* in Serbia was monitored by the EU through the work of the parliament, government and independent regulatory bodies. Additionally, given problems with statehood in the country, the bloc traced changes to the Constitution, pointing out discrepancies with European standards (EC 2007d: 6; EC 2012b: 6). Security institutions were identified as an important part of the state infrastructure that instead of supporting the country's transition to democracy and the rule of law was obstructing it (EC 2005c: 9-10). To change the situation, the EU insisted on the establishment of democratic control over the army, police and security forces more generally. As a result, progress reports of the European Commission regularly included a section on the civilian control of the security sector[157]. Although these sections are often criticised as superficial (Milic 2014: 53-54), they should not be disregarded as the EU used them to highlight weaknesses in the oversight mechanisms of the security sector in Serbia throughout the entire researched period, and if taken together they can be seen as an *EU guide on the democratic security governance.*

The basic structure of the security governance in the country was introduced with the 2006 Constitution, yet legislative and institutional changes continued to be added later, even after 2013. The Constitution granted security-related responsibilities to the National Assembly, i.e. parliament, executive actors, including the president who is the Commander in Chief of the SAF, judiciary[158], independent regulatory bodies and the public. The EU engaged with each branch of the security sector governance in Serbia, albeit neither comprehensively nor consistently. The parliament, according to Article 99 of the Constitution, decides on war and peace, supervises the work of security services and adopts strategic documents, such as the Defence Strategy. It also adopts legislation regulating the functioning of the security sector and approves its budgetary resources (Milic 2014: 74). As a traditionally weak institution in the Serbian political system (Ejdus 2010: 15), the parliament was closely monitored by the EU. Its security functions were regularly characterised as limited, weak and inconsistent (EC 2006f:9; EC 2009b: 8; EC 2011a: 11). When the Committee for Defence and Security was constituted in 2007, the European Commission started expressing concern over its limited resources, lack of specialist staff and broad jurisdiction, covering defence, internal affairs and intelligence issues (EC 2007d: 9; EC 2010d: 9). In a way, the division of this body into the Defence and Internal Affairs Committee and Security Services Control Committee, in 2010, was a response to the EU criticism (EC 2011a: 23). While the split was welcomed by the EU, the parliamentary oversight in Serbia in 2013 was still modest (EC 2012b: 9; EC 2013b: 10). Apart from advising the National

Assembly on organising the work of its security committee(s), the EU influenced parliamentary control of the security sector in Serbia indirectly through activities aimed at strengthening the country's parliamentary democracy. For example, it advised on changes to key legislation to harmonise it with European standards[159] and created opportunities for MPs and parliamentary staff to participate in study visits to Brussels and Strasbourg (Milic 2014: 59-60). It should be noted that in most cases staff of parliamentary committees on security issues were not targeted specifically but benefited from EU support alongside their colleagues from other parliamentary bodies (ibid.).

Executive bodies responsible for the civilian control of the security sector in Serbia were targeted by the EU even less consistently. The Ministry of Defence, Ministry of Interior and National Security Council (NSC) as key governmental bodies overseeing security matters received varying degrees of EU attention. The MoD, that was mostly non-functional during the Milosevic era and for at least three years after, was approached by the EU regarding three issues: internal organisation, financial management and preparation for future membership. The former two points, pursued, for instance, through demands to integrate the office of the Chief of Staff of the Armed Forces and the budget and procurements departments into the MoD (EC 2007d: 9) were meant to increase the transparency of the military. To assist Serbia with the preparations for challenges of the membership, the EU encouraged the establishment of new sections in the MoD such as a specialised CSDP Unit within the Directorate for Security Policy (EC 2011a: 127). Overall, however, the EU did not have a comprehensive approach to the MoD.

Initially, it looked as if the Serbian MoI, whose role was strengthened by the 2005 Law on Police, would be approached in the same way. The EU monitored changes in the internal organisation of the MoI (EC 2007d: 41) and criticised poor coordination of its policies with other ministries (EC 2008c: 10). Yet from 2008, the EU started increasingly emphasising flaws in the internal control of the police, provided by the MoI, and demanding the Ministry to overhaul its practices to become a normal part of the public administrative system (EC 2012c: 3-6). Eventually, it combined forces with other key external actors in the Serbian police reform, such as Norway, Sweden and DCAF, to assist the country with the reform of human resource management in the MoI, which if implemented successfully, "can completely alter the work of the police forces in Serbia" making them more transparent, accountable and professional (Elek, Tasik and Djordjevic 2015: 23). At the same time, the NSC, a coordinating body set up in direct response to the EU's ICTY conditionality in 2006, barely received any attention from the EU despite numerous structural flaws[160] (EC 2007d: 9).

The EU also contributed to the civilian oversight of the security sector in Serbia by supporting independent regulatory bodies, such as the Ombudsman and Commissioner for Free Access to Public Information (EC 2008c: 11) and development of a working anti-corruption policy. The work of the Anti-Corruption Agency (ACA), a body responsible for corruption preventive measures including in the police, for example, benefited from the European Commission's support that incorporated training, sharing of best practices and help with IT systems (EC 2013c: 8). Additionally, the EU left impact on the management of Serbia's security actors through advice on amending the public procurement legislation (ICLG 2017).

In terms of public oversight of the security system, until recently the EU's contribution was mostly indirect. The European Union used CARDS and IPA to develop independent media and enable civil society's participation in governmental decision-making processes (Aigner, O'Connor and Kacapor-Dzihic 2013: 60). It also pressured the Serbian government to be more transparent with the public through legislative practices, e.g. it played an important role in the adoption of the 2009 Law on Confidentiality of Data (Ejdus 2010: 24). In other words, by investing in the growth of Serbia's civil society and pushing the government for openness, the EU indirectly aided growing public interest in the security sector that had operated under the veil of secrecy for decades. When Serbia received a membership status, however, the EU started influencing civil society organisations (CSOs) working in the security sphere more directly, thus contributing to enhanced public expertise in security issues. For example, in 2013, CSOs with interest in security issues were involved in screening exercises for Chapters 23, 24 and 31 and invited to briefings with the EU negotiating team (OCCS 2014: 1-3). These activities were organised by the Office for Cooperation with Civil Society, opened in 2011, in response to EU pressure. Even more, in May 2013 a group of six Serbian NGOs created the coalition "prEUgovor" to monitor Serbia's progress with the political criteria and Chapters 23 and 24 (PrEUgovor n.d.). This network, while closely observing the Serbian government responses to the EU SSR-related conditionality and offering it recommendations on areas of improvement, often goes beyond EU requirements and picks up on issues, omitted by the Commission reports[161]. In short, between 1999 and 2013 the EU influenced Serbia's security governance through a variety of direct and indirect activities and policies, without a single comprehensive SSR strategy in place. Nonetheless, its engagement with this area of the reform, became more refined with time, just like its focus on cooperation with the ICTY.

The issue of *war legacy* goes to the heart of SSR in Serbia, although its overall significance is broader[162]. While the security top brass, closely linked to the paramilitary, shared responsibility for the development of the strategy of war crimes on the territory of former Yugoslavia with the political leadership of the country (Vankovska and Wiberg 2003: 249), the security sector as a whole was implicated in its execution (Gow and Zverzhanovski 2013: 127). Despite the presence of the war crimes legacy in Croatia and BiH, the Serbian case stands out due to the extent of the crimes on both temporal and territorial scales (ibid.: 152). In 1991-1995 Serbia was involved in the conflicts in Croatia and BiH, and after a short break, in Kosovo in 1998-1999.[163]

The EU acknowledged the importance of war crimes legacy for Serbia early on, calling on Belgrade to cooperate with the ICTY nearly from the moment of the tribunal's emergence (Dobbels 2009: 7). Yet until the early 2000s, these calls were left unanswered. Although the RA made contractual relations with the EU conditional on cooperation with the ICTY in 1997, Milosevic ignored the requirement, much like the policy itself. It was not until the launch of the SAP and promise of membership that the EU got important leverage over Serbia in this respect. Even then, the Union waited several years before starting to demand Serbia's compliance with ICTY conditionality more forcefully. It was the USA that urged the arrest of Milosevic, indicted by the ICTY in 1999 for his role in the Bosnian and Kosovo wars and called for the adoption of a law on cooperation with The Hague (Stojanovic 2009: 63). The EU's unwillingness to deal with the war crimes legacy can be partly explained by the sensitivity of the issue and partly by the Union's focus on trying to keep Serbia and Montenegro together.

The EU made its first serious attempt to change Belgrade's relationship with the ICTY in late 2004, soon after a post-DOS government, headed by Kostunica, introduced the policy of "voluntary surrender" that combined bribes and blackmail to convince those accused by the tribunal to surrender (Gow and Zverzhanovski 2013: 154). Brussels threated Serbia and Montenegro with a negative decision of the Feasibility Study, that could leave the country behind other Western Balkan states in the SAP. Combined with the US financial pressure, the EU's threat provided Kostunica with enough motivation to convince 16 war crimes suspects to hand themselves to The Hague between October 2004 and April 2005 (Dobbels 2009: 21-22). In April 2005, the SCG received a positive Feasibility Study as a reward from the EU, but by autumn the same year Belgrade's policy of "voluntary surrender" reached a dead end, unable to persuade the remaining six suspects with links to Serbia[164] to surrender. With the Croatian general Gotovina captured in December 2005, Serbia became the only Western Balkan country failing to commit to cooperation with the ICTY (ibid.). Even the adoption of a long-awaited law on freezing the assets of ICTY indictees in April 2006 failed to persuade the EU of Belgrade's commitment to the issue, leading it to suspend the SAA talks with the SCG in May 2006 (EC 2006f: 15). The EU's decision was announced only a few weeks before the Montenegrin referendum, giving Podgorica's push for independence more validity (Popovic et al 2011: 29).

Serbia's poor results in dealing with The Hague in this period can be mostly explained by three factors: the manipulation of the issue by political elites, rudimentary character of SSR in the country and weak coordination among external actors. With the ICTY being highly unpopular among the Serbians[165], many political actors manipulated the issue to revive anti-Western sentiments and boost their own popularity (Spoerri and Freyberg-Inan 2008: 358-362). Given the high political cost of the ICTY issue as demonstrated, for example, by the demise of Djindjic[166], the political elites explained cooperation with the tribunal as something required by external actors, not as a way towards reconciliation in the Balkans (Gow and Zverzhanovski 2013: 154). Moreover, without a comprehensive SSR, cooperation with the ICTY was a challenging task even for the elites willing to deal with the war crimes legacy as they simply did not have full control over the entire security sector. Finally, the Serbian leadership felt that it could get away with non-compliance since the international community was unable to speak with one voice on the issue, especially in 2000-2005. For instance, when the USA refused to release 100 million USD of aid to Serbia in March 2004 due to its poor cooperation with The Hague, the EU provided Belgrade with 279 million EUR the same month (Edmunds 2007: 228).

When the EU suspended the SAA negotiations with the SCG in May 2006, it quickly became clear that Serbia, instead of coming closer to the ICTY, was moving farther away from it. With the dissolution of the SCG, start of negotiations over the status of Kosovo and death of Slobodan Milosevic in The Hague, the country saw the resurgence of radicalisation and nationalism, led by the SPS and SRS that vocally opposed any kind of cooperation with the tribunal and denounced EU conditionality as extortion (Ostojic 2014: 98). To prevent further radicalisation of the country, and avoid destabilisation of the region, the EU had to soften its position. Instead of the arrest of Mladic, the initial key requirement for resuming the SAA talks, Brussels asked Belgrade to demonstrate a substantial improvement in cooperation with The Hague (B92 2007). Proof of such improvement was found in the Action Plan on cooperation with the ICTY, the National Security Council (NSC), both created in 2006, and arrest of Zdravko Tolimir, a Bosnian Serb military intelligence leader in May 2007. Acknowledging progress made by Belgrade, Brussels reopened the SAA negotiations with Serbia on 13 June 2007.[167]

Although the Action Plan was a deficient formality (EC 2006f: 15), two other measures proved crucial for establishing a working relationship with the tribunal. Thus, the NSC, set up as a coordinating body for police and all four branches of the Serbian intelligence community[168] under the supervision of the president, was a sign of strengthened civilian control of the security sector; the arrest of General Tolimir signalled the start of break-down of clandestine protection networks for ICTY fugitives (Gow and Zverzhanovski 2013: 157). The EU was partly behind these improvements as it refused to move forward with the SAA until all the suspects were moved to The Hague (hence, the delay with the ratification of the document even after the capture of former Bosnian Serb President Karadzic in 2008) and proactively pushed for a shift of power over the security agencies from Prime Minister Kostunica, by that time cautiously pro-European, to President Tadic, an open proponent of reforms (Ostojic 2014:103). Having obtained control over the Security and Information Agency (BIA) through the NSC, Tadic who held the presidential office since 2004, managed to arrest five remaining indictees between 2007 and 2011. This was a slow process that demanded a significant weakening of the Military Security Agency (VBA), which until 2008 provided formal, although ostensibly unsanctioned by the government[169], protection to Mladic and other war crime suspects (Gow and Zverzhanovski 2013: 156-160). The last two fugitives, Ratko Mladic and Goran Hadzic were transferred to The Hague in 2011, opening Serbia a door to EU candidate status. Yet after 2011, the ICTY issue did not disappear: the EU continued monitoring Serbia's cooperation with the tribunal, focusing on investigations of support networks that had harboured the fugitives and access to information and witnesses (EC 2012b: 18; EC 2013b: 11).

By 2013, cooperation with the ICTY produced some important results: 46 war crimes suspects, including high-profile army and police officers were transferred to The Hague (Ostojic 2014: 58) and most Serbian elites (except for the rump SRS, whose most prominent members set up a pro-European Serbian Progressive Party (SNS) in 2008), came to terms with the need to cooperate with the ICTY (ibid.: 106). While the views of the public did not improve significantly[170], the political leadership no longer openly opposed the tribunal's work. Moreover, one of the biggest achievements of ICTY conditionality, that was actively, though inconsistently promoted by the EU since the end of 2004, was the establishment of full democratic and civilian control over the security sector (Gow and Zverzhanovski 2013: 166). The removal of criminal elements implicated in the war crimes from the security sector and break-down of support networks in the intelligence community eliminated the last obstacles on the way to democratic security governance in the country. The polarisation of the Serbian political scene and the status of Kosovo introduced extra complexity to the issue in Serbia, yet the progress achieved is not insignificant, and the EU was instrumental in it. Working alongside other external actors, most notably the USA and NATO, the EU contributed into making Serbia's security sector more professional, transparent and accountable. There is still, however, work to be done, e.g. security archives need to be opened and a regional dialogue to be reinvigorated. According to experts, the EU has the potential and right tools to play a constructive role in this process, however, until now it has been unable to summon the will to do so.[171]

The final area through which the EU influenced the political level of SSR in Serbia is *regional cooperation*. To highlight the importance of this issue for Serbia, which the EU views as a country playing a key role in the Western Balkans (EC 2008b: 9), the regional dimension was incorporated into the sections of annual reports examining progress made by the country in meeting the Copenhagen political criteria. In SSR, regional dimension was most visibly encouraged by the EU in four spheres: police cooperation, border security, war crimes legacy and Kosovo question.

The emphasis on police and border cooperation materialised relatively early when Serbia was still part of the SCG. It was one of the ways for the EU to facilitate capacity-building in the region, especially to fight organised crime, while also working towards building trust and reciprocity among former adversaries. Financial aid for regional cooperation in the JHA area was initially provided under regional CARDS programmes, and from 2007 through Multi-Beneficiary assistance under IPA. An example of an early regional initiative that included Serbia was the 2004 CARDS project "Policing systems, police co-operation and the enhancement of the fight against main criminal activities", implemented and co-financed by the Council of Europe (DEURS 2004). The EU also placed value on the development of formal relations between the Serbian police and police services in neighbouring countries of the Western Balkans and beyond. For instance, signing and enforcement of agreements on police cooperation and cooperation in the fight against organised crime with Albania, Austria, BiH, Croatia, the FYROM, Hungary, Montenegro (EC 2009b: 22; EC 2010e: 8; EC 2011a: 108), and establishment of a joint contact centre for police and customs cooperation with Bulgaria and Romania were seen as positive developments (EC 2010d: 21). Additionally, the EU supported Serbia's commitment to police cooperation via non-EU regional initiatives, such as the Regional Strategic Document and Action Plan on Justice and Home Affairs 2011-2013 developed within the framework of the SEECP (EC 2011a: 35). In terms of border security, the EU prioritised the prevention of illegal migration and development of an effective border management system within the regional, and from 2012, EU-wide IBM concept (DEURS 2004). Apart from regional actions already mentioned in previous chapters, the EU put strong emphasis on joint border patrols alongside the common borders with such neighbours as FYROM, Montenegro, BiH and Croatia as well as alongside the Administrative Boundary Line with Kosovo (EC 2010d: 50).

Concerning the war crimes legacy, the EU's main focus was on addressing the "regional impunity gap" (EC 2010e: 57) by monitoring domestic trials and encouraging Serbia to exchange information on war crimes with other countries and players of the region, such as Croatia, BiH and EULEX (EC 2009b: 20). With BiH and Croatia instigating two separate lawsuits for genocide against the FRY in the Criminal Court of Justice (ICJ) in 1993 and 1999 (Ostojic 2014: 87), it was important for the EU to ensure Serbia was willing to look past disagreements and could cooperate with its neighbours on the sensitive issue of war crimes. The inclusion of Kosovo into regional security cooperation was another area of contention in the Western Balkans. Having refused to recognise Kosovo's unilateral declaration of independence in 2008, Serbia opposed its participation in regional meetings and projects, including in the area of security. In such circumstances, the EU's first task was to get Serbia to subscribe to the inclusiveness of regional cooperation, which it did in the run-up to the March 2012 European Council that granted Serbia candidate status (EC 2012b: 19). Consequently, the focus shifted to technical security cooperation, such as integrated management of border/boundary crossing points (ibid.).

The overall aim of the EU's emphasis on the regional dimension has been the facilitation of trust and reciprocity among the Western Balkan states. In a way, all three elements of the political level of SSR supported by the EU were pursuing this goal. Unfortunately, the efforts to improve the transparency of Serbia's security sector, deal with the legacy of war crimes and build working regional relations were not attempted by the EU as a single programme or strategy, which diminished their value. The uncertainty surrounding Serbia's statehood and lack of stability on the internal political scene did not help matters either. Furthermore, the Kosovo issue raised more questions for Serbia's SSR. With Belgrade making state territorial integrity central for all its policies and taking the decision of military neutrality that limited NATO's impact on defence reform, SSR took a back seat in the government priorities. The EU-moderated dialogue with Pristina improved the situation slightly in 2013 by delivering the "First agreement on principles governing the normalisation of relations", complemented with a comprehensive implementation plan. Until the issue of Kosovo is resolved fully, however, the uncertainty will keep surrounding both the country' future and the development of its security sector.

In terms of the political level of SSR, Serbia has gone a long way: it achieved full democratic and civilian control over the security sector and built a system of security governance based on extensive legal documents and numerous institutions, that have been honed to meet (though not always successfully) standards set by the EU. In 2013, however, as well as at the time of writing there was still a gap between theory and practice: parliamentary control over the military was rather limited, system of human resources management in the MoI—underdeveloped and public scrutiny of security matters — insufficient. This meant further engagement of the EU in the political level of Serbia's SSR was needed after 2013. The remainder of the section will determine if the situation was any different with the organisational level of the reform.

Organisational level

Defence reform in Serbia, as explained above, was delayed due to a power struggle inside the DOS coalition and uncertainty over the future of the FRY/SCG as the army was one of the federal/State Union level institutions. Moreover, the Kosovo conflict contributed to strained relations with NATO, eliminating the possibility for the Alliance to play a leading role in the reform like it did in other states of the region. Although NATO supported defence reform through PfP, the country never experienced the full scale of its assistance. Serbia's decision to pursue military neutrality in February 2008 gave the EU a unique opportunity to spearhead military reform. Nevertheless, the bloc was not ready to take on such responsibility, given its relative inexperience in the sphere. Moreover, the absence of a clear break with the previous regime in the armed forces[172], Serbia's reluctance to deal with the ICTY and continuation of ties with the army of the RS made the prospect of dealing with defence reform in the country unattractive for the EU (Edmunds 2007: 214). At the same time, the persistence of nationalist sentiment and rise of radicalism in Serbia prevented it from committing fully to the idea of European integration, and as a result excluded the country from participating in CSDP structures until it received the candidate status in 2012. Even more, the intensification of military cooperation between Serbia and Russia added more wariness to the EU – Serbia relations (Milic 2014: 62).

Despite all of this, the depth and breadth of the EU's engagement with the Serbian defence sector has been growing and is most visible in four areas: legal advice, post-conflict aid, technical assistance and training and sharing best practices. The EU has been tracing the development of Serbia's defence legislative framework since the moment it identified defence reform as one of the priorities for the SCG in the first European Partnership (Council of the

EU 2004). To confirm its interest in the reform, the EU included it under short- and mid-term priorities into European Partnership 2006 (Council of the EU 2006a) and 2008 (Council of the EU 2008) for Serbia, after its separation from Montenegro. Initially, the EU encouraged Serbia to adopt strategic documents such as a defence strategy and national security strategy, which were released in October 2009[173] (EC 2010d: 9), and fundamental laws on defence, required by the constitution, such as the Law on the Army of Serbia, Defence Law, both adopted in December 2007, the Law on the Military Security Agency and the Military Intelligence Agency, Law on Civilian Service and Law on the Use of the Army and other Defence Forces in Multinational Operations outside Serbia, all from October 2009 (EC 2011a: 22). The European Commission expressed satisfaction with the state of Serbia's legislative framework for defence reform only in 2010 (EC 2010d: 9). At a later stage, the EU placed more emphasis on the adoption of legislation enabling the country's integration into CSDP and harmonisation of its position with EU standards in such areas as trade in arms and military equipment/dual use goods/small arms and light weapons (SALW), non-proliferation and arms control regimes, etc (EC 2012b: 63; EC 2013b: 59). In this respect, by 2013 Serbia achieved mixed results. On the one hand, it adopted several key acts allowing it to participate in CSDP missions[174], exchange classified information with the EU[175] or cooperation with the European Defence Agency (EDA)[176], accepted principles of the 1998 EU Code of Conduct on Arms Exports (SEESAC 2010a) and released a new law on dual-use goods in 2013 (EC 2014a: 62). On the other, at the end of 2013 it was still lacking a new law on trade of arms and military equipment, and its application for joining the Wassenaar Arrangement on export controls for conventional arms and dual-use goods and technologies was pending (ibid.). These issues, however, are closely monitored under Chapter 31, and were not tackled during the studied period. According to a former MoD employee and leading security expert in Serbia, legislative changes is one of the biggest achievements of the EU and process of European integration as a whole in the defence sphere[177].

Post-conflict and technical assistance, provided by the EU to the Serbian military was mostly linked to the issue of SALW and development of the country's capacities in the CSDP framework. Additionally, the EU provided minor support to Serbia with de-mining, but its contribution to tackling the problem was less significant than in many other Western Balkan countries. For instance, the European Commission allocated 2 million EUR specifically for mine clearing action in Serbia for the first time only in 2006, while in Croatia it first got involved in de-mining in 1998 (GICHD 2008: 35). Such low engagement on part of the EU can be explained by a smaller scale of the problem in Serbia, persisting perception of the country as an aggressor responsible for regional violence of the 1990s and the fact that most of the burden for mine-clearing activity was undertaken by the Slovenia-based ITF (ibid.: 21).

The problem with proliferation of small arms in Serbia was much more acute than with mines, and hence demanded larger assistance. The number of SALW on the territory of the SFRY prior to the outbreak of hostilities in 1991 was more than six million (Griffiths 2010: 184). Although there are no official data confirming the amount of SALW available on the territory of Serbia after the Kosovo conflict, it is believed that nearly four million illegal weapons were circulating in the Western Balkans at the time, most of them in Serbia (Bjelotomic 2017). Even in 2013, it was estimated that there were between 200, 000 and 900, 000 of SALW in the country (Centar 2015). It is not surprising therefore that the EU was eager to assist Serbia with tacking this problem. Although initially the EU offered SALW assistance to Serbia directly (Poitevin 2013:7), with time it switched to working through South Eastern and Eastern Europe Clearinghouse for the Control of Small Arms and Light Weapons (SEESAC) that holds a mandate from the UNDP and RCC (SEESAC 2017). Cooperation between SEESAC and the EU has been developing since 2002[178] in the EUSAC framework[179], and in Serbia has been mainly focused on planning and conducting activities of SALW controls for the purposes of collection or seizure and destruction and creating conditions for the safe disposal of state-owned surplus SALW stockpiles (SEESAC 2010a). It should be mentioned, however, that many actions under EUSAC had a regional dimension as the EU considers SALW to be a regional problem. Another important point to make is that the EU has been one of many external actors, involved in SALW action in Serbia. The USA and NATO Maintenance and Supply Agency also offered considerable support (Griffiths 2010: 181).

What concerns developing Serbia's capacities for participating in the CSDP, these activities intensified after the country received the candidate status in 2012. Since then, Serbia was given many opportunities to improve its defence capabilities in the field of crisis management and learn more about CSDP (MoD RS 2014). An important role in this respect was played by the EDA that signed the Administrative Agreement with the Serbian MoD in December 2013. Unfortunately, the activities implemented under this agreement fall outside the scope of this study as Serbia joined the first EDA project only in 2016 (EDA 2016). Still, Serbia managed to benefit from some defence training and exchange programmes offered by the EU before 2013. Besides, the SAF was offered numerous training opportunities by other actors. For example, it participated in the partnership programme with the Ohio National Guard, ongoing since 2006, NATO's PfP (MoD RS 2016) and bilateral exchanges with individual EU member states (IHS 2016). Serbia has also been developing relations with partners from the East such as China that signed the Military Cooperation agreement with the country in 2008 and Russia, Serbia's long-standing partner (Pavlicevic 2011: 9).

The EU's training opportunities were different to those offered by other external actors, as they were aimed at preparing Serbia to be part of its own security infrastructure. Thus, Serbia was given a chance to participate in CSDP missions, which it joined in 2011 by sending two members to the EU NAVFOR *Somalia – ATALANTA* and EUTM Somalia, in the development of the Battlegroup concept, the conference on which it attended in March 2012 for the first time, and given access to key EU military bodies, such as the European Union Military Committee, that opened its meetings to representatives of the Serbian MoD since 2012 (EC 2012b: 63). The opening of CSDP to Serbia was described by Catherine Ashton, the then EU

High Representative on Foreign Policy, as "a sign of mutual trust" between the EU and the country (Euractiv 2011).

In short, the EU's impact on Serbia's defence reform in 1999-2013 was mostly felt in the legislative sphere, post-conflict and technical assistance and CSDP-specific activities. While showing only limited interest in the strategic side of the reform, the EU focused on preparing Serbia for membership and making it a functional state—a goal, impossible to achieve without finding a solution to the Kosovo issue. Moreover, over the past years, Serbia has been developing close military cooperation with Russia by signing a series of agreements on security and defence (Milic 2014: 63), joining the Russia-led Collective Security Treaty Organisation as an observer in 2013 (EC 2013b: 59) and holding regular joint military exercises (Glavonjic 2014). Most security experts interviewed in Serbia expressed concern over these developments and called on the EU to challenge this cooperation more forcefully, fearing that it could further delay Serbian accession to the bloc.[180]

Police and border reforms in Serbia, both part of Justice and Home Affairs in the SAP, were approached by the EU less cautiously yet still reluctantly, given the strained relationship with the security elites. The leading role in *police reform* was initially taken by the OSCE that commissioned the "Study on Policing in the Federal Republic of Yugoslavia" in 1991 (Monk 2001) and organised follow-up activities on the basis of six priority areas, identified by the study[181] (Downes 2004: 7). As Serbia progressed in its membership talks, the EU assumed a more active role in its police reform, and even started offering the country strategic guidance on policing. The latter was the result of the 2011 Council decision to place the rule of law at the centre of enlargement policy (EC 2012d: 4) and growing frustration in Brussels with the lack of results in the reform despite nearly a decade of support.

From the times of the FRY and onwards, the EU framed police reform in Serbia as an element of reform of the public administration, thus insisting that police work should follow the same standards as the rest of public administration—an idea central to the concept of SSR (EC 2002c: 7). In 1999-2013, the EU's impact on the Serbian police reform was felt most through technical assistance, post-conflict support, legislative advice and training. Like elsewhere in the region, the EU chose to start with technical support, avoiding sensitive areas and often acting as a supporting actor to other external players. Thus, in 2001-2002 the bloc, through its monitoring mission EUMM[182], provided logistical support to the OSCE mission to the FRY while the latter was training officers for the MEPE in South Serbia (Caruso 2007: 82-83) and from 2002, through the CARDS programme, began funding projects aimed at rehabilitating Serbia's police infrastructure, damaged in the wars (Particip GmbH 2009: 52). For instance, under CARDS 2002, law enforcement agencies were given around 4.7 million EUR for technical assistance and under CARDS 2004 they received nearly 2.7 million EUR for infrastructure and forensic equipment (ibid.). The initial aim of the EU's technical assistance was to strengthen the administrative and professional capacity of the Serbian police service by contributing to its demilitarisation, and modernisation of its work (EC 2005c: 50; EC 2008b: 50; EC 2009b: 10).

The EU's capacity-building activities in this sphere have become more refined with time as the Union started promoting better coordination and specialisation in the police. The reorganisation of the service that was slowly implemented after 2000 not only led to the removal of certain elements (e.g. the disbandment of the JSO) and creation of others (e.g. the Gandermerie in 2001), but also to the emergence of a more decentralised structure. This structure that included the MoI and General Police Directorate at the top, 48 regional command police centres in the middle and 161 police stations at the bottom (Rose 2011: 73), was characterised by poor coordination and connectivity, which the Commission saw as a major obstacle to dealing with organised crime, corruption and war crimes (EC 2008c: 51). It called for legislative action to clarify the division of responsibilities between different law enforcement services and units of the Directorate (ibid.: 52) and advised the government to develop an IT system linking the police with the courts and prosecution (EC 2013b: 51). The reform of human resource management in the Serbian MoI, actively promoted by the EU alongside other donors, has the potential to improve the coordination and transparency of the police, yet at the time of writing it was still not complete. Specialisation can also boost the service. The EU has been promoting it by focusing on the development of specialised services of the criminal police, e.g. services for combating organised crime, financial investigations and high-tech crime (EC 2010d: 52; EC 2013b: 51) and enhancement of investigative capacity in war crimes (EC 2011a: 33). The CARDS 2004 project "Prevention of economic crime", also known as PACO Serbia, and 2010 IPA Project "Against Money Laundering and Terrorism Financing in Serbia" are examples of the EU initiatives aimed at improving specialisation of the police in cooperation with other relevant institutions such as the Ministry of Finance (EC 2010f: 1, 11). Two observations can be made about the EU's technical assistance to the Serbian police. First, it was predominantly geared towards capacity-building in the areas of corruption, organised crime and war crimes; and second, it was provided in an *ad hoc* manner, without a clear strategy in place. Unsurprisingly, at the end of the studied period the European Commission was only partially satisfied with the level of cooperation and information flow between Serbia's law enforcement agencies and identified a number of problem areas with specialised services, e.g. it criticised the underdevelopment of intelligence-led policing in the country (EC 2012b: 54; EC 2013b: 51).

The second observation was also true for the EU's engagement with the Serbian legislation on policing and its role in the country's police reform more broadly until 2011, when the Union started prioritising a comprehensive approach. It took Belgrade five years of post-Milosevic period to adopt the Law on Police (2005) and several attempts to adjust it to the EU standards. Nonetheless, in 2013, the work on the law was still pending. Apart from emphasising the deficiencies of the main legal document regulating the work of the police in annual progress reports (EC 2008c: 51; EC 2010d: 52), the EU offered Serbia financial support and policy advice to amend it through IPA. Still, even the 2016 version of the Law, that resulted from projects funded by the EU and Swedish International Development Cooperation Agency (SIDA) (Elek, Tasik and Djordjevic 2015: 20), was not yet fully harmonised with the EU requirements (Poznatov 2016).

The EU's assistance achieved more results in relation to laws in the sphere of organised crime. Thus, the EU influenced the adoption of the National Anti-Corruption Strategy in 2005 and its updated version in 2013, the National Strategy for combating trafficking in human beings in 2006, the National Strategy to Fight Organised Crime in 2009, the Criminal Code in 2006 and its amendment in 2009, and the Criminal Procedure Code in 2011 (PrEUgovor 2013: 4; EU 2007d: 43; EC 2011a: 108). More broadly, a long-awaited Law on Private Security, adopted in 2013 was also a response to the EU demands (Petrovic and Milosevic 2017; CEAS 2013). After granting Serbia the status of a candidate state, the EU has been relying on Chapter 24 to harmonise the country's legislation on internal affairs and direct police reform as a whole. Until then, however, the EU's approach to legislation in the sphere was sporadic and led by desire to eradicate organised crime and corruption from the country and its police service. While the focus on organised crime remained strong after 2011, the EU significantly strengthened the emphasis on human resources, operational capacities and police cooperation with the start of membership negotiations (MoI RS 2016: 126).

Finally, the European Union attempted to influence police reform in Serbia trough training and sharing best practices. In the early post-Milosevic period, training was provided to improve the level of professionalism among police officers and enhance their digital literacy. Like in Croatia, many supply contracts offered by the EU contained a training element. For example, the 2004 CARDS programme provided the Criminal Police in Serbia with forensic equipment and training on its use (EC 2004a: 11). A strong emphasis in this respect was placed by the EU on regional projects as they were believed to help Serbia find a common language with its neighbours. Such initiatives as "Development of reliable and functional policing systems and enhancing combating main criminal activities and police cooperation", funded under CARDS 2002/2003 and "Regional cooperation in Criminal Justice: Strengthening capacities in the fight against cybercrime", part of the 2010 Multi-beneficiary IPA, were implemented to harmonise police practices in the Western Balkans (EC 2010f: 11-12).

Still, EU efforts to enhance police education in Serbia were not very visible as a variety of courses, seminars and workshops on ethics, human rights and modern security threats were organised by the OSCE as well as many local and international NGOs (Trivunovic 2004: 254-255). Moreover, until 2004-2005 the reform of police education was tackled in Serbia on a piecemeal basis. Only after the MoI opened a directorate for professional education in 2004 and drafted a Strategy for developing the education and training police system in 2005, did noticeable changes start to occur (Petrovic 2006: 10). Thus, the Police High School in Sremska Kamenica, Vojvodina was transformed into the Basic Police Training Centre, open to men and women from all ethnic backgrounds, in 2006 (Ristovic 2007), the Advanced School of Internal Affairs and Police Academy were integrated into the Academy of Criminal and Police Studies later that year (ACPS 2022) and the curricular for both establishments were modernised and demilitarised (Rose 2011: 87-88). These changes[183] were impelled and coordinated by the OSCE, whereas the EU was involved in the process mostly indirectly as membership in the bloc provided an overarching stimulus for police reform.[184] Thus, the OSCE training courses were aimed at introducing the Serbian police to EU standard practices (ibid.), while the efforts to overhaul police education were meant to change the police culture in the country, helping it absorb social values and human rights principles, respected by EU member states (Downes 2004: 7).

With the OSCE guiding the transformation of Serbia's police education system, by 2008 the EU shifted its attention to the improvement of internal control in the MoI and law enforcement agencies. The IPA 2007 project "Police Reform: Internal Control", for example, implemented in 2008-2010, targeted the MoI's Section of Internal Control of Police to share the EU best practices to promote professionalism and prevent misuse of power in the service (EC 2012c: 5). A training element was also included into the 2012 IPA project "Modern concept of Human Rights Management in the Ministry of Interior of the Republic of Serbia" that was part of a more strategic approach undertaken by the EU in conjunction with other donors to enhance professional development and institutional capacity of the police after 2011 (ibid.). According to an expert on the Serbian police reform, this latter project, which ended in 2016, gave the Serbian MoI tools to manage the HR system more effectively and efficiently[185]. Another tool employed by the EU to assist the Serbian police in achieving transparency and accountability, found inside the bloc, was the promotion of cooperation and information exchange with Europol, the EU law enforcement agency, and CEPOL, the EU Agency for Law Enforcement Training. Unfortunately, in the studied period the cooperation with the former was minimal and with the latter non-existent. Officially, Serbia started engaging with Europol after signing a strategic cooperation agreement in 2008, however, the relationship lacked substance until 2014 when an operational agreement was concluded (EC 2014a: 54). CEPOL included Serbia into a first exchange programme only in 2014 (ibid.; CEPOL n.d.).

Additionally, it is worth highlighting that police reform in Serbia was influenced by the Kosovo question. As part of an effort to normalise relations between Belgrade and Pristina, the EU made police cooperation one of the focal points of the Dialogue it moderated between the two sides. Progress in the area was slow as initially the Serbian MoI was refusing not only any direct contact with Kosovo police structures, but even the recognition of the EULEX mandate (EC 2008b: 51). Although Serbia signed a special cooperation protocol with EULEX in 2009, cooperation between the actors was restricted to the areas of combating organised crime and cross-border issues (Elek 2015: 9). "The First Agreement on Principles Governing the Normalisation of Relations" signed by Belgrade and Pristina in April 2013, brought the EU another small but important victory: Serbia agreed to dismantle parallel security institutions it was keeping in northern municipalities of Kosovo and cooperate with Pristina regarding the integration of the security personnel into the Kosovo structures (Guzina and Marijan 2014: 8). Moreover, in December 2013 Serbian and Kosovar leaders agreed that the role of an acting regional police commander for Kosovo's northern municipalities should be given to a local Kosovar Serb (Andric 2013). Overall, in 2013 Serbia and Kosovo were only starting to cooperate on police issues.

Still, compared to the reform of the army, police reform in Serbia in 1999-2013 experienced a stronger EU influence. Although initially the EU gave preference to non-sensitive, technical issues, with time it became more comfortable engaging in more complex areas. After 2011, when the focus of the enlargement policy was placed on the rule of law, and the country received a candidate status, the bloc searched for more comprehensive solutions to remaining problems. With many external players active in the Serbian police reform, the European Union did not lead it per se, but provided a stimulus for transformation through the membership perspective. As one of the interviewed security experts put it, "the EU is the reason why we are doing (all) these [reforms]"[186]. By 2013, the police reform in Serbia achieved a lot, but was still incomplete. On the one hand, the institutional framework for law enforcement and fight against organised crime was mostly in place and legislation largely harmonised with the EU standards. On the other, skill shortages in specialised police services and gaps in inter-agency and regional police cooperation persisted (EC 2013b: 51).

Border reform experienced even stronger EU impact, although its process was also non-linear. In the FRY and SCG, border security was a joint responsibility of the federal/State Union army and republican police and was therefore affected by tensions between Belgrade and Podgorica until 2006. Border delineation disputes with neighbours, including BiH and Croatia, and poor conditions at most border crossing points (BCPs), where infrastructure was either severely outdated or destroyed by the NATO bombing campaign, made the task of improving border security in Serbia additionally difficult (Bakic and Gajic 2006: 24). The unresolved status of Kosovo added another obstacle, which became graver with Kosovo's unilateral declaration of independence in 2008. Given the geo-strategic importance of Serbia for the stability of the region and its location on the Balkan route that exposed not only Balkan countries but also EU states to dangers of organised crime, border reform in the country was identified by the EU as an early and urgent priority (EC 2002c: 27). Working alongside other external actors, such as NATO, the OSCE, Stability Pact and DCAF, the EU emerged as the leader of the reform since all externally promoted efforts in the area were geared towards preparing the FRY, SCG and eventually Serbia for EU membership. Starting from 2003, when Serbia subscribed to the Ohrid Process on Border Security, the overarching framework of the reform was decided by the EU's Integrated Border Management concept, formally adjusted to the context of the Western Balkans in 2004 (Bakic and Gajic 2006: 24). The IBM Guidelines obliged Serbia to develop effective systems of border control, trade facilitation and cross-border cooperation to ensure the country had "open, but controlled and secure borders" (Trauner 2007: 27). The EU also insisted on the demilitarisation of borders since border security in the bloc was seen as an area of policing, rather than defence (Council of the EU 2006b: 3; Bakic and Gajic 2006: 24). Given the JNA/VJ's history with violence and war crimes, the salience of border demilitarisation in Serbia was even greater than in many other Western Balkan countries. The withdrawal of the military from border control points in Serbia, however, did not happen immediately: the process was protracted, chiefly thanks to uncertainties surrounding Serbia's statehood.

Although strategic documents on demilitarisation were prepared by the Serbian MoI with the assistance of external donors, including the EU's EAR, in 2001-2002, the police started assuming control of the country's BCPs only in 2005 (Rose 2011: 96, 98). It is notable that the first control posts to be demilitarised were those on the border with Hungary, the only border Serbia shared with an EU member state at the time. From there, the focus shifted onto BCPs along borders with pre-accession countries, Romania and Bulgaria, and only afterwards to borders with other Western Balkan states such as Croatia and BiH (ibid.: 98). Such sequence was not accidental but determined by the EU's prioritisation (EC 2002c: 29) as the IBM concept was meant not only to enable the Western Balkan states approach border issues in a coordinated manner, but also to improve the security of the EU's external borders (IBM Guidelines 2007: 13, 18).

Despite having an overarching framework for border reform, the EU chose to approach it from a technical aspect first. On the one hand, it was a way of supporting Serbia in dealing with some of the biggest gaps in its border control without impinging on any sensitive issues. On the other, it was an opportunity to rehabilitate key European transport routes, ruined by years of neglect and war. The Serbian part of the so-called Corridor X, for example, an important route running between Austria and Greece, was restored not just for the benefit of the country, but also for the normalisation of passenger and goods flows in Europe. Moreover, it is worth remembering that while the IBM concept promotes a comprehensive vision of border management, it is mostly technical in nature (IBM Guidelines 2007: 2). After all, in the EU the control of external borders is a responsibility of individual member states, and not a supranational policy (Council of the EU 2006b: 3). This meant that Serbia, while required to adhere to the same values and standards in border management as EU member states, had the freedom to decide on the specifics of its border security system[187].

In 2001-2006, 73% of the CARDS budget allocated to border issues in Serbia, was spent on infrastructure projects, with the rest going towards supply contracts and supervision contracts for infrastructure measures (Particip GmbH 2009: 53). In 2001, 2002 and 2004 the EU launched projects to restructure and upgrade BCPs at Horgos, Batrovci and Presevo, all affecting the Serbian part of Corridor X and in 2007 started supervising renovation works of border crossing facilities at Dimitrovograd railway station, also along Corridor X (EC 2008d: 10). In 2005, the EU invested in the restructuring of veterinary and phytosanitary services, assisting the latter with the adoption of legislation, training of staff and provision of equipment for BCPs (ibid.: 11). The emphasis of the EU's assistance shifted from technical issues to a more comprehensive approach in 2006[188], when Serbia and Montenegro parted their ways. Apart from the fact that Belgrade achieved full control over issues that previously required Podgorica's approval, there were two main reasons for this change. First, in 2006 Serbia adopted a national IBM strategy and corresponding Action Plan that defined the country's border management framework, roles and responsibilities of border services, and their goals and priorities (IBM Strategy 2006). These documents were meant to help Serbia achieve full control of its borders and assume responsibilities of EU membership, when time came. The EU provided help not only with drafting the IBM strategy, but also with its implementation. Thus, within the 2006 CARDS project "Implementation of Integrated Border Management Strategy", it conducted analysis of the country's legal framework on border issues, assisted with the design of a new Human Resources Management System, carried out training of key personnel and developed curricular for staff involved in the IBM activities (EC 2012e: 7). Second, a more diverse approach to border security in Serbia materialised because of an improved understanding of the regional context by the EU. Having implemented "The Regional CARDS Programme for Western Balkan—Multi-Year Indicative programme 2002-2006", the EU established not only that Western Balkans lacked a comprehensive approach to border management, but also that their border problems were inextricably linked (EC 2008d: 11). As a result, the question of Serbia's border security, became integrated with the border security of the region. To preserve stability in the Western Balkans and boost the region's economic and political development, the EU urged Serbia to improve cooperation in the field of border management with its neighbours and resolve existing border disputes (IBM Strategy 2007: 9). While Serbia agreed to these demands in principle, it did not hurry to deliver on them. This was not only because the country's government still struggled to reconstruct border control infrastructure in many areas, but also because its attention was directed towards other burning issues such as the worsening of situation in Kosovo.

By 2008, Serbia's borders were demilitarised and fully under control of the border police, coordinated by a restructured Border Police Directorate within the MoI. Despite these achievements, more progress was needed in relation to legislation, technical capacities of agencies involved in border management, staffing, provision of equipment to the border police and border disputes with neighbours (EC 2008c: 48; EC 2009b: 51). To provide the country with an incentive to tackle these issues and prevent it from falling behind other Western Balkan states, Serbia, alongside Albania, FYROM and Montenegro[189], was invited to start a dialogue with the EU on visa liberalisation in January 2008 (EC 2008e: 2). As a result, for the next two years border reform in the country was dominated by the visa liberalisation process. The Roadmaps on visa-free travel for Western Balkan states identified four areas requiring change: document security, illegal migration, public order and security, and external relations issues connected to the movement of persons (EC 2008f). For Serbia, this *inter alia* meant introduction of biometric travel documents and improvement of document security; adoption and implementation of asylum, migration and visa policies, aligned with the EU standards; functional policies to fight organised crime, corruption and terrorism and improved judicial and law enforcement cooperation with EU member states, Balkan neighbours and relevant international agencies (ibid.). Serbia fulfilled the formal requirements of the roadmap by the end of 2009 and received the right of visa-free travel to the Schengen area in December 2009 (EC 2010d: 49). Although the country aligned its legislation on border control with the Schengen Border Code, its border control and management systems remained underdeveloped (ibid.). Their weaknesses were exposed, for example, by significant rise of unfounded asylum applications by Serbian citizens after the opening of Schengen borders, which prompted the Commission to introduce a post visa liberalisation monitoring mechanism (EC 2012b: 52).

To fully understand the relative slowness of border reform in Serbia, one needs to acknowledge the gravity of situation in the field. After four wars, infrastructure at border crossing facilities, professionalism of staff ensuring border security, as well as relevant legislation were in a dire state that could not be transformed quickly. Unsurprisingly, Belgrade remained dependent on external aid and guidance, which the EU continued to provide throughout the studied period and beyond. Having addressed the most acute infrastructure and equipment needs of Serbian BCPs with CARDS, the EU continued to support the development of administrative and operational capacity at border control facilities with IPA, yet with a stronger emphasis on the three pillars of the IBM, i.e. improving intra-service, inter-agency and international cooperation. Thus, thanks to the IPA 2008 project "Development of the Information System for Border Crossing Control", Serbia updated infrastructure for border crossing checks and started developing an integrated information system for the Border Police Directorate (EC

2012e: 7). It was also under the influence of the EU that a cooperation agreement in the field of IBM was signed between the MoI, Ministry of Finance and Ministry of Agriculture, Forestry and Water Management in 2009 (MoI RS 2016: 76). On the international level, the European Commission insisted on connecting all border crossings in Serbia to the Interpol system (I-24/7) and improving cooperation with Frontex, the European Border and Coast Guard Agency. Since 2009, Frontex has been engaging Serbian border staff in joint operations, regular exchanges of information and best practices as well as training activities, trying to raise their professionalism (EC 2012b: 53).

Training opportunities were offered to the border police through other channels, too. The first specialised training was offered by a precursor of the Border Police Directorate, Directorate for Border Police, Aliens and Administrative Affairs in 2003 (Rose 2011: 104). An important contribution into the development of curricular for educating staff involved in the IBM activities was made through the CARDS 2006 project, "Implementation of Integrated Border Management Strategy" which not only provided training for key personnel but also offered guidance on updating the Human Resources Management System of the border police (EC 2012c: 5). Overall, there were two areas of training prioritised by the EU in this area: training border personnel to work with modern technologies and to remove corruption from the border control and management service (ibid.).

Like in other aspects of SSR, legal approximation in border security was highly valued by the EU. After Serbia adopted the IBM Strategy under the EU guidance, as part of the visa liberalisation process, it adopted many other important documents, such as the Law on Protection of State Border (2008), Law on Foreigners (2008), Law on Travel Documents (2008), Migration Management Strategy (2009) and Law on Migration Management (2012) (MoI RS 2016: 78). As mentioned above, effective asylum, migration and visa policies were demanded by the EU in Serbia as part of the process, too. In fact, Serbia had to fulfil the same requirements as Croatia and other Western Balkan states with respect to these areas. While the requirements were predominantly the same, Serbia did not have the capacity to address them quickly. Thus, in 2013 it struggled to implement its asylum policy, formulated in 2007, as there was still no adequate asylum processing, the Asylum Office operated on an *ad hoc* basis and the list of safe non-EU countries was not fully aligned with the *acquis* (EC 2013b: 50). Although migration and visa policies were relatively more advanced, they were still below the expected standard (ibid.). Serbia was also behind Croatia in terms of implementing the IBM strategy. In November 2012, the Serbian government adopted a new version of the strategy to accommodate the Commission's conditions for a stronger IBM Coordination body (ibid.). Yet even that strategy was still based on the Western Balkans IBM Guidelines, and not harmonised with the EU IBM concept (MoI RS 2016: 77), meaning that more changes could be expected in the area in the future.

Finally, border reform in Serbia was affected by several border demarcation disputes. Serbia disagreed with Croatia over the border at the Danube River and two small islands near the town of Vukovar, and over the border along the Drina river with BiH (Milekic and Zivanovic 2017). In 2008, it paused the process of border delineation with Montenegro in protest of the latter's decision to recognise Kosovo's independence, while FYROM's border demarcation agreement with Kosovo was met with a dose of hostility (EC 2011a: 36). The European Commission monitored these disagreements through annual progress reports urging Serbia to solve them, but not willing to interfere otherwise in what it saw as bilateral issues (EC 2006f: 17-18; EC 2011a: 36; EC 2013b: 13). With no *aquis* on border delineation, the EU avoided drawing a link between Serbia's border arguments and its progress in the membership talks. As a result, disputes with Croatia and BiH remained unresolved in 2013. Yet looking at Croatia's experience, it is likely that the EU will display more interest in this matter as Serbia gets closer to the prospect of membership. The question of managing the boundary[190] between Serbia and Kosovo, however, could not wait that long. Border cooperation has been identified by the EU as one of the priorities of the Belgrade—Prisitina Dialogue. Thanks to exposing the parties to consistent pressure and keeping negotiations technical, the EU received first tangible results by 2013. Not only did Belgrade and Pristina opened joint interim crossing points, but their respective Border Police Departments became the only law enforcement units cooperating directly (Elek 2015: 9). Both developments were achieved through signing the IBM agreement in December 2012 and its associated implementation protocol in February 2013 (Kursani 2015: 8). Prior to that, all exchanges on border issues between the two sides were mediated by EULEX. While significant, these achievements did not solve all problems: the IBM agreement was yet to be implemented, permanent BCPs to be established and border patrols to be transferred from regular police to the border service (Elek 2015: 9).

In short, border reform in Serbia was approached by the EU in a most comprehensive manner, which materialised with a slight delay in 2006. By encouraging Serbia to adopt a national IBM strategy, based on the IBM Guidelines for the Western Balkans, it steered the country towards the same benchmarks as the rest of the region. It promoted intra-service, inter-agency and international cooperation. Thanks to financial help under CARDS and IPA, Serbia updated infrastructure and equipment at most BCPs, developed information exchange networks between the border police and all other agencies involved in border management and control, introduced changes into national legislation to bring it closer to EU standards and raised the level of professionalism of border guards and staff at the Border Police Directorate. The EU also played a key role in establishing direct communication channels between the border police in Serbia and Kosovo. Nonetheless, in 2013 border reform was not complete: asylum, migration and visa policies were still underdeveloped, border disputes with Croatia and BiH unresolved and the IBM strategy, even updated, not aligned with the EU IBM concept.

Conclusion

In the period from 1991 to 2013, Serbia went from an aggressor, causing havoc in its neighbourhood, to a candidate state for EU membership. The transformation it underwent, although remarkable, is still unfinished, much like security sector reform that in many ways reflects the country's development. The Serbian security sector, largely inherited from the SFRY, was manipulated by Milosevic to support the goals and policies of his regime. Between 1991 and 1995 the army, police, security agencies and various paramilitary units were used in the Slovenian, Croatian and Bosnian wars, including the design and implementation of ethnic cleansing strategies. The rare attempts to bring change to the work and management of the FRY and Serbia's security structures such as Serbianisation and decommunisation of the army or militarisation of the police were aimed at bringing them closer to the regime, and further from standards found in democratically governed states. With Milosevic and his allies sponsoring illicit economic and military networks to side-step the UN and EU sanctions, Serbia as one of the poles of the Balkan regional conflict formation, spread animosity and instability in the Western Balkans. Although after the end of hostilities in Croatia and BiH, Milosevic tried to position himself as a peace-maker and was seemingly committed to principles of reciprocity, regional cooperation and good neighbourliness, promoted by international initiatives, peace in the region did not last. With the outbreak of violence in Kosovo in 1998-1999, the fragile security regime in the Western Balkans collapsed. In 1995-1999, the VJ and Serbian police saw minimal change, mostly linked to reduction in numbers of personnel and minor restructuring of forces. The NATO bombing campaign as well as the UN and EU sanctions not only weakened the country's security sector but also led to anti-Western sentiment among its leadership that added another obstacle to externally-led SSR efforts after the electoral defeat of Milosevic in 2000.

As a result of uncertainty surrounding Serbia's statehood, the severity of the war crimes legacy and internal power struggle, Serbia grappled with initiating change in the security sector for several years after the ousting of Milosevic. Despite a slow take-off, by 2013, SSR in the country has seen some important results: legal frameworks on the military, policing and border security were largely harmonised with international and EU standards, the security sector as a whole was put under democratic and civilian control, the army was slimmed down and professionalised, the police were depoliticized and modernised, borders demilitarised, cooperation with the ICTY recognised as satisfactory and relations with Kosovo, at least in the areas of policing and border security, started gaining definition. While these achievements do not mean that the country's SSR is complete, they signal that Serbia was ready to move away from the status of a pariah state and willing to change to join the EU/Europe security community. By 2013, the Serbian political and security elites have not only formally committed to the values of rule of law, transparency and accountability, shared by the EU member states, but also started demonstrating the first signs of political responsiveness and predictability of behaviour which Deutsch recognised as essential conditions of a security community. These signs became more recognisable after 2008, when the nationalist movement was weakened by a split in the Radical Party and European integration recognised as a key goal by most influential political players.

The commitment to the European idea of the country's political leadership *inter alia* has strengthened the EU's role in Serbia's SSR. As between 1991 and 1999, except for some brief periods, the EU relations with Serbia were characterised by a punitive character, it was not easy for the bloc to get involved in the reform. Having introduced independent sanctions against the FRY, supported the UN sanctions and NATO bombing campaign, and delivered a blow to the Milosevic plan for Greater Serbia via the Arbitration Commission, the EU chose to approach sensitive issues like security cautiously. Besides, the lack of real change in the immediate post-Milosevic period, resurgence of nationalism and cumbersome structure of the SCG that emerged as a direct result of EU pressure meant that domestically there was little appetite for SSR, too. After overcoming initial hesitation, the first steps of the EU in Serbia's SSR were directed at technical issues such as rehabilitating the infrastructure at border crossings and updating police equipment. With time, the scope of the EU's influence has grown considerably: not only did it frequently engage in military, police and border police reforms, but it made a significant contribution into the political level of SSR and finding a solution to the issue of war crimes. Bearing in mind the content of this chapter, the EU's involvement in

Serbia's SSR between 1991 and 2013 can be summarised in five points.

First, *the EU did not settle into the role of an SSR actor in Serbia easily*. This was not only because Brussels did not get a chance to initiate change in security sector in the 1990s or continued to treat Belgrade with suspicion even after the Bulldozer Revolution, but also because Serbian political elites were not fully committed to the idea of Euro-Atlantic integration until at least five years after the departure of Milosevic. Without reciprocity, the EU's security governance attempts could not bear fruit.

Second, *SSR in Serbia,* just like in Croatia, *was used by the EU as a member state-building tool.* The pressure on Serbia to bring its army, police and border police under democratic and civilian control, as well as in line with international, and often EU-specific, standards increased as the country made progress in the accession talks. Yet, the EU was unable to help Serbia reach the level of security found inside the bloc, hence the offer of a candidate status and not membership in 2012. Apart from disagreements with Montenegro over the future of their partnership and strong nationalist sentiments, Serbia's progress (in accession process as well as SSR) was slowed down by its reluctance to cooperate with the ICTY and the Kosovo question. If the former issue was mostly resolved in 2011 with the last two ICTY fugitives been transferred to The Hague, the latter was still open in 2013 and even getting heated at the time of writing. It is widely believed that without reaching a mutually favourable agreement on the status of Kosovo, Serbia cannot become a fully functional state nor complete its security sector reform[191].

Third, *despite having a unique opportunity to lead military reform in Serbia, the EU dealt with the strategic elements of the reform reluctantly*, choosing to focus on the same aspects of the reform, as elsewhere in the region, where such opportunity was denied by the strong presence of NATO. It therefore confirmed its preference to dealing with soft security issues over hard security.

Fourth, *the EU showed varying levels of interest and involvement in the three studied elements of SSR*, with border reform receiving the most consistent and comprehensive attention from Brussels, police emerging as a firm priority towards the end of the studied period, and defence issues being tackled from the point of CSDP infrastructure. The EU's interest in the reform underwent considerable transformation, yet the bloc did not attempt a more comprehensive approach, even though according to experts, it had the tools for it.[192]

Fifth, *the regional dimension of SSR in Serbia was approached by the EU extra carefully* due to the importance of the country for the stability of the Western Balkans and its influence over Kosovo's participation in regional initiatives. The Serbian political elites were encouraged to make security cooperation with their neighbours a priority on bilateral and regional levels. Although there is still a long way to go before the Western Balkans can be seen as a tension-free zone, the security situation in the region in 2013 was mostly peaceful, and Serbia, as one of the regional poles, under the guidance of the EU, played a significant role in achieving this point.

---

117 Serbia was involved in the conflicts in Slovenia (1991), Croatia (1991-1995), Bosnia and Herzegovina (1992-1995) and Kosovo (1998-1999) (Ejdus 2010: 10).

118 The complexity of networks piercing through the Western Balkans and uniting the region into a regional conflict formation in the first half of the 1990s, made it very hard to disentangle the conflicts and single out a single side responsible for violence.

119 Serbia does not pursue membership in NATO. For the discussion of Serbia's military neutrality, see Ejdus (2014).

120 When necessary, references to the situation in Montenegro and Kosovo will be provided.

121 In a referendum on 1 March 1992, 62 per cent of Montenegrin citizens voted to stay in union with Serbia, while most opposition parties boycotted the vote (Noutcheva 2012: 68). For a detailed discussion of the Montenegrin politics after the SFRY disintegration and Podgorica's relations with Belgrade, see Bieber (2003).

122 Serbia's development during this period can also be seen within the framework of state failure clusters, see Wolff (2011).

123 Seselj was also in charge of the Serbian Chetnik Movement, for details see Kaldor (2012:49).

124 According to some estimations, by the end of 1998 around 300,000 Kosovars fled their homes, and more than 700 were killed (Ramet 2002: 319; NATO 2016).

125 For a detailed analysis of the Kosovo war, including the NATO air campaign, see Judah (2002).

126 While damaging the FRY's security resources, the NATO bombing improved the VJ's image domestically: after surviving the 78-day attack the army was seen as a strong and professional force.

127 Serbia and Montenegro, despite staying together, took diverging paths after the split of the governing DPS party in Montenegro and election of Djukanovic as president in 1997 (Noutcheva 2012: 69).

128 The level of Serbian involvement in the wars in Croatia and BiH is a matter of debate (Ostojic 2014: 21-22). For further discussion, see Gagnon (2004) and Hoare (2004).
129 To prevent the disintegration of Yugoslavia and to manage the conflicts, the EU employed a variety of diplomatic instruments that did not prove successful. These instruments are briefly overviewed in Chapter 4; for a more detailed analysis of the EU's role in the Balkans in 1991-1995, see Glaurdic (2011) and Ginsberg (2001: 57-104).
130 All the EU sanctions against the FRY, except for the arms embargo, were suspended in 1995.
131 While the WEU assisted the UN sanction regime on its own initiative, without a formal request from the EU, it can still be included into this analysis as part of the EU effort, based on its commitment to "be developed as the defence component of the European Union" in 1991 at Maastricht (WEU 1991:1).
132 In April 1993, the UN extended its sanction regime to the Bosnian-Serbs after their refusal to back a new peace plan, proposed by the US. Milosevic agreed to support sanctions against the RS in August 1994 to avoid the economic collapse of the FRY (Lopez 2000: 75).
133 Other factors included the conflict environment and post-communist transition (Andreas 2005: 337).
134 For a detailed analysis of all opinions and discussion of the legality of the Badinter Commission's work, see Craven (1996).
135 For the texts of Opinions 1-10, see (CoY AC 1992).
136 Opinion 3 was not attempting to solve border disputes between former Yugoslav republics. States could be recognised without their borders being fully defined (Blockmans 2007: 145).
137 At the start of the 1990s, Montenegro was not a self-sufficient republic, but dependent on the Yugoslav and Serbian economy (Hadzi-Vidanovic and Djuric 2007:16). Besides, with the Montenegrin government and President being closely associated with Milosevic, Montenegro's decision to stay part of the transformed Yugoslavia in 1992 was not surprising (ibid.). The cracks in Serbia – Montenegro relations started appearing only in 1997, after the split in the Montenegro's ruling DPS.
138 See UNSC Resolution 820, adopted on 17 April 1993.
139 Although Serbia and Montenegro remained together within the FRY, Montenegro did not participate in the Kosovo conflict (Noutcheva 2012: 69).
140 In May 1999, 430, 000 refugees from Kosovo were in Albania and 200, 000 in FYROM; Bosnia and Montenegro were also affected, but numbers there were significantly lower (IMF 1999).
141 For a full list of the EU's autonomous restrictive measures, see ICG (2000: 3-6); Buchet de Neuilly (2008).
142 For the assessment of the decision-making processes that led to the adoption of these sanctions, see de Vries (2002).
143 This was the case for the UN that imposed the new embargo on the FRY with Security Council resolution 1160 of 31 March 1998.
144 The KLA relied heavily on clandestine networks with Albania to acquire weapons, for the analysis of its supply chains, see Perritt (2008: 110-129).
145 This category also included a ban on international flights to and from Yugoslavia, but these restrictions are omitted from the work due to them not targeting the security sector directly. For the same reason, the EU financial sanctions are

not considered here either. It should be noted, however, that to a certain degree financial sanctions hurt the security elites in Serbia as the latter were closely linked to the regime and were often owners of substantial capital. For the discussion of these categories see de Vries (2002).
146 See Council of the EU (1998a).
147 The list included not only security officials, but all persons considered to be closely associated with Milosevic and responsible for repressive activity in Kosovo, see Council of the EU (1999b, 1999c, 2000a, 2000b, 2000c, 2000d).
148 Exceptions applied to humanitarian action and diplomatic/consular missions, including NATO aircraft, see Council of the EU (1999d).
149 Interviews of the author with Serbian civil society representatives and former military personnel in Belgrade, conducted in September 2016.
150 For the discussion of the EU's role in the emergence of the State Union of Serbia and Montenegro, see Tocci (2007: 81-88).
151 February 2008 saw some violent clashes over the declaration of independence by Kosovo, yet the Serbian government vowed to use only peaceful means to contest the issue (EC 2008b: 50-51).
152 Interview of the author with a representative of Serbian civil society working on SSR issues, conducted in September 2016.
153 Interview of the author with an OSCE official involved in SSR activities in Serbia, conducted in September 2016.
154 Interview of the author with a security expert working at the Serbian MoI, conducted in September 2016.
155 For an example of such report see EC (2006f).
156 IPA II covers the period from 2014 to 2020 but is outside the scope of this study.
157 Initially, progress reports focused on the civilian oversight of the army, but from 2007 they started monitoring the oversight of the security sector more broadly.
158 Judiciary control is omitted from this study.
159 One of the most prominent examples of a legal provision changed under EU pressure was ending the practice of "blank resignations", which required MPs to sign resignation letters that could be activated by their political parties at any time (EC 2011a: 10).
160 For problems with the organisation and functioning of the NSC, see Milic (2014: 76).
161 For example, see PrEUgovor (2013: 11-31).
162 The issue of war crimes in former Yugoslavia is first and foremost linked to transition justice, see Ostojic (2014) and Kandic (2005).
163 For more information on war crimes in Kosovo and Operation "Horseshoe", launched by Serbs, see House of Commons (2000).
164 These included Bosnian Serbs.
165 In 2005, two thirds of Serbs believed that the tribunal was biased against Serbia (BCHRSM 2005).
166 While causes of Djindjic's murder are disputed, it is widely believed that his willingness to cooperate with the ICTY was one of the reasons behind his killing (Ostojic 2014: 78-79).
167 It is worth noting that the EU was not the only international actor that softened its attitude towards Serbia: NATO acted first in November 2006 by inviting the country to join PfP, despite the lack of progress with the ICTY issue at the time (NATO 2006).

168 These included the Security and Information Agency, Military Intelligence Agency, Military Security Agency and Archives and Information Service (Gow and Zverzhanovski 2013: 159).
169 The question whether the political leadership of Serbia knew about the protection provided to ICTY indictees by the security apparatus after 2002 (and to what extent) remains open. For further discussion, see Gow and Zverzhanovski (2013: 156-170).
170 According to the 2012 opinion poll of the OSCE, 40 % of respondents perceived the ICTY as anti-Serb, while 66% believed the establishment of the tribunal was unnecessary (BalkanInsight 2012).
171 Interviews conducted by the author with a leading human rights campaigner and prominent political analyst, conducted in Belgrade and Sarajevo in September 2016.
172 The absence of change can be seen on the example of General Pavkovic, who remained the Chief of Staff of the VJ until 2002, despite his involvement in war crimes (Griffiths 2010: 188).
173 The first National Defence Strategy was adopted when Serbia was part of the SCG in 2004 (Edmunds 2007: 161).
174 Framework Participation Agreement for participation in CSDP missions and operations (2011).
175 Agreement on Exchange of Classified Information (2012).
176 Administrative Agreement with the European Defence Agency (2013).
177 Interview conducted by the author in September 2016 in Belgrade, Serbia.
178 In the studied period, it has been regulated by Council Decisions 2002/842/CFSP, 2003/807/CFSP, 2004/791/CFSP and 2010/179/CFSP, and from 2013 by Council Decision 2013/730/CFSP.
179 EUSAC stands for EU Support of SEESAC Disarmament and Arms Control Activities in South East Europe.
180 Interviews conducted in September 2016 in Belgrade and 2021 via Zoom.
181 These included organised crime, accountability, community policing, education development, forensics and border policing.
182 The EUMM that succeeded the ECMM in 2000 opened office in Belgrade in 2001 (Caruso 2007: 87).
183 For a detailed discussion of the police education reform in Serbia see Petrovic (2006) and Rose (2011: 87-88).
184 Interview with security experts with experience in Serbia's police reform, conducted in Belgrade in September 2016.
185 Interview conducted in Belgrade in September 2016.
186 Interview conducted in Belgrade in September 2016.
187 This system still has to comply with EU standards as on accession to the bloc, the Schengen acquis on external borders take precedence over the IBM guidelines.
188 After 2006, the EU continued providing technical assistance to Serbia's border police, but it was no longer the key focus of its engagement with border security.
189 BiH was able to join the dialogue in 2008 too, but later than its four neighbours.
190 As Serbia does not recognise the independence of Kosovo, it insists on the term "boundary", while Kosovo prefers the term "border" (Milekic and Zivanovic 2017). To preserve neutrality the EU refers to the IBM cooperation between two sides as the Integrated Border/Boundary Management (EC 2012b: 19).

191 Interviews conducted with security experts in Belgrade, September 2016.
192 Interviews with security experts in Belgrade in September 2016 and on Zoom in 2021.

Chapter 6
Security Sector Reform in Bosnia and Herzegovina

Introduction

Already in 2002, security sector reform (SSR) in BiH was described as "an unprecedented experiment" (King, Dorn, and Hodes 2002), yet even twenty years later, this experiment was not complete. This chapter discusses the EU's contribution to SSR in Bosnia, following the approach undertaken to the case studies of Croatia and Serbia. Before proceeding with the analysis, however several key factors are discussed that have shaped the reform in the country. These include: the legacy of war, the structural framework introduced by the Dayton Peace Accords (DPA), strong international presence and divergent visions of the state's future among the political elites of the two entities making up BiH.

The Bosnian war, that lasted from April 1992 to November 1995, was the bloodiest of all conflicts fought on the territory of the former Yugoslavia in the 1990s (Bassuener 2005: 102). It displaced more than 2 000 000 and left around 100, 000 dead (Ahmetasevic 2007). During the war, military forces, paramilitary actors and the police of all three sides—the Bosnian government, the Bosnian Serbs and Bosnian Croats—routinely engaged in human rights violations and war crimes (King, Dorn, and Hodes 2002: 8). Some actors were also complicit in ethnic cleansing[193] that already in 1992 was identified as a goal, not a consequence of the Bosnian war[194] by the UN envoy Tadeusz Mazoviecki (Caruso 2007: 34). After the violence stopped, Bosnia's security sector was "fragmented, overpoliticised and structured along ethnic lines" (Perdan 2006: 180), and therefore in dire need of dealing with the legacy of war, which could not leave SSR unaffected.

The DPA, concluded in November 1995, provided both an enabling and restricting framework for SSR. While it included requirements for certain elements of the reform, such as military confidence-building measures and police restructuring, it ignored others, e.g. issues of border security, judiciary, and intelligence (King, Dorn, and Hodes 2002: 9). Moreover, by creating a weak state with two strong entities, the DPA introduced limitations on the level of change accessible to SSR. Security sectors of the two entities, the Federation of Bosnia and Herzegovina (hereinafter Federation or FBiH) and Republika Srpska (hereinafter RS), existed in parallel to each other with minimal contact. With time, the international community realised that this fragmentation not only wasted money, but also threatened the stability of the country and security of wider Europe. This led to the rise of centralising approaches, which brought about a single army and state-level Ministry of Defence and built the unified border police. The police reform, however, ran into unsurmountable difficulties when the international community, by that time led by the EU, could not justify requirements for centralisation of the service neither with the DPA provisions, nor through the *acquis*. SSR in BiH, therefore, has been affected by tensions between the decentralised system of security governance developed by the DPA and centralising approaches favoured by the international actors (Marijan 2017: 10). Nowhere in the region the link between SSR and state-building has been as clear as in BiH.

Similarly, the international role in Bosnia's SSR has been unprecedented. Thanks to the institutional structure, established by the DPA, and political divisions among the leadership of two entities, external actors were driving forward not just some, but all reforms in the security sector (Vetschera 2005: 37). NATO's Implementation Force (IFOR) and Stabilisation Force (SFOR), the OSCE, the High Representative (HR)[195], his Office (OHR), and the UN Mission in BiH (UNMIBH) were all given mandates to engage in SSR-related activities. Although the EU had no special role under the DPA, it still worked to contribute to the improvement of the security situation in the country, and in the early 2000s assumed a leadership role in SSR. Although the external pressure brought some important results in Bosnia's SSR, the extent of external involvement in the reform attracted a lot of criticism. The international community is often blamed for poor coordination of its efforts, inadequate mechanisms of accountability, politicisation of the reform, and disregard for local ownership (Marijan 2017: 9-10, 38; Weller and Wolff 2006: 5).

Finally, SSR in Bosnia has been affected by continuing tensions between the two entities. With the Federation seeking closer integration, and the RS refusing to give up the idea of joining a Greater Serbia or achieving independence, the development of security agencies on the state- and entity-level has been closely connected with the question of the BiH's statehood. Since the country announced its intention to join the EU, the political elites on both sides have tried to develop a common vision of the country's future, yet by 2013 these attempts failed to obtain substance. Considering everything said above, this chapter takes a closer look at SSR in BiH. It starts with an overview of changes in the security sector in 1991-2013 and continues with the analysis of the EU's contribution into the process.

Security sector reform in BiH: from the shadows of war to the challenges of state-building

Following the periodisation of regional development, presented earlier, the analysis of Bosnian SSR starts with the time when the Balkan subcomplex represented a regional conflict formation. Before the war, Bosnia's security sector was part of the bigger security structure of Yugoslavia. This meant that BiH did not have its own army as defence was handled by the JNA. On the other hand, the republic had a Territorial Defence Force, that was used as a base for forming the Army of Bosnia-Herzegovina (ABiH) in May 1992 (Kaldor 2012: 46-48). The Patriotic League, set up by Alija Izetbegovic in 1991 as an organ of self-defence, and numerous paramilitary units were also incorporated into the ABiH in 1992; the army command was centralised only in 1993 under the leadership of Prime Minister Haris Silajdzic (ibid.; Caruso 2007: 33).

In fact, none of the three ethnic factions had consolidated forces when the war broke out in April 1992 (Hadzovic, Dizdarevic and Kapidzic 2011: 12). The Serbian side, that established Serb autonomous regions in September 1991 and announced independence of the Serb Republic of BiH on 7 April 1992, relied on an armed militia, created by the Serbian Democratic Party (SDS BiH) and direct support from the JNA (Caruso 2007: 33; Ramet 2002: 205). Formally, the JNA withdrew from the territory of BiH in May 1992, but nearly 70, 000 of its troops transferred to the Bosnian Serb Army (VRS), which was set up in Pale on 12 May (Kaldor 2012: 47). The Croatian Defence Council (HVO) became the official military of Herceg-Bosna, when the latter proclaimed independence on 3 July 1992, and was formed out of militia set up by the Croatian Democratic Union (HDZ BiH) (ibid.). All three armies were heavily reliant on paramilitaries and foreign mercenaries, and none of them had the monopoly of force on the territories they controlled. The forces became more regularised and centralised towards the end of fighting (ibid.). According to different estimates, between 175, 000 and 430, 000 people were recruited for the war effort in BiH (Pietz 2006a: 156-157). The discrepancy can be explained by fluctuations of troops during different stages of fighting[196] and the inclusion or exclusion of non-regular forces. Thus, in 1994 the VRS consisted of around 100, 000 people, including professionals, volunteers and mercenaries from Bulgaria, Russia and Ukraine (Heinemann-Grüder, Pietz and Duffy 2003: 9). In 1994-1995, the HVO had around 50, 000 fighters and could rely on 15, 000-20, 000 soldiers seconded by the Croatian Army, while the ABiH had around 90, 000 troops, not counting nearly 3, 000 Islamic fighters at the end of the war (ibid.). The number of paramilitaries was especially difficult to estimate, but they were used by each of the sides.[197]

Such a mixture of regular and irregular forces and proliferation of clandestine networks, developed to overcome sanctions imposed by the EC/EU and UN, contributed to criminalisation of life in Bosnia and turning the country into a typical element of an RCF in the first half on the 1990s. Criminal networks were used by all sides of the conflict to acquire military equipment and weapons, though Bosniaks and Bosnian Croats were dependent on them more. This is because the VRS inherited equipment from the JNA and controlled most of the JNA's weapon stores in BiH (Kaldor 2012: 48). The VRS and HVO could also count on mostly covert, but still substantial support from the rump Yugoslavia and Croatia respectively. The situation in Bosnia was not helped by the chaotic nature of fighting, where parties were alternating between cooperation and hostilities (Hadzovic, Dizdarevic and Kapidzic 2011: 12). At the start of the war, Bosniaks and Bosnian Croats fought together against the Bosnian Serbs, yet after the release of the Vance-Owen Plan in 1993, that suggested the division of BiH into ethnically-based cantons, Croats and Bosniaks turned against each other (Kaldor 2012: 47). This war within the war formally ended in March 1994 with the signing of the Washington Agreement, which established a Bosniak-Croat Federation (Caruso 2007: 37).

The police played an important part in the conflict, too. The blurred division of responsibilities between security actors in BiH between 1991 and 1995 is another factor that qualifies the country as part of an RCF. During the war and immediately after, the police were split into parallel structures along ethnic lines (Wisler 2005: 140). The Bosniak police were based in Sarajevo and responsible for the central districts of Bosnia; the Bosnian Croat police controlled the Western parts of the country, the territory of the Croatian Herzeg-Bosna Republic, while Bosnian Serbs had their headquarters in Pale and controlled the rest of the country (ibid.). With the division between the police and military being fluid, tasks carried out by both forces were often interchangeable (ICG 2005: 7). The militarisation of the police and rapid increase in their size (in 1995, there were 45,000 police officers in the country) led to the loss of professionalism in the forces (Wisler 2005: 148; Perdan 2006: 186).

Borders in BiH during this time were porous and used by each side (sometimes, in cooperation with others) for smuggling and trafficking activities (Kaldor 2012: 51). Before the war, Bosnia had neither an international border, nor a border force, that is why during the war border security was a joint responsibility of the police and army (Hills 2006: 198). For instance, already in 1991, the border of the Serb autonomous regions in BiH were secured by the JNA, and later by the VRS (Ramet 2002: 205).

In short, between 1991 and 1995, the security situation in BiH was dominated by pre-war and war contexts. After the start of hostilities in April 1992, the military and police were split along ethnic lines and played a key role in supporting the strategic goals of the warring factions. For Bosnian Serbs and Bosnian Croats this was the removal of other ethnic groups from the territories they secured to attach the latter to respective homelands, i.e. Serbia and Croatia (Caruso 2007: 34). For the Bosniaks, it was the preservation of Bosnia's integrity (ibid.). Through their engagement in the war effort and criminal, sanction-busting activities, the armed and police forces of all three sides contributed to the spread of military, political and economic networks that turned the Western Balkans into a highly unstable and dangerous regional conflict formation.

The war had a devastating effect on the country and its security sector(s). It was stopped by the Dayton Peace Accords, formally the General Framework Agreement for Peace in Bosnia and Herzegovina (GFAP), initialled on 21 November 1995 at Dayton, Ohio, and signed several weeks later in Paris. The DPA established a highly decentralised state consisting of two entities, the Federation of Bosnia and Herzegovina and Republika Srpska (GFAP 1995). The Federation was further divided into ten cantons, each with considerable autonomy, while the RS adopted a central constitutional model (Wisler 2005: 139). Both entities were "ethnically derived" and held most powers usually found in a state, such us defence, taxation and justice (Bassuener 2005: 103). The DPA contained 11 annexes that provided a starting point for several areas of reform in BiH, including reform of the security sector[198]. Given the circumstances in which the Agreement was negotiated, i.e. "at a point when no party had either fully achieved its war aims or had been comprehensively defeated in military terms" (Weller and Wolff 2006: 3), it provided only minimal requirements for SSR. The immediate post-war goals were to preserve the unity of BiH and prevent the relapse into violence (King, Dorn, and Hodes 2002: 8). Therefore, in 1995-1999, SSR was restricted by the stabilisation and confidence-building agenda of the international community.

Military reform was conceived by the DPA "in terms of a division and balance of power" between the entities (Caparini 2006: 24). NATO's 60,000-strong IFOR was tasked with the separation of entities' forces and overseeing the withdrawal of heavy weapons to cantonment areas to prevent a resumption of hostilities (GFAP 1995). It was given a broad mandate to monitor and ensure BiH's compliance with the DPA's military aspects, included into Annex 1A. Although it could get involved in public security issues such as arresting war criminals, IFOR preferred to stay away from these tasks (Bassuener 2005: 104). SFOR that replaced IFOR in 1996 with 32,000 troops and stayed in the country till the end of 2003, developed a more proactive approach, reflected among other things in better coordination of its activities with the OHR (Bassuener 2015: 85). To address the military imbalance in the country, measures were taken to build capacity of the Federation's Army and improve arms control in both entities. Thus, the Train and Equip Programme, implemented by the US private military company Military Professional Resources Incorporated (MPRI), between 1996 and 2003, strengthened the Army of the Federation by updating its equipment, sharing best practices and reducing tensions between Bosniaks and Bosnian Croats (Pietz 2006a: 162). By targeting only one entity, however, the programme polarised the state militarily, spreading mistrust among Bosnian Serbs and undermining integration process (Caparini 2006: 25). It should also be mentioned that after the signing of the DPA, Bosnian Croats and Bosnian Serbs continued receiving financial support and intelligence from Croatia and the FRY respectively, making balanced relations between the armed forces in BiH more challenging (Pietz 2006a: 158).

The arms control issues were mostly coordinated by the OSCE under Annex 1B. It negotiated the Agreement on confidence and security-building measures in BiH under Article II of the Annex in January 1996 (Vienna Agreement), and the Agreement on Sub-Regional Arms Control under Article IV in June 1996 (Florence Agreement) (Caruso 2007: 52). The Vienna Agreement, signed by the Bosnian state and two entities, was aimed at achieving military transparency and cooperation in the country (Vetschera 2005a). The Florence Agreement, discussed earlier, introduced limitations on heavy weaponry and military strength not only of BiH and its two entities, but also of Croatia and the FRY (ASAC 1996). It was one of the steps undertaken by the international actors to foster a security regime in the Western Balkans. Although, all sides showed commitment to the Agreement initially, the FRY withdrew its support during NATO's bombing campaign in March 1999 (Boese 1999). By the time it resumed its participation in the initiative in July 1999, the incipient regional security regime had failed. Despite this, the two agreements, implemented under the vigilant supervision of the OSCE, were largely seen as a success (Vetschera 2005a). Together with the IFOR and SFOR activities, they provided the first building blocks for defence reform in Bosnia (Marijan 2016: 18).

Nonetheless, external actors did not cover all urgent needs of the post-war defence sector. For example, there was no comprehensive strategy for the demobilisation of combatants (King, Dorn, and Hodes 2002: 10). As a result, sporadic actions were taken to reduce the military forces in the entities, yet numbers of soldiers mostly fell due to the disintegration of armies rather than a controlled process of demobilisation (Pietz 2006a: 157). Hence, by June 1996, nearly 100, 000 left the ABiH, 45, 000 — the HVO[199] and 150, 000 — the VRS (World Bank 1996: 1). In the five-year period after the war, around 370, 000 combatants were demobilised (Pietz 2006a: 157).

Overall, most attempts to initiate change in defence matters between1995 and 1999 were concentrated on the level of entities as the Constitution of BiH, contained in Annex IV of the DPA, did not define defence as a state competency. The only state-level institution envisioned by Dayton and established in June 1997 was the Standing Committee on Military Matters (SCMM)[200] (Vetschera and Damian 2006: 29). Consequently, defence reform in BiH at this period was limited. Considering the international community's preoccupation with preserving peace in the country, and the political leadership of the entities focusing on the consolidation of their powers, this is hardly surprising (Bassuener 2005: 101). It is important to note that, despite the constitutional changes brought about by the DPA, the political elites in the country remained largely unchanged. Three major nationalist parties — the Bosniak Party of Democratic Action (SDA), the Serbian Democratic Party (SDS BiH) and the Croatian Democratic Union (HDZ BiH) — that won the first free elections in 1990 and led their respective ethnic groups during the war, won all, but the 2000, post-conflict elections until 2002 (Koneska 2014: 83). The dominance of nationalist parties exacerbated divisions among the two entities and three ethnic groups further. In such environment, refugee returns and cooperation with the ICTY remained low (Bassuener 2005: 106). The situation was not helped by slow police reform.

After the war, the entities structured their police forces according to two different models (Padurariu 2014: 3). In the Federation, the police were decentralised, with every canton having its own Ministry of Interior. These bodies were highly autonomous and powerful, while the Federation MoI had limited competences for organised crime, inter-cantonal cooperation, anti-terrorism and VIP protection (Wisler 2005: 140). The RS, on the other hand, chose a centralised model with a single MoI that was in full control of the crime prevention and law enforcement in the entity (ICG 2002: 9). When in March 1999, the Arbitration Tribunal in Vienna gave the city of Brcko a status of a district within BiH, but not subject to either entity (Hadzovic, Dizdarevic and Kapidzic 2011: 57), the number of police forces in Bosnia rose to thirteen (Wisler 2005: 140). With a few exceptions, these police forces were ethnically homogeneous, highly criminalised and boasting close links to local political parties (Berg 2016: 23). To assist BiH with maintaining "civilian law enforcement agencies operating in accordance with internationally recognized standards", Annex XI of the DPA tasked the UN with setting up an International Police Task Force (IPTF) (GFAP 1995). Originally, the IPTF was given a limited mandate, which allowed it to monitor activities of the police, advise and train personnel, as well as assess threats to public order and advise government bodies on effective law enforcement (ibid.). As a non-executive mission, without coercive power[201], it could not significantly change police practices in the country (Donais 2006: 175).

This mandate was extended in 1996 with UNSC Resolution 1088 that allowed the mission to investigate or assist with investigating human rights abuses among the law enforcement personnel (NATO1997). Its work was further improved when the Bonn Conference of the Peace Implementation Council (PIC) on 9-10 December 1997 granted additional powers to the High Representative (GFAP 1995). The PIC's decision that came to be known as the "Bonn powers" recognised the HR as "the final authority in theatre regarding interpretation" of the DPA's provisions on civilian aspects of peace implementation (OHR 1997). In such circumstances, the IPTF became more confident and started to acquire some real authority (Donais 2006: 177). From 1996, it focused its efforts on three main elements of the reform: restructuring of police forces, vetting police officers and promoting minority recruitment.

Given different approaches to policing in the entities and varying openness of their leadership to reforms, the IPTF had to move at different speeds in the Federation and RS. In the former, with the 1996 Bonn-Petersberg Agreement, it demanded the reduction of police force from 32, 750 to 11, 500, and set quotas for minority recruitment at 28 per cent, which reflected the pre-war 1991 census (Donais 2006: 177-178). In the latter, the Framework Agreement of Police Restructuring, Reform and Democratization was signed only in December 1998. It stipulated the need to cut down the numbers of police officers from 12, 000 to 8, 500, and set the targets for non-Serb recruits at 20 per cent, based on the turnout of minorities in the first local elections of 1997 (Bieber 2010: 9-10). While the reduction of forces was achieved in both entities within a few years, the targets for minority recruitment remained unattainable. The Agreements also allowed the IPTF to conduct a certification programme that screened police officers for involvement in war crimes or repeated cases of misconduct, and de-authorised those that were found guilty of these offences (Donais 2006: 177).

When studying police reform in BiH, two cases need to be mentioned separately: Mostar and Brcko. In Mostar, from 1994 till 1996, the WEU police contingent was deployed to assist the EU unify the city after the end of conflict between the Bosnian government and Bosnian Croats (Bieber 2010: 10). Although, the WEU mission had to create a single police force, it achieved limited results by the end of its mandate. In Brcko, that was under full international protectorate since 1997 and received a special status in 1999, the IPTF and OHR had more freedom to reform the police, which allowed them to achieve a multi-ethnic and diverse police force by 1999 (ibid.: 10-11). Apart from the IPTF, police reform in Bosnia was also promoted by other external actors, such as the Council of Europe, European Commission, OSCE, UNHCR, and Stability Pact (ICG 2002: 7). Unfortunately, the quantity of aid programmes did

SECURITY SECTOR REFORM IN BOSNIA AND HERZEGOVINA 241

not translate into quality, as most of the time donor actions were uncoordinated (Wisler 2005: 148).

Despite difficulties in initiating change in Bosnia's numerous police agencies, police reform in the country between 1995 and 1999 achieved considerably more than border reform. After the war, state borders in BiH were controlled by the MoI of the RS and Ministries of Interior at entity and cantonal levels of the Federation (Hadzovic, Dizdarevic and Kapidzic 2011: 22). Thirteen ministries altogether oversaw Bosnian border control. The infrastructure at border crossings was very poor because the country had no external borders as part of Yugoslavia, while the cooperation and exchange of information between different Ministries was practically non-existent due to the legacy of war (Hadzovic 2009: 42). This made Bosnia vulnerable to trans-border and organised crime, which threatened the rest of Europe, too (King, Dorn, and Hodes 2002: 20). Due to the complexity and sensitivity of border issues, the international community preferred to focus on technical matters first. For example, the EU worked with the OHR through the Customs and Fiscal Assistance Office (CAFAO) to develop customs systems in BiH, compliant with European standards (ibid.: 21). It was not, however, until 1997 that the question of state border police was raised (Hills 2006: 196). At the Bonn Conference, the PIC invited the OHR and IPTF to assist local Bosnian authorities in preparing legislation on a state border agency (Hadzovic 2009: 42). Although the RS initially resisted the idea, as it feared this legislation could be used to revise the BiH constitution, in November 1999 under international pressure all three members of the BiH Presidency signed the "New York Declaration", thus proclaiming their support for the establishment of a unified State Border Service (SBS) (ibid.: 42-43).

To sum up, BiH saw first attempts at SSR immediately after the signing of the DPA. Efforts in this area were led by external actors, entrusted with specific peace-building tasks at Dayton. Given the degree of devastation left in the country by the war, the international community first focused on preservation of peace and decreasing tensions between the three dominant ethnic groups (Hadzovic, Dizdarevic and Kapidzic 2011: 41). Unsurprisingly, the military aspects of the DPA initially received more attention and support, yet with the increase of the HR's powers in 1997, civilian aspects started gaining more prominence.

After the initial stability in BiH was secured, the international community started prioritising the strengthening of common institutions, while SSR emerged as one of the key elements of statebuilding. It was employed as a political tool for transforming decentralised Dayton structures and bringing Bosnia into the Euro-Atlantic institutions (Marijan 2016: 7). A confluence of several factors in the early 2000s, among which – the change of regimes in Croatia and Serbia, appointment of a strong-minded HR and the increased role of the EU in the country – created conditions for introducing important changes into the work of Bosnian security actors. In defence, to help the Federation and RS achieve smaller, more affordable armies, in 2001-2002, SFOR carried out and the OSCE supervised a downsizing exercise (Marijan 2016: 18), which reduced the number of soldiers in the country to 19, 000 (Perdan 2006: 189). Nonetheless, two separate armies kept draining the budget, costing the state five per cent of GDP yearly (Caparini 2006: 25). When the financial concerns were coupled with the requirements for joining NATO's PfP Programme, it became clear that BiH had to establish state-level defence institutions (Koneska 2014: 87). An opening for this change occurred in August 2002[202], when Serb military leaders were found to be involved in illegal arms transfers from the aircraft factory ORAO to Iraq, thus violating the UN embargo (Vetschera and Damian 2006: 32). In response, in May 2003, HR Paddy Ashdown established the Defence Reform Commission (DRC) that brought together representatives of both entities and international community to discuss ways of establishing state command and control of Bosnia's armed forces (OHR 2003).

The Commission finished work and published its report in September 2003 (Vetschera and Damian 2006: 34). Based on the report, the Parliamentary Assembly of BiH adopted the Defence Law on 1 December 2003 that assigned supreme operational and administrative control and command over the armed forces in BiH to the Presidency and established a state MoD (ibid.). Nonetheless, the entity MoDs were not abolished and remained in charge of most military matters (Koneska 2014: 90). Although the results achieved by the DRC were modest, they made further changes possible. When in December 2004, EUFOR *Althea* that substituted NATO's SFOR, discovered evidence of the VRS harbouring Ratko Mladic from the ICTY, Ashdown revitalised the reform (ibid.: 91-92). He brought back the DRC and tasked it with drafting the legislation for establishing a single army (ibid.). He also emphasised cooperation with the ICTY, which was unsatisfactory in the country (ICG 2005: 3). The DRC released the final report on 18 July 2005, which led to the transfer of responsibilities for defence from the entities to the state of BiH, the abolition of entity MoDs and compulsory military service from January 2006, and the creation of the unified Armed Forces of Bosnia and Herzegovina (AFBiH) (ibid.: 77, 79). The new army's strength is mandated at 10, 000 active-duty soldiers, 1,000 civilians and 5, 000 reservists (Bassuener 2015: 91). In recognition of the gained results, NATO invited BiH to join PfP in 2006 and the Membership Action Plan (MAP) in 2010 (NATO 2017). NATO's pull is widely recognised as one of the main factors explaining the success of military reform in BiH (Koneska 2014: 94). Other reasons included: the informal setting of the DRC; the achievement of compromise as a final arrangement, which did not allow either of the entities to tilt the balance of power in its favour; consensus among all Bosnian political elites that the reform was necessary (ibid.: 90) and the ability of the international community to act in unison (Marijan 2016: 20).

While considerable progress was achieved by 2006, in 2013 the country did not assume full responsibility for its defence. In December 2004, EUFOR *Althea* took over the role of enforcing Annex 1A of the DPA (Bassuener 2015: 89). Since 2010 it has also been providing confidence-building and training support to the AFBiH, while contributing to a safe and secure environment in BiH (EUFOR BiH 2016). EUFOR is responsible for tactical aspects of defence reform in the country, while NATO, that kept small headquarters in Sarajevo, oversees the strategic elements[203]. After the focus shifted from defence reform, Bosnia witnessed a slowed down progress in this area (Bassuener 2015). Politicisation, dealing with the legacy of war crimes and unresolved property ownership issues between the state and entities remained a source of concern. Compared to the starting point in 1995, however, the achievements of defence reform in BiH are undeniable. Police reform, on the other hand, was less transformative.

The IPTF remained the leader of police reform until the end of 2002. It dedicated its final years to promoting democratisation and depoliticization of the police forces, as well as finalising the certification process[204] (Padurariu 2014: 4). The latter de-authorised between 1,500 and 2,000 officers, 190 of whom were suspected of committing war crimes (Koneska 2014: 120). As the process was finished in a rush (Bieber 2010: 9) and was not followed up with UN-sanctioned criminal proceedings, it did not lead to considerably higher levels of popular trust in the police (Collantes-Celador 2005: 371). It was still an important step towards overcoming the legacy of war and making the police forces in both entities more professional. The depoliticization and democratisation agenda[205] of the IPTF in 2000-2002 was pursued through the appointment of independent police commissioners and police chiefs, co-location at senior levels (Wisler 2005: 151) and the accreditation of police agencies according to democratic policing standards (Padurariu 2014: 4). Additionally, the IPTF contributed to building first state-level law enforcement institutions in BiH—the State Border Police (SBS) in 2000 and the State Information and Protection Agency (SIPA)[206] in 2002 (ibid.). Both became operative under the HR's decisions and were initially weak. When the IPTF finished work, and declared the police in BiH "fit for Europe" (UNMIBH 2002), it achieved some important results: the police in the Federation and RS were "pacified" and no longer seen as a major public threat (Donais 2006: 173); they were also slimmed down and introduced to modern standards in policing through trainings and reopening of police academies in Sarajevo and Banja Luka (Perdan 2006: 194; Padurariu 2014: 6). Still, the biggest challenges of police reform were left unanswered: the political control over the policing system was not removed, and the fragmented structure left untouched (Muehlmann 2009: 142).

The European Union Police Mission (EUPM)[207], which substituted the IPTF in January 2003, had too weak a mandate to tackle the reform on its own (EEAS 2012). Hence, the restructuring effort was initiated by HR Ashdown, who by that time also acted as the EU Special Representative (EUSR). He set up the Police Restructuring Commission (PRC) in July 2004, asking it to develop "a single structure of policing" for BiH (OHR 2004). Headed by the former Belgian PM Wilfred Martens, the commission also tried to bring BiH closer to the fulfilment of the three principles of policing set by the EU for starting SAA negotiations. These required: (1) exclusive state-level competence for all police matters; (2) no political interference in policing; and (3) local policing areas (LPA) designated according to technical and functional criteria (ICG 2005: 5).

Without a political opening, such as presented by the ORAO affair in defence reform, the PRC was unable to bring domestic elites to support centralisation of the police[208]. Marten's report, released after the PRC ended in December 2004 concluded that no consensus was reached on the issue. In October 2005, thanks to a watered-down proposal by RS President Dragan Cavic that in essence was "a deal to make a deal" (Bassuener 2015: 90), the EU conceded that enough progress was achieved in the reform to start SAA negotiations. Although Cavic's agreement envisioned the establishment of a Directorate for Police Restructuring Implementation (DIPR), it did not contain any other executive provisions or commitment to re-designing the LPAs so that they could cut across the inter-entity boundary line (IEBL) (Koneska 2014: 125). For two years, the reform efforts, championed by the HR/EUSR and the EU, were blocked by senior politicians from both entities, most notably by then RS PM Milorad Dodik and Bosniak member of the BiH Presidency Haris Silajdzic (Bassuener 2015: 90). Only in October 2007, when the Mostar Declaration was signed, the stalemate ended. The Declaration and a follow-up Action plan led to the adoption of two laws on policing[209] and establishment of seven new state-level agencies (Berg 2016: 28). This allowed the EU to sign the SAA with BiH in 2008 (ibid.). Police reform, however, remained unfinished[210]: instead of creating a leaner policing system, resistant to politicisation and conducive to inter-entity cooperation, the police structure in the country became even more cumbersome (Koneska 2014: 133).

After changes of 2007-2008, the EU continued attempts to bring change to the Bosnian police, but the reform was transferred into local ownership (Hadzovic, Dizdarevic and Kapidzic 2011: 85). The EUPM provided technical and legislative support until 2012. After that, the EU Delegation/Office of the EU Special Representative took over the assistance with the fight against organised crime, regional cooperation and police-criminal justice system relations (Padurariu 2014: 7-8). The Delegation has also been placing a strong emphasis on preparing Bosnia for EU membership[211], a theme, which is even more clearly discernible in relation to border reform.

Having laid the foundation for the state-level border police at the end of the 1990s, the international community did not ease pressure on BiH until the service became fully operational (King, Dorn, and Hodes 2002: 21). Although the DPA did not contain provisions on border security, the OHR used Article III of Annex 4, which allows the establishment of additional institutions to support the country's international character, to justify border reform (Hadzovic 2009: 43). The SBS became operational in June 2000 (Hadzovic, Dizdarevic and Kapidzic 2011: 58), and took full control over the BiH borders in December 2002 (BPBiH n.d.). While responsibility for setting up the SBS was given to the UNMIBH, the work of the new border service was based on "the EU-style norms, structures and objectives" from the start (Hills 2006: 196). With the launch of the Ohrid Process in 2003, Bosnia subscribed to the Integrated Border Management strategy, developed by the EU for Western Balkan countries (Trauner 2011: 27). When created, the SBS was under the civilian oversight of the Ministry of Civil Affairs and Communication (Arndt 2000: 36), yet in 2004 with the adoption of the new Law on State Border Service, it was put under the jurisdiction of the Ministry of Security (MoS) of BiH, set up in February 2003 (BPBiH n.d.). Already within a few years of its deployment, the SBS had noticeable impact on border security: it considerably reduced the levels of illegal migration and increased customs revenues (King, Dorn, and Hodes 2002: 22). As a multi-ethnic service that adheres to the requirements for ethnic representation (Hadzovic 2009: 45), the SBS/border police also contributed to raising the profile of the law enforcement agencies in the country (Donais

2006: 179). In 2008-2009, it implemented important reforms in strengthening the rule of law, combating organised crime, illegal migration and corruption, and applying Schengen-style border management, as the result of which BiH was granted a visa-free regime with the EU in 2010 (Council of the EU 2010). Despite certain challenges, such as dependence on external support and politicisation of rule of law in the country, it is widely accepted that border reform has been the most successful of all security sector reforms in Bosnia[212] (Marijan 2016: 29; Collantes-Celador and Juncos 2012: 216).

To conclude, it is possible to say that Bosnia's SSR produced mixed results by 2013. On the one hand, the country established a unified professional army under the control of the state-level MoD, set up the Ministry of Security, developed the multi-ethnic border police and adopted key security legislation. The level of cooperation achieved in defence and border security would have been inconceivable immediately after the war. On the other hand, the police forces in the entities remained politicised and highly divided. Although, they were "pacified", professionalised, trimmed and introduced to democratic standards of policing, the law enforcement agencies from the Federation and RS find it difficult to cooperate or coordinate their activities. Moreover, the introduction of several state-level bodies, such as SIPA or DIPR added more complexity to the already cumbersome system. The overview of SSR in BiH suggests that the state only partially meets the essential conditions of an element in a security community, defined by Deutsch. Although leaders of both entities formally subscribe to the values of democracy, human rights, the rule of law and future in the EU[213], in practice they resist the implementation of reforms that could lead to their attainment. What Deutsch labelled as "responsiveness" does not yet characterise the country's security sector, or three of its elements studied here. Finally, with the leadership of three ethnic groups struggling to find a common language, mutual predictability of behaviour is still weak. Problems with SSR contributed to the slowing down of Bosnia's integration into the Euro-Atlantic institutions. Having joined the PfP in 2006, BiH made practically no progress with the MAP (Bassuener 2015a: 5). Although the EU signed the SAA with BiH in June 2008, in 2013 the country was only a potential candidate after launching the High-level Dialogue on the Accession Process in 2012. It was therefore behind not only Croatia, by that time member of both NATO and the EU, but also Serbia that achieved the candidate status in 2012.[214] The next section will analyse the EU's impact on SSR in BiH.

The EU and BiH security in 1991-1995

As discussed in previous chapters, the European Community, found itself in the vanguard of the international effort to manage the Yugoslav crises. By the time the war broke out in Bosnia, the EC's leadership was waning, and the UN came to play a more prominent role in negotiating peace between the warring parties (Hill and Smith 2000: 360). As the situation in the Western Balkans "grew too complex and dangerous" to be solved through civilian diplomacy (Ginsberg 2001: 76), the EU-UN partnership was sidelined by the US and NATO[215], whose combined efforts stopped the violence in Bosnia in late 1995. Nonetheless, between 1991 and 1995, the EC/EU had an impact on the security situation in Bosnia, and, unlike in Croatia and Serbia, managed to get directly involved in reform of the country's security sector[216]. This impact was uneven, inconsistent and flawed, yet by no means insignificant (ibid.: 59). Without trying to fully assess the EU's response to the wars of Yugoslavia's dissolution[217], this section will focus on those aspects of the EU action in 1991-1995 that are most relevant for Bosnia's SSR, either due to their influence on Bosnia's statehood, security situation or security bodies. This action includes: the Badinter Commission and recognition of BiH as an independent state, the arms embargo, the deployment of the ECMM and the European Union administration of Mostar (EUAM).

When on 17 December 1991, the EC invited the Yugoslav republics seeking recognition to submit their applications by 24 December (Blockmans 2007: 116), it effectively signalled the acceptance of Yugoslavia's dissolution and emboldened Bosnia (and Macedonia) to declare independence (Ginsberg 2001: 78-79). It was the task of the Arbitration Commission, chaired by Robert Badinter, to assess these applications and present authoritative, yet non-binding opinions on several issues, ranging from statehood to succession (Craven 1996: 333-334). Opinion No 4 stipulated that BiH was not yet entitled to the recognition as a sovereign and independent state because "the will of the peoples of Bosnia-Herzegovina" was not "fully established" (CoY AC 1992). This decision, informed by the absence of support for the application[218] from the Bosnian Serbs (ibid.), was not an outright rejection as the Commission recommended holding a national referendum if BiH desired the assessment to be reviewed (ibid.). Thus, the EC did not deny Bosnia recognition, but delayed it and by doing so prevented Sarajevo from obtaining the international support in the face of imminent war (Ginsberg 2001: 81). The Arbitration also deepened the tensions between different ethnic groups in Bosnia. By ruling that the Serbian population in Bosnia (as well as in Croatia) did not have the right to self-determination in Opinion No 2 and recognising internal boundaries between the Yugoslav republics as frontiers under international law in Opinion No 3 (CoY AC 1992), the Badinter Commission, angered Bosnian Serbs and their patrons in Belgrade, on the one hand, and gave the Bosnian government encouragement to push for independence, on the other. Therefore, like in Croatia, the EC as a convenor of the Arbitration Commission, determined Bosnia's general shape and international personality as a state.

The referendum in BiH was held on 29 February and 1 March 1992: out of 64 per cent of the population who voted, 99.7 per cent supported the independence, while 31 per cent (mostly Bosnian Serbs) boycotted the plebiscite (Ginsberg 2001: 81). The EC had no choice but recognise the independence of BiH, which it did on 7 April (ibid.: 83). Once Bosnian Serbs realised the recognition was forthcoming, they decided to fight for territory, fearing the minority status in a new sovereign state (Andreas 2006: 72). It can be argued therefore that the Badinter Commission's decisions and the EC's subsequent actions on recognition invigorated Sarajevo's push for independence and hastened the coming of war to Bosnia (Ginsberg 2001: 81). Additionally, by recognising Bosnia as a sovereign state, the EC helped turn the conflict from a civil war to interstate war (ibid.: 79), making it impossible for the international community to ignore it (Gow 1997: 36).

If the recognition of BiH by the EC defined Bosnia's statehood, the arms embargo influenced the distribution of military power among the warring parties and contributed to the criminalisation of Bosnia's key security players. Having introduced the arms embargo against Yugoslavia in July 1991, the EC/EU member states put a strong emphasis on keeping it in place during the war in Bosnia, despite the USA's insistence on lifting the embargo for the Bosniak side (Ginsberg 2001: 77). The EU also supported the implementation of the UN arms embargo, introduced in September 1991 (Lopez 2000: 73), by cooperating with the OSCE and NATO. Measures, undertaken by the EU and UN to reduce the flow of arms in the region were first aimed at the prevention and then at limiting violence, instead they disproportionately disadvantaged the Sarajevo government and set the balance of military power in favour of Bosnian Serbs and, to a lesser extent, Bosnian Croats (ibid.: 74).

The RS could rely on the JNA's armaments and covert networks in Belgrade, while Bosnian Croats were supported by Croatia (Andreas 2006: 73). The Bosnian government was hit by the EU and UN arms embargos the most, due to its landlocked geographic position and weak financial standing (ibid.). It had to build its military arsenal practically from scratch and almost exclusively through illegal networks. Most weapons had to enter Bosnia through Croatia that not only charged substantial transhipment fees, but often acted as a supplier itself (Andreas 2005: 352). Other sources of illegal weaponry for the Bosnian government originated in the Middle East, in such countries as Iran, Sudan, Saudi Arabia and Libya (Pomfret 1996). Although Bosniaks struggled to acquire certain types of weapons, e.g. armour and artillery, through clandestine channels, by 1994-1995 they amassed enough strength to tip the military balance in their favour[219] (Andreas 2006: 83-84). Underground networks that allowed the Bosnian side to avoid defeat, while being disadvantaged by the EU and UN arms embargos, did not disappear with the end of conflict, but spread further to economy and society[220] (ibid.). Like in Croatia and Serbia, therefore, the EU's activities in support of the arms embargoes, introduced by its member states and the UN, unintentionally contributed to the criminalisation of the Bosnian state. It would be unfair to say, however, that the EU's position on the arms embargo had exclusively negative impact. There is evidence to suggest that lifting of the embargo could have led to the escalation of violence and made the Bosnian government less inclined to support a diplomatic solution to the conflict (National Intelligence Council 1994).

Two remaining aspects of the EC/EU action in BiH in 1991-1995 considered here — the deployment of the ECMM and EUAM — involved the bloc's active engagement on the ground. The ECMM was brought to BiH, after opening operations in Slovenia and Croatia, on 1 October 1991 (Blockmans 2007: 129). Its work followed the same principles and faced the same difficulties as in Croatia[221], creating "a real and symbolic link" (Ginsberg 2001:69) between Bosnia and the Western Balkans, on the one hand, and the EU and international community, on the other. Although unable to stop the conflict, the ECMM demonstrated that Bosnia mattered to the outside world. The mission's work provided the EU with first-hand information on the situation in the country shaping the bloc's policy towards Bosnia and the region (EU Council Secretariat 2007). The mission's monitors came in close contact with the Bosnian security actors during the war, thus collecting valuable experience for postwar SSR. This experience in many cases was put into use when former EC monitors joined international institutions in BiH working on bringing change to the country's security sector, e.g. SFOR, EUPM or European Delegation to BiH[222]. ECMM's work in 1991-1995 therefore contributed to Bosnia's SSR, although mostly indirectly.

A more direct link can be established between SSR in Bosnia and the activities of the EU administration of the town of Mostar[223], which was the first major action under the CFSP. When in May 1994 the EU formally accepted the invitation of the parties to the Washington Agreement to help with the unification and reconstruction of Mostar (Court of Auditors 1996: 3), the historic capital of Herzegovina, it also took on the task to unify the town's divided police forces (Blockmans 2007: 182-183). This task was entrusted by the Council of the EU to the WEU Police Force (WEUPOL), deployed to Bosnia in September 1994 (Yarwood et al 1999: 7). The mission was also mandated to monitor the demilitarisation of Mostar with UNPROFOR, restore and maintain public order together with the local police and provide the latter with training (Court of Auditors 1996: 14). From the start, the WEUPOL faced difficulties in fulfilling its mandate partly caused by the lack of resources (Reichel 2000: 15), partly by the opposition to unification in the Bosnian Croat-controlled West Mostar (Court of Auditors 1996: 4). Nonetheless, by the end of 1995, it achieved first results. It established a joint operations centre, improved police communications and organised patrols on the demarcation line between two parts of the city with the East Mostar police and the West Mostar police (ibid.). No joint patrols were taken by West and East Mostar police forces together, despite an agreement signed on 18 September 1995 (ibid.).

Most of the WEUPOL's achievements were therefore of technical character. The objectives set for the mission and EUAM more broadly were incredibly ambitious: achieving unification of Mostar and its police forces within two years would have been challenging even for a more experienced actor with access to military instruments. The EU had neither the appropriate experience in crisis management, nor military tools to back up its requirements (Juncos 2013: 108). The WEUPOL's deployment and implementation was still important for both Bosnia and the EU. Bosnia received a clear signal that it had a partner in the EU, while the EU gained experience in crisis management that informed the development of its civilian CSDP missions, the first of which was deployed in Bosnia in 2003.

Overall, in 1991-1995 the EC/EU had uneven impact on BiH. Initially, it worked to prevent violence in the country, while later focused on finding a peaceful solution to the conflict and managing its consequences. Through opinions of the Arbitration Commission and recognition of Bosnia as an independent state, the EU not only confirmed Bosnia's statehood, but also hastened the coming of war to the country and made it impossible for the international community to stand aside. Having given up the leadership position when the war took a grip of BiH, the EU continued influencing the security situation on the ground through the arms embargo, ECMM and administration of Mostar. Although the embargo disadvantaged the Bosnian government and unintentionally led to the criminalisation of the security sector and life in the country, it also arguably prevented the escalation of violence. The ECMM and EUAM established a direct link between Bosnia and Brussels, giving the latter an opportunity to learn crisis management and conflict resolution through practice. Moreover, the WEUPOL as an element of the EUAM allowed the EU to gain experience in SSR, before the bloc even had a vision on the reform.

The EU's impact on SSR in BiH in 1995-1999

Although the DPA gave Brussels no mandate in the post-conflict BiH, the EU, "as part of equitable burden-sharing" chose to contribute to the implementation of civilian aspects of the peace agreement and continue its humanitarian aid in the country (European Council 1995). There were three main reasons that prompted the EU to remain engaged in the country, despite its earlier failures. First, the EU wanted to assist with the normalisation of life and post-conflict reconstruction in Bosnia to speed up the return of 750, 000 Bosnian refugees its member states accepted during the war (EC DGIA 1998). Second, it was a way of bolstering its credibility in the country and region after failing to prevent the violence in the early 1990s, and third, it was an attempt to prevent the spread of instability and animosity from the Western Balkans to the EU member states. Thus, the EU covered part of the costs for the establishment and running of the Office of High Representative[224] and used its Presidency and the Commission to influence the work of the PIC (GAC 1995). In 1995-1999, the EU engaged with Bosnia's SSR by continuing the initiatives launched in the previous period, such as the arms embargo, the ECMM and WEUPOL, and starting some new endeavours, such as de-mining and the Regional Approach.

The EU embargo on arms, munitions and military equipment, as discussed in previous chapters, remained in place towards BiH, Croatia and the FRY, even after the end of the Bosnian war and lifting of the UN embargo (Blockmans 2007: 153). In July 1999, the EU lifted the embargo on exports of small arms to the police in BiH and transfers of de-mining equipment (SIPRI 2012) but kept the ban on other types of arms and military equipment in BiH till 2006. By maintaining these restrictive measures, the EU contributed to the arms control and confidence-building activities, promoted by the OSCE under the Sub-regional arms control agreement (McCausland 1997), and therefore to the incipient security regime in the Western Balkans, which sadly failed to take hold. In the postwar period, the ECMM was also meant to contribute to confidence-building in Bosnia and reciprocity in the Western Balkans. Its mandate was expended to supervise the implementation of the DPA provisions concerning the return of refugees, protection of human rights and other inter-ethnic issues (Juncos 2013: 70). In 1997, the mission's headquarters were moved from Zagreb to Sarajevo, reflecting the importance placed by the EU on normalisation of the situation in Bosnia (Oliver 2005: 175). With missions in neighbouring countries closing, the ECMM in Bosnia had the biggest representation of monitors, spread around the country in five coordination centres (ibid.). However, the ECMM's role in the country remained limited due to continuing problems over its management (it was still run by the EU presidency and had no permanent coordinating body) and the inability of Brussels to clearly identify the direction and position of the mission among other bodies of the international community (ibid.: 177). This led to the ECMM being used mainly for collecting information on the security situation in BiH, without having a leverage to impact the latter.

After 1995, the WEUPOL managed to bring the police in Mostar closer together, yet only after the EUAM considerably reduced its ambitions for the unification of the town under the pressure of Bosnian Croats. The Rome agreement, signed on 18 February 1996, significantly diminished the size of the central zone in Mostar and opened doors for first joint patrols between the police forces from western and eastern parts of the town (ICG 2000a: 9-10). Joint patrols started in March 1996, the Joint Police Headquarters opened in late April (Winn and Lord 2001:92), and in August the WEUPOL published a plan for the Unified Police Force of Mostar (UPFM) of 380 officers (Juncos 2013: 106). When on 15 October 1996, the WEUPOL finished its operation, Mostar had three police agencies:

East and West Mostar Police and the UPFM (Winn and Lord 2001: 92-93). Although the latter was given the mandate to act throughout the town, it operated only within the central zone (ibid.). The unified police, created by the WEU contingent, was therefore different to the promised goal of a service capable of ensuring public safety and freedom of movement in a unified city (Cameron 1999: 53). Having established the UPFM and improved police infrastructure, the WEUPOL achieved limited success. Apart from the ambitious goals, set by the EUAM, the WEUPOL's modest record can also be explained by the EU's insistence on taking a technical approach to a politically charged question of police unification in the divided town. Moreover, the EUAM was the first major CFSP joint action and coordination of the UPFM was the first task delegated by the EU to the WEU after signing the Maastricht Treaty (Blockmans 2007: 185). That is why the mission suffered from poor coordination and lack of strategic guidance. It was still an important experience for the EU, not least since it used elements of SSR as a tool of postconflict transformation.

One of the new SSR-related tasks undertaken by the EU in Bosnia after the war was de-mining. Although the responsibility for a mine action programme fell to the UNMIBH, the EU found ways to contribute to the UN effort, as well as provide help to local actors directly. The bloc was the main donor of the United Nations Mine Action Centre (UNMAC), opened in June 1996 and put under the BiH government ownership in July 1998 (EC DGIA 1998: 5). It also continued supporting the Bosnia Herzegovina Mine Action Centre (BHMAC) that substituted the UNMAC in 2002 (BHMAC n.d.). Moreover, the EU was the only external actor that directly engaged with the Civil Protection Authority (CPA), that dealt with civilian bomb disposal in BiH under the supervision of the military (Mansfield 2017: 21). In 1997, it provided equipment and trained 18 clearance teams and 9 explosive ordnance disposal teams through cooperation with the CPA (ICRC 1998). The Union also allocated nearly 1.5 million USD to the work of two de-mining NGOs – HELP and Oktol to assist with the reconstruction of water supply and infrastructure in several residential areas (ibid.). In 1998, in cooperation with the World Bank the EU produced the "Bosnia and

Herzegovina—National Mine Action Plan" that outlined the key priorities of de-mining in the country (Mansfield 2017: 22). Like in Croatia, in BiH, the EU saw mine clearance as a prerequisite for returns of refugees and displaced persons, as well as a way of making land safe for agriculture, reconstruction and development (ibid.). Also like in Croatia, the EU's efforts contributed to the development of defence and civilian expertise in de-mining among local actors.

On the regional level, SSR elements were introduced via the Regional Approach (RA). In BiH, the RA placed a special emphasis on the political level of the reform, as well as certain aspects of police and border reforms, touching upon defence reform superficially. Introduced in 1996, the RA's primary objectives were to assist the successful implementation of the DPA and Erdut Agreement and "create an area of political stability and economic prosperity" (EC 1999). The DPA envisioned a decentralised state with a few common institutions and policy areas[225] (GFAP 1995). The EU used the RA to monitor the development of these institutions and policies, seeing them as a prerequisite for consolidated statehood, which Bosnia was lacking (EC 1999a: 13). It is interesting to note that while the EU was not directly involved in the formation of common institutions[226], it often provided funding for institution-building programmes, e.g. for the Council of Ministers (EC 1998c: 7). In terms of the security sector, the Union singled out control of the military and police by "democratic political means" as a fundamental requirement for democratisation process in the country (EC 1998: 2).

The police, border services and the army were given varying degrees of attention by the RA. Having recognised the IPTF's leadership in police reform, the EU still chose to closely monitor the area. It observed the restructuring and training of the police forces in both entities (EC 1998: 2), denounced the inefficiency of law enforcement services in fighting organised crime, deplored human rights violations by police officers (EC 1998c:4) and argued for the application of the principle of equal protection by law (EC 1997a: 4). In the sphere of border reform, the EU insisted on BiH determining official border crossings with Croatia and the FRY (EC 1998c:

6), advocated the removal of unauthorised check-points that obstructed the freedom of movement between the entities (EC 1998: 3) and pressed for increasing the efficiency of border controls (EC 1999a: 5). Additionally, the EU supported the work done by the OHR and IPTF on introducing the state border police to Bosnia and developing a whole-state customs system via the CAFAO project (EC 1997a: 4; EC 1998c: 7). Defence reform, that at the time was linked to the military dimensions of the DPA, was seen by the EU as a success (EC 1999a: 5). However, cooperation with the ICTY that bore importance not only for the military but for SSR in general, was largely perceived as sub-standard, especially in the RS (EC 1997a: 5). Although limited progress could be observed in the country after 1998, with SFOR taking on a more active role in arresting the indictees, the EU was not satisfied with Bosnia's cooperation with the tribunal (EC 1998c: 7). Still, it was unwilling to apply negative conditionality to invigorate the process. Just like in Croatia and the FRY, the Regional Approach in Bosnia was mainly used as a monitoring exercise rather than a transformative tool. If in the former two cases, the implementation of the initiative was obstructed by the regimes, suspicious of the EU, in BiH, it was side-lined by other efforts of the international community to build peace in the war-torn country. Despite discussions of the EU assuming the leadership of post-conflict crisis management in Bosnia, including through WEU-led military and police missions[227], the bloc settled for a supplementary role to actors entrusted with peace-building credentials by the DPA.

In short, in 1995-1999 the EU, although without a clear mandate from the DPA, focused on the normalisation of life and post-conflict reconstruction in Bosnia. Elements of SSR, attempted by Brussels, were subordinated to these larger goals as well. For example, the WEUPOL, de-mining activities and RA were promoted as a way of dealing with the legacy of war, that was precluding the return of refugees and displaced persons and assisting Bosnia in becoming a functional state. It is important to note that the EU's SSR-related endeavours in BiH were not isolated from its activities in the sphere in the rest of the Western Balkans. The arms embargo, the ECMM, de-mining and certain RA conditions were not unique to the Bosnian situation, but applied in the neighbouring countries, too. The EU thus contributed to the emergence of rudimentary reciprocity between the Western Balkan states, which is crucial for the sustainability of a security regime. Unfortunately, there was not enough will among the local actors or commitment on the EU's part, that was still finetuning the CFSP and still lacking a military muscle, to solidify the regime in the region.

The EU's impact on SSR in BiH in 1999-2013

The EU's profile in BiH started rising with the launch of the SAP in June 1999. In February 2002, when the HR of the international community was given "a double hat", allowing him to act as an EU Special representative, the Union's position in Bosnia was strengthened further (Noutcheva 2012: 95). If previously the EU supported the PIC reform agenda in a subordinate role, with the double-hatting of the HR, it was given the power to shape the reform process in BiH, ensuring the compliance not only with Dayton, but also with the SAP (Chandler 2006: 35). By the time the EUPM succeeded the IPTF in January 2003 and EUFOR *Althea* took over responsibilities of NATO's SFOR in December 2004, the EU's leadership in the country was confirmed (Dowling 2008: 181). By 2005, the Union was involved "in every level of BiH policy preparation and implementation" (Chandler 2006: 39). Despite this strong position, however, it did not manage to accelerate Bosnia's European integration. Although negotiations on SAA started in November 2005, the document was only signed on 16 June 2008 (EC 2008g: 4). Bosnia's Europeanisation process was hampered by problems with police restructuring and inability of political elites reach to consensus on constitutional changes that would allow Bosnia to function without support of the international community. As a result, in 2013, Bosnia remained a potential candidate for the EU membership.

Despite the slowness of the integration process, in 1999-2013, Bosnia benefited from an extensive SSR agenda promoted by the EU. Thanks to the intensive use of the CFSP and CSDP instruments, that complemented the Commission's reform endeavours, the EU approached SSR in BiH more forcefully and comprehensively than in the two other studied countries. This does not mean, however, that it had a single vision for the reform: like in Croatia and Serbia, requirements for SSR need to be extracted from various EU initiatives. Before looking at sources of SSR conditionality in Bosnia, a few words should be said about the EU agents facilitating the reform in the country. Although the Commission oversaw the SAP, and therefore SSR-related conditions, linked with the process, it had to share its influence in Bosnia with the EUSR, representing the CFSP and Council of the EU (Noutcheva 2012: 95). The fact that the EUSR's post was merged with that of the HR in 2002-2011 increased both the EU's leverage over the reform processes and complexity of its engagement in the country. On the one hand, through double-hatting of the HR and EUSR, the EU received direct access to Bosnian political process and thus to elements of SSR, on the other — it led to confusion among local elites who found it difficult to differentiate between the mandates given to the HR/EUSR by the international community and the EU. To remove this confusion and increase the coherence of EU activities in Bosnia, the EUSR was decoupled from the HR in 2011[228] (Juncos 2013: 135). It should also be mentioned that the EUSR's role underwent several changes in the studied period: it was strengthened with new tasks and more resources through amendments to the original mandate (Council of the EU 2002b), which *inter alia* enabled the post-holder to better engage with other CFSP actors present in the country, namely the EUMM, EUPM and EUFOR (Juncos 2013: 136). As until its closure in 2007, the EUMM, known as ECMM until 2000, continued to focus on mostly the same tasks as in the previous period (EU Council Secretariat 2007), it does not require additional analysis here. The EUPM and EUFOR, on the other hand, deserve special attention. They were launched in Bosnia to strengthen the EU's role in the country by promoting its values and norms (Juncos 2005: 99) and contributed to border, police and defence reforms in the country. It is this contribution that is studied below.

As relations between the EU and Bosnia evolved, the requirements for SSR developed, too. First, EU conditionality, demanding changes in the running and oversight of elements of the security sector, was presented to the BiH government in the 2000 Road Map and 2003 Feasibility Study. The former explicitly called for the introduction of the State Border Service (ESI 2000), while the latter emphasised the importance of police reform for integration into the bloc (EC 2003c). From 2004, key reform priorities including SSR, identified by the EU, were communicated to BIH through the European Partnership that was updated on two occasions: in 2006 and 2008. The annual progress reports, released by the European Commission were instrumental in holding BiH accountable. SSR provisions can be found in sections on political criteria and European standards in Justice, Freedom and Security. As BiH did not achieve a candidate status in the studied period[229], the Commission's reports were not upgraded to include more detailed SSR requirements through Chapters 23, 24 and 31, like they were in Croatia and Serbia. Similarly, with the SAA being enforced only in 2015, demands for defence, police and border reforms[230] formulated in the document, remain outside the scope of this study. On the other hand, in Bosnia, regularly updated mandates of the EUSR, EUPM and EUFOR served as an important source of information of the bloc's SSR conditionality.

To help ease the financial burden of running demanding security sector reforms, the EU offered BiH substantial support via the CARDS National Programme and CARDS Regional Programme in 2001-2006, and the Instrument for Pre-Accession Assistance (IPA) that included the Multi-Beneficiary Assistance from 2007[231]. CARDS programmes, whose entire budget for Bosnia reached 503 million EUR, funded SSR-related projects in such areas as JHA, IBM and de-mining (Berenschot and Imagos: 2013: 150). IPA, that allocated 659 million EUR to Bosnia in 2007-2013, continued supporting these areas, but only through two out of its five components: (1) Transition Assistance and Institution-Building and (2) Regional and Cross-border Cooperation (Juncos 2012: 64). The limitations on funding were imposed due to Bosnia's potential candidacy. Bosnia's security sector also benefited, although indirectly, from allocations to the EU's CSDP missions — the EUPM and EUFOR. The diversity of tools used by the EU to promote SSR in BiH allowed it to influence the reform on both — political and organisational — levels.

Political level

The EU's approach to the political level of SSR in Bosnia was closer to that applied in Serbia, than Croatia. This is because the fragility of the state created by Dayton prompted the EU to pay considerable attention to the country's governance system, demanding its overhaul to help Bosnia become a fully functioning state (EC 2003c: 6). The uncertainty over Serbia's statehood, as explained in the previous chapter, added an extra dimension to the EU's SSR agenda in the country, too. Yet while in Serbia this dimension was mostly removed after the peaceful dissolution of the State Union in 2006[232], in Bosnia, the EU, continued calling for consolidating the state and implementing a constitutional reform[233], that would allow domestic elites to take full responsibility for the state governance, throughout the studied period. In the security sector, *state consolidation* by the EU was mostly promoted through requirements for strengthening security competences of the common state and establishing effective coordination mechanisms between various levels of government (EC 2013e: 6). Still, trying to respond to unique needs of the complex Bosnian state (EPRS 2017: 7) did not prevent the Union from engaging in the same three areas of the political level of SSR in Bosnia as in Croatia and Serbia, namely *oversight of the security sector, cooperation with the ICTY and regional cooperation.*

Although the Constitution of BiH, incorporated into the DPA, established a basic state structure with most of security competences delegated to the entity-level, Bosnia developed all significant measures of control as a result of a series of reforms, sponsored by the international community (Hadzovic and Dizdarevic 2012: 52). Thus, the system of state parliamentary oversight, represented by the Joint Committee on Defence and Security (JCDS) and Joint Committee on Supervision of the work of Intelligence and Security Agency of BiH, emerged from defence and intelligence reforms respectively.[234] The JCDS, established in December 2003 with a mandate to monitor the implementation of the national security and defence policy and oversee the activity of the army (EPRS 2017: 8), benefited from the EU's impact only marginally (Berg 2016: 26). Although the European Commission regularly monitored the committee's work, it did not target it directly. Instead, it was the OSCE that provided training and information assistance to committee members (Marijan 2016: 30). The EU, however, left indirect impact on the system of parliamentary oversight in Bosnia by supporting the development of parliamentary democracy in general. Within the SAP framework, regular visits for members of BiH's Parliamentary Assembly were arranged to the European Parliament and advice was offered on improving the efficacy, efficiency and transparency of the parliamentary work (EC 2007e: 5; EC 2009c: 6). For instance, in 2007, both Houses of BiH's Parliament amended their rulebooks on advice of the HR/EUSR (EC 2008g: 9). Additionally, under CARDS and IPA, the state Parliament in BiH was offered programmes to build capacity of its members and administrative staff. For the most part, these focused on technical assistance, like IPA 2010 "Document Management System", yet became more versatile with the enforcement of the SAA (EC 2016d). Although entity parliaments and the parliament of Brcko also have committees for overseeing security matters, in the studied period, the EU did not engage with them directly (EPRS 2017: 8).

The EU's engagement with the executive system of control over Bosnia's security was even more complex. On the state level, this system was established through laws, regulations and amendments to entity constitutions to include the Presidency of BiH, entrusted with supreme command and control over the AFBiH, MoD, in charge of the administrative organisation of defence and overall defence policy[235], and Ministry of Security (MoS), responsible for the protection of international borders, dealing with crimes of international or inter-entity character and harmonisation of activities between the entity Ministries of Interior and the MoI of the Brcko District[236]. It was the MoS that attracted substantial attention and resources of the EU. The ministry was important for establishing an effective system of border management in BiH and coordination of law enforcement functions on the state level. When police reform came against the opposition of Bosnian Serbs and had to be reconfigured to allow Bosnia progress within the SAP, the significance of the MoS grew further. The EU supported the establishment of the ministry, its operationalisation (EC 2003: 26c), and evolution (Tolksdorf 2014: 65).

The EUPM provided capacity-building and assistance with support functions, such as human resources management and budgeting (Padurariu 2014: 8), while the European Commission offered generous funding for the implementation of the legislative and institutional frameworks that expanded the MoS mandate in 2008. For instance, one component of the IPA 2008 project "Support to the Police Reform Process" assisted with the operationalisation of the Directorate for Coordination of Police bodies, one of the seven new state-level agencies established in response to the EU conditionality (EC 2016d: 7). The EU funding was also used to build sustainable working relationships between the MoS and other state ministries, such as the Ministry for Foreign Affairs and Ministry for Human Rights and Refugees (EC 2009d). In contrast to this extensive engagement with the MoS, the EU showed limited interest in the work of the MoD, occasionally commenting on its development in annual reports, and letting NATO guide its development (EC 2006g: 12; EC 2007e: 12). Like in the sphere of parliamentary control, executive oversight of the security sector in BiH also involves the level of entities and Brcko district, e.g. presidents of the entities, entity/cantonal governments and ministries of affairs of entities/cantons (Hadzovic and Dizdarevic 2012: 53). Although initially the EU preferred to focus on the state-level only, after the adoption of the 2008 police laws, it started providing IPA funds to harmonise the state-level policing with lower levels of governance (EC 2009c: 60; MoS BiH 2013).

In terms of the oversight of the security sector by independent bodies and the public, the EU's support to these areas has been mostly indirect. Thus, the EU closely followed the establishment of the state-level Ombudsman office and abolishment of the entity ombudsmen (EC 2009c: 11), provided financial assistance for strengthening the institutional and administrative capacities of the Data Protection Agency and bringing it closer to European data protection standards (EC 2010g: 16), assisted with the implementation of the Public Procurement Law and establishing a comprehensive public procurement system in BiH, as well as monitored the work and development of the Anti-Corruption Agency, Communications Regulatory Agency, Parliamentary Military Commissioner and Public Auditors Office (EC 2016e). Although these measures were not explicitly linked to SSR, they indirectly contributed to the reform as they promoted transparency and accountability of the state apparatus and its key sectors, including security. Nonetheless, some of the EU activities in this sphere could be linked more directly to SSR. For instance, the Public Complaints Board, the Board for Complaints of Police Officials and the Independent Police Board of BiH not only appeared as the result of the EU conditionality on police reform, but also benefited from the Commission and EUPM's support (EC 2011b: 57). Additionally, the EU supported public scrutiny over security matters by promoting independent media and the development of civil society in BiH more generally. Media bodies and CSOs were the beneficiary of assistance via CARDS and IPA, as well the Civil Society Facility. The EU prioritised increasing the capacity of CSOs, improving their democratic role, building networks between the entities and across the region, and mobilising civil society for the fight against organised crime (Berenschot and Imagos: 2012: 56).

Overall, the EU's input into the development of the system of *oversight of the security sector* in Bosnia has been mixed: on the one hand, it engaged directly with the matter by supporting the MoS and independent policing agencies, on the other — it focused on improving the efficiency and transparency of the state administration and capacity-building of civil society and media, contributing to democratisation of the Bosnian state and its security sector as a result. To an extent, the EU's engagement with this element of SSR in Bosnia was affected by the unique nature of the Bosnian state. This uniqueness also found reflection in *cooperation with the ICTY*.

Having identified cooperation with The Hague as an early priority in the SAP (EC 2003c: 10), the EU had to deal with two opposing approaches to the matter in the country: the Federation was arguably the only player in the region that actively supported the tribunal's work[237], while the RS did not capture a single indictee until 2005 (Hartman 2009: 77). While trying to maintain single-state conditionality, the EU had to recognise this discrepancy and single out the RS as the entity holding back BiH from finding a resolution to the legacy of war crimes (Noutcheva 2012: 127). The gravity and scale of war crimes committed on the territory of BiH, as well as the role of the security sector in perpetuating these, meant that SSR in the country could not be completed without full compliance with the ICTY conditions. To highlight the importance of the issue, the EU did not allow Bosnia to move ahead within the SAP without satisfactory cooperation with The Hague. Unlike in Croatia and Serbia, however, in Bosnia it was not the ICTY question that delayed the SAA, but police reform (Hartman 2009: 77). Cooperation with the ICTY, although slow, progressed quicker than the reform of the police. Under increased pressure from NATO and the EU, the RS started transfers of war crime suspects in 2005 and in 2007 Carla Del Ponte announced that BiH's compliance with the tribunal was satisfactory (ibid.). The EU reached the same conclusion in 2008 (EC 2008g: 21). Moreover, the ICTY's evidence suggested that no more fugitives were hiding on the RS territory after 2006, prompting the EU and international community increase the pressure on Serbia[238], whose security networks provided cover to many of the indictees remaining at large, including the Bosnian Serb military leader Ratko Mladic (Gow and Zverzhanovski 2013: 156). Even so, the ICTY conditionality remained high on the list of the EU priorities. After 2008, when Radovan Karadzic, the RS president during the war, was arrested in Belgrade, the Commission kept insisting that both entities continue providing access to witnesses and archives, freeze economic assets of the indictees, investigate support networks that protected fugitives and improve cooperation on domestic trials (EC 2009c: 21; EC 2011b: 20; EC 2013e: 20).

In the ICTY-related matters, the European Commission relied on the support of the HR/EUSR, EUPM and EUFOR. It is notable that the HR could use the Bonn powers to dismiss officials obstructing cooperation with The Hague. Although the EU advocated the phaseout of these powers, it usually supported such actions regarding the indictees (Noutcheva 2012: 127). The EUPM supported the ICTY conditionality mostly indirectly by promoting police reform, while EUFOR was given a mandate to contribute more openly via tracing and arresting indicted war criminals (Knauer 2011: 9). With time, the EU agencies learnt to speak with one voice on the issues of war crimes in Bosnia, while also coordinating their approaches with other external actors present in the country. In general, by insisting on cooperation with the ICTY, the EU helped Bosnia's security sector to become more professional, accountable and transparent. Nonetheless, even with all indictees transferred to The Hague[239], the issue of war legacy in BiH remains resolved only partially, leaving a shade over SSR.

Finally, the EU promoted *regional cooperation* as an element of the political level of SSR. Namely, it emphasised the importance of regional relations in policing, border management and on the issue of war crimes. While encouraging constructive relationships between Western Balkan states and in broader SEE, the EU recognised a special link between BiH, Croatia and Serbia. Connected by the war legacy and ethnically identical populations, the three states, and their security relations, often deserved special attention on part of the EU (EC 2003c: 18). The regional context in which Bosnia existed became more favourable for normalisation of relations between former adversaries in 1999-2000. With the death of Tudjman and electoral defeat of Milosevic, building bridges became easier, although not simple.

To allow Bosnia to progress towards the EU, the European Commission required proof of improved and evolving neighbourly relations. In the sphere of policing, an important piece of evidence were agreements concluded by Bosnia with other Western Balkan states, which could be of a generic nature, e.g. police cooperation agreements with Croatia, Montenegro, Macedonia and Serbia (EC 2008g: 23-24; EC 2012f: 22), or dedicated to more specific issues, such as cooperation in fighting organised crime and terrorism concluded with Albania, Macedonia and Serbia (EC 2010h: 23-24). The EU monitored not just the signing and ratification of such agreements, but also closely followed their implementation. Moreover, it encouraged Bosnia to go beyond bilateral protocols to set up wider networks outside the Western Balkans, e.g. Bosnia's 2011 decision to establish a network of police officers in the countries of the region, EUROPOL and certain EU member states was seen as an achievement (ibid.). Similarly, the Union commended the conclusion of a protocol between BiH, Montenegro and Serbia to start a joint centre for police cooperation in Trebinje in December 2013 (EC 2014b: 24).

Regional cooperation on border security was identified as equally important. Such activities as joint supervision of borders, e.g. with Croatia, or joint border patrols and regular meetings between border police, e.g. with Montenegro and Serbia, were greeted by the EU as a sign of normalisation of relations in a highly sensitive area (EC 2007e: 22; EC 2009c: 23, 56). The EU also wanted Bosnia to demonstrate commitment to the IBM on the regional level, that is why it monitored the signature and implementation of protocols on strengthening IBM cooperation with neighbouring states (EC 2010h: 24). Additionally, Bosnia was invited to join regional initiatives, developed by the EU agencies, e.g. the Frontex Western Balkan risk analysis network (ibid.: 54), and non-EU bodies, e.g. MARRI, owned regionally but receiving financial help from the EU, and SEECP that covers broader SEE region (EC 2012f: 22; EC 2011b: 22). In terms of dealing with the legacy of war crimes, Bosnia had to improve cooperation on exchange of evidence and transfer of suspects with Croatia and Bosnia (EC 2009c: 22). It was a way of addressing the regional impunity gap and speeding up the process of reconciliation in the Western Balkans. Provision of adequate victim and witness protection, cooperation between courts and prosecutors from Bosnia, Croatia and Serbia and extradition agreements were also meant to help with the achievement of reconciliation (EC 2010h: 21-22; EC 2013e: 22). While insisting on close cooperation on war crimes, the EU was mindful of the "special parallel relationships" existing between BiH's entities and Serbia and Croatia. Although the latter was publicly denounced by Zagreb, the former remained a source of concern (EC 2003c: 18).

In short, all three elements of the political level of SSR in Bosnia, supported by the EU, have targeted the improvement of security governance system in the country and security relations in the Western Balkans. In Bosnia, the EU efforts to strengthen the civilian and democratic control over security bodies were accompanied by calls for an overhaul of the weak constitutional system, created by Dayton to allow BiH to become a functioning state, capable of fulfilling demands of the integration process into Euro-Atlantic institutions. As political elites in BiH failed to reach consensus on the constitutional reform, a comprehensive system of oversight, with parliamentary, executive, judiciary and independent measures of control, built under supervision of external actors, including the EU, remains fragile. Cooperation with the ICTY and neighbouring countries on security matters also produced mixed results: while the level of cooperation achieved by 2013 would have been inconceivable right after the Bosnian war, it still lacked stability and irreversibility, leaving Bosnia's security sector vulnerable. The EU invested a lot of effort and finances into enhancing the good governance of BiH's security sector and harmonisation of the country's security relations with other Western Balkan states, especially Croatia and Serbia. Nonetheless, its work on the political level of SSR is not finished.

Organisational level

Having provided an important, although mixed, input into the political level of SSR in BiH, the EU engaged with the organisational level of defence, police and border reforms in the country even more vigorously. In *defence reform*, the DRC was convened by the HR, who also acted as the EUSR at the time. Moreover, the discovery of evidence by EUFOR in December 2004 that Ratko Mladic had been supported in hiding from the ICTY by the VRS, enabled the HR/EUSR to extend the mandate of the DRC, leading to the abolishment of the entity ministries of defence and establishment of a single state command structure of the military as well as a single army (Koneska 2014: 91-92). Although the contribution by the EU actors is important to acknowledge, it should not be overemphasised, as it was NATO's PfP conditionality that was leading defence reform in Bosnia initially (Vetschera and Damian 2006: 31). With time, as EUFOR's mandate evolved to include capacity-building activities and Bosnia's membership in NATO became less certain, due to the RS leadership choosing to side with Serbia (Bassuener 2015a: 5), the EU's role in Bosnia's defence reform grew. According to some security experts, the EU now leads defence reform in BiH "operationally" or "tactically", while NATO is still responsible for the strategic level[240]. In 1999-2013, the EU's impact on the reform is discernible in four key areas: policy and legal advice, training, technical assistance and support with overcoming the war legacy.

Policy advice was provided by the EU through EUFOR *Althea* and through EC annual reports. The latter monitored the implementation of key legislation in the sphere of defence and demanded harmonisation of BiH's legal acts with the EU's strategies and policies. For instance, the 2004 European Partnership called on Sarajevo to implement the Law on Defence as a matter of priority (Council of the EU 2004a). The Commission regularly criticised the outdated character of the BiH Demining law, that Bosnia was unsuccessfully trying to update with the help of UNDP since 2008 (EC 2011b: 20, AETS Consortium 2015: 31), and expressed dissatisfaction with the development of legislation on SALW (EC 2008g: 57). To comply with the EU requirements, BiH included activities and obligations from the EU Strategy on SALW (Council of the EU 2006c) into its SALW Control Strategies for 2006-2012 and 2013-2016 (MoS BiH 2016: 5). The general policy guidance was still left by the EU to NATO, which after admitting BiH to the PfP programme in 2006 continued closely cooperating with the state, although the 2010 invitation to join the Membership Action Plan (MAP) was still not acted upon in 2013, pending the resolution of the immovable defence property issue (NATO 2017). As the transfer of immovable defence property from entity to state level was identified by the PIC as one of the conditions for closing the OHR, the EU closely monitored it, too (EC 2008g: 12; EC 2013e: 7). EUFOR's input into the defence policy of BiH was more direct, yet its role in defence reform was still supplementary to NATO's (Bertin 2008: 74). EUFOR took over SFOR's responsibilities in December 2004, receiving the executive mandate to oversee the implementation of Annexes 1-A and 2 of the DPA under UNSCR Resolution 1575. The mandate, that had to be renewed annually under Chapter 7 of the UN Charter, identified four key military and four supporting tasks for the EU's third military operation[241] (Council of the EU 2004b). While the key tasks focused on deterrence, contributing to a safe and secure environment, supporting the OHR in peace implementation, conducting information operations and managing the residual aspects of the DPA, e.g. de-mining and weapons collections; supporting tasks included activities to fight organised crime, assistance in defence reform and support to the ICTY with tracing indictees (ibid.). Although defence reform assistance was initially given little attention by EUFOR, with changes to the mandate which were introduced four times in the studied period, the task moved up the operation's agenda. EUFOR was providing policy advice to the MoD and AF-BiH on gender equality and human rights (Pulko, Muherina and Pejic 2016:103) and on the development of normative frameworks for managing stockpiles of ammunition, weapons and explosives (Carapic, Chaudhuri and Gobinet 2016: 21). It is important to emphasise that EUFOR's policy advice was closely coordinated with NATO that kept small headquarters in Bosnia after the departure of SFOR to focus on defence reform and some operational supporting tasks like counter-terrorism and detention of persons indicted by the ICTY (Juncos 2013: 153). Moreover, NATO played a significant role in EUFOR's overall development.

The launch of EUFOR Althea was made possible thanks to the previous work of NATO's IFOR and SFOR that stabilised the security situation in the country, allowing the EU to enter a relatively risk-free environment (Peen Rodt and Wolff 2012: 142; Pulko, Muherina and Pejic 2016:93). Established as a Berlin Plus operation, EUFOR could also rely on NATO common assets and capabilities such as communication and information systems (Bertin 2008: 73). Furthermore, with nearly 80 per cent of SFOR troops coming from Europe and staying in Bosnia under EUFOR command after a change of insignia, EUFOR could settle down quickly (ibid.: 64). Despite some hiccups during the transition and minor overlaps in activities, EUFOR and NATO's cooperation has been working well (Peen Rodt and Wolff 2012: 148). While maintaining close working relations with NATO242, EUFOR aimed to support Bosnia on its journey towards the EU integration, especially as it was designed to be part of the EU's comprehensive approach to the country and the Western Balkans (European Council 2004). The alignment of EUFOR's activities with those of other EU actors present in BiH improved with time.

One of the biggest changes to EUFOR's mandate was introduced in January 2010, when the list of operation's tasks was extended to include non-executive capacity-building and training support for BiH authorities (Council of the EU 2010a), practically turning *Althea* into a military-civilian operation from a purely military one (Pulko, Muherina and Pejic 2016:93). In September 2012, the operation further reconfigured its focus to capacity-building and training of the AFBiH, while retaining its executive obligations, including support in maintaining a safe and secure environment in Bosnia[243] (EUFOR BiH 2016). Although some criticised the introduction of non-executive tasks (Bassuener 2015: 101), many welcomed this development as a step in the right direction (Knauer 2011: 12; Juncos 2013: 157). This is mostly because the introduction of the capacity-building element to EUFOR allowed the EU to become more actively engaged in the country's SSR and gave it new tools to assist BiH in becoming a security provider (Pulko, Muherina and Pejic 2016:94). One of the key goals pursued by EUFOR in this respect was building professionalism and capacity of the AFBiH to ensure it could perform a conventional army role and act as a humanitarian actor (ibid.). A new component, Mobile Training Teams (MTT), established within EUFOR, was used as a main tool for capacity-building, focusing on providing the BiH army with knowledge, technical expertise and mentoring assistance at tactical, operational and strategic levels (AETS Consortium 2015: 28). To facilitate local ownership of defence reform, the MTTs worked to transfer responsibility for the future training courses to the Bosnian authorities (Carapic, Chaudhuri and Gobinet 2016: 21-24). In 2010-2013, the EU also organised several rounds of "Rapid Response" exercises that involved Over-the-Horizon forces and EUFOR troops to train the AFBiH to deal with internal security threats (Bassuener 2015: 101). Overall, capacity-building and training support provided by EUFOR was a useful contribution into the AFBiH's self-sustainability (Pulko, Muherina and Pejic 2016:94).

Technical assistance to defence reform was provided by the EU mostly regarding post-conflict reconstruction and modernisation of the army. Thus, EUFOR provided advice on inventory maintenance and management, while MTT trainings often focused on assisting the AFBiH staff with acquiring skills necessary for operating new equipment (Carapic, Chaudhuri and Gobinet 2016: 24). It was not an easy task as the AFBiH lacked resources for procurement and EUFOR could not purchase the equipment either (Pulko, Muherina and Pejic 2016: 100). To alleviate the problem, EUFOR used its own assets to train the AFBiH (ibid.) or relied on equipment donations from participating MTT countries (Carapic, Chaudhuri and Gobinet 2016:21). By dealing with residual tasks of the DPA such as supervision of storage sites and disposal of surplus weapons, EUFOR contributed to technical aspects of defence reform, too (EC 2007e: 12). With the downsizing of the operation, however, responsibility for these areas was transferred to local actors (Juncos 2013: 157). The bulk of the EU's technical assistance concentrated on dealing with the issue of small and light weapons. The EU considered the lack of control over this area to be an obstacle to the establishment of the rule of law, sustainable economic development and human security in the country (Hadzovic, Krzalic and Mihajlovic 2013: 8). Uncontrolled presence of SALW also drained the MoD budget and posed a threat to civilians (AETS Consortium 2015: 9). Like in the rest of the region, in BiH, the EU worked through the EUSAC framework within SEESAC. It supported SALW collection campaigns, raising awareness among the BiH citizens about dangers of SALW and unexploded ordnances, improved security of storage sites and promoted regional cooperation (SEESAC 2013; SEESAC 2014). In many cases, EUSAC activities had a regional dimension that apart from improving regional security was also aimed at rebuilding trust and achieving reconciliation in the Western Balkans.

The size of the threat posed by SALW in BiH prompted the EU to look for additional ways of tackling the issue. Thus, it provided nearly 5 million EUR under the Instrument for Stability (IfS) to support the UNDP's "Small Arms Control and Reduction Project in BiH", the two phases of which in 2008-2009 and 2009-2011 destroyed over 8, 300 tonnes of ammunition (AETS Consortium 2015: 9). In 2013, a follow-up programme was launched by the UNDP and OSCE, for which the EU allocated 3.9 million EUR under the IfS (ibid.). By supporting these actions, the EU contributed to the security, safety and development prospective of individuals and local communities, affected by the problem (Council of the EU 2014). Unfortunately, in 2013, with nearly 1.2 million firearms spread around the country, 89 per cent of which were in civilian possession, the problem was still lacking resolution (Hadzovic, Krzalic and Mihajlovic 2013: 10).

The situation was somewhat similar in the sphere of de-mining. In 2013, 1,219 km2 remained contaminated despite continuous efforts of local and international actors to remove the mine threat from BiH (Mine Action Review 2014). Since 1996, the EU has been a key stakeholder in Bosnia's de-mining process, having spent around 40 million EUR in the period to 2013 (AETS Consortium 2015: 3). While EUFOR restricted its engagement in mine action over time, the European Commission continued supporting the sector through donations under CARDS, IPA and Anti-Personnel Landmines (APL) programmes (EC 2008i: 8). Under CARDS[244], the EU allocated funds to strengthen the CPA capacities to conduct de-mining projects independently under the entity supervision and under APL[245], assisted BiH authorities with the removal of anti-personnel land mines. Problems with inter-entity coordination of CPA activities and lack of transparency in the work of the BHMAC, the agency supervising mine-related issues on the state level, undermined the effectiveness of the EU's mine action under CARDS and APL (Mine Action Review 2014). Nonetheless, the EU kept supporting de-mining in BiH through IPA. Even more, it increased the variety of projects on offer. Specifically, it funded projects on mine clearance and technical survey (e.g. under IPA 2007, 2008 and 2011), mine risk education (e.g. IPA 2008 project managed by "Posavina without mines"), mine victim assistance and land release (both under IPA 2011) (AETS Consortium 2015: 59). While the bloc closely aligned its mine action support with local strategies, the most recent of which was released in 2009, and managed to achieve most results set within individual projects, BiH still lacks the capacity and resources to make the mine threat an issue of the past (ibid.: 31). Without an updated legal framework, reformed and more transparent BHMAC, Bosnia is unlikely to reach a proclaimed goal of becoming mine-free by 2019. Apart from assisting with de-mining and SALW problem, the EU's post-conflict support focused on cooperation with the ICTY. As already mentioned, the EUFOR's mandate included the search for persons indicted for war crimes by the ICTY (Council of the EU 2004b), which was widely perceived as one of its key contributions into stabilisation and peace-building in Bosnia (Knauer 2011: 17).

To conclude, the EU played an active role in Bosnia's defence reform in 1999-2013, acting through the European Commission, HR/EUSR and EUFOR. The latter's presence gave the EU an opportunity to promote change in BiH's defence sector more directly than it did in Croatia and Serbia. Nevertheless, its efforts came secondary to those of NATO that remained in charge of defence reform in the country. In 2013, BiH remained dependent on external provisions of security, although local ownership considerably increased in the sphere, partly thanks to EUFOR's work.

In *police reform*, the EU quickly assumed the leadership role, although in 2000 the operational level was still handled by the IPTF, while the OHR managed the reform strategically. In 2003, the EU not only launched the EUPM, that worked "to establish sustainable policing arrangements under Bosnia ownership" (Council of the EU 2002a), but also named police reform among sixteen political conditions Bosnia had to satisfy to start negotiations on the SAA (EC 2003c: 41). In 2004, police reform became part of the EU's political conditionality, when the EU Commissioner for External Relations Chris Patten presented Bosnian authorities with the list of three policing principles, they had to fulfil to sign the SAA (Patten 2004). It is widely believed that these principles originated in the OHR and made their way into the SAP under the pressure of Paddy Ashdown, the then HR/EUSR, who considered centralisation of the police an important step in the state-building process of BiH (Muehlmann 2009: 156; Noutcheva 2012: 167; Tolksdorf 2014: 65). For the EU, at least initially, centralisation was not the only possible way of dealing with inefficient policing in BiH. A functional review, financed by the European Commission and released in June 2004, found that the presence of fifteen law enforcement agencies (thirteen police forces and two state-level institutions, SBS and SIPA), was not the core problem, but one of many in BiH (ICMPD and TC

Team Consult 2004). The study offered three possible models for restructuring the Bosnian police: (1) single national police with 5-7 regions; (2) two entity police forces, the Brcko District police, SIPA, SBS and several state-level coordinating bodies, but no cantonal forces; and (3) a bottom-up approach that would keep all the law enforcement bodies in the country while developing several state-level support institutions (ibid.: 118).

Once the first, top-down, model was identified by the HR/EUSR as most suitable[246] and three policing principles were made part of the SAA negotiations, the EU had to find a way to move police reform in BiH forward. The task proved problematic, as the bloc was neither willing to impose the reform, nor able to convince local elites to adopt it voluntarily. Imposition, for example through the HR's Bonn powers, was opposed by the European Commission due to the sensitivity of the matter and complexity of the reform's implementation (Noutcheva 2012: 125, 161). Securing support of domestic actors was out of reach, too. Both normative and efficiency arguments used by the EU and HR/EUSR to help parties reach consensus within the PRC and later the Directorate for the Implementation of Police Restructuring (DIPR), set up in 2006, lacked substance. The presence of decentralised police forces in many EU states and EU's insistence on police decentralisation in other Western Balkan states allowed Bosnian Serbs, who obstructed the reform the most[247], reject European standards as an adequate justification for the centralised police in BiH. The efficiency argument, while difficult to counteract, was not powerful enough on its own to coax Bosnian elites into re-drawing the LPA boundaries. Besides, many in the RS considered police restructuring to be an attempt at constitutional restructuring of the state and therefore actively resisted it (Collantes-Cellador 2009). A perceived threat to their autonomy and identity[248] fed Bosnian Serb opposition to establishing new LPAs by crossing the inter-entity boundary. While the EU wanted BiH to overcome constitutional weaknesses of Dayton and saw a more centralised model as preferable, it lacked the mandate to demand such changes[249] (Noutcheva 2012: 60). Without such a mandate and in circumstances of increasingly volatile domestic and fragile regional environment, the EU had to lower the bar for police reform on several occasions. In 2005, with the start of accession talks with Croatia, and the launch of SAA talks with Serbia and Montenegro, BiH was the only Western Balkan state[250] without a contractual relationship with the EU (ibid.: 126). To avoid the country's isolation, the EU accepted a watered-down proposal, developed by the RS President Cavic, as compliant with the three principles and recommended starting SAA negotiations on 21 October 2005. In 2007, with the political crisis brought about by reforms of the then HR/EUSR Miroslav Lajcak, who tried to relax veto mechanisms in BiH, and upcoming independence of Kosovo threatening to upset the regional balance, the EU settled for a compromise that promised to establish seven new state-level coordination bodies and made restructuring of the police conditional on the future constitutional reform (Tolksdorf 2013: 23-24). By lowering demands, the EU, on the one hand, rescued the SAA with Bosnia, and on the other, damaged the credibility of its conditionality. Nonetheless, even with the failure of the police restructuring, the EU managed to leave important impact on police reform in BiH, which although focused on the question of centralisation in 2005-2008, involved other aspects, too.

The EU provided policy and legal advice to police reform through several channels. Having included the three principles of policing into the SAP, the European Commission provided a general framework for the reform. By supporting the PRC financially and refusing to sign the SAA without an agreement on police restructuring, the Commission also tried to shape the progress of the reform, yet without resorting to the direct imposition techniques[251]. The HR/EUSR Ashdown, who convened the PRC, and his successors who continued the efforts to restructure the police, Christian Schwarz-Schilling and Miroslav Lajcak[252], represented the EU as well, although their EUSR hat was relatively unknown to the public (Muehlmann 2009: 157). The political elites, on the other hand, were familiar with the EU credentials of the HRs, as the latter regularly referred to EU conditionality and EU standards when facilitating the reform. Moreover, the European Commission supported the implementation of decisions and laws adopted as part of police reform. It did so not only by monitoring progress and identifying gaps in strategic policing documents through annual reports (EC 2009c: 58; EC 2010h: 14, 57-58; EC 2013e: 52), but also through allocating funds to the EU Delegation to BiH via CARDS and IPA. Although most of this work focused on technical assistance and capacity-building, there were also projects offering policy and legal support to Bosnian authorities. In 2008, for example, after the BiH Parliament adopted two laws envisaged in the Mostar Declaration, the EU commissioned a team of rule of law experts to work in the EU Delegation office in Sarajevo on supporting local actors in the implementation of these laws and on legal harmonisation between the state, entity, Brcko district and cantonal levels.[253] After the end of the EUPM's mandate in 2012, a Law Enforcement Section was established in the Delegation, to continue providing strategic and policy advice on policing and wider rule of law issues, as well as support Bosnian law enforcement agencies through technical assistance.[254]

The EUPM[255] provided policy and legal advice too, although cautiously at first. Launched in January 2003, the mission had a limited mandate to monitor, mentor and inspect the Bosnian police to align their practices with international standards and contribute to peace implementation in BiH (Merlingen and Ostauskaite 2006: 61). Even without a mandate to contribute to police reform, the EUPM worked with the OHR on different concepts of police restructuring from the start of the PRC (Muehlmann 2009: 143). The Head of the EUPM was also a member of the PRC. Furthermore, in 2003-2005, the mission helped with drafting and implementing laws and other expert advice on police matters (Juncos 2013: 144). Although the IPTF considerably improved operational capabilities of many of the BiH police forces, very little was done to develop support functions of the police (Metz 2010: 59). The EUPM attempted to change the situation by investing into policy planning, budgeting and human resources management (ibid.). While these contributions were important, they were also limited as in the first years of existence the EUPM struggled to find an identity. To ensure continuity, 119 IPTF experts and the IPTF Commissioner stayed on to work for the EUPM (Padurariu 2014: 6). Although this smoothed the transition, it also made it difficult for the EUPM to develop an independent profile (Merlingen and Ostauskaite 2006: 61). Tensions with EUFOR over the fight with organised crime also contributed to the EUPM's identity problems. EUFOR, having converted the SFOR's Multinational Specialised Unit into the Integrated Police Unit, used it to fight illegal activities such as weapons smuggling and drug trafficking (ibid.: 56-57), which undermined the EUPM's efforts in the field. The situation improved in 2005-2006, when the EUPM, EUFOR and the EUSR agreed on Seven Principles on Coordination and Operational Guidelines that made the EUPM a leading CSDP actor for tackling organised crime in BiH, while EUFOR was prescribed a supporting role (Juncos 2013: 140). Additionally, in 2006, the EUPM received stronger powers for dealing with organised crime and given a mandate to assist police reform (Tolksdorf 2013: 23). The mission therefore helped with the implementation of the 2008 police laws and establishment of the Directorate for Coordination of Police Bodies (Juncos 2013: 145). It was also thanks to the EUPM assistance that state-level police agencies, such as SIPA and SBS/border police became fully operational (Padurariu 2014: 8). Overall, however, the EUPM paid more attention to training activities and technical assistance. It was engaged in educating and instructing local police officers through a variety of projects, many of which, at least initially, were based on co-locating EUPM personnel at mid and senior levels of BiH police agencies (Collantes-Celador 2009). Although co-location practices became less common after the first renewal of the EUPM's mandate in 2006, the EUPM continued prioritising raising professionalism levels of the BiH police and developing managerial skills among police leadership (Metz 2010: 60).

While some of the EUPM projects, such as the Police Education and Training Programme launched in 2004, focused exclusively on capacity-building, many others included a training component alongside other tasks (Merlingen and Ostauskaite 2006: 67). These latter projects could be roughly divided into initiatives promoting specialisation and modernisation of BiH's law enforcement. Specialisation was necessary for achieving effectiveness in dealing with different types of crimes. The crime police programme that combined basic criminal investigation training with training in the criminal procedure code and the criminal justice programme that mentored court police officers are examples of the EUPM initiatives promoting specialisation (ibid.: 65-66). Modernisation was meant to help the Bosnian police overcome not only the legacy of war, but also move from the socialist past to the European future. Although the IPTF conducted some important work in this respect, the fractured nature of the country's police forces meant more needed to be done. The EUPM assisted police officers on all levels to improve their IT and communication skills, acquire competence in intelligence-led policing and independent law enforcement according to the best EU and international standards (EEAS 2012). One of the biggest achievements of the EUPM was the engagement with the policing staff in all parts of BiH through regional and field offices (ibid.). Unfortunately, accomplishments of the mission were undermined by its project-based approach, that although at times attempted a long-term structural reform, especially through its capacity-building activities, mostly dealt with specific disconnected issues (ibid.; Juncos 2013: 142).

A broader approach to police reform was pursued by the European Commission that worked to prepare BiH for the EU membership through CARDS and IPA projects. Due to initial gaps in coordination between the EU Delegation, that managed such projects, the EUPM, EUSR and other external actors engaged in police reform in BiH, such as the OHR and USAID, as well as due to the lack of uniformity in police matters across the two entities, the Commission's approach also had limitations. Overall, the European Commission projects and those of the EUPM pursued similar goals — strengthening the sustainability and independence of BiH's law enforcement agencies, harmonising their practices and improving efficiency of their work. Moreover, in both, technical assistance played an important role. Thanks to CARDS and IPA funding, various police bodies in BiH acquired modern equipment, adopted rules and procedures for exchanging information and improved connectivity between each other through the introduction of shared databases. For example, through projects funded by the European Commission, BiH aquired the Criminal Analysis Network — a central database for storing all intelligence data and a telecommunications system that connects police units throughout the country

(Dimireva 2010). While these initiatives considerably improved the work of the Bosnian police, they did not solve the issue of structural fragmentation that plagued the sector's development. As observed by several interviewees with experience in police reform in BiH, police coordination and cooperation remain weak not only between the entities, but also between cantons in the Federation.[256]

Technical assistance provided by the EUPM produced similar results: although it contributed to the improved professionalism and accountability of the police in BiH, more harmonised policing practices in different parts of the country and operationalisation of state-level bodies, it did not overcome the divisions (Merlingen and Ostauskaite 2006: 66-67; Padurariu 2014: 7-10). It is worth noting that the EUPM's engagement in technical assistance developed with the evolution of the mission's mandate that was updated four times between 2006 and 2012. Thus, if at first, the EUPM emphasised standardisation and accountability of the police, with the introduction of the second mandate, it prioritised the development of capabilities for fighting organised crime and centralisation of Bosnian law enforcement, while at the end, it facilitated cooperation between the police and criminal justice system (Padurariu 2014: 7). To achieve coherence of action between different police bodies in the entities and Brcko District, the EUPM invested in standardised record keeping systems, financial management systems, based on models from EU member states, and harmonised recruitment processes (Merlingen and Ostauskaite 2006: 69-70). To ensure effective fight against organised crime, the EUPM developed guidelines on intelligence-led policing and procedures for data protection, assisted local actors in planning and conducting investigations, often relying on EUFOR's capabilities, and supported the development of investigative powers of SIPA (ibid.: 66; Juncos 2013: 140; Padurariu 2014: 8). Having achieved an extension of SIPA's competences through lobbying for a stronger mandate together with the OHR, the EUPM assisted the agency's work through advice and mentoring on effective management of data, cooperation with the Court of BiH, the Prosecutor's Office and lower-level police institutions (Metz 2010: 59-60; Becirevic and Cehajic 2013: 48). The fight against organised crime and strengthening capabilities of state-level institutions remained at the centre of the EU attention even after the departure of the EUPM in 2012.

In terms of post-conflict assistance, the EU's impact after 2000 was limited. The EUPM, unlike the IPTF could not dismiss local police officers deemed to be involved in war crimes or obstructing cooperation with the ICTY (Merlingen and Ostauskaite 2006: 63). The Head of the mission could recommend the dismissal of individual officers to the OHR, yet this practice was used on very few occasions (Juncos 2013: 143). Nonetheless, the EUPM made some impact on this area through improving cooperation between the police and judiciary, which led to higher confidence of the ICTY in the latter.[257]

Overall, for the most part of the third studied period, the EU led police reform efforts in BiH though the SAP conditionality, a double-hatted position of the HR/EUSR and its first civilian mission, the EUMP[258]. The inability of the bloc to justify requirements for centralisation of the police with the provisions of the DPA, the *acquis* or its own practices in other countries and get all its agencies present in Bosnia act in unison damaged the reform efforts. To prevent BiH from falling behind other Western Balkan states, Brussels had to settle for a compromise, postponing the finalisation of police restructuring until the domestic elites agree on a broader constitutional revision. Although the EU was unable to complete the process of restructuring, it contributed to the reform in many other ways, which are often overlooked. By 2013, the European Commission and EUPM strengthened the local ownership of the reform, improved the professionalism and accountability of the local police forces, as well as their crime fighting capabilities, and were instrumental in harmonising legislation on the state, entity, cantonal and Brcko District levels. The changes achieved "advanced the transformation of the Bosnian police from an instrument of ethnic warfare into a professional service" (Merlingen 2009: 162). Still, the biggest challenges facing the police in Bosnia, i.e. politicisation and fragmentation, were left unanswered, rendering police reform in the country incomplete, which it will remain while BiH is undergoing the process of state-building. Having linked the integration process with the reform, the EU would not be able to abandon it half-way without sustaining considerable reputational damage.

The final aspect of SSR in BiH considered here is *border reform*. Although border reform was started by the PIC in 1997 and managed for the first few years by the OHR and UN[259], it was transferred into the EU's ownership already in 2003. This happened thanks to the launch of the EUPM, which from the onset took on several border security improvement projects (Eralp 2012; 101) and due to BiH committing to the EU standards of border control at the Ohrid Border Conference and consequently to the Guidelines for IBM in the Western Balkans, released by the Commission in 2004. Even before 2003, the EU's impact on border security was noticeable: while the European Commission pressed for the establishment of the SBS in the Road Map to allow BiH progress in the SAP, the UNMIBH's Border Police Department and the IPTF ensured that the SBS's operational model was based on EU standards and norms (Hills 2006: 198). Although the SBS could control BiH's external borders already in 2002, the agency was still weak and in need of guidance when the IPTF left the country (Skogstrom 2006). The EU's assistance therefore was crucial to ensure it was fully operational and relied on a well-developed policy and legal framework. Established by a law, imposed by the HR in 2000, the SBS's legal basis was fragile. Due to several amendments to the Law on the State Border Service in 2004 and 2007, that were partly inspired by the EU requirements, partly by the need to improve the efficiency of the service, the SBS, renamed the border police in 2007, strengthened its position among the state-level law enforcement agencies of BiH (BPBiH n.d.). Moreover, many laws specifying competences of BiH's border police, were either adopted or underwent changes to satisfy EU conditionality, e.g. the Law on border control was adopted in 2009, and Law on movement and stay of aliens and asylum, was released in 2003, and updated in 2008 and 2012 under EU pressure (EC 2009c: 55; EC 2008g: 54; MoS BiH 2015: 72-73).

Moreover, the EU's support was crucial for the development and implementation of BiH's IBM strategy to pursue the creation of open and secure borders (Collantes-Celador and Juncos 2012: 204). The first national Strategy on IBM, adopted in July 2005, benefited from the 2002 CARDS regional project "Support to and Coordination of Integrated Border Management Strategies", while the 2008 revised version of the strategy and Action Plan on the IBM directly resulted from the 2005 CARDS project "EU Support for the Implementation of the Integrated Border Management Strategy for Bosnia and Herzegovina" (EC 2008j). With the launch of IPA in 2007, the European Commission continued supporting the IBM strategy in Bosnia. Later projects such as the IPA 2008 "Support for the Implementation of the BiH IBM Strategy and Action Plan" addressed not only harmonisation of the BiH IBM legislation with EU standards and development of common risk analysis, but also coordination of work between all institutions involved in the concept (DEUBiH 2012; DEUBiH 2015). Apart from the border police, the IBM in Bosnia involves the Indirect Taxation Authority (ITA), State Veterinary Office, State Plant Health Administration of BiH, Service for Foreigners' Affairs and three Border Inspectorates established at the entity level and the Brcko Disctrict (DEUBiH 2015). The MoS is the national coordinator for the implementation of the IBM strategy. As explained in chapters on SSR in Croatia and Serbia, the IBM concept in the Western Balkans focuses on three pillars: intra-service cooperation, inter-agency cooperation and international cooperation. Although CARDS projects started addressing the second and third pillars in addition to the first one, it was IPA that contributed to improved cooperation between different services involved in border management in BiH and development of their international connections the most (Collantes-Celador and Juncos 2012: 205). Thus, one of the elements of the above-mentioned IPA 2008 project supported the development of a clear communication and coordination structure between the border management agencies in the country (IPA 2008k: 5-7). It is worth mentioning that the EUPM supported the development of the IBM legal framework through its own projects (Skogstrom 2006; Eralp 2012: 101), yet its assistance was more extensive in the areas of capacity-building and technical aid.

In terms of policy and legal advice, the analysis of the EU's influence cannot be complete without considering reforms introduced by the Roadmap for visa liberalisation. In June 2008, the European Commission set requirements for substantial reforms to be implemented in four key areas to allow BiH citizens visa-free travel to the Schengen zone (EC 2008l). The areas that included document security, illegal migration, public order and security, and external relations and fundamental rights brought about technical (e.g. improved infrastructure for asylum procedure) and legal changes (e.g. harmonisation of criminal codes on all levels, implementation of the Law on citizenship, Law on data protection, National Anti-Corruption Strategy, etc.) (Populari and ESI 2009). Despite a demanding character of these reforms, leaders from both entities showed unanimity in supporting their implementation (Noutcheva 2012: 130). The tangible promise of visa-free travel to the Schengen zone temporarily united the camps that were normally in opposition. It would be wrong the assume, however, that the reforms went smoothly. In May 2009, Bosnia scored lowest among other Western Balkan states participating in the process[260], which prevented it from achieving a visa-free Schengen travel at the end of 2009 with Macedonia, Montenegro and Serbia that emerged as reform leaders (Knaus 2009). To catch up with the neighbours, within only several months, BiH implemented colossal changes to the sensitive area of security: it introduced biometric passports; adopted key legislation on issues ranging from border control to prevention of financing terrorist activities; and improved working relations with EU member states, neighbouring countries and EU agencies involved in policing, justice and border matters — Eurojust, Europol and Frontex[261] (ibid.). This allowed the European Commission to recommend visa liberalisation for Bosnia in November 2010 (Noutcheva 2012: 130). The experience of reforms in 2008-2010 challenged the image of Bosnia as a dysfunctional state and confirmed the EU's SSR capabilities. By holding BiH accountable to the same benchmarks as the rest of the region and by offering a real incentive, based on European standards supported by the *acquis*, the EU demonstrated it could persuade Bosnian elites to implement even highly demanding reforms of the security sector (Knaus 2009). After the visa liberalisation process was successfully completed by BiH, the EU continued promoting the harmonisation of BiH legislation on border management with the EU standards, especially in terms of the IBM[262], and conditioning of the BiH border police to work according to best Schengen practices (DEUBiH 2015a).

Policy and legal work in BiH's border control went hand in hand with capacity-building and technical assistance. As already mentioned, the EUPM played an important role in both. It entered Bosnia at a time, when the country's security situation was mostly stable, but state-level security institutions, including the SBS, were still fragile. Entrusted with helping the locals develop a working common policing space, the EU's police mission identified the SBS development among its key priorities (Merlingen and Ostauskaite 2006: 71). Capacity-building programmes, run by the EUPM encompassed technical training, projects for higher management and specialised training to combat organised crime. The scope and focus of technical exercises varied considerably: some programmes provided on-demand training to border guards on how to detect forgery (ibid.) or use high-tech surveillance equipment, often donated by the EU states, while others offered advice to separate agencies involved in the IBM on regulations, procedures and standards they required to implement to comply with the EU guidelines (Eralp 2012: 101). Similarly, these agencies were offered help in developing working relations between each other, e.g. EUPM used the co-location procedure to improve coordination between the ITA, SIPA and other policing bodies (Padurariu 2014: 10). Co-location was also used to develop the management capacity of senior SBS officers. Thus, a 70-strong co-location team, mostly from Germany, mentored top border officers on ways to delegate authority, transparency in decision-making and importance of planning and risk analysis for effective border control (Merlingen and Ostauskaite 2006: 71). Focus on the management level, just like in police reform, was perceived by the EUPM to be of key importance for developing local ownership in border security (Skogstrom 2006). Capacity-building programmes with the emphasis on fighting cross-border organised crime, including trafficking of arms, persons and drugs, became more common after the update of the EUPM mandate in 2006 (Padurariu 2014: 8). Improved capacities for fighting organised crime and corruption were also among the main goals of projects funded by the European Commission through CARDS and IPA, as demonstrated by the CARDS 2006 project "Support to the State Border Service" and elements of the IPA 2010 "The EU

Support to Law Enforcement in BiH" (EC 2006h; DEUBiH 2015b). These projects were often more ambitious and comprehensive than projects of the EUPM, as they contained various other elements e.g. technical and policy assistance.

Technical assistance to the SBS/border police was of utmost importance, too, as BiH had no experience of managing external borders until 1995. The country's needs in this respect were also heightened due to war damage. The EUPM and European Commission-funded projects offered the Bosnian border police modern equipment, databases, infrastructure for forensics and biometrics as well as support with constructing border crossing points (BCPs)/closing illegal crossings. Initially, at least for the Commission, supply projects were prioritised. Thus, supply of surveillance and protection equipment was ensured through CARDS 2001 and 2002 programmes, while CARDS 2003 funds were allocated for the acquisition of an Automatic Fingerprint Identification System, supply of hardware for Weapons Database System, national DNA Database System and Criminal Analysis Network (EC 2006h). By the time IPA was launched, the Bosnian border police had basic equipment, and the focus shifted onto the infrastructure necessary to comply with the Schengen requirements and improvement of connectivity and cooperation between different border services. The EU support was crucial for connecting separate databases on migration and border control existing in BiH into a single network, improving data exchange between numerous police agencies in Bosnia[263]. Similarly, the EU demands and financial assistance were behind the development of the integrated system of control of state border crossings (CSBS) that connected all international BCPs in BiH by 2013 (EC 2013e: 49). The EUPM, while not providing the equipment to the border police, offered substantial operational support to border management agencies on maintaining it, e.g. through inventory management[264]. Working on developing local ownership, it refused to get involved in guarding the borders (Eralp 2012; 101). EUFOR, however, during the first two years in BiH, did not shy away from patrolling borders and organising operations to tackle trans-border crime (Friesendorf and Penksa 2008: 683). It also provided the SBS with high-tech equipment, e.g. aerial military maps and night-vision goggles, and trained the border police in using it (ibid.).

One of the areas of technical assistance that remained topical till the end of the studied period was linked to border crossings. Thanks to more than 12 million EUR under CARDS 2001-2004, BiH constructed and equipped BCPs in several key locations such as Orasje, Gradina—Jasenovac and Kamensko (ITABiH 2007). Work on more BCPs continued even after 2013 (EC 2013e: 49). Blocking illegal border crossings along Bosnia's 1,551 km state border was a similarly challenging task that BiH could not complete on its own. The length of the state border and geography of the country created favourable opportunities for cross-border organised crime that exploited weaknesses in the country's border control. Having made the first financial contribution into the elimination of unauthorised BCPs towards Croatia in 2003 (Court of Auditors 2007), the EU continued prioritising this area of border reform even a decade later. Thanks to the EU assistance, all illegal border crossings towards Croatia were closed by 2009[265] and by 2013—towards Montenegro, leaving only the closure of unauthorised BCPs on the border with Serbia pending (EC 2013e: 49). Securing the Croatian border first was not accidental, as from June 2013 it became the external border of the EU. Support to Bosnia's border crossings therefore, as well as technical assistance to the country's border police in general, was used as a tool for developing security structures and capacities needed for achieving an effective line of defence for the EU (Hills 2006: 198).

Another area of border security that attracted the EU's attention was the issue of border delineation. Although a small country, Bosnia has one of the longest state borders in Europe. After the war, it had only two neighbours—Croatia and the FRY, which after 2006 turned into three: Croatia, Serbia and Montenegro. None of the three neighbours had a ratified demarcation agreement with BiH in 2013[266], and all had unresolved border disputes. Montenegro disagreed with BiH over the Sandzak area[267], Serbia—over the meandering Drina River and the area around Bajina Basta, while Croatia had a long list of disputes with Bosnia[268], among which issues around the Bosnian coast-line around Neum and Croatian Port of

Ploce were the most contentious (Gosar 2012: 90-92). Like in Serbia and Croatia, the EU monitored existing border disputes in BiH through progress reports of the European Commission, while approaching them as bilateral problems (EC 2013e: 21-22). Nonetheless, the involvement of the bloc was necessary to facilitate agreements on border management between BiH and Croatia on the eve of the latter's joining the EU. In general, the EU's role in finding a solution to Bosnia's border disputes was minimal, which can change with BiH gaining the status of a candidate for membership in the bloc.

To conclude, the EU in BiH approached border reform in a similar way to border reforms in Croatia and Serbia. It provided policy and legal advice on the implementation of the IBM strategy (first in line with the concept for the Western Balkans, then for the EU), harmonisation of BiH legislation with the Schengen practices and improvement of cooperation with its member states and agencies. It also invested substantial resources into capacity-building of all services involved in border management, modernisation of equipment and infrastructure at BCPs and development of data and information exchange networks, necessary for managing borders, as well as achieving effective asylum and migration policies. While criticising border disputes with neighbours in European Commission's progress reports, the EU preferred not to link them with the process of integration into the bloc. It is important to acknowledge that in Bosnia, unlike in Croatia and Serbia, the European Commission's efforts to improve border security were supported by Council instruments, namely the EUPM and EUFOR. The EUSR was promoting the reform, too. Compared to other elements of security sector in BiH, border security is often presented as the area that had the most robust and comprehensive reform, and the EU contribution plaid an important role in the process.[269]

Conclusion

Compared to Croatia and Serbia, the transformation experienced by Bosnia in 1991-2013 is simultaneously less and more substantial. On the one hand, 18 years after the war, BiH could not yet fully exercise its sovereignty due to the continuing civilian and military presence of the international community in the country. Moreover, the process of Euro-Atlantic integration produced limited results: having joined NATO's PfP in 2006 and received invitation for the MAP in 2010, Bosnia's relationship with the alliance stalled, while decade-long negotiations with the EU did not even result in a candidate status. On the other hand, the country reached stability after the most violent conflict seen in Europe since World War II, developed institutions normally found in a democracy and implemented a rage of demanding reforms. Given the devastation left by the war in 1995 and weak statehood created by Dayton, these achievements are not insignificant. The process of BiH's development in the studied period was therefore rather uneven. SSR reflects this unevenness, too.

In the sphere of defence, instead of three separate conscription-based armies at the end of the war, BiH now has a unified professional army under a single chain of command and civilian oversight. There are also the single state-level border police, responsible for border management and security, as well as implementation of the EU's IBM standards in cooperation with other border management services. The only security service that resisted centralisation was the police. Although several state-level agencies, such as SIPA and Directorate for Coordination of Police Bodies were established, both entities kept their own police forces organised according to two different models. This is not to say police reform brought no results: professionalism of police officers and efficiency of policing in the Federation and RS were considerably improved, largely thanks to the UN's IPTF and EU's Police Mission. Nonetheless, Bosnian police agencies are still highly politicised and disconnected, which means police reform and SSR in the country more generally remain incomplete.

The unfinished SSR is of concern to the EU, which linked elements of the reform to the promise of membership in the bloc and made Bosnia a testing ground for its civilian and military crisis missions. Even when in 2022, BiH was offered a conditional offer of a candidate status, it was linked to the fulfilment of SSR requirements. With the help of EUFOR *Althea* and the EUPM, double-hatting of the HR as EUSR, as well as a growing profile of the SAP, by 2013, the EU evolved into the leader of border and police reforms and a tactical guide of defence reform in Bosnia. Unfortunately, the SSR agenda, promoted by the EU did not bring the local elites fully together. While Bosniak, Bosnian Croat and Bosnian Serb leaders (as well as most of the opposition) agreed on the future of BiH in the EU, they disagreed on what was needed to achieve the membership. As certain elements of SSR put an emphasis on centralisation, the RS leadership and to, a lesser extent, Bosnian Croat elites feared this could lead to the reduced autonomy of the ethnic groups they were representing and eventual restructuring of the state. The link between SSR and state-building in BiH is the most visible and problematic among the studied Western Balkan states. Until the two entities and three key ethnic groups agree on the future constitutional shape of the country, the EU, and entire international community, will have to accept a limited character of the reform in the country. Based on the analysis presented in the chapter, five considerations can be drawn about the EU's role in SSR in BiH.

First, it should be highlighted that *EU's SSR agenda has been closely intertwined with SSR activities undertaken by other external actors*. Both the EUPM and EUFOR benefited from the groundwork, conducted by the UN and NATO respectively, while the missions cooperated with these, and many other actors, to fulfil their constantly evolving mandates. Joining the HR and EUSR positions in 2002-2011 brought the EU even closer to the rest of the international community which mostly worked in unison on peace and state-building in BiH. This closeness, while largely seen as beneficial to Bosnia, made it difficult to differentiate the EU's SSR efforts in the country and introduced an element of confusion for local actors that could not always tell whose conditionality they were fulfilling. Moreover, as police restructuring illustrated, the overlapping of reform agendas undermined the EU's credibility and opened its conditionality to criticism.

Second, *in BiH, the EU had a wider choice of tools for promoting SSR than in Croatia and Serbia*. Alongside the financial help and conditions coming from the European Commission, Bosnian SSR was influenced by the Council that acted through the EUSR, EUPM and

EUFOR. This allowed the EU to approach border, police and defence reforms in BiH more deeply and consistently.

Third, by engaging in SSR in Bosnia, *the EU demonstrated an ability to adapt and learn* (Juncos 2013). From an actor marginally involved in de-mining and police reform in a single town, that was providing support to others, it evolved into an agenda setter. Even when the SAP started guiding the region and BiH's development, the EU kept adapting to the situation on the ground. For instance, it updated the mandates of the EUPM and EUFOR on several occasions. It also adjusted requirements for police restructuring in 2005 and 2008 when it became clear no consensus would be reached on the reform. Although these actions are often criticised as a sign of weakness, the critics forget that the EU was unable to justify centralisation requirements through the *acquis* or common practices in the bloc. Failure to compromise therefore could have led to the isolation of BiH.

Fourth, *SSR in Bosnia, just like SSR in Croatia and Serbia, was used as a means of member state-building*. Yet the distant nature of the membership promise, the absence of *acquis* behind certain demands and weakness of the state made the "pull of Brussels" less effective in Bosnia than in its neighbouring countries. The disagreements between political elites in the country regarding the future shape of BiH introduced another layer of difficulty for SSR and other reforms. Conflicting visions of the Bosnian statehood, promoted by the political leadership of the entities, undermine the EU's efforts to bring BiH into the EU family. As long as there is no consensus between the entities on the constitutional structure of the state, Bosnia's place in the embryonic security community emerging in the Western Balkans is threatened.

Finally, *the EU's SSR efforts in BiH had a clear regional dimension*. Whether it was cooperation with the ICTY, joint border controls or police cooperation to fight organised crime, the EU encouraged BiH officials to work closely with their neighbours. Special attention was paid to BiH's relations with Serbia and Croatia, due to their role in the war of 1992-1995 and the influence they retained over their ethnic populations in the country. In the absence of regional trust, the EU's impetus was important for establishing working relations between key security bodies of the three former adversaries, trying to substitute the link of the legacy of war with the promise of membership in the bloc.

---

193 Forceful expulsion, imprisonment or killing of other ethnic populations to achieve ethnic homogeneity (Bassuener 2005: 103).
194 The role of each side in ethnic cleansing is still disputed, although the Serbian and Croatian sides are widely seen as primary aggressors. For further discussion, see Kaldor (2012: 44, 54).
195 The HR was designated by the DPA to facilitate and coordinate civilian aspects of the peace settlement. The holder of the post is accountable to the Peace Implementation Council, an ad hoc international body with 55 members. For more on these institutions, see GFAP (1995) and UN (1995).
196 For the discussion of troop levels in BiH, see Heinemann-Grüder, Pietz and Duffy (2003: 8-9).
197 For the discussion on the role of paramilitaries in the war, see Kaldor (2012: 49-50). For a detailed analysis of the war parties and their strategies, see Hoare (2004).
198 For a detailed assessment of the DPA as a peace-building and state-building tool see Weller and Wolff (2006), Keil and Kudlenko (2015).
199 Although in theory the Army of the Federation was united, in practice it was divided into a Bosniak and Bosnian Croat elements.
200 Presidency was entrusted with the civilian oversight of the armed forces but could not perform the task due to the division of armies between the entities.
201 For the discussion of the IPTF's original mandate and how it was negotiated in Dayton, see ICG (2002: 4-5; Holbrooke 1999: 251-252).
202 Prior to this, the international community, attempted to transform the SCMM, into a state Ministry of Defence. As the change posed some constitutional problems, it failed, see Vetschera and Damian (2006: 31-32).
203 Interviews with an MoD official and former NATO employee conducted by the author in Bosnia in September 2016 and a Bosnian security expert in 2021 on Zoom.
204 For a comprehensive analysis of the process, see ICG (2002: 51-55).
205 For details, see ICG (2002: 7).
206 In 2004, SIPA's mandate, largely thanks to the EUPM, was extended and acquired investigative capabilities which was reflected in its new name—State Investigation and Protection Agency (Padurariu 2014: 8).
207 For a more detailed analysis of the EUPM, see the next section.
208 The support for police reform was strongest among the Bosniaks, while the RS actively resisted the idea of centralisation and the Bosnian Croats opposed the transfer of police competences to the state-level more cautiously (Koneska 2014: 123).
209 The Law on Directorate for Coordination of Police Bodies and Agencies for Support to Police Structure of Bosnia and Herzegovina and Law on Independent and Supervisory Bodies of Police Structure of Bosnia and Herzegovina (Koneska 2014: 132).
210 For discussion of the reasons behind the failure of police restructuring, see the next section.

211 Interview of the author with an employee of the EU Delegation in Bosnia, conducted in September 2016.
212 Interview with a security expert from Bosnia in 2021.
213 The question of NATO membership is more contentious.
214 BiH received a candidate status to the EU on 15 December 2022.
215 The Contact Group also contributed to the peaceful solution of the conflict, for its role, see Schwegmann (2000: 5-8).
216 Although on a limited scale of one town, Mostar, see below.
217 For comprehensive studies on this subject, see Ginsberg (2001) and Lucarelli (2000).
218 BiH, or then the Socialist Republic of Bosnia-Herzegovina, asked the EC to recognise the republic on 20 December 1991 (Ginsberg 2001: 81).
219 The Washington Agreement concluded with the Bosnian Croats in 1994, also contributed to this shift, as well as Croatian offensives in 1995. See Chapter 4.
220 For the criminalising effects of sanctions see Andreas (2005).
221 See Chapter 4.
222 Interview of the author with an employee of the EU Delegation in Bosnia, conducted in September 2016.
223 For a comprehensive analysis of the EUAM, see Juncos (2013: 99-110) and Reichel (2000); for peace-building in Mostar, see Moore (2013).
224 The HR, on insistence of the EU, has always been a European and was occasionally required to report to Brussels. This led some researchers to see the OHR as an EU body, e.g. see Ginsberg (2001), Szewczyk (2010). Here, however, the OHR is approached as an EU instrument only between 2002 and 2011, when the HR was officially combined with the post of the EUSR.
225 For a full list of state competencies in BiH, see Annex IV GFAP (1995).
226 The process was overseen by the OHR.
227 For the scenarios giving the EU a bigger role in post-war BiH, see Juncos (2013: 110-113).
228 Having de-coupled the EUSR from the HR, the EU combined the former with the post of the Head of the EU Delegation.
229 The European Commission recommended granting Bosnia the candidate status only on 12 October 2022, provided the completion of a range of demands, including in SSR.
230 These can be found under Title VII Justice, Freedom and Security (Art. 78-85), as well as in more general sections under Title II Political Dialogue (Art. 10-13) and Title III (Art. 14-17) (SAA 2015).
231 Other smaller instruments, such as the Instrument for Stability, were also used.
232 The Kosovo issue keeps the validity of uncertainty for Serbia.
233 While admitting the importance of the DPA for stopping the violence in the country and establishing peace, the EU argued for the change of the Bosnian Constitution presented in Annex IV of the agreement. The latter was seen as a hindrance to establishing a self-sustaining state in Bosnia, independent from the international community. To assist the Bosnian elites to reach consensus on a new constitutional arrangement, the EU worked closely with the USA and launched several rounds of talks in 2009 and 2013. Unfortunately, these did not bring any results. For more on the constitutional reform, see Noutcheva (2012: 163); EC (2013e: 6).
234 As intelligence reform is not covered by the study, the second committee is not part of the analysis.

235 For a detailed description of defence responsibilities of the Presidency and MoD, see Law on Defence of BiH (2005).
236 See Law on Ministries and Other Bodies of Administration of Bosnia and Herzegovina (2003).
237 Although the Federation as an entity was willing to cooperate with the ICTY, the Bosnian Croats have not always shared this vision (EC 2003c: 10).
238 Serbia's cooperation with the ICTY also covers issues relating to the RS and Croatian Serbs, as Belgrade was held accountable for their transfer to The Hague, see Chapter 5. Similarly, Zagreb was seen to be responsible for Bosnian Croats, which reduced the pressure on BiH.
239 For the assessment of the ICTY's impact on transitional justice in Bosnia, see Vukusic (2015).
240 Interviews with an MoD official/former NATO employee and security expert conducted by the author in Sarajevo in September 2016.
241 Here, EUFOR is analysed from the point of view of its contribution into BiH's defence reform, for a broader evaluation of the operation, see Bertin (2008), Knauer (2011), Pulko, Muherina and Pejic (2016), Juncos (2013: 147-159).
242 For a closer look on EUFOR−NATO relations, see Juncos (2013: 153-155).
243 Mandate changes were accompanied by the reduction of the troop levels (from 7, 000 troops in 2004, only 600 were left in BiH in 2012, supported by the Over-the-Horizon forces) and altered force structure. These amendments can be partly explained by the reduced threat of large-scale violence in BiH, and partly by the lack of a common vision for the future of the operation among EU member states, for details see Knauer (2011: 12-16) and Juncos (2013: 150).
244 CARDS 2001-2004 provided around 4.5 million EUR for building the CPA capacities (Ramboll Management 2008: 45).
245 In 2006-2008, 3 million EUR was allocated for these purposes (EC 2008i: 9).
246 The choice can be partly explained by the success of defence and intelligence reforms which overcame divisions in BiH. For further discussion of Paddy Ashdown's motivations and role in police reform, see Muehlmann (2009: 155-157), Metz (2010: 89).
247 Bosniaks, the biggest supporters of police centralisation, on several occasions stalled the reform by refusing to compromise or calling for the abolition of the entity-structure. Bosnian Croats, although mostly favouring more central policing, were worried about losing influence over Croat-dominated areas, and thus were content with the Bosnian Serb opposition (Metz 2010: 75, 91).
248 For Bosnian Serbs, the police, rather than the army, was a symbol of their identity (interview with a security expert in Sarajevo, September 2016).
249 In the absence of acquis on policing, the EU's leverage in the sphere was limited. Moreover, the SAP negotiations were supposed to be of technical character and did not give the EU any right to demand changes to constitutional structure of a (potential) candidate state.
250 Apart from Kosovo.
251 Interview with a former employee of the EUPM and EU Delegation to BiH, conducted in September 2016.
252 Schwarz-Schilling had insignificant impact on the reform, while Lajcak tried to replicate Ashdown's forceful approach. For more details, see Koneska (2014: 128-133).
253 Interview with a former employee of the EU Delegation to BiH, conducted in September 2016.

254 Interview with a senior staff member of the EU Delegation to BiH, conducted in September 2016.
255 Like EUFOR, the EUPM is analysed here from the point of its contribution into SSR only, for a broader discussion, see Merlingen and Ostrauskaite (2006: 52-78), Juncos (2013: 137-147), Padurariu (2014).
256 Interviews with a former and current employee of the EU Delegation to BiH, conducted in September 2016.
257 Interview with an employee of the EU Delegation to Bosnia conducted in September 2016.
258 EUFOR contributed to the reform too through its attempts to fight organised crime.
259 Interview with a senior OHR employee, conducted in September 2016 in Sarajevo.
260 Only Kosovo was not included in the process.
261 For a full list of reforms see Populari and ESI (2009). For the assessment of visa-liberalisation process in the Western Balkans, see Kacarska (2012).
262 The IBM strategy and Action Plan were aligned with the EU's IBM concept in 2016.
263 Interview with a former employee of the EU Delegation to BiH, conducted in September 2016.
264 Interview with a former employee of the EUPM and EU Delegation to BiH, conducted in September 2016.
265 Interview with a former employee of the EU Delegation to BiH, conducted in September 2016.
266 Although Croatia and BiH signed a treaty on state border in 1999, it was never ratified (Klemencic 1999).
267 The solution to the issue was reached in 2015, allowing BiH and Montenegro sign a demarcation agreement (Tomovic: 2015).
268 See Gosar (2012: 91-92).
269 Interviews with a senior OHR employee, a senior employee of the Delegation of the EU to BiH and a former employee of the Delegation, conducted in September 2016 in Sarajevo. An interview with a security expert on Western Balkans in 2021 on Zoom.

Chapter 7
Conclusion

Comparative analysis of the EU's involvement in SSR in Croatia, Serbia and BiH

To conclude the analysis, the book compares the EU's impact on SSR in Croatia, Serbia and Bosnia. The comparison is *focused* as it deals with two level of SSR – political and organisational, and three aspects of the reform in all three cases (defence, police and border reforms) and *structured* (George 1979), as it is guided by the Regional Security Complex Theory (RSCT) that allows to distinguish three periods of analysis within the chosen timeframe: 1991-1995, when the Balkan subcomplex represented a case of regional conflict formation (RCF), 1995-1999, the time of an incipient security regime, and 1999-2013, an emerging embryonic security community within the EU/Europe RSC. The analysis, provided here, is therefore cross-temporal and cross-spatial,[270] which is essential from the point of view of complex security governance.

As mentioned in previous chapters, the first period, from 1991 to 1995, differs from the other two as its context does not create favourable conditions for security sector reform. Although SSR is applicable to a range of environments, it is not typical for the context of open warfare and interconnected conflicts, characteristic of an RCF. It is still important to analyse this period to determine whether the security sectors of the three case studies had different starting points of SSR, to define factors that enabled or held back the EU's engagement in the reform, and to assess the evolution of the EU as a security actor in the region. Besides, it is during this period that the EU attempted SSR in the Western Balkans for the first time, although on a limited scope of one town in BiH. While this experience is examined below, the analysis starts with the EU instruments that influenced the security development of the three states, which are identified as precursors of the bloc's impact on the political level of the reform. These instruments include the

Arbitration Commission on Yugoslavia, arms embargo, the European Community Monitoring Mission (ECMM) and sanctions against the SFRY/FRY.

The Arbitration or Badinter Commission defined the general shape and international personality of Croatia, Serbia and BiH by ruling that internal boundaries between Yugoslav republics could be regarded as international borders. By convening the commission, the EU, then still the EC, at least in the eyes of regional players, bore responsibility for its decisions, although as demonstrated by Croatia's case, it did not follow them blindly. It was not surprising therefore that Badinter's ruling denying the Serbian populations in Croatia and BiH the right to self-determination, contributed to the spread of anti-EU sentiments among the Serbs.[271] The arms embargo imposed by the EC/EU on Yugoslavia in July 1991 was another EU instrument, applied to all three states. It was meant to prevent the spread of violence in the region, but instead, combined with the UN embargo, introduced in September 1991, tilted the military balance in favour of the FRY (dominated by Serbia), disadvantaging Croatia and BiH, and unintentionally contributed to the criminalisation of the security sectors of the three states and their societies more broadly. The FRY inherited the JNA and most of the military equipment and weapons from the SFRY, while Croatia and BiH had to build their armies practically from scratch in the conditions of war. The police, which represented a republican service in the SFRY, and paramilitary groups, using criminal networks piercing the Balkans, were of utmost importance in this process. Moreover, in BiH the security sector was divided between the three warring ethnic groups – Bosniaks, Bosnian Serbs and Bosnian Croats. While the former group were left to their own devices, the latter two could count on support from Belgrade and Zagreb respectively. Trying to treat all post-Yugoslav states in the same way, the EU successfully resisted calls for lifting the embargo for Bosniaks. These actions, although criticised by the USA, have contributed to preventing the escalation of violence and reaching a diplomatic solution to the Bosnian war.

Despite efforts to act as an impartial mediator, the EU, as the rest of the international community, singled out the FRY/Serbia as the main aggressor in the Yugoslav conflicts of the 1990s. As a result, it excluded Belgrade from programmes offered to other Balkan states and used punitive economic measures to pressure Milosevic to cooperate. Thus, the ECMM that created real and symbolic links between the EU and individual Balkan states, including Croatia and BiH, did not open its offices in the FRY, whereas the economic sanctions that cut off financial aid and stopped trade relations with the whole of Yugoslavia in October 1991, were enforced only against Serbia and Montenegro after November 1991. These actions isolated the Milosevic regime and consolidated the anti-EU sentiment in the FRY.

It should also be mentioned that by placing the ECMM in Croatia and BiH, Brussels received unique insight into the security situations in these countries, yet in the absence of appropriate tools, was unable to apply the information collected to bring peace to the region. This inability to stop the violence and manage the crises contributed to the loss of trust in the bloc among Western Balkan states. Consequently, negative attitudes to the EU were not restricted to the FRY, but spread around Croatia and BiH, too. In such circumstances, the EU's attempts to manage the results of conflicts were met with suspicion and doubt, which can be observed in treatment of the EU administration of Mostar (EUAM) that includes the only example of the bloc's involvement in the organisational level of SSR during the first period. As part of its mandate, the EUAM promised to unite the town's police, divided between the Bosniak-controlled eastern and Croat-controlled western parts. The completion of the task was entrusted to the WEU Police Force (WEPOL) that started work in September 1994. Yet by the end of 1995, the WEU contingent, acting on the EU's behalf, achieved only modest results. It improved police communication infrastructure, established a joint operations centre and organised separate patrols with the East and West Mostar police forces. The progress was limited due to several reasons, most importantly, a mismatch between the ambitious goal and tools available for its achievement. With no previous experience in crisis management, limited resources to support the WEUPOL and lack of military power to back up its demands, the EU could not unite the deeply fractured town and its police in two years.

In short, the EU's SSR activity in 1991-1995 in the Western Balkans was minimal. Only BiH experienced the EU's impact on police reform in Mostar towards the end of the war. This is not surprising, considering the lack of instruments in the EU toolbox for dealing with military conflicts and hostile regional context. Most of the EU's efforts at this time were aimed at stopping the violence, finding a peaceful solution to the conflicts, and managing their consequences.

The end of the wars of Yugoslavia's dissolution changed the EU goals in the Western Balkans to promoting stabilisation and normalisation of life in the region. With the launch of the Regional Approach (RA) in 1996, the EU also set to facilitate regional cooperation, reconciliation and good neighbourly relations. Elements of SSR it attempted in 1995-1999 were therefore subordinated to these goals. During this period, when the international community tried to pacify the Western Balkans and substitute regional rivalry with reciprocity, typical of security regimes, the EU showed growing interest in the functioning and management of the security sectors of Croatia, Serbia and BiH. The political level of the reform was affected mostly indirectly through the continuation of the arms embargo, work of the ECMM in Croatia and BiH, the RA conditionality and return of punitive actions against the FRY/Serbia with the break-out of war in Kosovo. All of these activities touched upon security practices of the studied countries, although none was guided by SSR considerations. After all, the EU's concept of the reform was still missing.

The arms embargo, applicable to the three studied countries, and some of the autonomous EU sanctions against the FRY targeted security sectors in more obvious ways than the ECMM and RA. The embargo was kept by Brussels, despite the lifting of the UN restrictions in November 1995. This decision, explained by desire to protect international personnel engaged in peace-building activities in post Yugoslav states, allowed the EU to contribute to arms control and confidence-building measures, coordinated by the OSCE in Croatia, Serbia and BiH. With the start of the Kosovo conflict, however, the ban, strengthened by the 1998 Council decision to prohibit the export of equipment that could be used for internal repression of terrorism to the FRY, led to the exacerbation of the anti-EU sentiment among Serbian authorities and security elites. Travel restrictions that directly affected the FRY's security sector leadership and oil embargo that aimed to deny the FRY army the means to conduct military operations had a similar effect. The feelings of mistrust and hostility towards the EU became aggravated among FRY security actors after the bloc prevented the security top brass from travelling freely to its member states and tried to cut off supplies to the military in the face of NATO's bombing. These attitudes lingered even after the end of the Milosevic era, making the EU's SSR activities more problematic. On the other hand, the EU's punitive measures weakened the Milosevic regime and isolated Serbia even from its FRY partner, Montenegro.

The ECMM in Croatia and BiH contributed to the stabilisation of the countries by monitoring the implementation of the Erdut Agreement and the DPA. While continuing to provide a link between the countries and the EU, it lacked the tools and ambition to influence their security sectors more directly. The Regional Approach, as a more comprehensive EU policy, covering all Western Balkan states, was better suited to approach SSR. While emphasising sectoral issues, including in the sphere of policing, border security and to a lesser extent defence, the RA contained requirements for establishing a system of democratic governance in Croatia, the FRY and BiH, which is one of the key elements of the political level of SSR. For example, in the cases of Croatia and BiH, the RA reports directly called for the removal of political influence over the police and army and insisted on the introduction of democratic civilian control over the security sector. Given differences in state consolidation in Croatia, the FRY and BiH, the RA's priorities for the countries' political systems differed. Thus, in BiH, the EU emphasised building common institutions, while in Croatia and the FRY, it focused on the separation of powers and good governance. In all three states, however, the RA promoted the emergence of functional states, where human rights are protected, and public security is provided, not threatened, by the security sector. Another element of the Regional Approach that was equally applicable to all case studies and important for SSR was the requirement to cooperate with the ICTY. Due to the unfavourable standing of the tribunal among most ethnic groups in Croatia, Serbia and BiH[272] and the lack of will in the EU to use coercive power or negative conditionality to improve regional relations with The Hague, the requirement was largely ignored. Speaking more broadly, the RA in Croatia, Serbia (as part of the FRY) and BiH and its SSR conditionality were also mostly ignored by local actors, prompting the EU to use the approach as a monitoring tool. If in the former two cases, the implementation of the RA was obstructed by the semi-authoritarian regimes, suspicious of the EU, in BiH it was side-lined by other efforts of the international community building peace in the war-torn country under the DPA framework.

The EU's impact on the organisational level of SSR in 1995-1999 was similarly limited. It provided financial assistance and policy advice to Croatia and BiH to help with the post-conflict transformations of their defence sectors, police and border services. Serbia, however, received no direct or indirect support for its security sector reform. This was because it chose to deal with the Kosovo issue through violence, instead of looking for a peaceful solution, reclaiming the "pariah status" it tried to shed via the peace-making efforts of Milosevic in the mid-1990s. Even so, the EU monitored the practices of the country's police, criticising them for unprofessionalism and disregard for human rights, and endorsed the normalisation of border relations with its neighbouring states through the RA reports.

In Croatia and BiH, defence reform was promoted through support for mine clearance action and research on de-mining. In the former, the EU acted through the WEU Demining Mission as it was still lacking a defence policy of its own, and in the latter, it assisted the UN and provided direct support to de-mining NGOs and local authorities. In BiH, it also contributed to the development of the strategic documents for dealing with the mine threat. These activities contributed to a safer environment in the countries, improved refugee returns and the development of civilian and military expertise on de-mining. In police reform, while recognising the leadership of the UN and OSCE in Croatia and BiH, the EU argued for professionalisation of the services and introduction of democratic policing, respectful of human rights and intolerant to organised crime. Additionally, in Bosnia, the WEUPOL further improved infrastructure, offered training opportunities to the police of West and East Mostar and established the Unified Police Force, capable of acting only in the central zone of the town. The mission's achievements, like in the previous period, were mainly technical as the EU refused to recognise that police unification in the divided town was a politically-charged issue. It was still an important experience, as it allowed the EU to use elements of SSR as a tool of post-conflict transformation. Border reform in all three states was seen as an important step to regional reconciliation. The EU provided advice on restoration of border controls and introduction of international standards into the work of their border services. In Croatia and BiH, it also supported the development of customs services, which demonstrates that even before the introduction of the Integrated Border Management (IBM) for the Western Balkans, the EU understood border security in broad terms.

Overall, in 1995-1999, the EU showed more interest in elements of SSR in Croatia, Serbia and BiH than at the start of the 1990s. Its activities in the area were subordinated to the goals of post-conflict reconstruction and regional reconciliation. During this period, the bloc's relations with Serbia deteriorated further over the Kosovo conflict, leaving the country without even limited support for its defence, police and border reforms from the Union. Punitive measures introduced by the EU against the FRY and Serbia after 1998, such as the travel ban and oil embargo, while isolating and weakening the Milosevic regime, aggravated the anti-EU attitudes in the country and made them common in the security sector. Although Croatia and BiH were offered SSR support by the EU, it was limited and irregular. The European Union was content playing a supporting role to either local actors or other members of the international community. Besides, its foreign policy was only taking shape and defence policy would only develop after the Kosovo war. At the same time, the countries remained distrustful of the EU after its failure to manage Yugoslavia's dissolution. Tudjman's semi-authoritarian regime was wary of the RA, seeing it as an attempt at a new Yugoslavia, and the fragmented BiH had enough DPA conditions to fulfil without having to deal with the requirements from the EU, that had no special role under the peace agreement. It should also be emphasised that this period demonstrates the emergence of discrepancies between the three case studies: Croatia spent the post-war period strengthening its statehood, although under semi-authoritarian rule; Serbia, while remaining part of the FRY, started moving further away from Montenegro, and descended into violence over the status of Kosovo; and BiH, under the supervision of the international community, faced the dilemma of making the two entities and three ethnic groups work within the framework of a common state. The differences between the states would become more prominent in the next period, affecting their relationship with the EU, including in the sphere of SSR.

After the end of the Kosovo conflict, with the launch of the Stability Pact and Stabilisation and Association Process (SAP), the Western Balkan states were offered an opportunity to integrate into the EU. The death of Tudjman and electoral defeat of Milosevic created a further opening for regional transformation and reconciliation. Croatia, Serbia and BiH did not use these opportunities equally, which is reflected in different levels of integration into the EU they achieved by 2013. Croatia joined the bloc in July 2013, Serbia was granted a candidate status in March 2012, while BiH was still a potential candidate at the end of the researched period, receiving the candidate status only in 2022 (EC 2022). In terms of SSR, differences can also be detected on both political and organisational levels, although in many cases the EU's approach to the reform was similar in all three countries. Thus, on *the political level*, the EU promoted three elements of the reform in Croatia, Serbia and BiH: *the oversight of the security sector, cooperation with the ICTY* and *regional cooperation.*

The oversight of the security sector was approached by the EU through support for and advice on establishing parliamentary, civilian and public control measures over different security agencies of the three countries. In Serbia and BiH, however, this aspect of the reform was supplemented by demands for state consolidation.

While Croatia, having achieved territorial integrity in 1998 with the reintegration of Eastern Slavonia, did not experience any serious challenges to its statehood, the same cannot be said about Serbia and Bosnia. Serbia existed within four different configurations, i.e. the SFRY, FRY, State Union of Serbia and Montenegro (SCG) and the Republic of Serbia, between 1991 and 2013, which put a strain on its development as a functioning state. Although BiH maintained the same shape after 1995, the state created by Dayton was fractured, weak and not self-sustaining. The EU's insistence on state consolidation in Serbia and BiH is therefore not surprising. In the sphere of security reform this demand took different forms for the two states. In Serbia, where defence and border security were a joint responsibility of the federal and later SCG government, the EU advocated clear separation of powers between the federal/State Union and republican levels and harmonisation of security practices with Montenegro. When the SCG ceased existence in 2006, and Serbia parted ways with Montenegro, the EU switched to prioritising the promotion of good security governance as an element of democratisation and Europeanisation of the state apparatus. The same approach was applied to Croatia but starting from 2000. In BiH's security sector, state consolidation was about building/strengthening common state institutions and establishing effective coordination between different levels of government. Even though by 2013 the army and border police were centralised, the unfinished restructuring of the police and absence of constitutional reform to remove the external influence over the state's governance system, meant that the question of state consolidation remained significant for Bosnia's SSR even after 2013.

The analysis of the EU's impact on the oversight of security sectors in Croatia, Serbia and BiH cannot be complete without evaluating the character of this impact and motivation for it. The three cases demonstrated that the EU tended to influence parliamentary, civilian and public control through a mixture of *indirect* and *direct measures*. For example, in all three states, parliamentary control over security bodies have been strengthened thanks to the EU's efforts to support the development of their parliamentary democracies, while public control was improved through its assistance for the development of independent regulatory bodies, media and civil society. Some of the EU's actions were directly aimed at improving the oversight of the security sector, e.g. as demonstrated by the EU's attention to the work of the Committee for Defence and Security in Serbia and its role in the transformation of the latter into two more specialised bodies, the Defence and Internal Affairs Committee and Security Services Control Committee. In none of the three cases, however, was the EU found to follow a coherent and comprehensive programme while approaching the political level of SSR (or SSR in general). The motivation for its actions in the sphere can be explained by the need to prepare Croatia, Serbia and BiH for future membership in the bloc. Transparent and accountable security sectors are seen by the EU as a prerequisite of functioning states that can fulfil demands of the integration process into Euro-Atlantic institutions. As Croatia, Serbia and BiH progressed with their EU membership talks at a different pace, Brussels demonstrated different levels of engagement with their security reforms, which is even more evident on the organisational level, compared below.

The second element of the political level of SSR affected by the EU is linked to the work of the ICTY. Cooperation with this *ad hoc* court of law had significance for SSR in Croatia, Serbia and BiH for three main reasons. First, the tribunal's work led to the dismissal of security personnel, embroiled in war crimes, and therefore professionalisation of security agencies. Second, it contributed to the achievement of full civilian control over the security sector by dismantling the protection networks harbouring fugitives. Finally, by encouraging the states to tackle the legacy of war, it promoted restoration of trust and peace in the region. Although the EU supported the ICTY nearly from the moment of its establishment in 1993 and included cooperation with the tribunal into the RA and SAP conditionality, it started actively insisting on the improvement of this cooperation in Croatia, Serbia and BiH only around 2004-2005. Given differences in the scale and gravity of war crimes in each country and coercion from other members of the international community, there were some differences in the ways the EU promoted cooperation with the ICTY in the three studied countries. Nonetheless, they did not affect the essence of the EU's ICTY conditionality. The EU demanded Croatia, Serbia and BiH to capture and transfer indictees to The Hague, provide security guarantees to witnesses, develop functional channels of communication with the tribunal and investigate support networks. While most of the public in Croatia, Serbia and the RS in BiH remained opposed to the ICTY, the state elites of the three states had to eventually accept the necessity of cooperation with the court. The emphasis of the EU on the matter within the SAP is one of the key reasons behind this change.

The third and final element of the political level of SSR, promoted by the EU in the Western Balkans is regional cooperation. In Croatia, Serbia and BiH, it was mostly facilitated in three areas: policing, border security and dealing with the legacy of war. The latter involved cooperation between the states not only on matters relating to the ICTY, but also to domestic trials. In Serbia, relations with Kosovo were added as an extra requirement, as the EU wanted to ensure the latter was able to participate in regional initiatives, too. In general, the EU endorsed regional cooperation on security issues to build the capacity of Croatian, Serbian and Bosnian security actors, introduce them to international and EU standards in policing and border security and develop trust and reciprocity in the region. It is important to acknowledge that the EU's attention to the regional dimension of SSR became more visible in the organisational level of the reform in 1999-2013 as well. Finally, it should be pointed out that while the EU prioritised cooperation between the Western Balkan states and specifically Croatia, Serbia and BiH, considering their shared past and identical ethnic populations, it also encouraged the development of working security relations with a broader SEE area.

The organisational level of SSR in 1999-2013, like during the previous period, is divided into defence, police and border reforms. In defence reform, the EU's footprint was the least visible in Croatia, where NATO assumed leadership in 2000, and most noticeable in BiH, where the bloc used not only the European Commission's conditionality but relied on efforts of the EUSR (who acted as the HR of the international community in 2002-2011) and EUFOR *Althea* to promote the reform. In Serbia, for a long time the EU avoided engagement with defence issues due to the constitutional and legal uncertainty surrounding the FRY and SCG, and strong anti-EU sentiment among the top brass, mentioned above. The peaceful break-up of the SCG and Serbia's decision not to pursue NATO membership, prompted the EU to show more interest in the area. Using priorities, set out in the European Partnerships in 2006 and 2008, it demanded Belgrade adopt some strategic legislation in the sphere of defence. Once this was achieved, however, the EU switched to supporting defence reform in the country from the point of its own security infrastructure, particularly CSDP and Battlegroups. In fact, in all three countries the EU's efforts at defence reform were closely linked to preparing them for demands of EU membership. In BiH, given the distance of the membership perspective and the weakness of the state, EUFOR was also used to promote self-sustainability of the recently unified army. To address the membership requirements for Croatia, Serbia and BiH, help Serbia establish a legal defence framework, compatible with the EU standards, and strengthen the sustainability of the Bosnian army, the EU used policy advice, training, technical assistance and post-conflict support. The latter two categories were often combined. For example, in Croatia and BiH, the EU spent considerable financial resources (from the mid-1990s to 2013, around 20 million EUR and 40 million EUR respectively) on mine clearance action and developing de-mining expertise. Serbia received less support in this sphere due to a smaller scale of the mine threat and persisting perceptions of the country as an aggressor. It should also be highlighted that the EU's technical and post-conflict assistance had a strong regional dimension. Thus, the problem of small and light weapons, tackled by the EU in Croatia, Serbia and BiH mostly in cooperation with the UNDP, was approached through various regional projects, while de-mining programmes often focused on territories, lying between several Western Balkan states. The importance of regional context was also recognised in the context of CSDP.

While the EU's role in defence reform in the Western Balkans should be acknowledged, it is important to understand that it was still limited. The bloc did not try to compete with NATO and was content with supporting the Alliance's endeavours. Even in BiH, where it carved itself a special place in defence thanks to EUFOR, and in Serbia, where NATO's impact was restricted due to its role in the Kosovo war, the EU preferred to focus on non-strategic elements of the reform. In Croatia, its focus remained firmly on its own security infrastructure.

In police reform, the EU's involvement was more prominent. This is because policing, just like border security, is part of Justice and Home Affairs, an area of priority for the Western Balkans. The EU relied on the SAP to raise the profile of police reform in all three countries and used four areas to promote its implementation, namely: policy and legislation, training and sharing best practices, technical assistance and post-conflict assistance. There were three other important similarities in the EU's treatment of the reform in Croatia, Serbia and BiH, which were linked to the issue of organised crime, regional cooperation and patterns of engagement with other external actors in the field. Fight against organised crime provided an overarching theme for a bulk of the EU efforts to build the capabilities of the local police services, equip them with the skills and technologies necessary to deal with different types of criminal activities, ranging from drug trafficking to terrorism, and develop legislative frameworks, compatible with international and EU standards. To tackle the transnational nature of organised crime and help law enforcement agencies, representing the former adversaries, to build a working relationship, the EU promoted regional cooperation in policing through CARDS and IPA projects, as well as its CSDP missions. Croatia, for example, contributed to the EUPM in BiH and EULEX in Kosovo. What concerns the EU's relations with other external actors, involved in police reforms, e.g. the OSCE and the UN, they followed the same pattern in all researched countries. From a supporting actor that did not usually consider the work done by others, which often led to overlaps and wasted funds, the EU evolved into a leader of police reform that not only coordinated its efforts with other agents, but also often relied on them to promote its own procedures and policies.

Having acknowledged similarities in the EU's approaches to police reforms in Croatia, Serbia and BiH, it is important to analyse *differences*. These are most clearly discernible in specific aspects of the four reform areas and general approaches to the reform in the studied countries. Although the EU focused on the same areas of the reform, i.e. policy advice, training, technical and post-conflict assistance, in all three states, it prioritised different aspects of these areas, which could partly be explained by different levels of development and post-conflict reconstruction achieved by each state by 1999-2000, and partly their closeness to the membership in the bloc. Thus, in Serbia, technical assistance was for a long time understood by the EU in terms of modernisation and demilitarisation, while in Croatia nearly from the start of the third period, it was about specialisation of the police and preparation for the demands of membership. In Croatia and until 2011 in Serbia, the EU applied a project-based approach to police reform. In BiH, it combined a project-based approach with a long-term structural reform. The development, achieved by the Croatian police thanks to internal and external effort, by the early 2000s, the emergence of strong support for the EU membership soon after Tudjman's death and the strength of Croatia's statehood meant that the country had a good foundation for fulfilling EU requirements on transforming its policing and could progress fast with the reform. By 2013, it was deemed to have created an effective, although still developing, institutional and legislative framework on policing, reaching the standards found inside the EU. In Serbia, the fractured political scene, poor exposure to externally led programmes in the immediate post-Milosevic period and continuing challenges to its statehood (first within the FRY and SCG, then over the status of Kosovo) rendered the EU's project-based approach to police reform only partially successful. With the Council's decision to reinvigorate the focus on the rule of law in the Western Balkans in 2011 and Serbia's achievement of a candidate status in 2012, the EU started moving towards a more strategic and comprehensive approach to the reform. The results achieved by 2013, however, were not enough to finalise police reform in the country, as Serbia still lacked developed infrastructure and a fully operational legal framework on policing.

The EU's involvement in BiH's police reform stands out from its approaches in Croatia and Serbia not only because its first civilian mission, EUPM, spent nearly ten years trying to improve standards of policing in the country, but also because it identified police reform as one of the key conditions for the membership negotiations. In BiH, therefore, the EU defined the general framework of police reform. Having chosen a top-down model for restructuring the police in Bosnia's two entities, however, the bloc was unable to convince domestic actors to adopt it. Without the *acquis* on policing or precedent of supporting centralisation of the police in other Western Balkan states, the EU conditionality was easy to oppose. In the Republika Srpska (RS), the opposition was the strongest. Fearing that the reform was just a pretext to change the state system, created by Dayton, the RS refused to support it, putting BiH's progress within the SAP at risk. To save the SAA talks from total collapse and BiH from isolation, the EU lowered its demands on several occasions and agreed to postpone the finalisation of police reform until BiH implements a constitutional reform. By 2013, the EU's support contributed to modernisation and professionalisation of law enforcement agencies in BiH, harmonisation of legislation on state, level, cantonal and Brcko District levels, and improved operational capacity of state-level institutions, e.g. SIPA. Nonetheless, it did not remove the problem of politicisation of the police nor lead it to self-sustainability. These issues are unlikely to be resolved until the country removes uncertainty surrounding its statehood. The EU, having invested considerable effort into the reform and linked it to the membership in the bloc, cannot abandon it without sustaining substantial reputational damage.

The final element of SSR analysed in this work is border reform. In the three studied countries, compared to defence and police reforms, it was promoted by the EU in the most comprehensive and consistent way. Considering the geographic closeness of the Western Balkans to the bloc and its vulnerability to organised crime, the EU, within the Ohrid Process, developed an overarching strategy for the region's borders security and labelled it the Integrated Border Management for the Western Balkans. The goal of this strategy is to develop a working system of well-coordinated national and regional agencies in border management. The presence of such framework enabled the EU to set the same benchmarks for border security in Croatia, Serbia and BiH, while promoting them through the already-familiar areas of legal approximation, training, technical assistance and post-conflict support. Although technical in nature, the IBM concept for the Western Balkans understood border security in broad terms by integrating border control, trade facilitation and border regional cooperation. After Croatia, Serbia and BiH achieved substantial progress in the implementation of their national IBM strategies, aligned with the IBM concept for the region, the EU started introducing them to the IBM concept, designed for the members of the bloc, which was to prepare them for the future in the borderless Schengen zone.

Given differences between the three states' experiences with border security, border reforms in each of them progressed at a different pace. Croatia emerged as a regional leader since its borders were never militarised and remained intact since 1998. In Serbia, with only minor changes introduced to border security after Milosevic's departure, the IBM took off only in 2006, when Belgrade gained full control over border issues that previously had to be coordinated with Podgorica. Kosovo's unilateral declaration of independence in 2008 returned the uncertainty into Serbia's border security. By the time that Croatia's border reform achieved levels of border security, compatible with international standards (although not those of the Schengen zone[273]), Serbia built a working border management system, but did not bring its asylum, migration and, to a lesser degree, visa policies in line with the EU's demands. BiH for a long time struggled to comply with the EU's IBM requirements as it had no experience in managing external borders until 1995, lacked a state-level border agency until 2000 and its borders sustained the biggest damage during the regional violence of the 1990s. With the help of the European Commission's projects, the EUPM and even EUFOR, BiH created a modern border service, which while still developing, is arguably the most resilient domestic security actor in the country.

An important part of border reform in the three countries was linked with the harmonisation of their visa policies with those of the EU. Croatia, like before, was in a better position than its neighbours. As the only Western Balkan country that was not placed on the negative visa list, it could adjust its visa, migration and asylum policies to EU requirements relatively quickly. Serbia and BiH, on the other hand, had to go through the visa liberalisation process between 2008 and 2010, which dominated their border reforms at the time. Although BiH found it more difficult to fulfil demands of the process at first, it managed to achieve a free-visa regime with the Schengen zone soon after Serbia.

Other important successes of the reform concern improved regional cooperation on border issues in the Western Balkans and support of the EU-led efforts by other members of the international community. By choosing to approach border security in all three states through a region-based IBM approach, the EU contributed to the emergence of reciprocal relations between their border management systems. Furthermore, these relations were promoted by other external actors, involved in border reform in Croatia, Serbia and BiH as the EU's IBM strategy for the Western Balkans was integrated in a broader regional initiative, the Ohrid Border Process. It is therefore possible to conclude that the EU's approach to border reform achieved bigger progress in the researched states[274] than defence or police reform thanks to a combination of factors, among which the emphasis on technical character of the reform, offer of tangible incentives, coordination of activities with the rest of the international community and use of the same conditions for all Western Balkan states deserve a special mention. Of course, border security in Croatia, Serbia and BiH remains a challenging topic mostly because of the unresolved border disputes, which the EU prefers to treat as bilateral issues in the absence of the *acquis* on border delineation, uncertainties surrounding Serbia-Kosovo relations and the lingering legacy of war. Even in such circumstances, however, the EU's contribution into border reform of the three states has been significant.

To conclude the comparative analysis[275], the chapter identifies factors that explain discrepancies between the results, achieved by the EU in SSR in Croatia, Serbia and BiH. On the surface, the EU's involvement in the political and organisational levels of the reform followed similar approaches in all three countries. On the political level, the EU promoted the development of good security sector governance, cooperation with the ICTY and regional relations. On the organisational level, defence, police and border reforms focused on policy and legal advice, capacity-building, technical assistance and post-conflict reconstruction. Moreover, clear goals guided the EU's engagement with the Western Balkans during the three periods defined with the RSCT's help: in 1991-1995, it was mostly concerned with stopping the violence through peaceful means; in 1995-1999, it sought ways to stabilise the region and normalise life there, while in 1999-2013, it worked on the integration of the regional states into its institutions. A closer look at SSR in Croatia, Serbia and BiH reveals that similarities in the EU's approaches were not enough to achieve similarities in results. Keeping in mind that in complex systems, causality remains problematic and that no analysis, no matter how comprehensive is able to identify a full causal chain, given the uncertainty and non-linearity of social development, four main factors explaining differences in SSR in the studied countries are identified, namely: *lasting presence of war legacy, nature of statehood, proximity of the EU's membership and involvement of other members of the international community in SSR.*

While all three states went through wars, the damage they sustained (actual and reputational) were different. Croatia, under a strong leadership that made the war part of national mythology started recovering soon after the 1992 UN-negotiated ceasefire, although its territorial integrity would be restored only in 1998. Serbia, having engaged in four regional conflicts between 1991 and 1999, emerged as a piranha state, condemned and shunned by most of the international community until the early 2000s, while BiH was hit by violence so hard it required military and civilian international involvement to build peace between its two entities. Thus, *the legacy of war*, although for different reasons, left a more lasting impact on Serbia and BiH than Croatia, affecting not only their ability to respond to the EU's SSR demands, but also the nature of their relationship with the bloc. For example, in Serbia, the EU's punitive measures during the 1990s created a strong anti-EU camp in the security sector which made the EU's engagement with the country's SSR challenging. The questions of *statehood and state consolidation* are also closely linked to legacy of war. The fact that Serbia existed in four different configurations between 1991 and 2013 and is still in dispute with Kosovo over the latter's status introduced an extra dimension into the EU's approach to the country's SSR. The same as Bosnia's reluctance to undergo a constitutional reform to achieve full control over its governance. Although, formally, BiH is independent, its sovereignty is undermined by the presence of the OHR. Croatia, whose statehood remained unchallenged since the end of the war, presented a much simpler case for the EU's SSR. The nature of statehood of the studied countries therefore influenced the nature of the EU's engagement with SSR there, making the bloc introduce additional requirements for the reform when states lacked consolidation or had their sovereignty challenged.

Proximity of the EU's membership promise is the third factor identified here. The analysis demonstrated that after 1999, the EU used SSR as a member state-building tool to create resilient and functioning states, capable of joining the bloc. Through SSR, the EU was encouraging elites in Croatia, Serbia and BiH to subscribe to the values shared by its member states, develop effective security institutions and reciprocal relationships between them as well as learn to act according to the same rules and principles, thus promoting the emergence of elite security community. The changes demanded by the EU in the security sector were therefore not just technical but held high political cost for domestic actors. The closer the country was to membership, the higher was the incentive for its elites to implement SSR. The further it was—the more the elites resisted, fearing the loss of public support and consequently power over the EU conditionality. The proximity of membership also reinvigorated the EU, prompting it to pay closer attention to SSR issues in countries that moved closer to the prospect of membership. The choice of a more comprehensive approach to police reform in Serbia after 2012 demonstrates this point.

Finally, the *involvement of other external actors* in SSR in Croatia, Serbia and BiH had significance for the EU's performance in the field. It was not only because this involvement defined the level of progress achieved by the security sectors in the Western Balkans by the time the EU emerged as the regional leader, but also because it influenced the character of the EU's engagement with SSR in the studied countries. For instance, as NATO was guiding defence reform in Croatia, the EU only approached this aspect of SSR from the point of its own security architecture, while in Serbia it had to provide some strategic advice. The presence of other members of the international community was also important for coordination purposes. Although the EU developed a well-coordinated approach to border reform that was supported by other participants of the Ohrid Process, it struggled for a long time with coordinating its activities in police reform with other actors, involved in the area such as the OSCE and the UN, which led to unnecessary overlapping, wasted funds and confusion among regional actors.

As can be seen, each of the identified factors—the legacy of war, nature of statehood, closeness of the membership perspective and presence of other external actors—had an impact on the EU's engagement with SSR in Croatia, Serbia and BiH and the results this involvement achieved. While it is possible to identify other contributing factors, the analysis conducted here singled out these four as having the most significance for the three studied cases. The sections that follow summarise the main findings of the book and offer several observations on the EU's security governance in times of complexity.

Changes in the character of security interdependence in the Western Balkans and the EU's SSR efforts in 1991–2013

Having approached the Western Balkans as a sub-complex within the European regional security complex (RSC), this work traced the development of the region on the spectrum of security interdependence between 1991 and 2013. The analysis demonstrated that in the studied period, the region went through considerable transformation, moving from the pole of enmity to the pole of amity. This transformation was not a linear or straightforward process: it was accompanied by complex changes of relations between states of the region and with the outside world as well as the evolution of the EU as an actor.

CONCLUSION 317

Between 1991 and 1995, the Western Balkans developed into a regional conflict formation (RCF), whose security situation was dominated by a combination of closely interlinked conflicts that could not be easily untangled. Paradoxically, the networks that connected the Western Balkan states into an RCF, brought the region closer to a wider Europe by exposing it to transnational threats like organised crime and illegal migration. Although the European Community (EC) was first to respond to the Balkan crises of the early 1990s, it was unable to manage them. Undergoing transformation into the EU, it lacked a fully operative foreign and security policy, unity among its members and, most importantly, a military muscle to resolve the violent conflicts. The USA and NATO had to step in to stop the violence in 1995, putting an end to the strategy of containment, pursued by the international community in the Balkans in 1991-1995. By using negotiation and imposition, external actors, led by the USA and under growing influence of the EU, started stabilising the Balkan subcomplex. Various regional initiatives, including the Dayton Peace Accords (DPA) and Regional Approach, worked to introduce members of the subcomplex to the principles of regional cooperation, good neighbourliness, transparency and reciprocity. Had they taken root, the region could have developed into security regime. This did not happen, however, as the legacy of war was inadequately addressed, while the international community could not agree on what constituted the region and continued treating it as an area, separate from the rest of Europe.

The Kosovo conflict of 1998-1999 acted as a watershed moment for the Western Balkans: it exposed limits of reactive and selective responses, utilised by the international community previously, and demonstrated that the region was of key importance for the security and stability of the EU. The European Union emerged as the leading actor in the development of the Western Balkans at the end of the 1990s, trying to prevent the spread of transnational threats from the region to its member states, repair the reputational damage sustained through the failure of its early efforts to manage the crises and compensate the diminishing interest in regional affairs on part of the USA. With the launch of the Stability Pact and the SAP, the bloc started working on strengthening the statehood of Western Balkan states and fostering amicable relations between them. By exposing the Western Balkan leaders to its regional and bilateral initiatives, it helped the Balkan subcomplex to transform into an embryonic security community that is based not on common identity (as a mature type), but on elite cooperation. This research project therefore argues that *between 1991 and 2013 the security situation in the Western Balkans changed drastically from largely negative and dominated by war to mostly positive and peaceful*. This change was achieved under the pressure of the international community, which from the end of 1999 has been led by the EU.

To evaluate the contribution of the EU into the improved security situation in the Western Balkans, the study analysed its influence on the transformation of regional security sectors, captured by the concept of security sector reform. SSR covers polices and activities promoting effective and efficient provision of state and human security within a framework of good and democratic governance. In the context of this work, *SSR is seen as a tool of complex security governance that can be used by internal and external actors to change the nature of security interdependence in states and regions, helping them move from the pole of enmity to the pole of amity*. The European Union has been engaged in conceptualisation and implementation of security sector reform since the 1990s. As a versatile instrument that is based on foreign, security and development policies, over the years SSR was used by the EU as an element of conflict-prevention, peace-building, democratisation, sustainable development, state-building and even member state-building.

As part national, part transnational policy, SSR can be applied by the EU as a tool of integration that aligns the work and management of the security sectors of non-EU states with EU values and norms. Currently, it is widely believed that SSR epitomises European integration, externalises the success of the EU as a security community and can be applied as a security community-building instrument (Spence 2010: 93, Ekengren 2010: 103). By studying the EU's impact on SSR in the Western Balkans between 1991 and 2013, it was demonstrated that the EU's engagement with the reform in the region had not always had the potential to be used as such an instrument. It developed from trial and error; and in 2013 as well as at the time of writing, it was still evolving. After all, the bloc started engaging in SSR-related activities in the Western Balkans before its concept of SSR was formulated, and its experience with the reform was not nearly as comprehensive as was prescribed by its theoretical framework. According to the latter, SSR is a multi-sector and long-term process, aimed at achieving accountable, effective and efficient security sectors that operate under civilian control and adhere to the principles of good governance, transparency and the rule of law.

As EU approaches to SSR on the state level were compared above, it only remains to summarise their implementation on the regional level. In 1991-1995, the context of open warfare that engulfed most of the Balkan subcomplex, leading many of its members to lose domestic monopoly over their security sectors, created no opening for the reform. The EU, that lacked capabilities and unity among its member states to prevent violence or effectively manage Yugoslavia's dissolution, did not yet see the Western Balkans as a distinct area in need of a regional approach. Most of the bloc's activities at this time were focused on finding a peaceful solution to conflicts between (post)-Yugoslav states and providing them with humanitarian aid. It is therefore impossible to speak about the use of SSR in the Western Balkans on the regional level between 1991 and 1995. The end of wars, however, brought about through a combination of diplomatic effort, exercised by the USA and Contact Group and NATO's intervention, changed this situation. When the EU released its Regional Approach, it was the first time the Western Balkans was formally recognised as a distinctive group, different from CEE and the rest of SEE. The RA was also the first instrument used by the EU to formulate requirements for the regional level of SSR. In general, this regional SSR conditionality was directed at normalisation of the work of security sectors in the Western Balkans. The focus was placed on post-conflict stabilisation and fostering good-neighbourly relations. It also promoted reciprocal relations that form the basis of security regimes. As the security regime did not take hold in the region, it is difficult to judge what aspects of SSR are typical for this type of an RSC. It is possible, however, to comment on elements of the reform applied by the EU to promote a shift from war to peace in the region.

The RA's SSR conditionality mostly concerned the work of the police (professionalisation, modernisation, cultivation of police culture respectful of human rights and intolerant to organised crime), border services (post-war reconstruction, introduction of international and EU standards of border management and normalisation of relations between states of the region), judiciary (securing its independence and professionalism) and in the case of Croatia, the FRY and Bosnia cooperation with the ICTY. While the EU commented on defence issues in certain Western Balkan states, it did not attempt to formulate region-wide requirements for the sphere. This is not surprising, as there was still no EU-wide security and defence policy. The RA also contained requirements for good governance of the security sector that differed from state to state, reflecting diverse levels of state consolidation in the region. In short, through the RA framework, the EU prioritised activities that could professionalise and modernise security sectors, as well as make the rule of law and respect of human rights commonly accepted in the Western Balkans. The bloc promoted harmonisation of relations between states of the region, hoping to turn them into good neighbours that would refrain from violence to solve future disagreements between each other, and choose peaceful means instead. Nonetheless, such reciprocity did not emerge in the region before 1999.

While SSR-related demands of the RA should be recognised, it is important not to overemphasise them. References to elements of the reform were disjointed and scattered around policy documents. This was one of the main reasons why SSR did not take off on the regional level in the Western Balkans in the immediate postwar period. The fact that the initiative was not fully supported and, in certain cases, opposed by regional actors, like Croatia and the FRY, contributed to the lack of effectiveness of the RA-supported SSR, too. Finally, it is noteworthy that the EU's RA activities were poorly coordinated with other external initiatives that promoted regional approaches to SEE. Such coordination was difficult in the absence of agreement in the international community on the definition of the Balkan subcomplex.

After the Kosovo conflict, the EU's approach to SSR started getting more coordinated and coherent. Having offered the Western Balkan states the prospect of membership and launched the Stabilisation and Association Process to support their integration, the EU confirmed that the future of the region lay in the bloc. Between 1999 and 2013, the Union came to explicitly acknowledge the importance of SSR for the reconstruction, stabilisation and Europeanisation of the region. If in the previous period, it tackled the reform timidly, hoping that security sectors in the Western Balkans would transform eventually, almost as a by-product of general conditionality, after 1999 it recognised SSR as a distinct reform agenda, in need of a targeted approach. This recognition was not immediate but gradual, since the Union was still in the process of formulating its SSR vision. Furthermore, it is worth noting that some of the EU's initial attempts to refine the concepts of the reform, developed by the Council and European Commission, took place in the Western Balkans. Thus, in 2006 two consecutive EU presidencies held high-profile events on SSR in the region that discussed not only regional SSR needs, but also the future of the EU as an SSR actor.

The EU used two main channels during this period to promote the reform regionally: the SP and SAP. The SP, launched by the bloc, but transferred into the OSCE ownership until it became regionally owned in 2008, had a broader coverage than the SAP, as it included Moldova, Bulgaria, Romania as well as the Western Balkans, while the SAP only focused on the latter group. Nonetheless, with time many of the SP SSR-related initiatives, such as the Migration, Asylum, Refugees Regional Initiative, developed an exclusive emphasis on the Western Balkan states. The EU provided strategic guidance and financial assistance to such projects. The SAP linked the stabilisation of the Western Balkans with the process of integration into the EU, thus introducing a new element into regional SSR. In addition to being used for post-conflict reconstruction, peace-building, democratisation and sustainable development, SSR also became an instrument of EU integration and member state-building. The SAP therefore does not set out to cultivate a separate

Western Balkan identity but strives to Europeanise the Western Balkans and make it part of the EU/Europe security community.

Deutsch identified three essential conditions for the success of security community: *compatibility of main values held by the political elites inside the community, political responsiveness and mutual predictability of behaviour*. The EU's involvement with regional level of SSR in the Western Balkans after 1999 has been pursuing the fulfilment of these conditions. The framework of the SAP has been used to bring the Western Balkan elites to congruent values by insisting they adopt "the values and models on which [the EU] is founded" and adopt social, economic and political rights and liberties shared by EU member states (Council of the EU 2000). Transparency, accountability and good security governance have been among the main values promoted in the sphere of security. By agreeing to pursue membership in the bloc and follow the SAP conditionality, the Western Balkan elites have agreed to adhere to values, shared inside the EU. Political responsiveness, which is understood through building effective and efficient institutions, was facilitated through the organisational level of SSR. In 1999-2013, the EU encouraged security and political elites of the Western Balkans to become more responsive to each other through capacity-building, assistance with modernisation and professionalisation of their security sectors and development of support functions of their defence bodies, police services and border management systems. Finally, mutual predictability of behaviour required regular contact between security sectors of the Western Balkan states. The EU endorsed such contact through regional projects and initiatives that exposed regional players to the principles and standards guiding the functioning and management of security systems in its own member states. As the main recipients of the SAP conditionality were political elites and not entire societies, the EU's endeavours to harmonise relations between Western Balkan states led to the emergence of an embryonic or elite security community in the region. SSR efforts in this type of an RSC can be seen to show equal attention to issues of governance and functioning of the security sectors. Thus, within the SAP, the EU emphasised the need for democratic and civilian oversight as well as efficiency and effectiveness of the Western Balkan security sectors, trying to build functioning states, whose security systems would be compatible with the security systems of the bloc's members.

In short, *the EU's regional approach to SSR in the Western Balkans evolved* considerably throughout the studied period: if in the early 1990s, the Union was unable to deal with the reform due to the hostile environment and lack of capabilities, in the mid-1990s it promoted elements of SSR, even without having a formal framework on the reform, as an instrument of stabilisation and from 1999-2000, while still working on the conceptualisation of the reform agenda, applied it as an instrument of integration into the bloc and member state-building. Between 1991 and 2013, the EU *learned to be an actor of SSR by doing*. Its *evolution* was by no means perfect, not only because the concepts, formulated by the Council and Commission in 2005-2006, were not united into a single programme or because the practical application of the reform was not as comprehensive as the concepts suggested but first and foremost because clean and perfect evolution is not possible in the complex world. In the context of *uncertainty, cognitive challenges, complex risks,* and constant *adaptability* to growing vulnerabilities, that define social (and natural) relations, evolution is never complete, while learning and adaptation are constantly present. Thus, the EU's engagement with the reform has been non-linear and messy, like all relations in complex systems.

Although compared to the RA period, in 1999-2013, the EU's SSR-related regional projects were more frequent and better coordinated, they were rarely presented as part of the SSR agenda. Despite this, the objectives and outcomes of such initiatives were normally aligned with the reform concepts, accepted by the EU. By promoting good governance, accountability and efficiency of security systems in the Western Balkans, through the SP and SAP projects, the EU contributed to developing *positive security relations* between the states of the region. When SSR started to be applied as a member state-building tool, the Western Balkan elites were introduced to security practices of EU member states that as members of the mature security community tend to solve their disputed peacefully, without resorting to violence. This application can therefore be linked to the emergence of an elite security community in the region, whose members choose peaceful cooperation, too, but because of the policies pursued by decision-making elites, not due to the common identity. The fact that security community, that emerged in the Western Balkans, was contingent on elites deserves special attention. Particularly, in light of the regional development in the decade after 2013, the ending point of this research. With the region showing signs of democratic stagnation and some of its elites displaying populist and authoritarian tendencies, it is important to understand that an elite security community can unravel easily unless practices, typical of this form of security governance, penetrate non-elite communities. Without the involvement of the local level, states of the region cannot find the resilience that is needed not simply for surviving in the world of constant change but also learning from this change and transforming into stronger, more effective members of the international community (Korosteleva and Petrova 2021).

Changing security landscape in the Western Balkans and security governance in times of complexity

Having studied over twenty years of the EU — Western Balkan relations, what have we learnt about the EU as a security actor and the security dynamics of the region? The first lesson is that of co-evolution: by engaging in SSR in the Western Balkans on regional and state levels, the EU not simply contributed to the improved regional security situation but also evolved as a security actor. Throughout the studied period, the EU continued developing by building up its foreign, security and defence toolbox and *learning by doing*. Thus, it developed CFSP and CSDP in many respects in response to the rapidly changing situation in the Western Balkans, employed its first CSDP missions in the region and honed the concept of SSR in the "field laboratory" of Western Balkan states. It is customary to criticise the bloc for its failures in the region, but it is rarely acknowledged that it mostly had acted within its capabilities at the time, while balancing its own (often emergent) policies with the work of other international actors and simultaneously learning to speak with one voice on the international arena. Co-evolution therefore is one of the defining elements of the EU's governance of security risks, emanating from the Western Balkans.

The second lesson is about the contextual character of complex security governance. The context, composed of temporal and spatial elements, had a great impact on the ways in which the EU had engaged in SSR in the studied period and will continue influencing its security governance in the future. What is more, this context is multi-layered[276], which means that it includes different levels, e.g. local, state, regional and global. Changes on any of the levels can affect the EU's engagement with its Western Balkan partners and how they respond to this engagement in a myriad of ways. While many examples of the importance of context can be extracted from the main body of the book, to illustrate the point here, examples are drawn from the current situation in the region. For instance, the local level has gained prominence in Bosnia due to the growing fears over the secession of one of its entities—Republika Srpska. This prompted the EU to engage more actively with elites below the state level (NSC 2022). On the regional level, tensions between Western Balkan states have also become more prominent, compared to 2013: e.g. in August 2022, NATO and the EU had to intervene into the dispute between Serbia and Kosovo regarding the identity documents, required for crossing the border between them. While NATO oversaw the removal of roadblocks, set up by Serbs living in the North of Kosovo, the EU mediated a deal over the movement of citizens across the border (BBC 2022) The deal helped to defuse tensions, but also demonstrated the EU's limitations as it still lacked a long-term plan for "the lasting settlement of the issue" (Bechev 2022). In terms of the global context, the security situation in the Western Balkans in 2022 was more obviously affected by Russia and China, both global powers, than a decade before. For instance, Russia has further strengthened its military ties with Serbia, selling it weapons, aircraft and anti-aircraft systems (Karastanovic 2022), which in turn has affected the EU's engagement with the country's defence reform. Close ties with Russia, not only in Serbia, but also BiH and Montenegro were also observed in gatherings of far-right groups in support of Russia's invasion of Ukraine (ibid.). Thus, the context in the region continues changing and the EU will have to continue learning and adapting to keep the region inside its zone of peace.

The third and final lesson considered here concerns the effects of EU security governance. It is important to acknowledge and accept (including for the bloc itself) that the EU, as a complex system, that engages with other complex systems (in the context of this work, the Western Balkan states) is not in control of the impact it has. The effects of complex systems are also complex, and can materialise in nonlinearities, indirect effects, feedback, contingencies and unintended consequences.[277] No matter what type of effects a system produces, another thing to bear in mind is that they are likely to be non-reversible or not easily amendable. For example, the unintended consequence of the arms embargoes, introduced by the EU in the 1990s, are still felt in the second decade of the 2000s. While preventing the conflicts from escalation, they also contributed to the spread of organised crime, which remains one of the key problems in the region[278], and not only in states that are still seeking membership in the bloc but also Croatia, despite it having joined the EU a decade ago[279]. It also affects the EU itself. For this reason, when studying security governance of complexity, it is suggested here that security is approached not as control, but as resilience, as a process of self-governance, which recognises the importance of relations between elements of a system and between systems. What is more, it is crucial to recognise that security relations are not one-sided but reciprocal. For example, recipient of EU policies can later have an impact on these policies and their implementation as was seen on the case of de-mining in Croatia: having benefited from EU support in de-mining, Croatia developed valuable expertise it continues sharing with the EU and outside of it in the framework of CSDP missions and operations.

While these observations are made on the basis of the study of EU SSR efforts in the Western Balkans, they could be applicable to the study of complex security governance more broadly. This research demonstrated that in the world of increasing vulnerability, uncertainty, complexity and ambiguity, also known as the VUCA-world (Burrows and Gnad 2017), security governance is closely intertwined with *co-evolution, context (or timescapes)* and *resilience*.

270 For the values of temporal variance in comparative research, see Bartolini (1993).
271 The self-proclaimed Croatian entity in BiH, Herzeg-Bosna, was also denied recognition on the same grounds.
272 Bosniaks were the exception.
273 The country joined the Schengen area on 1 January 2023.
274 While they still displayed certain discrepancies in development.
275 Summary of the EU's impact on SSR in Croatia, Serbia and Bosnia in 1991-2013 is provided in Annex II.
276 Interview with a security expert from Croatia in 2021.
277 For details of each effect, see Jervis (2012).
278 Interviews with security experts in Croatia, Bosnia and Serbia in 2016, and on Zoom in 2021.
279 Interview with a regional SSR expert in 2021.

Bibliography

ACPS (2022) *The Academy of Criminalistic and Police Studies* [online]. Available from: http://www.kpa.edu.rs/en/ [Accessed 10/06/2022].

Adler, E. (1998). Seeds of Peaceful Change: the OSCE's Security Community-Building Model. In: E. Adler and M.N. Barnett, eds., *Security Communities*. Cambridge: Cambridge University Press, pp. 119-160.

Adler, E. and Barnett, M.N. (eds.) (1998) *Security Communities*. Cambridge: Cambridge University Press.

AETS Consortium (2015) *Self-Evaluation of the Projects "Support to Mine Action and Ammunition Destruction"* [online]. Available from: https://europa.ba/wp-content/uploads/2015/10/Final-Evaluation-Report-29092015.pdf [Accessed 19/10/2021].

Ahmetasevic, N. (2007) Bosnia's Book of the Dead. *Justice Report* [online]. Available from: http://www.justice-report.com/en/articles/bosnia-s-book-of-the-dead [Accessed 12/08/2022].

Aigner, D., O'Connor, S. and Kacapor-Dzihic, Z. (2013) *Ex-Post Evaluations of CARDS Programmes in the Western Balkans (Albania, Bosnia and Herzegovina, Croatia, Serbia, Montenegro, Kosovo, and the former Yugoslav Republic of Macedonia)* [online]. Kielce: EPRD. Available from: http://www.evropa.gov.rs/Documents/Home/DACU/12/193/Ex-post%20CARDS%20in%20WB%20final%20report.pdf [Accessed 01/04/2022].

Andreas, P. (2005) Criminalizing Consequences of Sanctions: Embargo Busting and Its Legacy. *International Studies Quarterly*, 49(2), pp. 335-360.

Andreas, P. (2006) The Clandestine Political Economy of War and Peace in Bosnia. In: M.A. Innes, ed., *Bosnian Security after Dayton: New Perspectives*. London and N.Y.: Routledge, pp. 71-95.

Andric, G. (2013) Serb to Run Police in North Kosovo. *BalkanInsight* [online]. Available from: http://www.balkaninsight.com/en/article/belgrade-pristina-reach-deal-on-kosovo-north-police [Accessed 21/04/2022].

APMBC (Anti-Personnel Mine Ban Convention) (2013) *Statement of the Republic of Croatia on Mine Clearance* [online]. 13MSP to APMBC, Geneva, 2–5 December 2013. Available from: https://www.apminebanconvention.org/fileadmin/APMBC/MSP/13MSP/day4/11b_ARTICLE_5_EXTENSION_GRANTED_-_Croatia.pdf [Accessed 12/12/2021].

Armstrong, A. and Rubin, B.R. (2002) *Policy Approaches to Regional Conflict Formations*. N.Y.: Centre on International Cooperation.

Armstrong, A. and Rubin, B.R. (2005) The Great Lakes and South Central Asia. In: S. Chesterman, M. Ignatieff and R. Thakur, eds., *Making States Work: State Failure and the Crisis of Governance.* Tokyo: United Nations University Press, pp. 79-101.

Arndt, K. (2000) Management Selection for the State Border Service for Bosnia and Herzegovina. *36th IAMPS*, pp. 35-42.

ASAC (1996) *Agreement of Sub-Regional Arms Control*, Florence, 14 June 1996.

Associated Press (1996) U.N. Formally Ends the Sanctions on Yugoslavia. *New York Times* [online]. Available from: http://www.nytimes.com /1996/10/02/world/un-formally-ends-the-sanctions-on-yugoslavi a.html [Accessed 09/06/2022].

Ayoob, M. (1986) *Regional Security in the Third World.* London: Croom Helm.

Ayoob, M. (1995) The Third World Security Predicament: State Making, Regional Conflict, and the International System. Boulder, CO: Lynne Rienner.

Bailes, A.J.K. (2010) The Quest for an EU Approach for Security Sector Reform. In: M. Ekengren and G. Simons, eds., The Politics of Security Sector Reform: Challenges and Opportunities for the European Union's Global Role. London and N.Y.: Routledge, pp. 65-79.

B92 (2007) Bildt: EU Policy Depends on the Election [online]. Available from: https://www.b92.net/info/vesti/index.php?yyyy=2007&mm =01&dd=15&nav_id=227709&nav_category=11&order=priority [Accessed 09/08/2022].

Baker, J. and DeFrank, T. (1995) The Politics of Diplomacy. New York: Putnam.

Bakic, B. and Gajic, N. (2006) *Police Reform in Serbia: Five Years Later.* Balkans Series 06/21. Swindon: Conflict Studies Research Centre.

BalkanInsight (2012) *Serbs Defensive over War Crimes, Survey Shows* [online]. Available from: http://www.balkaninsight.com/en/article/Serbian -attitudes-towards-war-crime-prosecution [Accessed 09/08/2022].

Ball, N. (1998) Spreading Good Practices in Security Reform: Policy Options for the British Government. London: Safeworld.

Ball, N. (2010) The Evolution of the Security Sector Reform Agenda. In: M. Sedra, ed., The Future of Security Sector Reform. Ontario: GIGI, pp. 29-44.

Barany, Z.D. (1991) Civil-Military Relations in Communist Systems: Western Models Revisited. Journal of Political and Military Sociology, 19 (1), pp. 75-99.

Baric, S. (2006) The Croatian Armed Forces and NATO. Balkans Series 06/20. Swindon: Conflict Studies Research Centre.

Bartolini, S. (1993) On Time and Comparative Research. Journal of Theoretical Politics, 5(2), pp.131-167.

Bassuener, K. W. (2005) Lost Opportunities and Unlearned Lessons — the Continuing Legacy of Bosnia. In: A. H. Ebnöther and P. Fluri, eds., *After Intervention: Public Security Management in Post-Conflict Societies — From Intervention to Sustainable Local Ownership.* Vienna and Geneva: Bureau for Security Policy at the Austrian Ministry of Defence, National Defence Academy, Vienna and Geneva Centre for the Democratic Control of Armed Forces, Geneva in co-operation with PfP-Consortium of Defence Academies and Security Studies Institutes, pp. 101-138.

Bassuener, K. W. (2015) Virtual Deterrence — BiH's Institutionalized Insecurity and the International Flight from Responsibility. In: S. Keil and V. Perry, eds., *State-Building and Democratization in Bosnia and Herzegovina.* London and N.Y., pp. 85-107

Bassuener, K. W. (2015a) *The Armed Forces of Bosnia and Herzegovina: Unfulfilled Promise.* Policy Note No 04. Berlina and Sarajevo: Democratization Policy Council.

Bassuener, K. W. (2021) The EU's Humiliating Failure in Bosnia. Carnegie Europe. [online]. Available from: https://carnegieeurope.eu/strategiceurope/85705Serb [Accessed 11/09/2022].

BBC (2022) Serbia-Kosovo ID document row settled, says EU. [online]. Available from: https://www.bbc.co.uk/news/world-europe-62702819 [Accessed 11/09/2022].

BCHRSM (Belgrade Centre for Human Rights and Startegic Marketing) (2005) *Public Opinion in Serbia: Attitudes towards the ICTY* [online]. Available from: http://www.bgcentar.org.rs/bgcentar/eng-lat/wp-content/uploads/2005/10/Attitudes-towards-war-crimes-the-ICTY.ppt [Accessed 09/09/2022].

Bechev, D. (2006) Carrots, Sticks and Norms: the EU and Regional Cooperation in Southeast Europe. *Journal of Southern Europe and the Balkans,* 8(1), pp.27-43.

Bechev, D. (2011) *Constructing South East Europe.* Houndmills, Basingstoke, Hampshire: Palgrave Macmillan.

Bechev, D. (2012) Dynamics and Achievements of Regional Cooperation. In: C. Solioz and P. Stubbs, eds., *Towards Open Regionalism in South East Europe.* Baden-Baden: Nomos Publishers, pp. 71 – 88.

Bechev, D. (2022) The Latest Kosovo-Serbia Tensions Reveal the EU's Diplomatic Limits, Carnegie Europe. https://carnegieeurope.eu/2022/08/25/latest-kosovo-serbia-tensions-reveal-eu-s-diplomatic-limits-pub-87755 [Accessed 15/10/2022].

Becirevic, E. and Cehajic, M. (2013) Politics, Policing and Security Sector Reform in Post-War Bosnia and Herzegovina. In: T. Flessenkemper and D. Helly, eds., *Ten Years after: Lessons from the EUPM in Bosnia and Herzegovina 2002-2012*. Paris: ISS, pp. 44-50.

Benedek, W., Daase, C., Dimitrijevic, V. and van Duyne, P. (Eds.) (2010) *Transnational Terrorism, Organized Crime and Peace-Building: Human Security in the Western Balkans*. New York: Palgrave Macmillan.

Berenschot and Imagos (2013) *Thematic Evaluation of Rule of Law, Judicial Reform and Fight against Corruption and Organised Crime in the Western Balkans – Lot 3* [online]. Final Main Report. Available from: https://ec.europa.eu/neighbourhood-enlargement/sites/near/files/pdf/financial_assistance/phare/evaluation/2013_final_main_report_lot_3.pdf [Accessed 15/04/2022].

Berg, L.A. (2016) From Weakness to Strength: The political Roots of Security Sector Reform in Bosnia and Herzegovina. In: U. C. Schroeder and F. Chappuis, eds., *Building Security in Post-Conflict States: The Domestic Consequences of Security Sector Reform*. Oxon: Rotledge, pp. 17-32.

Bertin, T. (2008) The EU Military Operation in Bosnia. In: M. Merlingen and R. Ostrauskaite, eds., *European Security and Defence Policy*. London: Routledge, pp. 61-77.

Bhaumik, S., Gang, I. and Yun, M. (2006). Ethnic conflict and economic disparity: Serbians and Albanians in Kosovo. *Journal of Comparative Economics*, 34(4), pp.754-773.

BHMAC (Bosnia and Herzegovina Mine Action Centre) (n.d.) *BHMAC Organization Chart* [online]. Available from: http://www.bhmac.org/?page_id=704&lang=en [Accessed 03/11/2021].

Bilandzic, V. (2006) *Parliamentary Control of Defence and Security Sector in South East Europe* [online]. Report EP/EXPOL/B/2005/34. Directorate-General for External Policies of the Union Directorate B – Policy Department. Available from: http://www.pedz.uni-mannheim.de/daten/edz-ma/ep/06/pe381.387-en.pdf [Accessed 23/04/2022].

Bieber, F. (2003) Montenegrin Politics Since the Disintegration of Yugoslavia. In: F. Bieber, ed., *Montenegro in Transition: Problems of Identity and Statehood*. Baden-Baden: Nomos, pp. 11-42.

Bieber, F. (2010) *Policing the Peace after Yugoslavia: Police Reform between External Imposition and Domestic Reform* [online]. GRIPS State-Building Workshop 2010: Organizing Police Forces in Post-Conflict Peace-Support Operations, January 27-28th, 2010. Available from: http://www.grips.ac.jp/r-center/en/discussion_papers/10-07/ [Accessed 02/10/2022].

Bieber, F. and Daskalovski, Z. (2003) *Understanding the war in Kosovo*. London: Routledge.

Bjelotomic, S. (2017) Illegal Weapons in Serbia: Tragic Legacy of 1990s. *Serbian Monitor* [online]. Available from: http://serbianmonitor.com/en/society/28599/illegal-weapons-serbia/ [Accessed 09/08/2022].

Bjola, C. (2001) *NATO as a Factor of Security Community Building*. EAPC-NATO 2000/01 Report.

Bideleux, R. and Jeffries, I. (2007) *The Balkans: A Post-Communist History*. London: Routledge.

Blockmans, S. (2007). *Tough Love: The European Union's Relations with the Western Balkans*. Thesis (PhD), Leiden University.

Boese, W. (1999) Belgrade to Abide by Sub-Regional Arms Control Agreement. *Arms Control Association* [online]. Available from: https://www.armscontrol.org/act/1999_07-08/belja99 [Accessed 07/05/2022].

BPBiH (Border Police of Bosnia and Herzegovina) (n.d.) History [online]. Available from: http://www.granpol.gov.ba/Content/Read/49?title=Historijat [Accessed 22/12/2021].

Brenner, M. (1992) The EC in Yugoslavia: A Debut Performance. *Security Studies*, 1(4), pp. 586-609.

Bretherton, C. and Vogler, J. (2005) *The European Union as a Global Actor*. 2nd ed. London: Routledge.

Bojicic-Dzelilovic, V. and Kostovicova, D. (2013) Europeanisation and Conflict Networks: Private Sector Development in Post-Conflict Bosnia-Herzegovina. *East European Politics*, 29(1), pp.19-35.

Bojicic-Dzelilovic, V., Kostovicova, D. and Randazzo, E. (2016) *EU in the Western Balkans: Hybrid Development, Hybrid Security and Hybrid Justice* [online]. Security in Transition SiT/WP/03/16. Available from: http://www.securityintransition.org/wp-content/uploads/2016/02/WP03_Balkans_FinalEditedVersion.pdf [Accessed 10/07/2022].

Bourne, M. (2014) *Understanding Security*. London: Palgrave Macmillan.

Buchet de Neuilly, Y. (2008) *European External Relations Fields: The Multi-Pillar Issue of Economic Sanctions against Serbia* [online]. Paris: CRPS. Available from: http://citeseerx.ist.psu.edu/viewdoc/download?doi=10.1.1.591.9161&rep=rep1&type=pdf [Accessed 02/05/2022].

Burrows, M., and O. Gnad. (2017) Between 'Muddling Through' and 'Grand Design': Regaining Political Initiative—The Role of Strategic Foresight. *Futures* 97: 6–17.

Busek, E. and Kuehne, B. (eds.) (2010) *From Stabilisation to Integration: The Stability Pact for South Eastern Europe*. Vienna: Bohlau.

Buzan, B. (2007) *People, States and Fear: An agenda for International Security Studies in the Post-Cold War Era*. 2nd ed. Colchester: ECPR Press.

Buzan, B. and Waever, O. (2003) *Regions and Powers: The Structure of International Security*. Cambridge: Cambridge University Press.

Buzan, B., Waever, O. and de Wilde, J. (1998) *Security: A New Framework for Analysis*. London: Lynne Rienner.

Cameron, F. (1999) Foreign and Security Policy of the European Union: Past, Present and Future. Sheffield: Sheffield Academic Press.

Cantori, L.J. and Spiegel, S.L. (1970) The International Politics of Regions: A Comparative Approach. Englewood Cliffs: Prentice Hall.

Caparini, M. (2006) Security Sector Reform in the Western Balkans [online]. Istanbul: TESEV. Available from: http://tesev.org.tr/wp-content/uploads/2015/11/Security_Sector_Reform_In_The_Western_Balkans.pdf [Accessed 09/09/2022].

Carapic, J., Chaudhuri, P. and Gobinet, P. (2016) Sustainable Stockpile Management in Bosnia and Herzegovina: The Role of EUFOR Mobile Training Team for Weapons and Ammunition Management. Working Paper 24. Geneva: Small Arms Survey and Swiss Verification Unit.

Carlsson, I. (1992) A new International Order Through the United Nations. *Security Dialogue*, 23(4), pp. 7–11.

Caruso, U. (2007) Interplay between the Council of Europe, OSCE, EU and NATO. Bozen: European Academy.

Cascone, G. (2008) ESDP Operations and NATO: Co-operation, Rivalry or Muddling-Through? In: M. Merlingen and R. Ostrauskaite, eds., *European Security and Defence Policy: An Implementation Perspective*. London: Routledge, pp. 143–158.

CEAS (Centre for Euro-Atlantic Studies) (2013) *Serbia: Law on Private Security* [online]. Policy Brief. Available from: https://www.ceas-serbia.org/images/2015-i-pre/AOG_Policy_Brief_I_-_September_2013_-_Law_on_Private_Security.pdf [Accessed 15/08/2022].

Centar (2015) *EU and SEESAC Help Serbia Combat Illegal Weapons* [online]. Project: Targeting Weapons—Misuse of Weapons in Serbia. Available from: http://publicpolicy.rs/arhiva/985/eu-and-seesac-help-serbia-combat-illegal-weapons?lang=en#.WoA3DiXFLIX [Accessed 08/09/2021].

CEPOL (n.d.) *External Partners* [online]. Available from: https://www.cepol.europa.eu/who-we-are/partners-and-stakeholders/external-partners [Accessed 18/08/2021].

Chanaa, J. (2002) *Security Sector Reform: Issues, Challenges and Prospects*. Adelphi Paper 344. Oxford: Oxford University Press for the International Institute for Strategic Studies.

Chandler, D. (2006) From Dayton to Europe. In: D. Chandler, *Peace without Politics? Ten Years of International State-Building in Bosnia*. London and N.Y.: Routledge, pp. 30-43.

Chandler, D. (2018) *Ontopolitics in the Anthropocene: An Introduction to Mapping, Sensing and Hacking*. Abingdon: Routledge.

Churruca Muguruza, C. (2008) *European Union Support for Security Sector Reform: The Added Value of the EU as a Global Security Actor*. Cuadernos de Estrategia, 138, pp. 73-109.

Cillliers, P. (2001) Boundaries, Hierarchies and Networks in Complex Systems. *International Journal of Innovation Management*, 5(2), pp.135-147.

Closa Montero, C. (2007) *Study on Democratic Control of Armed Forces: Who Controls?* European Commission for Democracy through Law (Venice Commission). Study No. 389.

Collantes-Celador, G. (2005) Police Reform: Peacebuilding through 'Democratic Policing'? *International Peacekeeping*, 12(3), pp.364-376.

Collantes-Celador, G. (2009) *Becoming 'European' Through Police Reform: A Successful Strategy in Bosnia and Herzegovina?* [online]. Available from: http://openaccess.city.ac.uk/13771/ [Accessed 22/11/2021].

Collantes-Celador, G. and Juncos, A. (2011) Security Sector Reform in the Western Balkans: The Challenge of Coherence and Effectiveness. In: In: M. Ekengren and G. Simons, eds., *The Politics of Security Sector Reform: Challenges and Opportunities for the European Union's Global Role*. London and N.Y.: Routledge, pp. 127-154.

Collantes-Celador, G. and Juncos, A. (2012) The EU and Border Management in the Western Balkans: Preparing for European Integration or Safeguarding EU external borders? *Southeast European and Black Sea Studies*, 12(2), pp.201-220.

Collier, D. (2011) Understanding Process Tracing. *Political Science and Politics*, 44 (4), pp. 823-830.

de Coning, C. (2018) Adaptive Peacebuilding. *International Affairs*, 94(2), pp. 301-307.

Constitution of the Federal Republic of Yugoslavia (1992) Sluzbeni list (SRS), 1992-04-27, no 1, pp. 1-11.

Constitution of the Republic of Croatia (1990), Narodne Novine, no. 56.

Constitution of the Republic of Croatia (2001) Narodne Novine, no. 41.

Constitution of the Republic of Croatia (2010) Narodne Novine, no. 76.

Constitution of The Republic of Serbia (2006) Official Gazette of the RS No 98.

Cottey, A. (2009) The Kosovo War in Perspective. *International Affairs*, 85 (3), pp. 593-608.

Cottey, A. (2012) The Other Europe: Regional Security Governance in Europe's East. In: S. Breslin and S. Croft, eds., *Comparative Regional Security Governance*. London: Routledge, pp. 44-71.

Council of the EU (1991) Council Regulation (EEC) No 3300/ 91 of 11 November 1991 Suspending the Trade Concessions Provided for by the Cooperation Agreement between the European Economic Community and the Socialist Federal Republic of Yugoslavia. *Official Journal of the European Union*, L 315, 15.11.1991, pp. 1-2.

Council of the EU (1991a) Council Regulation (EEC) No. 3567/91 of 2 December 1991 Concerning the Arrangements Applicable to the Import of Products Originating in the Republics of Bosnia-Herzegovina, Croatia, Macedonia and Slovenia. *Official Journal of the European Union*, L 342, p. 1.

Council of the EU (1996) 96/184/CFSP: Common Position of 26 February 1996 Defined by the Council on the Basis of Article J.2 of the Treaty on European Union Concerning Arms Exports to the Former Yugoslavia. *Official Journal of the European Union*, L 58, pp.1-2.

Council of the EU (1998) 98/240/CFSP: Common Position of 19 March 1998 defined by the Council on the Basis of Article J.2 of the Treaty on European Union on Restrictive Measures against the Federal Republic of Yugoslavia. *Official Journal of the European Union*, L 95, pp. 1-3.

Council of the EU (1998a) 98/725/CFSP: Common Position of 14 December 1998 Defined by the Council on the Basis of Article J.2 of the Treaty on European Union on Restrictive Measures to be Taken against Persons in the Federal Republic of Yugoslavia Acting against the Independent Media. *Official Journal of the European Union*, L 345, pp. 1-2.

Council of the EU (1999) 1999/319/CFSP: Council Decision of 10 May 1999 Implementing Common Position 1999/318/CFSP Concerning Additional Restrictive Measures against the Federal Republic of Yugoslavia. *Official Journal of the European Union*, L 123, pp. 3-11.

Council of the EU (1999a) 1999/318/CFSP: Common Position of 10 May 1999 Adopted by the Council on the Basis of Article 15 of the Treaty on European Union Concerning Additional Restrictive Measures Against the Federal Republic of Yugoslavia. *Official Journal of the European Union*, L 123, pp. 1-2.

BIBLIOGRAPHY 337

Council of the EU (1999b) 1999/424/CFSP: Council Decision of 28 June 1999 Amending Decision 1999/357/CFSP Implementing Common Position 1999/318/CFSP Concerning Additional Restrictive Measures against the Federal Republic of Yugoslavia. *Official Journal of the European Union*, L 163, pp. 86-93.

Council of the EU (1999c) 1999/612/CFSP: Council Decision of 13 September 1999 Amending Decision 1999/424/CFSP Implementing Common Position 1999/318/CFSP Concerning Additional Restrictive Measures against the Federal Republic of Yugoslavia. *Official Journal of the European Union*, L 242, pp. 32-39.

Council of the EU (1999d) Council Regulation (EC) No 900/1999 of 29 April 1999 Prohibiting the Sale and Supply of Petroleum and Certain Petroleum Products to the Federal Republic of Yugoslavia (FRY). *Official Journal of the European Union*, L 114, pp. 7-9.

Council of the EU (1999e) Council Regulation (EC) No 2111/1999 of 4 October 1999 Prohibiting the Sale and Supply of Petroleum and Certain Petroleum Products to Certain Parts of the Federal Republic of Yugoslavia (FRY) and Repealing Regulation (EC) No 900/1999. *Official Journal of the European Union*, L258, pp. 12-18.

Council of the EU (2000) Council Joint Action of 16 November 2000 on the holding of a meeting of Heads of State or of Government in Zagreb (Zagreb Summit). *Official Journal of the European Union*, L 290, 17/11/2000, p. 54.

Council of the EU (2000a) 2000/177/CFSP: Council Decision of 28 February 2000 Amending Decision 1999/319/CFSP Implementing Common Position 1999/318/CFSP Concerning Additional Restrictive Measures against the Federal Republic of Yugoslavia. *Official Journal of the European Union*, L 56, pp. 2-20.

Council of the EU (2000b) Council Decision of 22 May 2000 Amending Decision 1999/319/CFSP Implementing Common Position 1999/318/CFSP Concerning Additional Restrictive Measures against the Federal Republic of Yugoslavia. *Official Journal of the European Union*, L 122, pp. 7-26.

Council of the EU (2000c) Council Decision of 5 June 2000 Amending Decision 1999/319/CFSP Implementing Common Position 1999/318/CFSP Concerning Additional Restrictive Measures against the Federal Republic of Yugoslavia. *Official Journal of the European Union*, L 134, pp. 1-20.

Council of the EU (2000d) Council Decision of 3 August 2000 Amending Decision 1999/319/CFSP Implementing Common Position 1999/318/CFSP Concerning Additional Restrictive Measures against the Federal Republic of Yugoslavia. *Official Journal of the European Union*, L 200, pp. 1-20.

Council of the EU (2001) Council Common Position of 26 February 2001 amending Common Position 2000/696/CFSP on the maintenance of specific restrictive measures directed against Mr Milosevic and persons associated with him and repealing Common Position 98/725/CFSP. *Official Journal of the European Union*, L 57, pp. 3-4.

Council of the EU (2002) Council Joint Action 2002/211/CFSP of 11 March 2002 Appointing Lord Paddy Ashdown as the European Union Special Representative in Bosnia and Herzegovina. *Official Journal of the European Union*, L 70, p. 7.

Council of the EU (2002a) Council Joint Action 2002/210/CFSP of 11 March 2002 on the European Union Police Mission. *Official Journal of the European Union*, L 70, pp. 1-6.

Council of the EU (2004) 2004/520/EC: Council Decision of 14 June 2004 on the Principles, Priorities and Conditions Contained in the European Partnership with Serbia and Montenegro including Kosovo as Defined by the United Nations Security Council Resolution 1244 of 10 June 1999. *Official Journal of the European Union*, L 27, pp. 21-34.

Council of the EU (2004a) 2004/515/EC Council Decision of 14 June 2004 on the Principles, Priorities and Conditions Contained in the European Partnership with Bosnia and Herzegovina. *Official Journal of the European Union*, L 221.

Council of the EU (2004b) *Concept for the European Union (EU) Military Operation in Bosnia and Herzegovina (BiH)*. Brussels, 29 September 2004, 12576/04.

Council of the EU (2005) EU Concept for ESDP support to Security Sector Reform (SSR). Brussels, 12566/4/05.

Council of the EU (2006) Draft Council Conclusions on a Policy Framework for Security Sector Reform. Brussels, 9967/06.

Council of the EU (2006a) 2006/56/EC: Council Decision of 30 January 2006 on the Principles, Priorities and Conditions Contained in the European Partnership with Serbia and Montenegro Including Kosovo as Defined by the United Nations Security Council Resolution 1244 of 10 June 1999 and Repealing Decision 2004/520/EC. *Official Journal of the European Union*, L 35, pp. 32-56.

Council of the EU (2006b) *Integrated Border Management; Strategy Deliberations*. Brussels, 13926/3/06.

Council of the EU (2006c) *EU Strategy to Combat Illicit Accumulation and Trafficking of SALW and their Ammunition*. Brussels, 5319/06.

Council of the EU (2008) 2008/213/EC: Council Decision of 18 February 2008 on the Principles, Priorities and Conditions Contained in the European Partnership with Serbia Including Kosovo as Defined by United Nations Security Council Resolution 1244 of 10 June 1999 and Repealing Decision 2006/56/EC. *Official Journal of the European Union*, L 80, pp. 46–70.

Council of the EU (2010) *Visa liberalisation for Albania and Bosnia and Herzegovina*. Brussels, 8 November 2010, 15957/10, PRESSE 294.

Council of the EU (2010a) *2992nd Council meeting – Foreign Affairs*. Press Release: Council Doc. 5686/10 (Presse 10), Brussels, 25 January 2010.

Council of the EU (2014) Fifteenth Progress Report on the implementation of the EU Strategy to Combat Illicit Accumulation and Trafficking of SALW and their Ammunition – (2013/I) (2014/C 178/02). *Official Journal of the European Union*, C 178, pp. 2-8.

Court of Auditors (1996) Special Report No 2/96 Concerning the Accounts of the Administrator and the European Union Administration, Mostar (EUAM) Accompanied by the Replies of the Commission and the Administrator of Mostar. *Official Journal of the European Union*, C 287, Volume 39.

Court of Auditors (2007) Special Report No 5/2007 on the Commission's Management of the CARDS Programme together with the Commission's Replies. *Official Journal of the European Union*, C 285, pp. 1-23.

CoY AC (Conference on Yugoslavia Arbitration Commission) (1992) Opinions on Questions Arising from the Dissolution of Yugoslavia. *International Legal Materials*, 31, pp. 1494-1527.

Craven, M. C.R. (1996) The European Community Arbitration Commission on Yugoslavia. *British Yearbook of International Law*, 66, (1), pp. 333-413. CROMAC (n.d.) *IPA* [online]. Available from: https://www.hcr.hr/en/ipa.asp [Accessed 19/12/2021].

Daalder, I.H. (1996) Fear and Loathing in the Former Yugoslavia. In: M.E. Brown, ed., *The International Dimensions of Internal Conflict*. Cambridge: MIT Press, pp. 35-68.

DCAF (2006) *European Union Presidency Seminar on Security Sector Reform (SSR) in the Western Balkans*. Vienna, 13–14 February 2006. Food for Thought Paper (on file with author).

Delevic, M. (2007) *Regional Cooperation in the Western Balkans*. Chaillot Paper No 104. Paris: ISS.

DEUBiH (Delegation of the EU to Bosnia and Herzegovina) (2012) *EU Support to the Integrated Border Management in BiH* [online]. Available from: http://europa.ba/?p=12333 [Accessed 10/12/2021].

DEUBiH (Delegation of the EU to Bosnia and Herzegovina) (2015) *EU Support to Law Enforcement* [online]. IPA 2010 CRIS Number—2010/022-259. Available from: https://europa.ba/wp-content/uploads/2015/05/delegacijaEU_2012101515362548eng.pdf [Accessed 10/12/2021].

DEUBiH (Delegation of the EU to Bosnia and Herzegovina) (2015a) *EU Support to Law Enforcement* [online]. Special Edition. Available from: http://europa.ba/wp-content/uploads/2015/05/delegacijaEU_20 13121116102598eng.pdf [Accessed 10/12/2021].

DEUBiH (Delegation of the EU to Bosnia and Herzegovina) (2015b) *Newsletter Published by the EU Support to Law Enforcement Project* [online]. Issue IV. Available from: http://europa.ba/wp-content/uplo ads/2015/05/delegacijaEU_2014020323124741eng.pdf [Accessed 10/12/2021].

DEURS (Delegation of the European Union in the Republic of Serbia) (2004) *EU and Serbia and Montenegro: CARDS Regional* [online]. Available from: http://europa.rs/eu-assistance-to-serbia/the-cards-programme/regional/?lang=en [Accessed 12/08/2022].

Deutsch, K.W., Burrell, S.A., Kann, R.A., Lee, M., Lichterman, M., Lindgren, R. E., Lorwenheim, F. L., and Van Wagenen, R. W. (1957) *Political Community and the North American Area: International Organization in the Light of Historical Experience*. Princeton: Princeton University Press.

Dimireva, I. (2010) EU Assistance to Bosnia and Herzegovina. *EUbusiness* [online]. Available from: https://www.eubusiness.com/europe/bosnia/eu-assistance [Accessed 30/11/2021].

Dobbels, M. (2009) *Serbia and the ICTY: How Effective Is EU Conditionality?* EU Diplomacy Papers 6/2009. Bruges: College of Europe.

Donais, T. (2005) The Status of Security Sector Reform in South East Europe: An Analysis of the Stability Pact Stock-Taking Programme. In: E. Cole, T. Donais and P. H. Fluri, eds., *Defence and Security Sector Governance and Reform in South East Europe Self-Assessment Studies: Regional Perspectives*. Baden-Baden: Nomos Verlagsgesellschaft, pp. 221-251.

Donais, T. (2006) The Limits of Post-Conflict Police Reform. In: M.A. Innes, ed., *Bosnian Security after Dayton: New Perspectives*. London and N.Y.: Routledge, pp 173-190.

Dowling, A. (2008) EU Conditionality and Security Sector Reform in the Western Balkans. In: D. Spence and P. Fluri, eds., *The European Union and Security Sector Reform*. London: John Harper Publishing, pp. 174-199.

Downes, M. (2004) *Police Reform in Serbia Towards the Creation of a Modern and Accountable Police Service* [online]. Law Enforcement Department OSCE Mission to Serbia and Montenegro. Available from: http://www.osce.org/serbia/18310?download=true [Accessed 20/08/2022].

Dursun-Ozkanca, O. and Vandemoortele, A. (2012) The European Union and Security Sector Reform: Current Practices and Challenges of Implementation. *European Security*, 21(2), pp.139-160.

EDA (European Defence Agency) (2016) *EDA Chief Executive Visits Serbia* [online]. Available from: https://www.eda.europa.eu/infohub/press-centre/latest-news/2016/12/20/eda-chief-executive-visits-serbia [Accessed 11/08/2022].

Edmonds, M. (1988) *Armed Services and Society*. Leicester: Leicester University Press.

Edmunds, T. (2007) *Security Sector Reform in Transforming Societies: Croatia, Serbia and Montenegro*. Manchester and N.Y.: Manchester University Press.

Edwards, G. (1996) The Potential and Limits of the CFSP: The Yugoslav Example. In: E. Regelsberger; P. Schoutheete and W. Wessels, eds., *Foreign Policy of the European Union: From EPC to CFSP and Beyond*. Boulder: Lynne Rienner, pp. 173-195.

EEAS (2012) *European Union Police Mission in Bosnia and Herzegovina (EUPM)* [online]. Available from: https://eeas.europa.eu/archives/csdp/missions-and-operations/eupm-bih/pdf/25062012_factsheet_eupm-bih_en.pdf [Accessed 20/10/2021].

EEAS (2016) *Shaping of a Common Security and Defence Policy* [online]. Available from: https://eeas.europa.eu/topics/common-security-and-defence-policy-csdp/5388/shaping-of-a-common-security-and-defence-policy-_en [Accessed 25/01/2022].

EEAS (2022) *Military and Civilian Missions and Operations*. Available from: https://eeas.europa.eu/node/430_en [Accessed 25/08/2022].

Eekelen, W. van (2008) Security Sector Reform: CFSP, ESDP and the International Impact of the EU's Second Pillar. In: D. Spence and P. Fluri, eds., *The European Union and Security Sector Reform*. London: John Harper Publishing, pp. 108-125.

Ejdus, F. (2010) *Democratic Security Sector Governance in Serbia*. Frankfurt: Peace Research Institute Frankfurt.

Ejdus, F. (2014) Serbia's Military Neutrality: Origins, Effects and Challenges. *Croatian International Relations Review*, 20(71), pp. 43-69.

Ekengren, M. (2010) The Challenge of a Broadening Security Agenda for EU Security Sector Reform. In: M. Ekengren and G. Simons, eds., *The Politics of Security Sector Reform: Challenges and Opportunities for the European Union's Global Role*. London and N.Y.: Routledge, pp. 101-124.

Ekengren, M. and Simons, S. (eds.) (2011) The Politics of Security Sector Reform: Challenges and Opportunities for the European Union's Global Role. London and N.Y.: Routledge.

Elbasani, A. (2004) Albania in Transition: Manipulation or Appropriation of International Norms? Southeast European Politics, 5(1), pp. 24-44.

Elek, B. (2015) Towards More Effective Police Cooperation between Serbia and Kosovo. Belgrade: Belgrade Centre for Security Policy.

Elek, B., Tasic, D. and Djodjevic, S. (2015) Assessment of Police Integrity in Serbia. Belgrade: Belgrade Centre for Security Policy.

Erdut Agreement (1995) *Basic Agreement on the Region of Eastern Slavonia, Baranja and Western Sirmium*, A/50/757−S/1995/951.

ESI (European Stability Initiative) (2000) *EU Road Map: Steps to be Taken by Bosnia and Herzegovina to Prepare for a Launch of a Feasibility Study* [online]. Available from: http://www.esiweb.org/pdf/bridges/bosnia/EURoadMap.pdf [Accessed 01/10/2021].

EU Council Secretariat (2007) *Factsheet on European Union Monitoring Mission (EUMM)* [online]. Available from: http://www.europarl.europa.eu/meetdocs/2004_2009/documents/dv/sede100108eumm_/sede100108eumm_en.pdf [Accessed 19/08/2022].

EUFOR BiH (2016) *About EUFOR* [online]. Available from: http://www.euforbih.org/eufor/index.php/about-eufor/background [Accessed 10/10/2017].

Euractiv (2011) *Serbian Soldiers to Participate in EU Missions* [online]. Available from: https://www.euractiv.com/section/global-europe/news/Serbian-soldiers-to-participate-in-eu-missions/ [Accessed 12/08/2021].

European Commission (1996) Common Principles for Future Contractual Relations with Certain Countries in South-Eastern Europe. Brussels, COM(96) 476 final.

European Commission (1997) Agenda 2000−Commission Opinion on Slovenia's Application for Membership of the European Union. Brussels, DOC/97/19.

BIBLIOGRAPHY 343

European Commission (1997a) Regional Approach to the Countries of South-Eastern Europe: Compliance with the Conditions in the Council Conclusions of 29 April 1997. Brussels, 3 October.

European Commission (1998) Regional Approach to the Countries of South-Eastern Europe: Compliance with the Conditions in the Council Conclusions of 29 April 1997. Brussels, SEC(1998) 586.

European Commission (1998a) Regional Approach [online]. Memo/98/76. Available from: http://europa.eu/rapid/press-release_MEMO-98-76_en.htm [Accessed 12/07/2022].

European Commission (1998b) Regional Approach to the Countries of South-Eastern Europe: Compliance with the Conditions in the Council Conclusions of 29 April 1997. Brussels, COM(1998) 618 final.

European Commission (1998c) Regional Approach to the Countries of South-Eastern Europe: Compliance with the Conditions in the Council Conclusions of 29 April 1997. Brussels, SEC(98) 1727.

European Commission (1999) Commission Proposes a Stabilisation and Association Process for Countries of South-Eastern Europe [online]. Press release IP/99/350. http://europa.eu/rapid/press-release_IP-99-350_en.htm?locale=en [Accessed 12/07/2021].

European Commission (1999a) *On the Stabilisation and Association Process for Countries of South-Eastern Europe. Bosnia and Herzegovina, Croatia, Federal Republic of Yugoslavia, Former Yugoslav Republic of Macedonia and Albania.* Brussels, COM(1999) 235 final.

European Commission (2002) *The Stabilisation and Association process for South East Europe: First Annual Report.* Brussels, COM(2002)163 final.

European Commission (2002a) *Country Strategy Paper for Croatia 2002-2006: CARDS.*

European Commission (2002b) *Programme CARDS 2002 Financing Proposal for Croatia* (on file with author).

European Commission (2002c) *Federal Republic of Yugoslavia Country Strategy Paper.* Brussels.

European Commission (2003) *Proposal for a Council Regulation on the Establishment of European Partnerships in the Framework of the Stabilisation and Association process.* Brussels, COM(2003) 684 final.

European Commission (2003a) *Governance and Development.* Brussels, COM(2003) 615 final.

European Commission (2003b) *CARDS 2003 Financing Proposal for Croatia.*

European Commission (2003c) *On the Preparedness of Bosnia and Herzegovina to Negotiate a Stabilisation and Association Agreement with the European Union.* Brussels, COM(2003) 692 final.

European Commission (2004) *Amended CARDS National Action Programme for Croatia 2004.*

European Commission (2004a) *CARDS Action Programme 2004 for State Union of Serbia and Montenegro (SCG) / Republic of Serbia.*

European Commission (2005) *Croatia 2005 Progress Report.* Brussels, SEC (2005) 1424.

European Commission (2005a) *PHARE 2005 Project Fiche: Croatia* [online]. Available from: https://ec.europa.eu/neighbourhood-enlargement/sites/near/files/pdf/fiche-projet/croatia/bg-fm/2005/hr2005_6_1-pf-hr-and-police-academy.pdf [Accessed 21/03/2022].

European Commission (2005b) On the Preparedness of Serbia and Montenegro to Negotiate a Stabilisation and Association Agreement with the European Union. Brussels, COM(2005) 476.

European Commission (2005c) Serbia and Montenegro 2005 Progress Report. Brussels, SEC (2005) 1428.

European Commission (2006) A Concept for European Community Support for Security Sector Reform. Brussels, COM(2006) 253 final.

European Commission (2006a) Annexes to A Concept for European Community Support for Security Sector Reform. Brussels, SEC(2006) 658.

European Commission (2006b) Instrument for Pre-accession Assistance (IPA): Multi-Annual Indicative Planning Document (MIPD) 2008-2010 Multi-Beneficiary [online]. Available from: https://ec.europa.eu/neighbourhood-enlargement/sites/near/files/pdf/mipd_multibeneficiary_2008_2010_en.pdf [Accessed 30/07/2022].

European Commission (2006c) *Screening Report Croatia. Chapter 24 – Justice, Freedom and Security* [online]. Available from: https://ec.europa.eu/neighbourhood-enlargement/sites/near/files/pdf/croatia/screening_reports/screening_report_24_hr_internet_en.pdf [Accessed 30/07/2022].

European Commission (2006d) *Croatia 2006 Progress Report.* Brussels, SEC(2006) 1385.

European Commission (2006e) *PHARE 2006 Project Fiche – Draft: Croatia* [online]. Available from: https://ec.europa.eu/neighbourhood-enlargement/sites/near/files/pdf/fiche-projet/croatia/bg-fm/2006/hr2006.018-113.6.1-blue-border-surveillance-final-03-08-06_en.pdf [Accessed 21/03/2022].

European Commission (2006f) *Serbia 2006 Progress Report.* Brussels, SEC (2006)1389.

European Commission (2006g) *Bosnia and Herzegovina 2006 Progress Report.* Brussels, SEC (2006) 1384.

BIBLIOGRAPHY 345

European Commission (2006h) CARDS BA 06 IB JH 02 — Relaunch. *Support to the State Border Service of Bosnia and Herzegovina* (on file with author).

European Commission (2007) *Instrument for Pre-accession Assistance (IPA): Multi-Beneficiary Multi-Annual Indicative Planning Document (MIPD) 2007 – 2009.* Annex (on file with author).

European Commission (2007a) *Screening Report Croatia. Chapter 31 – Foreign, Security and Defence Policy* [online]. Available from: https:// ec.europa.eu/neighbourhood-enlargement/sites/near/files/pdf/ croatia/screening_reports/screening_report_31_hr_internet_en.pdf [Accessed 10/09/2022].

European Commission (2007b) *Project Fiche for PHARE: Combating Drugs Trafficking and Abuse. HR2007/03/24/7* [online]. Available from: https://ec.europa.eu/neighbourhood-enlargement/sites/near/fil es/pdf/croatia/ipa/hr2007_03_24_7_version_1482007_en.pdf [Accessed 12/03/2021].

European Commission (2007c) *Croatia 2007 Progress Report.* Brussels, SEC(2007) 1431.

European Commission (2007d) *Serbia 2007 Progress Report.* Brussels, SEC(2007) 1435.

European Commission (2007e) *Bosnia and Herzegovina 2007 Progress Report.* Brussels, SEC(2007) 1430.

European Commission (2008) *Western Balkans: Enhancing the European perspective.* Brussels, COM(2008) 127 final.

European Commission (2008a) *Croatia 2008 Progress Report.* Brussels, SEC(2008) 2694.

European Commission (2008b) *Enlargement Strategy and Main Challenges 2008-2009.* Brussels, COM(2008) 674 final.

European Commission (2008c) *Serbia 2008 Progress Report.* Brussels, SEC(2008) 2698 final.

European Commission (2008d) *Development of the Information System for Border Crossing Control in the Republic of Serbia* [online]. Standard Summary Project Fiche — IPA centralised programmes. Available from: https://ec.europa.eu/neighbourhood-enlargement/sites/near/fil es/pdf/serbia/ipa/2008/25-ministry_of_interior_border_it_en.pdf [Accessed 21/08/2021].

European Commission (2008e) *Roadmap on Visa Free Travel Opens EU Doors to Serbia.* Press Release IP/08/717. Brussels, 7 May 2008.

European Commission (2008f) Visa Liberalisation with Serbia: Roadmap.

European Commission (2008g) Bosnia and Herzegovina 2008 Progress Report. Brussels, SEC(2008) 2693 final.

European Commission (2008h) DECISION C(2008)8393 of 18/12/2008 Adopting the Multi-Beneficiary Programme 2b, for Projects Requiring a Financing Agreement under the IPA Transition Assistance and Institution Building Component.

European Commission (2008i) IPA National Programme 2008 Part II – Bosnia and Herzegovina. Fiche 5: Support to Mine Action Activities in Bosnia and Herzegovina [online]. Available from: https://ec.euro pa.eu/neighbourhood-enlargement/sites/near/files/pdf/bosnia_a nd_herzegovina/ipa/2008/ipa_2008_part_ii_05_de-mining_en.pdf [Accessed 21/11/2021].

European Commission (2008j) *IPA National Programme 2008 Part II – Bosnia and Herzegovina.* Fiche 5: Support for the implementation of the BiH Integrated Border Management (IBM) Strategy and Action Plan (on file with author).

European Commission (2008k) *IPA National Programme 2008 Part II – Bosnia and Herzegovina.* Fiche 19: Integrated Border Management and Support to the Indirect Taxation Authority [online]. Available from: https://ec.europa.eu/neighbourhood-enlargement/sites/near/file s/pdf/bosnia_and_herzegovina/ipa/2008/ipa_2008_part_ii_19_bo rder_management_indirect_taxation_authority_en.pdf [Accessed 11/12/2021].

European Commission (2008l) *Roadmap on Visa Free Travel Opens EU Doors to Bosnia and Herzegovina.* Press Release IP/08/874.

European Commission (2009) *Visa free travel for citizens of the former Yugoslav Republic of Macedonia, Montenegro and Serbia before Christmas* [online]. Press Release IP/09/1852. Available from: http://europa.eu/rapid/press-release_IP-09-1852_en.htm?locale=fr [Accessed 21/07/2021].

European Commission (2009a) *Croatia 2009 Progress Report.* Brussels, SEC(2009) 1333.

European Commission (2009b) *Serbia 2009 Progress Report.* Brussels, SEC(2009) 1339.

European Commission (2009c) *Bosnia And Herzegovina 2009 Progress Report.* Brussels, SEC(2009) 1338.

European Commission (2009d) *IPA 2007 Bosnia and Herzegovina* [online]. Available from: https://ec.europa.eu/anti-trafficking/eu-projects/ ipa-2007-bosnia-and-herzegovina-bih [Accessed 21/07/2022].

European Commission (2010) *Visa free regime for Albania and Bosnia and Herzegovina: the European Commission welcomes the Council's decision* [online]. Press Release MEMO/10/548. Available from: http://europa.eu/rapid/press-release_MEMO-10-548_en.htm?locale=en [Accessed 21/07/2022].

BIBLIOGRAPHY 347

European Commission (2010a) *Project Fiche 1 Support to the Operating Expenditures of the Regional Cooperation Council (RCC) Secretariat and Strengthening the RCC Secretariat* [online]. Available from: https://ec.europa.eu/neighbourhood-enlargement/sites/near/fil es/pdf/financial_assistance/ipa/2010/pf1_operating_costs_and_ strengthening_final.pdf [Accessed 21/07/2022].

European Commission (2010b) *IPA 2010 Croatia: Project Fiche HR-2010-01-36-04* [online]. Available from: https://ec.europa.eu/neighbour hood-enlargement/sites/near/files/pdf/croatia/ipa/2010/04_de-mining_programme_en.pdf [Accessed 01/08/2022].

European Commission (2010c) *Croatia 2010 Progress Report*. Brussels, SEC(2010) 1326.

European Commission (2010d) *Serbia 2010 Progress Report*. Brussels, SEC(2010) 1330.

European Commission (2010e) *Enlargement Strategy and Main Challenges 2010-2011*. Brussels, COM(2010) 660.

European Commission (2010f) *Project against Money Laundering and Terrorism Financing in Serbia* [online]. CRIS Number: 2009/021-765. Available from: https://ec.europa.eu/neighbourhood-enlargement/sites/ near/files/pdf/serbia/ipa/2010/5_financial_crime_ipa10.pdf [Accessed 11/08/2022].

European Commission (2010g) 2009 Annual Report on PHARE, Turkey Pre-Accession Instruments, CARDS and the Transition Facility. Brussels, COM(2010) 793 final.

European Commission (2010h) *Bosnia and Herzegovina 2010 Progress Report*. Brussels, SEC(2010) 1331.

European Commission (2011) *Instrument for Pre-Accession Assistance (IPA): Multi-Annual Indicative Planning Document (MIPD) 2011-2013 Multi-Beneficiary* [online]. Annex. Available from: https://ec.europa.eu/ neighbourhood-enlargement/sites/near/files/pdf/mipd_multiben eficiary_2011_2013_en.pdf [Accessed 30/07/2021].

European Commission (2011a) Commission Opinion on Serbia's Application for Membership of the European Union. Brussels, SEC(2011) 1208.

European Commission (2011b) Bosnia and Herzegovina 2011 Progress Report. Brussels, SEC(2011) 1206 final.

European Commission (2012) On the Main Findings of the Comprehensive Monitoring Report on Croatia's state of Preparedness for EU Membership. Brussels, COM(2012) 601 final.

European Commission (2012a) Comprehensive Monitoring Report on Croatia's State of Preparedness for EU Membership. Brussels, SWD(2012) 338 final.

European Commission (2012b) Serbia 2012 Progress Report. Brussels, SWD(2012) 333 final.

European Commission (2012c) IPA 2012 Serbia: Standard Twinning Project Fiche SR 12 IB JH 02. Annex C1 (on file with author).

European Commission (2012d) *Enlargement Strategy and Main Challenges 2012-2013*. Brussels, COM(2012) 600 final.

European Commission (2012e) *Police Reform and Migration Management* [online]. Project Fiche IPA National programmes / Component I: Serbia. Available from: https://ec.europa.eu/neighbourhood-enlargement/sites/near/files/pdf/serbia/ipa/2012/pf_2_police_reform_and_migration_management.pdf [Accessed 22/08/2022].

European Commission (2012f) *Bosnia and Herzegovina 2012 Progress Report*. Brussels, SWD(2012) 335 final.

European Commission (2013) Project Fiche – IPA Multi Beneficiary programmes: Component I. *International Cooperation in Criminal Justice: Prosecutors' Network* [online]. Available from: https://ec.europa.eu/neighbourhood-enlargement/sites/near/files/pdf/financial_assistance/ipa/2013/multi-beneficiary/pf_14_pn_ipa_2013_amend.pdf [Accessed 05/07/2021].

European Commission (2013a) *Croatia – Bosnia and Herzegovina: Agreements on Border Management Signed* [online]. Press Release. Available from: http://europa.eu/rapid/press-release_SPEECH-13-557_en.htm [Accessed 05/04/2022].

European Commission (2013b) *Serbia 2013 Progress Report*. Brussels, SWD(2013) 412 final.

European Commission (2013c) *National Programme for Serbia under the IPA – Transition Assistance and Institution Building Component for the Year 2013*. Twinning No. SR 13 IB JH 04 (on file with author).

European Commission (2013d) *National programme for Serbia under the IPA – Transition Assistance and Institution Building Component for the year 2013*. Twinning No SR 13 IB JH 05 (on file with author).

European Commission (2013e) *Bosnia and Herzegovina 2013 Progress Report*. Brussels, SWD(2013) 415 final.

European Commission (2014) *The European Union explained: International cooperation and development* [online]. Available from: https://europa.eu/european-union/topics/development-cooperation_en [Accessed 12/06/2022].

European Commission (2014a) *Serbia 2014 Progress Report*. Brussels, SWD(2014) 302 final.

European Commission (2014b) *Bosnia and Herzegovina 2014 Progress Report*. Brussels, SWD(2014) 305 final.

European Commission (2015) *Roadmap: Elements for an EU-wide Strategic Framework for Supporting Security Sector Reform (SSR)* [online]. Brussels. Available from: http://ec.europa.eu/smart-regulation/road maps/docs/2016_eeas_001_cwp_security_sector_reform_en.pdf [Accessed 09/05/2022].

European Commission (2016) Elements for an EU-wide strategic framework to support security sector reform. Brussels, JOIN(2016) 31 final.

European Commission (2016a) Enlargement: Accession criteria [online]. Available from: https://ec.europa.eu/neighbourhood-enlargement /policy/glossary/terms/accession-criteria_en [Accessed 01/08/2022].

European Commission (2016b) *Serbia* [online]. Available from: https://ec.europa.eu/neighbourhood-enlargement/countries/detailed-country-information/serbia_en [Accessed 18/06/2021].

European Commission (2016c) *Serbia 2016 Report*. Brussels, SWD(2016) 361 final.

European Commission (2016d) *Support to the Parliaments of Bosnia and Herzegovina in the EU Integration Tasks* [online]. Instrument for Pre-Accession Assistance (IPA II) 2014-2020. Available from: https://ec.euro pa.eu/neighbourhood-enlargement/sites/near/files/ipa_2016_39 653_3_bih_support_to_the_parliaments_of_bih_in_the_eu_integrat ion_tasks.pdf [Accessed 10/08/2021].

European Commission (2016e) Bosnia and Herzegovina: Strengthening Public Procurement System in Bosnia and Herzegovina Phase II – Developing the Capacities of Contracting Authorities [online]. Instrument for Pre-Accession Assistance (IPA II) 2014-2020. Available from: https://ec.europa.eu/neighbourhood-enlargement/sites/ne ar/files/ipa_2016_39653_1_bih_strengthening_public_procurement _system.pdf [Accessed 10/08/2022].

European Commission (2017) Identification of applicants (EURODAC) [online]. Available from: https://ec.europa.eu/home-affairs/whatwe-do/policies/asylum/identification-of-applicants_en [Accessed 01/04/2022].

European Commission (2022) 2022 Enlargement package: European Commission assesses reforms in the Western Balkans and Türkiye and recommends candidate status for Bosnia and Herzegovina [Accessed 16/10/2022].

European Commission DGIA (1998) *The European Union in Bosnia and Herzegovina: Repairinf, Reconstructing, Reconnecting.* Brussels: EC DGIA.

European Council (1995) Madrid European Council 15 and 16 December 1995, Presidency Conclusions. Annex 7: Declaration on Former Yugoslavia.

European Council (2004) European Security Strategy — Bosnia and Herzegovina Comprehensive Policy. Brussels, 17-18 June.

European Council (2016) Shared Vision, Common Action: A Stronger Europe: A Global Strategy for the European Union's Foreign and Security Policy [online]. Available from: http://europa.eu/globalstrategy/sites/globalstrategy/files/pages/files/eugs_review_web_13.pdf [Accessed 10/07/2022].

EPC (European Political Cooperation) (1991) Statement by an Extraordinary EPC Ministerial Meeting Concerning Yugoslavia (91/203) on 5 July 1991. European *Political Cooperation Documentation Bulletin,* Volume 7.

Eralp, D.U. (2012) *Politics of the European Union in Bosnia-Herzegovina: Between Conflict and Democracy.* Plymouth: Lexington Books.

Faleg, G. (2012) Beween Knowledge and Power: Epistemic Communities and the Emergence of Security Sector Reform in the EU Security Architecture. *European Security,* 21(2), pp.161-184.

Floudas, D. A. (1996) A Name for a Conflict or a Conflict for a Name? An Analysis of Greece's Dispute with FYROM. *Journal of Political and Military Sociology,* 24(2), pp. 285-321.

Fluri, P. (2003) Why the Federal Republic of Yugoslavia Ought to Apply for Joining the Partnership for Peace. In: M. Hadzic and P. Fluri, eds., *Security Inclusion of the Federal Republic of Yugoslavia into the Euro-Atlantic Community.* Belgrade: Centre for Civil-Military Relations, pp. 25-29.

Franc, R. and Medjugorac, V. (2013) *Support for EU Membership in Croatia has Fallen Dramatically since Accession Negotiations Began in 2003* [online]. LSE EUROPP. Available from: http://blogs.lse.ac.uk/europpblog/2013/04/02/croatia-euroscepticism/ [Accessed 22/05/2022].

Friesendorf, C. and Penksa, S. (2008) Militarized Law Enforcement in Peace Operations: EUFOR in Bosnia and Herzegovina. *International Peacekeeping,* 15(5), pp.677-694.

Fuerstenberg, M. (2010) *Conflict Beyond Borders: Conceptualizing Transnational Armed Conflict.* Braunschweig: Institute of Social Sciences.

GAC (1995) 1878th Council Meeting of the General Affairs Council, Conclusions on the Former Yugoslavia. Brussels, 31 October.

Gallagher, T. (2003) The Balkans after the Cold War: from Tyranny to Tragedy. Abingdon: Routledge.

Gagnon, V.P. (2004) *The Myth of Ethnic War: Serbia and Croatia in the 1990s.* Ithaka and London: Cornell University Press.

GFAP (1995) General Framework Agreement for Peace in Bosnia and Herzegovina, A/50/790−S/1995/999.

George, A. L. (1979) Case Studies and Theory Development: The method of Structured, Focused Comparison. In: P. G. Lauren, ed., *Diplomacy: New Approaches in History, Theory, and Policy.* New York: Free Press, pp. 43-68.

George, A. L. and Bennett, A. (2005) *Case Studies and Theory Development in the Social Sciences.* Cambridge, MA: MIT Press.

George, A. L., and McKeown, T. J. (1985) Case Studies and Theories of Organizational Decision Making. In: R. F. Coulam and R. A. Smith, eds., *Advances in information processing in organizations.* Greenwich, CT: JAI Press, vol. 2, pp. 21-58.

Gerring, J. (2012) The Case Study: What it is and What it Does. In: R. E. Goodin, ed., *The Oxford Handbook of Political Science* [online]. Available from: http://www.oxfordhandbooks.com/view/10.1093/oxfordhb/9780199604456.001.0001/oxfordhb-9780199604456-e-051 [Accessed 26/03/2021].

GICHD (Geneva International Centre for Humanitarian Demining) (2008) *Evaluation of EC-Funded Mine Action Programmes in South East Europe – 2002-2007* [online]. Available from: https://www.gichd.org/fileadmin/GICHD-resources/rec-documents/EvaluationEC-SE_Europe_-GICHD-Dec2008.pdf [Accessed 09/08/2021].

Ginsberg, R. (1999) Conceptualizing the European Union as an International Actor: Narrowing the Theoretical Capability–Expectations Gap. *Journal of Common Market Studies,* 37 (3), pp. 429–54.

Ginsberg, R. (2001) *The European Union in International Politics: Baptism by Fire.* Lanham, MD: Rowman & Littlefield.

Glaurdic, J. (2011) *The Hour of Europe.* New Haven, Conn.: Yale University Press.

Glavonjic, Z. (2014) Serbia, Russia to hold first joint military exercise. *Radio Free Europe* [online]. Available from: https://www.slobodnaevropa.org/a/serbia-russia-to-hold-first-joint-military-exercise/26682014.html [Accessed 11/08/2021].

Gledhill, J. and King, C. (2010) Institutions, Violence, and Captive States in the Balkan History. In: W. Van Meurs and A .Mungiu-Pippidi , eds., *Ottomans into Europeans: State and Institution Building in South-East Europe.* London: Hurst Publishers, pp. 245-275.

Glenny, M. (1996) *The Fall of Yugoslavia*. 3rd ed. London: Penguin books.

Glenny, M. (2009) *McMafia: Seriously Organised Crime*. London: Vintage.

Gnesotto, N. (1994) *Lesson of Yugoslavia*. Chaillot Paper No 14. Paris: Institute for Security Studies of WEU.

Goldstein, I. (1999) *Croatia: A History*. London: Hurst and Company.

Gow, J. (1997). *Triumph of the Lack of Will*. London: Hurst.

Gow, J. (2003) *The Serbian Project and Its Adversaries: A Strategy of War Crimes*. Lonodn: Hurst and Company.

Gow, J. and Zverzhanovski, I. (2013) Security, Democracy and War Crimes: Security Sector Transformation in Serbia. N.Y.: Palgrave Macmillan.

Gordon, C., Sasse, G. and Sebastian, S. (2008) Specific report on the EU policies in the Stabilisation and Association process [online]. Bozen: European Academy. Available from: http://www.eurac.edu/en/re search/autonomies/minrig/Documents/Mirico/24_SAP.pdf [Accessed 10/05/2022].

Gosar, A. (2012) Border Puzzle: The Results of Disintegration and EU Integration Processes on the Territory of the Former Yugoslavia. *Eurasia Border Review*, 3(1), pp. 81-100.

Gourlay, C. (2008) The Difficulties of a Donor: EU Financial Instruments, SSR, and Effective International Assistance. In: D. Spence and P. Fluri, eds., *The European Union and Security Sector Reform*. London: John Harper Publishing, pp. 80-107.

GRC (Government of the Republic of Croatia) (2012) Regulation on Public Procurement for Obtaining Safety and Security. Narodne Novine, No 89.

GRC (Government of the Republic of Croatia) (2012a) Programme of the Government of the Republic of Croatia for the Adoption and Implementation of the *Acquis* for 2012. Zagreb.

Griffiths, H. (2010) Serbia: Choosing between Profit and Security. In: A. Karp, ed., *The Politics of Destroying Surplus Small Arms: Inconspicuous Disarmament*. N.Y.: Taylor and Francis Group.

Gross, E. (2013) *Assessing the EU's Approach to Security Sector Reform (SSR)* [online]. Brussels: European Parliament. Available from: http://www.europarl.europa.eu/RegData/etudes/etudes/join/2013/4338 37/EXPO-SEDE_ET%282013%29433837_EN.pdf [Accessed 25/05/2022].

Guzina, D. and Marijan, B. (2014) A Fine Balance: The EU and the Process of Normalizing Kosovo-Serbia Relations. *CIGI Papers* [online], 23. Waterloo, ON: The Centre for International Governance Innovation. Available from: https://www.cigionline.org/sites/default/files/no23_0.pdf [Accessed 15/08/2022].

Hadzi-Vidanovic, V. and Djuric, B. (2007) *Country Specific Report: Conflict Settlement Agreement Serbia* [online]. Bozen: European Academy. Available from: http://www.eurac.edu/en/research/autonomies/minrig/Documents/Mirico/15%20Serbia.pdf [Accessed 13/04/2021].

Hadzovic, D. (2009) *The Office of the High Representative and Security Sector Reform in Bosnia and Herzegovina*. Sarajevo: Centre for Security Studies.

Hadzovic, D. and Dizdarevic, E. (2012) Bosnia and Herzegovina. In: F. Klopfer, D. Cantwell, M. Hadzic and S. Stojanovic, eds., Almanac on Security Sector Oversight in the Western Balkans. Belgrade: Belgrade Centre for Security Policy and Geneva Centre for the Democratic Control of Armed Forces, pp. 47-72.

Hadzovic, D., Dizdarevic, E. and Kapidzic, D. (2011) Context Analysis of the Security Sector Reform in Bosnia and Herzegovina 1990–2009. Sarajevo: Centre for Security Studies.

Hadzovic, D., Krzalic, A. and Mihajlovic, S. (2013) Small Arms Survey [online]. Available from: http://www.seesac.org/f/docs/SALW-Surveys/Small-Arms-Survey-20102011-Bosnia-and-Herzegovina-EN.pdf [Accessed 20/11/2021].

Hartman, F. (2009) The ICTY and EU conditionality. In: J. Batt and J. Obradovic-Wochnik, eds., *War Crimes, Conditionality and EU integration in the Western Balkans*. Paris: ISS, pp. 67-82.

Hasenclever, A., Mayer, P. and Rittberger, V. (1997) *Theories of international regimes*. Cambridge: University Press.

Hänggi, H. (2004) Conceptualising Security Sector Reform and Reconstruction. In: A. Bryden and H, Hänggi, eds., *Reform and Reconstruction of the Security Sector*. Muenster: LIT, pp. 3-18.

Hänggi, H. (2009) Security Sector Reform. In: Chetail, V., ed., *Post-Conflict Peacebuilding: A Lexicon*. Oxford: Oxford University Press, pp. 337-349

Hänggi, H. and Tanner, F. (2005) *Promoting Security Sector Governance in the EU's Neighbourhood*. Chaillot Paper No 80. Paris: ISS.

Heinemann-Grüder, A., Pietz, T. and Duffy, S. (2003) Turning Soldiers into a Work Force: Demobilization and Reintegration in Post-Dayton Bosnia and Herzegovina. Brief 27. Bonn: BICC.

Hill, C. (1993) The Capability–Expectations Gap, or Conceptualizing Europe's International Role. Journal of Common Market Studies, 31 (3), pp. 305-328.

Hill, C. and Smith, K.E. (eds.) (2000) *European Foreign Policy: Key Documents*. London and N.Y.: Routledge.

Hills, A. (2006) Crossing Boundaries: State Border Services and the Multidimensional Nature of Security. In: M.A. Innes, ed., *Bosnian Security after Dayton: New Perspectives*. London and N.Y.: Routledge, pp. 191-208.

Hoare, M. (2004) *How Bosnia Armed: From Milosevic to Bin Laden*. London: Saqi Books.

Hoist, C.S. (2000) Leg. Dev.: Prohibiting the Sale and Supply of Petroleum and Certain Petroleum Products to Certain Parts of the Federal Republic of Yugoslavia. *Columbia Journal of European Law* [online], 6(1). Available from: http://cjel.law.columbia.edu/print/2000/leg-dev-prohibiting-the-sale-and-supply-of-petroleum-and-certain-petroleum-products-to-certain-parts-of-the-federal-republic-of-yugoslavia/ [Accessed 29/07/2021].

Holbrooke, R. (1999). *To End a War*. New York: Modern Library.

House of Commons (2000) *Foreign Affairs – Fourth Report: Kosovo* [online]. Available from: https://publications.parliament.uk/pa/cm199900/cmselect/cmfaff/28/2802.htm [Accessed 03/08/2022].

Howorth, J. (2007) *Security and Defence Policy in the European Union*. Basingstoke, Hampshire: Palgrave Macmillan.

Howorth, J. (2014) *Security and Defence Policy in the European Union*. 2nd ed.Basingstoke, Hampshire: Palgrave Macmillan.

IBM Guidelines (2007) *Guidelines for Integrated Border Management in the Western Balkans: Updated Version* [online]. Available from: www.legislationline.org/documents/id/16809 [Accessed 21/06/2022].

IBM Strategy (2006) Integrated Border Management Strategy in the Republic of Serbia. *Official Gazette of the Republic of Serbia*, No 28.

ICG (International Crisis Group) (1999) *War in The Balkans: Consequences of the Kosovo Conflict and Future Options for Kosovo and the Region* [online]. Europe Report N°61. Available from: http://old.crisisgroup.org/en/regions/europe/balkans/kosovo/061-war-in-the-balkans-consequences-of-the-kosovo-conflict-and-future-options-for-kosovo-and-the-region.html [Accessed 11/06/2022].

ICG (International Crisis Group) (2000) *Sanctions against the Federal Republic of Yugoslavia* [online]. Briefing No 15. Available from: https://www.crisisgroup.org/europe-central-asia/balkans/serbia/sanctions-against-federal-republic-yugoslavia [Accessed 12/07/2022].

ICG (International Crisis Group) (2000a) *Reunifying Mostar: Opportunities for Progress* [online]. Briefing No 90. Available from: https://www.crisisgroup.org/europe-central-asia/balkans/bosnia-and-herzegovina/reunifying-mostar-opportunities-progress [Accessed 01/11/2021].

BIBLIOGRAPHY 355

ICG (International Crisis Group) (2002) *Policing the Police in Bosnia: A Further Reform Agenda* [online]. Report No 130. Available from: https://www.crisisgroup.org/europe-central-asia/balkans/bosnia-and-herzegovina/policing-police-bosnia-further-reform-agenda [Accessed 12/10/2021].

ICG (International Crisis Group) (2005) *Bosnia's Stalled Police Reform: No Progress, No EU* [online]. Europe Report No164. Available from: https://www.crisisgroup.org/europe-central-asia/balkans/bosnia-and-herzegovina/bosnias-stalled-police-reform-no-progress-no-eu [Accessed 12/10/2021].

ICLG (International Comparative Legal Guides) (2017) *Serbia: Public Procurement* [online]. Available from: https://iclg.com/practice-areas/public-procurement/public-procurement-2017/serbia [Accessed 01/08/2021].

ICMPD and TC Team Consult (2004) *Financial, Organisational and Administrative Assessment of the BiH Police Forces and the State Border Service* [online]. Available from: http://www.esiweb.org/pdf/bridges/bosnia/EU_Functional_Review_of_Police.pdf [Accessed 28/11/2021].

ICRC (International Committee of the Red Cross) (1998) *The Silent Menace: Landmines in Bosnia and Herzegovina* [online]. Available from: https://www.icrc.org/eng/assets/files/other/silent-menace-bosnia-herzegovina-57jp32-010298.pdf [Accessed 01/11/2021].

ICTY (2016) *Trial Judgement Summary for Radovan Karadzic* [online]. Available from: http://www.icty.org/x/cases/karadzic/tjug/en/160324_judgement_summary.pdf [Accessed 30/06/2021].

ICTY (2017) *Trial Judgement Summary for Ratko Mladic* [online]. Available from: http://www.icty.org/x/cases/mladic/tjug/en/171122-summary-en.pdf [Accessed 11/01/2022].

IHS (2016) Balancing Act: Serbian Armed Forces Update. *Jane's Defence Weekly* [online]. Available from: http://www.janes360.com/images/assets/154/64154/Balancing_act_Serbian_Armed_Forces_update.pdf [Accessed 11/08/2021].

Ilic, M. (2017) Croatia V. Slovenia: The Defiled Proceedings. *Arbitration Law Review* [online], 9(11). Available from: https://elibrary.law.psu.edu/cgi/viewcontent.cgi?referer=https://scholar.google.co.uk/&httpsredir=1&article=1208&context=arbitrationlawreview [Accessed 21/01/2021].

IMF (1999) *The Economic Consequences of the Kosovo Crisis: An Updated Assessment* [online]. Available from: https://www.imf.org/external/pubs/ft/kosovo/052599.htm#II [Accessed 17/06/2022].

ITABiH (Indirect Taxation Authority of Bosnia and Herzegovina) (2007) *Archive* [online]. Available from: http://www.uino.gov.ba/en/ Aktuelna_pitanja/Arhiva_vijesti_2007_1.html [Accessed 17/12/2021].

Ivkovic, S.K. (2004) Distinct and Different: The Transformation of the Croatian Police. In: M. Caparini and O. Marenin, eds., *Transforming Police in Central and Eastern Europe: Process and Progress*. Muenster: LIT, pp. 178-20.

Ivkovic, S.K. (2015) Police Integrity in Croatia. In: I.S. K. Ivkovic and M. Haberfeld, eds., *Measuring Police Integrity Across the World*. N.Y.: Springer, pp. 97-123.

Jackson, P. (2011) Security Sector Reform and State Building. *Third World Quarterly*, 32(10), pp. 1803-1822.

Jervis, R. (2012) System Effects Revisited. *Critical Review*, 24(3), pp. 393-415.

Jarvis, C. (2000) The Rise and Fall of Albania's Pyramid Schemes. *Finance and Development* [online], 37(1). Available from: http://www.imf.org/external/pubs/ft/fandd/2000/03/jarvis.htm [Accessed 12/10/2021].

Jayasundara-Smits, S. and Schirch, L. (2016) *EU and Security Sector Reform: Tilting at Windmills?* [online]. The Scoping Study. Whole of Society Conflict Prevention and Peacebuilding. Available from: http://www.woscap.eu/documents/131298403/131553554/Scoping+Study+-+SSR.pdf/6f83ac77-ef91-401c-98cc-60073c58942c [Accessed 12/06/2021].

Jervis, R. (1982) Security regimes. *International Organization*, 36(02), pp. 357-378.

Joseph, J. (2018) *Varieties of Resilience*. Cambridge: Cambridge University Press.

Jovic D. (2006) Croatia and the European Union: a Long Delayed Journey. *Journal of Southern Europe and the Balkans*, 8 (1), pp. 85-103.

Judah, T. (2002) *Kosovo: War and Revenge*. New Haven: Yale University Press.

Juncos, A. (2005) The EU's Post-Conflict Intervention in Bosnia and Herzegovina: (re)Integrating the Balkans and/or (re)Inventing the EU? *Southeast European Politics*, 6(2), pp. 88-108.

Juncos, A. (2012) Member State-Building versus Peacebuilding: The Contradictions of EU State-Building in Bosnia and Herzegovina. *East European Politics*, 28(1), pp. 58-75.

Juncos, A. (2013) *EU Foreign and Security Policy in Bosnia*. Manchester: Manchester University Press.

Kacarska, S. (2012) *Europeanisation through Mobility: Visa Liberalisation and Citizenship Regimes in the Western Balkans* [online]. Working Paper 2012/21. The Europeanisation of Citizenship in the Successor States of the Former Yugoslavia (CITSEE). Available from: http://www.citsee.ed.ac.uk/__data/assets/pdf_file/0003/108912/374_europeanisationthroughmobilityvisaliberalisationandcitizenshipregimesinthewester.pdf [Accessed 12/12/2021].

Kaldor, M. (2012) *New and Old Wars*. Cambridge: Polity Press.

Kandic, N. (2005). The ICTY Trials and Transitional Justice in Former Yugoslavia. *Cornell International Law Journal*, 38(3) [online]. Available from: https://scholarship.law.cornell.edu/cgi/viewcontent.cgi?referer=&httpsredir=1&article=1655&context=cilj [Accessed 11/08/2022].

Kanet, R. E. (1998) *Resolving Regional Conflicts*. Urbana: University of Illinois Press.

Karastanovic, A., ed. (2022) Western Balkans Security Report 2022 [online]. Available from: https://ascg.me/wp-content/uploads/2022/10/WB-security-report-ENG-2022-online-small-1.pdf [Accessed 16/10/2022].

Kavalski, E. (2008) Extending the European Security Community. London: Tauris.

Kavalski, E. (2009) Timescapes of Security: Clocks, Clouds, and the Complexity of Security Governance. World Futures, 65(7), pp. 527-551.

Kavalski, E. (2015) Inside/Outside and Around: Observing the Complexity of Global Life. In.: E. Kavalski, ed., World Politics at the Edge of Chaos: Reflections on Complexity and Global Life, Albany, NY: State University of New York, pp. 1-27.

Keil, S. and Arkan, Z. (eds.) (2015) The EU and Member State Building. Oxon: Routledge.

Keil, S. and Kudlenko, A. (2015) Bosnia and Herzegovina 20 Years after Dayton: Complexity Born of Paradoxes. *International Peacekeeping*, 22(5), pp.471-489.

Keil, S. and Stahl, B. (2013) A security community in the Balkans? The foreign policies of the post-Yugoslav states. Südosteuropa Mitteilungen, 2/2013, pp. 14-25.

Keil, S. and Stahl, B. (2014) Introduction: The Foreign Policies of the Post-Yugoslav States. In.: S. Keil and B. Stahl, eds., The Foreign Policies of Post-Yugoslav States: From Yugoslavia to Europe, Hampshire: Palgrave Macmillan UK, pp. 3-17.

Kerr, R. (2014) Lost in Translation? Perceptions of the ICTY in the Former Yugoslavia. In: J. Gow, R. Kerr and Z. Pajic, eds., Prosecuting War Crimes: Lessons and Legacies of the International Criminal Tribunal for the Former Yugoslavia. London: Routledge, pp. 103-115.

King, J., Dorn, A.W. and Hodes, M. (2002) An Unprecedented Experiment: Security Sector Reform in Bosnia and Herzegovina [online]. Safeworld. Available from: https://www.saferworld.org.uk/resources/publications/493-an-unprecedented-experiment [Accessed 17/09/2021].

Kintis, A. (1997) The European Union's Foreign Policy and the War in The Former Yugoslavia. In: M., Holland, ed., Common Foreign and Security Policy: the Record and Reforms. London: Pinter, 148-173.

Kirchner, E. (2011) The European Union as a Regional and Global Security Provider. In: E. Kirchner and R. Dominguez, eds., *The security Governance of Regional Organizations*. London: Routledge, pp. 25-45.

Kirchner, E. and Sperling, J. (2007) *EU Security Governance*. Manchester: Manchester University Press.

Klemencic, M. (1999) The Border Agreement Between Croatia and Bosnia-Herzegovina: The First but Not the Last. Boundary and Security Bulletin, 7(4), pp. 96-101.

Koneska, C. (2007) Regional Identity: The Missing Element in Western Balkans Security Cooperation. *Western Balkan Security Observer*, 7(8), pp. 82-89.

Koneska, C. (2014) After Ethnic Conflict: Policy-making in Post-conflict Bosnia and Herzegovina and Macedonia. Farnham: Ashgate.

Korosteleva, E.A. (2020) Reclaiming Resilience back: A local Turn in EU External Governance. Contemporary Security Policy, 41(2), pp. 241-262.

Korosteleva, E. and Petrova, I. (2021) 'Community Resilience in Belarus and the EU response', Journal of Common Market Studies Annual Review, 59 (4), pp. 1-13.

Knauer, J. (2011) EUFOR Althea: Appraisal and Future Perspectives of the EU's Former Flagship Operation in Bosnia and Herzegovina [online]. EU Diplomacy Paper 07/2011. Available from: https://www.coleurope.eu/research-paper/eufor-althea-appraisal-and-future-perspectives-eus-former-flagship-operation-bosnia [Accessed 10/05/2022].

Knaus, G. (2009) *Bosnia's Visa Breakthrough and the Power of Europe* [online]. Available from: http://www.esiweb.org/index.php?lang=en&id=67&newsletter_ID=42 [Accessed 12/12/2021].

Knezovic, S. and Mahecic, Z. (2012) Croatia. In: F. Klopfer, D. Cantwell, M. Hadzic and S. Stojanovic, eds., *Almanac on Security Sector Oversight in the Western Balkans*. Belgrade: Belgrade Centre for Security Policy and Geneva Centre for the Democratic Control of Armed Forces, pp. 73-100.

Knezovic, S. and Stanicic, M. (2011) *Context Analysis of the Security Sector Reform in Croatia 1989-2009*. Zagreb: Institute for International Relations.

Kursani, S. (2015) *Police Cooperation between Kosovo and Serbia*. Belgrade: Belgrade Centre for Security Policy.

Kusovac, Z. (2002) Yugoslav Army Embarks on Restructure Programme. *Jane's Defence Weekly*, 13 February 2002.

Lake, D. A. and Morgan, P.M. (1997) *Regional Orders: Building Security in a New World*. University Park: Penn State University Press.

Lampe, J. (2006) *Balkans into Southeastern Europe*. Basingstoke: Palgrave.

Landry, R. (1999) *The European Community Monitor Mission (ECMM) in Former Yugoslavia: Lessons Learned for OAU Civilian Missions*. ACCORD Occasional Paper No 5. Available from: http://pdf.usaid.gov/pdf_docs/PNACL721.pdf [Accessed 17/08/2021].

Lang, A. (2012) *European Union (Croatian Accession and Irish Protocol) Bill* [online]. House of Commons. Research Paper 12/64. Available from: http://researchbriefings.parliament.uk/ResearchBriefing/Summary/RP12-64 [Accessed 11/04/2022].

Larrabee, F.S. (1990) Long Memories and Short Fuses: Change and Instability in the Balkans. *International Security*, 15(3), pp. 58-91.

Law, D. (2007a) Intergovernmental Organisations and their Role in Security Sector Reform. In: D. Law, ed., *Intergovernmental Organisations and Security Sector Reform*. Muenster: LIT, pp. 3- 23.

Law, D. and Myshlovska, O. (2008) Evolution of the Concepts of Security Sector Reform and Security Sector Governance: the EU Perspective. In: D. Spence and P. Fluri, eds., *The European Union and Security Sector Reform*. London: John Harper Publishing, pp. 2-26.

Law on Defence of BiH (2005) Official Gazette of Bosnia and Herzegovina, 88/05.

Law on Ministries and Other Bodies of Administration of Bosnia and Herzegovina (2003) Official Gazette of Bosnia and Herzegovina, 5/03.

Lehne, S. (2004) Has the 'Hour of Europe' come at last? The EU's strategy for the Balkans. In: J. Batt, ed., *The Western Balkans: Moving on*. Chaillot Paper No 70. Paris: ISS, pp. 111-124.

Lindstrom, N. (2004) Regional Sex Trafficking in the Balkans: Transnational Networks in an Enlarged Europe. *Problems of Post-Communism*, 51(3), pp. 45-52.

Lopez, G.A. (2000) Economic Sanctions and Genocide: Too Little, Too Late, and Sometimes Too Much. In: Riemer, N., ed., *Protection Against Genocide: Mission Impossible?* Westport, CT: Praeger.

Lucarelli, S. (2000) *Europe and the Breakup of Yugoslavia*. The Hague: Kluwer Law International.

Lukic, R. (2008) Civil-Military Relations in Croatia (1990-2005). In: S.P. Ramet, K. Clewing and R. Lukic, eds., *Croatia since Independence: War, Politics, Society, Foreign Relations*. Munich: R. Oldenbourg, pp. 189-210.

Malcolm, N. (1994) *Bosnia: A Short History*. New York: New York University Press.

Manners, I. (2002) Normative Power Europe: A Contradiction in Terms? *JCMS: Journal of Common Market Studies*, 40(2), pp.235-258.

Mansfield, I. (2017) The Early Years of Demining in Bosnia and Herzegovina: Transfer to National Ownership. *The Journal of Conventional Weapons Destruction*, 21(1), pp. 20-23.

Marenin, O. (2005) *Restoring Policing Systems in Conflict Torn Nations: Process, Problems, Prospects*. DCAF Occasional Paper No 7. Geneva: Geneva Centre for the Democratic Control of Armed Forces.

Marenin, O. (2010) *Challenges for Integrated Border Management in the European Union*. DCAF Occasional Paper №17. Geneva: Geneva Centre for the Democratic Control of Armed Forces.

Marijan, B. (2016) *Assessing the Impact of Orthodox Security Sector Reform in Bosnia-Herzegovina* [online]. Centre for Security Governance. Available from: http://secgovcentre.org/wp-content/uploads/2016/11/Assessing_Orthodox_SSR_in_Bosnia_Sept_2016.pdf [Accessed 01/09/2022].

Marijan, B. (2017) *The Gradual Emergence of Second Generation Security Sector Reform in Bosnia-Herzegovina* [online]. Centre for Security Governance. Available from: http://secgovcentre.org/wp-content/uploads/2017/01/Second-Generation-SSR-in-Bosnia-Herzegovina-January-2017.pdf [Accessed 01/09/22].

MARRI (2022) *Migration, Asylum, Refugees Regional Initiative: About Us* [online]. Available from: http://marri-rc.org.mk/about-us/ [Accessed 07/07/22].

McCausland, J. (1997). Arms control and the Dayton Accords. *European Security*, 6(2), pp.18-27.

MDNL (Ministry of Defence of the Netherlands) (2007) *European Community Monitoring Mission (ECMM): European Union Monitoring Mission (EUMM)* [online]. Available from: https://www.defensie.nl/downloads/brochures/2009/05/01/european-community-monitoring-mission-ecmm-european-union-monitoring-mission-eumm [Accessed 25/08/21].

Meharg, S. and Arnusch, A. (2010) *Security Sector Reform: A Case Study Approach to Transition and Capacity-Building*. Carlisle, PA: Strategic Studies Institute.

Mertus, J. (1999) *Kosovo: How Myths and Truths Started a War*. Berkley and L.A., CA: University of California Press.

Merlingen, M. (2009) EUPM (Bosnia and Herzegovina). In: G. Grevi, D. Helly and D. Keohane, eds., European Security and Defence Policy: The First Ten Years (1999-2009). Paris: ISS, pp. 161-172.

Merlingen, M. (2013) The CSDP in the Western Balkans: From Experimental Pilot to Security Governance. In: S. Biscop and R. Whitman, eds., *Routledge Handbook of European Security*. London: Routledge, pp. 145-158.

Merlingen, M. and Ostauskaite, R. (2006) European Union Peacebuilding and Policing: Governance and the European Security and Defence Policy. London: Routledge.

Metz, C. (2010) The Role of the International Community in the Police Reform in Bosnia-Herzegovina 2004-2008. Vienna: National Defence Academy and Bureau for Security Policy at the Austrian Ministry of Defence and Sports in co-operation with PfP Consortium of Defence Academies and Security Studies Institutes.

MHRR BiH (Ministry of Human Rights and Refugees of Bosnia and Herzegovina). (2005) *Comparative Analysis on Access to Rights of Refugees and Displaced Persons* [online]. Sarajevo. Available from: http://www.mhrr.gov.ba/PDF/UporednaAnalizaEngleski.pdf [Accessed 11/05/2021].

Milekic, S. and Zivanovic, M. (2017) Border Disputes Still Bedevil Ex-Yugoslav States. *BalkanInsight* [online]. Available from: http://www.balkaninsight.com/en/article/border-disputes-still-bedevil-most-ex-yugoslav-states-07-01-2017-1 [Accessed 21/08/2021].

Milic, J. (2012) The Elephant in the Room: Incomplete Security Sector Reform in Serbia and its Consequences for Serbian Domestic and Foreign Policies. *The New Century* [online]. Belgrade: CEAS. Available at: https://www.ceas-serbia.org/images/prilozi/07-eng.pdf [Accessed 19/03/2021].

Milic, J. (2014). *The Missing Link: Security Sector Reform, 'Military Neutrality' and EU-integration in Serbia* [online]. The Balkan Trust for Democracy (BTD). Available from: http://www.democratizationpolicy.org/pdf/CEAS-DPC%20Study%20-%20The%20Missing%20Link.pdf [Accessed 19/03/2021].

Mine Action Review (2014) *Clearing the Mines: The Third Review Conference of the Antipersonnel Mine Ban Treaty* [online]. Available from: http://www.mineactionreview.org/assets/downloads/Clearing_the_Mines_2014.pdf [Accessed 29/11/2021].

Mitchell, M. (2009) Complexity: A Guided Tour. New York: Oxford University Press.

Mladenov M. (2014) An Orpheus Syndrome? Serbian Foreign Policy After the Dissolution of Yugoslavia. In: S. Keil and B. Stahl, eds., *The Foreign Policies of Post-Yugoslav States. New Perspectives on South-East Europe*. London: Palgrave Macmillan, pp. 147-172.

Mobekk, E. (2005) Police Reform in South East Europe. In: E. Cole, T. Donais and P. H. Fluri, eds., *Defence and Security Sector Governance and Reform in South East Europe Self-Assessment Studies: Regional Perspectives*. Baden-Baden: Nomos Verlagsgesellschaft, pp. 155-168.

MoD RS (Ministry of Defence of the Republic of Serbia) (2014) *Cooperation with the European Defence Agency* [online]. Available from: http://www.mod.gov.rs/eng/7514/saradnja-sa-evropskom-odbrambenom-agencijom-7514 [Accessed 11/08/2021].

MoD RS (Ministry of Defence of the Republic of Serbia) (2016) *A Decade of the Serbia – Ohio National Guard Partnership Programme* [online]. Available from: http://www.mod.gov.rs/eng/9948/decenija-programa-drzavnog-partnerstva-srbije-i-nacionalne-garde-ohajo-9948 [Accessed 11/08/2022].

MoF and MoI RC (Ministry of Finance and Ministry of Interior of the Republic of Croatia) (2010) *IPA 2010: Integrated Border Management – Further strengthening of enforcement capacities of the Customs and Border Police*. Twinning No HR/2010/IB/JH/03.

MoI RC (Ministry of Interior of the Republic of Croatia) (2010) *IPA 2010: Support to the alignment of the Croatian IBM Concept with EU IBM Concept*. Twinning No HR/2010/IB/JH/06TL.

MoI RC (Ministry of Interior of the Republic of Croatia) (2011) *IPA 2011: Strengthening Capacities of the Ministry of Interior to Combat Cybercrime*. Twinning No HR 11 IB JH 01.

MoI RS (Ministry of Interior of the Republic of Serbia) (n.d.) *Internal Affairs Sector: About Us* [online]. Available from: http://prezentacije.mup.gov.rs/sukp/sukp_en.htm [Accessed 23/05/2022].

MoI RS (Ministry of Interior of the Republic of Serbia) (2016) *Action Plan for Chapter 24* [online]. Available from: http://www.bezbednost.org/upload/document/akcioni_plan_za_poglavlje_24_-_mart_2016_.pdf [Accessed 15/08/2022].

Moore, A. (2013) *Peacebuilding in Practice: Local Experience in Two Bosnian Towns*. Ithaka and London: Cornell University Press.

Monk, R. (2001) *Study on Policing in the Federal Republic of Yugoslavia* [online]. OSCE. http://www.osce.org/spmu/16296?download=true [Accessed 20/08/2022].

Morgan, S. (2017) Croatia and Slovenia Continue Maritime Dispute after Arbitration Ruling. *EURACTIV* [online]. Available from: https://www.euractiv.com/section/enlargement/news/croatia-and-slovenia-continue-maritime-dispute-after-arbitration-ruling/ [Accessed 21/07/2022].

MoS BiH (Ministry of Security of Bosnia and Herzegovina) (2013) *Brcko District Police, Border Police and the Service for Foreigners' Affairs in the Common Building* [online]. Available from: http://msb.gov.ba/vijesti/saopstenja/default.aspx?id=10236&langTag=en-US [Accessed 05/10/2022].

MoS BiH (Ministry of Security of Bosnia and Herzegovina) (2015) *Bosnia and Herzegovina Migration Profile for the Year 2015* [online]. Available from: http://www.msb.gov.ba/PDF/MIGRATION%20PROFILE_2015_ENG.pdf [Accessed 02/12/2021].

MoS BiH (Ministry of Security of Bosnia and Herzegovina) (2016) *The Small Arms and Light Weapons (SALW) Control Strategy in Bosnia and Herzegovina (2016–2020)* [online]. Available from: http://msb.gov.ba/PDF/SALW_ENG%20FINAL_web.pdf [Accessed 05/10/2021].

Muehlmann, T. (2009) Police Restructuring in Bosnia-Herzegovina: Problems of Internationally-led Security Sector Reform. In: D. Chandler, ed., *Statebuilding and Intervention: Policies, Practices and Paradigms*. London and N.Y.: Routledge.

Mulchinok, N. (2017) *NATO and the Western Balkans*. https://link.springer.com/book/10.1057/978-1-137-59724-3 [Accessed 05/07/2022].

MUPRH (*Ministarstvo Unutarnjih Poslova Republike Hrvtske*) (2017) *EU Projects of the Ministry of the Interior from Cards, PHARE, IPA and Transition Facility Programmes* [online]. Available from: http://eufondovi.mup.hr/UserDocsImages/dokumenti/PROJECTS%20MoI%2031-01-2017%20tablica.pdf [Accessed 21/03/2022].

MWH Consortium (2008) *Thematic Interim Evaluation of the European Union Pre-Accession Assistance: Review of Twinning in Croatia* [online]. No. R/ZZ/TWI/0809. Available from: https://ec.europa.eu/neighbourhood-enlargement/sites/near/files/pdf/financial_assistance/phare/evaluation/final_version_-_r-zz-twi-0809_-_twinning_in_croatia_en.pdf [Accessed 20/09/2022].

National Intelligence Council (1994) *A Multilateral Lifting of the Arms Embargo on Bosnia: Political and Military Implications* [online]. Available from: https://www.cia.gov/library/readingroom/docs/1994-11-01.pdf [Accessed 10/10/2021].

NATO (1994) *Partnership for Peace: Framework Document* [online]. Press Release Annex to M-1(1994) 002. Available from: https://www.nato.int/cps/ic/natohq/official_texts_24469.htm [Accessed 07/02/2021].

NATO (2006) *Bosnia and Herzegovina, Montenegro and Serbia join NATO Partnership for Peace* [online]. Available from: https://www.nato.int/docu/update/2006/12-december/e1214a.htm [Accessed 12/08/2022].

NATO (2016) *Kosovo Air Campaign* [online]. Available from: https://www.nato.int/cps/bu/natohq/topics_49602.htm [Accessed 30/06/2022].

NATO (2017) *Relations with Bosnia and Herzegovina* [online]. Available from: https://www.nato.int/cps/ic/natohq/topics_49127.htm [Accessed 27/09/2022].

Neild, R. (2001) Democratic Police Reforms in War-torn Societies. *Conflict, Security and Development*. 1(1), pp. 21-43.

Nikitin, A. (2004) Partners in Peacekeeping. *NATO Review* [online]. Available from: https://www.nato.int/docu/review/2004/issue4/english/special.html [Accessed 07/02/2022].

Norris, J. (2005) *Collision Course: NATO, Russia, and Kosovo*. Westport, CT: Praeger.

Noutcheva, G. (2012) European Foreign Policy and the Challenges of Balkan Accession. New York: Routledge.

Novota, S., Vlasic, I., Velinova, R., Geratliev, K. and Borissova, O. (2009) European Funds for Croatian Projects: A Handbook on Financial Cooperation and European Union Supported Programmes in Croatia. Zagreb: Central Office for Development Strategy and Coordination of EU Funds.

NSC (New Strategy Center) (2022) Security Challenges in the Balkans, 6th edition [online]. Available from: https://www.newstrategycenter.ro/security-challenges-in-the-balkans-2022/ [Accessed 24/09/2022].

Obradovic-Wochnik, J. (2013) The Role of the ICTY in Promoting Reconciliation. In: E. Prifti, ed., The European Future of the Western Balkans: Thessaloniki@10 (2003-2013). Paris: EUISS, pp. 93-99.

OCCS (Office for Cooperation with Civil Society) (2014) Report on the Participation of CSOs in the Negotiation Process for the Accession of the Republic of Serbia to the European Union [online]. Available from: https://civilnodrustvo.gov.rs/upload/old_site/2012/10/Report-on-CSOs-participation-in-negotiating-process-in-Serbia-December.docx [Accessed 02/08/2022].

OECD (2004) Security System Reform and Governance. Paris: OECD Publishing.

OECD (2008) The OECD DAC Handbook on Security System Reform: Supporting Security and Justice. Paris: OECD Publishing.

OHR (Office of the High Representative) (1997) *PIC Bonn Conclusions* [online]. Available from: http://www.ohr.int/?p=54137&print=pdf [Accessed 09/10/2022].

OHR (Office of the High Representative) (2003) Decision Establishing the Defence Reform Commission [online]. Available from: http://www.ohr.int/?p=65835&print=pdf [Accessed 09/10/2022].

OHR (Office of the High Representative) (2004) *Decision Establishing the Police Restructuring Commission* [online]. Available from: http://www.ohr.int/?p=65507 [Accessed 09/10/2022].

Oliver, I. (2005) *War and Peace in the Balkans*. London: I.B. Tauris.

OSCE (2014) *Article IV of the Dayton Peace Accords* [online]. Available from: http://www.osce.org/cio/119597 [Accessed 12/01/2021].

OSCE (2016) *OSCE Marks 20th Anniversary of Sub-Regional Arms Control Agreement* [online]. Available from: http://www.osce.org/cio/246991 [Accessed 07/02/2021].

Ostojic, M. (2014) Between Justice and Stability: The Politics of War Crimes Prosecution in Post-Milosevic Serbia. Farnham, Surrey: Ashgate.

Ottaway, M. (2003) *Democracy Challenged: The Rise of Semi-Authoritarianism*. Washington, D.C.: Carnegie Endowment for International Peace.

PACE (1999) *Honouring of Obligations and Commitments by Croatia* [online]. Report 8353. Available from: http://assembly.coe.int/nw/xml/XRef/X2H-Xref-ViewHTML.asp?FileID=8687&lang=en [Accessed 02/11/2021].

Padurariu, A. (2014) The Implementation of Police Reform in Bosnia and Herzegovina: Analysing UN and EU Efforts. *Stability: International Journal of Security and Development*, 3(1), pp. 1-18.

Papadimitriou, D. (2001) The EU's strategy in the post-communist Balkans. *Southeast European and Black Sea Studies*, 1(3), pp. 69-94.

Particip GmbH (2009) *Retrospective Evaluation of CARDS Programmes in Serbia* [online]. The European Evaluation Consortium 2007. Available from: https://ec.europa.eu/neighbourhood-enlargement/sites/ne ar/files/pdf/financial_assistance/cards/evaluation-reports/04-fr_ cards_serbia.pdf [Accessed 19/01/2022].

Patten, C. (2004) *Letter from Rt. Hon. Christopher Patten, Member of the European Commission to Mr Adan Terzic, Prime Minister of Bosnia and Herzegovina* [online]. Available from: hhtp://www.ohr.int/ohr-dept/rule-of-law-pillar/prc/prc-letters/pdf/patten-letter.pdf [Accessed 01/02/2022].

Pavlakovic, V. (2008) Better the Grave than a Slave: Croatia and the International Criminal Tribunal for the Former Yugoslavia. In: S.P. Ramet, K. Clewing and R. Lukic, eds., *Croatia since Independence: War, Politics, Society, Foreign Relations*. Munich: R. Oldenbourg, pp. 447-477.

Pavlicevic, P. (2011) *The Sino-Serbian Strategic Partnership in a Sino-EU Relationship Context* [online]. Briefing Series — Issue 68. The University of Nottingham: China Policy Institute. Available from:

https://www.nottingham.ac.uk/iaps/documents/cpi/briefings/briefing-68-sino-serbian-partnership.pdf [Accessed 11/08/2022].

Pearl, J. (2015) Causes of Effects and Effects of Causes. *Sociological Methods and Research*, 44(1), pp. 149-164.

Peen Rodt, A. and Wolff, S. (2012) EU Conflict Management in Bosnia and Herzegovina and Macedonia. In: R.G. Whitman and S. Wolff, eds., *The European Union as a Global Conflict Manager*. London: Routledge, pp. 138-151.

Pellet, A. (1992) The Opinions of the Badinter Arbitration Committee A Second Breath for the Self-Determination of Peoples. *European Journal of International Law*, 3(1), pp. 178-185.

Perdan, S. (2006) Security Sector Reform: The building of Security in Bosnia and Herzegovina. *Conflict, Security & Development*, 6(2), pp.179-209.

Perito, R. M. (2009) *Afghanistan's Police: The Weak Link in Security Sector Reform*. USIP Special Report. Washington, D. C.: United States Institute of Peace.

Perritt, H.H. (2008) *Kosovo Liberation Army: The Inside Story of an Insurgency*. Chicago: University of Illinois Press.

Petrovic, J. (2006) Police Education Reform in Serbia. *Western Balkans Security Observer*, 1, pp.9-11.

Petrovic, P. and Milosevic, M. (2017) *Better Private Security in Serbia Remains a Far Cry* [online]. Private Security Research Collaboration in the Western Balkans. The Swiss National Science Foundation. Available from: https://www.ppps.dcaf.ch/sites/default/files/ressources/Final_PP_2017_BCSP%20%28Serbia%29.pdf [Accessed 15/08/2021].

Pietz, T. (2006) *Defence Reform and Conversion in Albania, Macedonia and Croatia*. Brief 34. Bonn: BICC.

Pietz, T. (2006a) Overcoming the Failings of Dayton. In: M.A. Innes, ed., *Bosnian Security after Dayton: New Perspectives*. London and N.Y.: Routledge, pp. 155-172.

Pippan, C. (2004) The Rocky Road to Europe: The EU's Stabilisation and Association Process for the Western Balkans and the Principle of Conditionality. *European Foreign Affairs Review*, 9(2). p. 219-245.

Poitevin, C. (2013) European Union Initiatives to Control Small Arms and Light Weapons: Towards a More Coordinated Approach. *Non-Proliferation Papers* [online], 33. EU Non-Proliferation Consortium. Available from: http://www.nonproliferation.eu/web/documents/nonproliferationpapers/cdricpoitevin52b1d44997305.pdf [Accessed 30/07/2022].

Pomfret, J. (1996) How Bosnia's Muslims Dodged Arms Embargo. *The Washington Post* [online]. Available from: https://www.washingtonpost.com/archive/politics/1996/09/22/how-bosnias-muslims-dodged-arms-embargo/b2d78043-3e34-46d9-babc-c4c335236aeb/?utm_term=.6cc66b46a633 [Accessed 27/10/2021].

Pond, E. (2013) Serbia Reinvents Itself. *Survival*, 55(4), pp.7-30.

Popovic, D., Petrovic, P., Odanovic, G. and Radoman J. (2011) *Context Analysis of the Security Sector Reform in Serbia 1989-2009*. Belgrade: Belgrade Centre for Security Policy.

Populari and ESI (2009) *Bosnian Breakthrough Scorecard – Schengen White List Conditions* [online]. Available from: http://www.esiweb.org/pdf/schengen_white_list_project_bosnian%20breakthrough%20-%20visa%20scorecard%20-%2028%20September%202009.pdf [Accessed 29/11/2021].

Portela, C. (2005) Where and Why does the EU Impose Sanctions? *Politique Européenne*, 17(3), pp.83-111.

Posen, B. (1993) The security dilemma and ethnic conflict. *Survival*, 35(1), pp. 27-47.

Pöysäri, P. (2007) Assessing Progress on Security Sector Reform in South East Europe—a View from the Finnish EU Presidency. In: A. H. Ebnoether, E. M. Felberbauer and M. Stanicic, eds., *Security Sector Reform in South East Europe – from a Necessary Remedy to a Global Concept*. Vienna and Geneva: National Defence Academy and Bureau for Security Policy at the Austrian Ministry of Defence in co-operation with Geneva Centre for the Democratic Control of Armed Forces and PfP Consortium of Defence Academies and Security Studies Institutes, pp. 31-35.

Poznatov, M. (2016) EU-aspirant Serbia Struggles to Dismiss Allegations of Police Corruption. *Euractiv* [online]. Available from: https://www.euractiv.com/section/enlargement/news/eu-aspirant-serbia-struggles-to-dismiss-allegations-of-police-corruption/ [Accessed 11/08/2021].

PrEUgovor (n.d.). *About us* [online]. Available from: http://preugovor.org/preUgovor/1121/About-us.shtml [Accessed 09/08/2021].

PrEUgovor (2013) *Written Contributions to the European Commission 2013 Progress Report on Serbia* [online]. Belgrade. Available from: http://www.bezbednost.org/upload/document/2013-10-01_eng_preunup_joint_progres_report_(final.pdf [Accessed 12/08/2021].

Pridham, G. and Gallagher, T. (eds.) (2000) *Experimenting with Democracy: Regime Change in the Balkans*. London and New York: Routledge.

Pugh, M. C. (2007). *Limited Sovereignty and Economic Security: Survival in Southeast Europe*. Bradford: University of Bradford, Department of Peace Studies. Transformation of War Economies Project Working Paper.

Pugh, M., Cooper, N. and Goodhand, J. (2004) *War Economies in a Regional Context: Challenges of Transformation*. Boulder and London: Lynne Rienner.

Pulko, I.B., Muherina, M. and Pejic, N. (2016) Analysing the Effectiveness of EUFOR Althea Operation in Bosnia and Herzegovina. *European Perspectives*, Journal on European Perspectives of the Western Balkans, 8(2/15), pp. 87-116.

Radan, P. (2000) Post-Secession International Borders: A Critical Analysis of the Opinions of the Badinter Arbitration Commission. *Melbourne University Law Review*, 24(1) [online]. Available from: http://www.austlii.edu.au/au/journals/MelbULawRw/2000/3.html [Accessed 11/08/2021].

Radeljic, B. (ed.) (2013) *Europe and the Post-Yugoslav Space*. London and N.Y. Routledge.

Ramboll Management (2008) *Ad Hoc Evaluation of the CARDS Programme Country: Bosnia and Herzegovina* [online]. Sectors: Democratic Stabilisation, Good Governance, Economic and Social Development. Available from: https://ec.europa.eu/neighbourhood-enlargement/sites/near/files/pdf/financial_assistance/phare/evaluation/ad_hoc_evaluation_cards_bih_en.pdf [Accessed 28/11/2021].

Ramet, S. (2002) *Balkan Babel: The Disintegration of Yugoslavia from the Death of Tito to the Fall of Milosevic*. Oxford: Westview Press.

Ramet, S. (2006) *The Three Yugoslavias*. Washington, D.C.: Woodrow Wilson Center Press.

Reichel, S. (2000) *Transitional Administration in Former Yugoslavia*. Discussion Paper P00-305. Berlin: Wissenschaftzentrum Berlin fuer Sozialforschung.

Riding, A. (1991) Conflict in Yugoslavia: Europeans Send High-Level Team. *New York Times* [online]. Available from: http://www.nytimes.com/1991/06/29/world/conflict-in-yugoslavia-europeans-send-high-level-team.html [Accessed 1/04/2021].

Ristovic, N. (2007) *Modernizing Police Education in Serbia* [online]. OSCE. Available from: http://www.osce.org/serbia/57565 [Accessed 18/08/2022].

Rochester, M. (1993) *Waiting for the New Millennium*. Columbia, SC: University of South Carolina Press.

Rose, C.A. (2011) *Who is Guarding Serbia's Borders? An Assessment of Serbia's Progress in Border Security Development and Reform*. Thesis (MA), Naval Postgraduate School, Monterey, CA.

Rose, R. (1976) On the Priorities of Government: A Developmental Analysis of Public Policies. *European Journal of Political Research*, 4, pp. 247-289.

Rozen, L. (2001) The Balkans: Failing States and Ethnic Wars. In: S. J. Flanagan, E. L. Frost and R. L. Kugler, eds., *Challenges of the Global Century: Report of the Project on Globalization and National Security*. Washington, D.C.: National Defence University, pp. 1055-1075.

SAA (2005) Stabilisation and Association Agreement between the European Communities and their Member States, of the one part, and the Republic of Croatia, of the other part. *Official Journal of the European Union*, L26, pp. 3-220.

SAA (2013) Stabilisation and Association Agreement between the European Communities and their Member States, of the one part, and the Republic of Serbia, of the other part. *Official Journal of the European Union*, L 278, pp. 14–471.

SAA (2015) Stabilisation and Association Agreement between the European Communities and their Member States, of the one part, and Bosnia and Herzegovina, of the other part. *Official Journal of the European Union*, L 164, pp. 2–547.

Sayari, S. (2000) Turkish Foreign Policy in the Post-Cold War Era: The Challenges of Multi-Regionalism. *Journal of International Affairs*, 54(1), pp. 169-182.

Schnabel, A. and Ehrhart, H-G. (eds.) (2006) *Security Sector Reform and Post-Conflict Peacebuilding*. Tokyo, N.Y., Paris: United Nations University Press.

Schwegmann, C. (2000) *The Contact Group and its Impact on the European Security Structure*. Occasional Papers No 16. Paris: Institute for Security Studies of WEU.

SEESAC (South Eastern and Eastern Europe Clearinghouse for the Control of Small Arms and Light Weapons) (n.d.) *Who We Are* [online]. Available from: http://www.seesac.org/About/ [Accessed 12/12/2021].

SEESAC (South Eastern and Eastern Europe Clearinghouse for the Control of Small Arms and Light Weapons) (2010) *Less Weapons, Less Tragedies* [online]. Available from: http://www.seesac.org/News-SALW/Less-Weapons-Less-Tragedies/ [Accessed 12/12/2021].

SEESAC (South Eastern and Eastern Europe Clearinghouse for the Control of Small Arms and Light Weapons) (2010a) *Serbia Adopts a National SALW Strategy* [online]. Available from: http://www.seesac.org/News-SALW/Serbia-adopts-a-national-SALW-Strategy/ [Accessed 08/08/2022].

SEESAC (South Eastern and Eastern Europe Clearinghouse for the Control of Small Arms and Light Weapons) (2013) *Results of the EU and SEESAC'S Arms Control Activities in the Western Balkans in 2010-2012* [online]. Available from: http://www.seesac.org/News_1/Results-of-the-EU-and-SEESACS-Arms-Control-Activities-in-the-Western-Balkans-in-2010-2012/ [Accessed 20/11/2021].

SEESAC (South Eastern and Eastern Europe Clearinghouse for the Control of Small Arms and Light Weapons) (2014) *SEESAC Supports the SALW Collection Campaign in Bosnia and Herzegovina* [online]. Available from: http://www.seesac.org/News-SALW/SEESAC-Supports-the-SALW-Collection-Campaign-in-Bosnia-and-Herzegovina/ [Accessed 20/11/2021].

SEESAC (South Eastern and Eastern Europe Clearinghouse for the Control of Small Arms and Light Weapons) (2017) *EU Support of SEESAC Disarmament and Arms Control Activities in South East Europe (EUSAC)* [online]. Available from: http://www.seesac.org/EUSAC/ [Accessed 08/08/2021].

Short, C. (2010) Foreword. In: M. Sedra, ed., *The Future of Security Sector Reform*. Ontario: GIGI, pp. 10-14.

Sikavica, S. (2001) The War-Time and Peace-Time Abuses of the Yugoslav Army. In: Helsinki Committee, ed., *In the Triangle of State Power*[online]. Available from: http://www.dentisty.org/helsinki-files-in-the-triangle-of-the-state-power-army-police.html [Accessed 20/05/2021].

SIPRI (Stockholm International Peace Research Institute) (2012) *EU Arms Embargo on the Former Socialist Federal Republic of Yugoslavia* [online]. Available from: https://www.sipri.org/databases/embargoes/eu_arms_embargoes/yugoslavia [Accessed 29/04/2022].

Sjøstedt, G. (1977) *The External Role of the European Community*. Westmead: Saxon House.

Solana, J. (2000) *Public Debate on Western Balkans* [online]. Intervention by High Representative of the Common Foreign and Security Policy to the General Affairs Council. Brussels. Available from: http://www.consilium.europa.eu/uedocs/cms_data/docs/pressdata/en/discours/gac%2010.7%20en.doc.html [Accessed 10/02/2021].

Solioz, C. and Stubbs, P. (2012) Regionalism in South East Europe and Beyond. In: C. Solioz and P. Stubbs, eds., *Towards Open Regionalism in South East Europe*. Baden-Baden: Nomos Publishers, pp. 15-48.

Spence, D. (2010) Prospects and Advantages of EU Security Sector Reform. In: M. Ekengren and G. Simons, eds., *The Politics of Security Sector Reform: Challenges and Opportunities for the European Union's Global Role*. London and N.Y.: Routledge, pp. 93-100.

Spoerri, M. and Freyberg-Inan, A. (2008) From Prosecution to Persecution: Perceptions of the International Criminal Tribunal for the Former Yugoslavia (ICTY) in Serbian Domestic Politics. *Journal of International Relations and Development*, 11(4), pp.350-384.

Stalvant, C.-E. (2011) Three Traditions and the Concept of Security Sector Reform. In: M., Ekengren and S. Simons, eds., *The Politics of Security Sector Reform: Challenges and Opportunities for the European Union's Global Role*. London and N.Y.: Routledge, pp. 15-21.

Stoessinger, J. G. (2001) *Why Nations Go to War*. Basingstoke: Macmillan.

Skogstrom, K. (2006) *EUPM Contribution to the Development of the State Border Police in Bosnia and Herzegovina* [online]. Available from: www.pecshor.hu/periodika/2006/VI/skogstrom_en.pdf [Accessed 10/12/2021].

Stojanovic, J. (2009) *EU Political Conditionality and Domestic Politics: Cooperation with the International Criminal Tribunal for the Former Yugoslavia in Croatia and Serbia*. Thesis (PhD), Central European University.

Strazzari, F. and Coticchia, F. (2012) The Phantom Menace. Transnational Organized Crime and the Shaping of the Western Balkans. In: C. Solioz and P. Stubbs, eds., *Towards Open Regionalism in South East Europe*. Baden-Baden: Nomos Publishers, pp. 147-174.

Szewczyk, B.M.J. (2010) *The EU in Bosnia and Herzegovina: Powers, Decisions and Legitimacy*. Occasional Paper No 83. Paris: ISS.

Tanner, M. (2010) *Croatia: A Nation Forged in War*. New Haven: Yale University Press.

Tocci, N. (2007) *The EU and Conflict Resolution. Promoting Peace in the Backyard*. London: Routledge.

Todorova, M. (1997) *Imagining the Balkans*. Oxford: Oxford University Press.

Tolksdorf, D. (2013) Police Reform and Conditionality. In: T. Flessenkemper and D. Helly, eds., *Ten Years after: Lessons from the EUPM in Bosnia and Herzegovina 2002-2012*. Paris: ISS, pp. 20-26.

Tolksdorf, D. (2014) Incoherent Peacebuilding: The European Union's Support for the Police Sector in Bosnia and Herzegovina, 2002–8. *International Peacekeeping*, 21(1), pp.56-73.

Tomovic, D. (2015) Montenegro and Bosnia are to Sign a Historic Demarcation Agreement by the end of August. *Balkan Insight* [online]. Available from: http://www.balkaninsight.com/en/article/montenegro-bosnia-to-sign-border-agreement-08-17-2015 [Accessed 10/12/2021]

Trauner, F. (2007) From Membership Conditionality to Policy Conditionality: EU External Governance in South-Eastern Europe. Paper presented to the "EU Consent" conference *"Deepening in an Enlarged Europe: Integrative Balancing in the New Member States"*. Budapest, Hungary, 16-17 November 2007 (on file with author).

Trauner, F. (2011) The Europeanisation of the Western Balkans: EU Justice and Home Affairs in Croatia and Macedonia. Manchester and N.Y.: Manchester University Press.

Trivunovic, M. (2004) Police Reform in Serbia. In: M. Caparini and O. Marenin, eds., Transforming Police in Central and Eastern Europe: Process and Progress. Muenster: LIT, pp. 242-261.

Tull, S.M. (2003) The European Union and Croatia: Negotiating "Europeanization" amid National, Regional, and International Interests. In: P.J. Kubicek, ed., The European Union and Democratisation. London: Routledge.

Ullman, R. (ed.) (1996) The World and Yugoslavia's Wars. New York: Council on Foreign Relations.

UN (1995) Conclusions of the Peace Implementation Conference Held at Lancaster House (London Conference) [online]. Available from: https://peacemaker.un.org/bosnialondonconference95# [Accessed 18/09/2021]

UNDP. (2002) Human Development Report: Deepening Democracy in a Fragmented World. N.Y. and Oxford: Oxford University Press.

UNMIBH (2002) Summary of UNMIBH Human Rights Office Activities. Sarajevo: UN Mission in Bosnia and Herzegovina.

UNODC (2020) Measuring organized crime in the Western Balkans [online]. Available from: https://reliefweb.int/report/bosnia-and-herzegovina/measuring-organized-crime-western-balkans [Accessed 18/09/2022]

The United Nations Security Council Resolution 713 (1991), 25 September 1991. Socialist Republic of Yugoslavia.

The United Nations Security Council Resolution 757 (1992), 30 May 1992. Bosnia and Herzegovina.

The United Nations Security Council Resolution 820 (1993), 17 April 1993. Bosnia and Herzegovina.

The United Nations Security Council Resolution 1088 (1996), 12 December 1996. The situation in Bosnia and Herzegovina.

The United Nations Security Council Resolution 1160 (1998), 31 March 1998. On the letters from the United Kingdom (S/1998/223) and the United States (S/1998/272).

The United Nations Security Council Resolution 1575 (2004), 22 November 2004. The situation in Bosnia and Herzegovina.

USAID, USDD and USDS (2009) *Security Sector Reform* [online]. Available from: https://www.state.gov/documents/organization/115810.pdf [Accessed 12/04/2021].

Usanmaz, E. (2018) Successful Crisis Management? Evaluating the Success of the EU Missions in the Western Balkans. *European Foreign Affairs Review*, 23(3), pp. 381-403

Uvalic, M. (2003) Economics: from International Assistance toward Self-Sustaining Growth. In: W. van Meurs, ed., *Prospects and Risks Beyond EU Enlargement Southeastern Europe: Weak States and Strong International Support*. Wiesbaden: Springer, pp. 99-115.

Vankovska, B. and Wiberg, H. (2003) *Between Past and Future: Civil-Military Relations in the Post-Communist Balkans*. London: I.B. Tauris.

Vayrynen, R. (1984) Regional Conflict Formations: An Intractable Problem of International Relations. *Journal of Peace Research*, 21(4), pp. 337-359.

Vetschera, H. (2005) *Security Sector Reform in Bosnia and Herzegovina and the Role of the International Community- Background, Development and Results* (unpublished manuscript on file with author).

Vetschera, H. (2005a) *Mission Accomplished in Bosnia and Herzegovina Agreement on Confidence and Security-Building Measures Declared Obsolete* [online]. OSCE. Available from: http://www.osce.org/secretariat/15974?download=true [Accessed 02/10/2021].

Vetschera, H. and Damian, M. (2006) Security Sector Reform in Bosnia and Herzegovina: The Role of the International Community. *International Peacekeeping*, 13(1), pp.28-42.

de Vries, A.W. (2002) European Union Sanctions against the Federal Republic of Yugoslavia from 1998 to 2000: A Special Exercise in Targeting. In: D. Cortright and G. A. Lopez, eds., *Smart Sanctions: Targeting Economic Statecraft*. Plymouth: Rowman and Littlefield Publishers, pp. 87-108.

Vucetic, S. (2001) The Stability Pact for South Eastern Europe as a Security Community-Building Institution. *Southeast European Politics*, 2(2), pp. 109-134.

Vukadin, I.K., Borovec, K. and Ljubin Golub, T. (2013) Policing in Croatia: The Main Challenges on the Path to Democratic Policing. In: G. Mesko, C. B. Fields, B. Lobnikar and A. Sotlar, eds., *Handbook on Policing in Central and Eastern Europe*. N.Y.: Springer, pp. 31-56.

Vukusic, I. (2014) Perceptions of the International Criminal Tribunal for the Former Yugoslavia in Croatia. In: J. Gow, R. Kerr and Z. Pajic, eds., *Prosecuting War Crimes: Lessons and Legacies of the International Criminal Tribunal for the Former Yugoslavia*. London: Routledge, pp.151-181.

Vukusic, I. (2015) Stresses and Failures of Transitional Justice in BiH: The Case of the ICTY. In: S. Keil and V. Perry, eds., *State-Building and Democratization in Bosnia and Herzegovina*. London and N.Y.

Wallander, C., Haftendorn, H. and Keohane, R. O. (1999) Introduction. In: H. Haftendorn, R. Keohane and C. Wallander, eds., *Imperfect Unions: Security Institutions over Time and Space*. Oxford: Oxford University Press.

Watanabe, L. (2010). *Securing Europe*. Houndmills, Basingstoke, Hampshire: Palgrave Macmillan.

Watkins, A. (2010) *Security Sector Reform and Donor Assistance in Serbia: Complexity of Managing Change*. Shrivenham: Defence Academy of the UK.

Weber, R. (2001) Police Organization and Accountability: A Comparative Study. In: A. Kadar, ed., *Police in Transition: Essays on Police Forces in Transition Countries*. Budapest: Central European University, pp. 39-70.

Webber, M., Croft, S., Howorth, J., Terriff, T., and Krahmann, E. (2004) The Governance of European Security. *Review of International Studies*, 30(1), pp. 3-26.

Weller, M. and Wolff, S. (2006) Bosnia and Herzegovina Ten Years after Dayton: Lessons for Internationalized State Building. *Ethnopolitics*, 5(1), pp.1-13.

Wessels, W., Maurer, A. and Mittag, J. (2003) *Fifteen Into One?: The European Union and its Member States*. Manchester: Manchester University Press.

WEU (1991) *Declaration on the Role of the Western European Union and Its Relations with the European Union and with the Atlantic Alliance*. Maastricht, 10 December 1991.

WEU (2000) *WEU today*, January. Brussels: WEU Secretariat-General.

Wheaton, K.J. (2000) Cultivating Croatia's Military. *NATO Review* [online]. Available from: https://www.nato.int/docu/review/2000/0002-04.htm [Accessed 11/03/2022].

Whitman, J. (2005) The limits of global governance. London: Routledge.

Winland, D. (2008) Ten Years Later: The changing Nature of Transnational Ties in Post-Independence Croatia. In: D. Kostovicova and V. Bojicic-Dzelilovic, eds., *Transnationalism in the Balkans*. London: Routledge, pp. 79-92.

Winn, N. and Lord, C. (2001) *EU Foreign Policy Beyond the Nation State: Joint Action and Institutional Analysis of the Common Foreign and Security Policy*. Basingstoke, Hampshire: Palgrave Macmillan.

Wisler, D. (2005) The Police Reform in Bosnia and Herzegovina. In: A. H. Ebnöther and P. Fluri, eds., *After Intervention: Public Security Management in Post-Conflict Societies – From Intervention to Sustainable Local Ownership*. Vienna and Geneva: Bureau for Security Policy at the Austrian Ministry of Defence, National Defence Academy, Vienna and Geneva Centre for the Democratic Control of Armed Forces, Geneva in co-operation with PfP-Consortium of Defence Academies and Security Studies Institutes, pp. 139-160.

Wolff, S. (2011) The regional dimensions of state failure. *Review of International Studies*, 37(03), pp. 951-972.

Woodward, S. (1995) *Balkan Tragedy: Chaos and Dissolution after the Cold War*. Washington, D.C.: Brookings Institution.

World Bank (n.d) *Croatia* [online]. Available from: https://data.worldbank.org/country/Croatia [Accessed 01/04/2022].

World Bank (1996) *Technical Annex to Bosnia and Herzegovina for an Emergency Demobilization and Reintegration Project (EDPR)*. Washington, D.C.: World Bank.

World Bank (2016) *Armed Forces Personnel, Total* [online]. Available from: https://data.worldbank.org/indicator/MS.MIL.TOTL.P1 [Accessed 10/05/2022].

Yalnazov, E. (2000) *The Role of NATO and the EAPC in Support of Lasting Peace and Regional Security Cooperation in Southeastern Europe*. NATO/EAPC 1998/2000 Report.

Yarwood, J. R. Seebacher, A., Strufe, N. and Wolfram H. (1999) *Rebuilding Mostar: Urban Reconstruction in a War Zone*. Liverpool: Liverpool University Press.

Zakosek, N. (2008) Democratization, State-building and War: The Cases of Serbia and Croatia. *Democratization*, 15(3), pp.588-610.

Annex I

An inventory of SSR activities, undertaken by the EU in the Western Balkans[280]

Reform area	Types of activities with examples
Political level	
General	Policy and legal advice to relevant institutions, e.g. parliaments, governments, ministries and law enforcement agencies on the issues of political control and improvement of good/democratic governance.
Civilian control	1. Assistance in adopting a national security strategy and policy. 2. Support for the establishment and reform of governmental and administrative bodies, responsible for the provision of civilian control, e.g. Ministry of Defence, Ministry of Interior, customs and fiscal administrations. 3. Assistance to ensure control of budgeting, management, accountability and auditing of security expenditure.
Parliamentary control	1. Policy and legal advice to parliaments and parliamentary commissions dealing with different aspects of security. 2. Training and sharing best practices (e.g. training members of parliament and parliamentary staff, organising study visits). 3. Technical assistance to parliamentary commissions working on security issues.
Public control	1. Assistance to civil society and media to improve expertise in the sphere of security and capacity to monitor the security sector bodies. 2. Assisting states with the development of independent regulatory bodies that could improve the transparency of the security sector.
Regional dimension	Facilitation of cooperation between security sectors of neighbouring states and states linked geo-strategically to build good neighbourliness, accountability and transparency.
The legacy of war crimes	Promotion of cooperation with the ICTY to facilitate reconciliation.

Organisational level	
General	Institutional support in adopting legal foundations for the security system.
Defence sector	1. Policy and legal advice (e.g. assistance in defining a defence policy, separating tasks between army and police; advice on organising defence structures, including their chain of command, finances and political control; defining military planning procedures). 2. Training and sharing best practices (e.g. training military personnel, including Chiefs of Defence and senior officers; training on democratic principles of modern armed forces, regarding human rights, gender issues, international (humanitarian) law; co-locating EU experts to Ministries of defence in partner countries to mentor, monitor and advise local authorities on defence policy). 3. Technical assistance (e.g. helping with the acquisition of modern non-lethal military equipment, establishing the mechanisms for procurement and maintenance) 4. Post-conflict assistance (e.g. reorganisation of the army for peaceful time; disarmament, demobilisation and reintegration as part of SSR)
Police	1. Policy and legal advice (e.g. conducting an assessment of policing needs; assistance in defining a policing strategy and policy, compatible with objectives of the Justice/Rule of Law sector; advice on organising police forces, including administration, budget control, transparency, accountability and political control). 2. Training and creating opportunities for social learning (introducing police to the principles of modern policing and police management with a special focus on international law, human rights and gender issues; offering special guidance to the police force during the period of transition; co-locating EU experts to the Ministry of Interior). 3. Technical assistance (e.g. helping with the acquisition of modern equipment,

		improving connectivity among law enforcement agencies).
	4.	Post-conflict assistance (e.g. assistance in delineating tasks and responsibilities between police and army).
Border control	1.	Policy and legal advice (e.g. assistance in assessing needs, objectives and rules for border and customs services; advice on adopting a strategy on border control and policies for its management; advice on organising the border and customs sector, including political control).
	2.	Training and sharing best practices (e.g. training customs officers and border guards on principles of good border control; training on human rights, international law and gender issues; co-locating EU experts to the national bodies responsible for border control and customs).
	3.	Technical assistance (e.g. help with equipping border control services with modern up-to-date technology, compatible with international standards).
	4.	Post-conflict assistance (e.g. assistance with restoring controls over borders).

---

280 The inventory is based on the provisions of the Council and Commission Concepts on SSR, using the adjusted model of Hänggi and Tanner (2005: 100-104).

Annex II

Comparison of the EU's impact on SSR in Croatia, Serbia and Bosnia between 1991 and 2013

Aspects of SSR	Croatia	Serbia	BiH
1991-1995			
Political level	The Arbitration Commission defined the general shape and international personality of the state. Croatian para-state in BiH was denied recognition.	The Arbitration Commission defined the general shape and international personality of the state. It also denied recognition to Serbian para-states in Croatia and BiH.	The Arbitration Commission defined the general shape and international personality of the state. Additionally, it internationalised the conflict and sped it up.
	The EU arms embargo (and the EU's support for the UN embargo) disadvantaged the state in the conditions of war and unintentionally contributed to the criminalisation of the security sector.	The EU arms embargo (and the EU's support for the UN embargo) set the military balance in favour of Serbia and unintentionally contributed to the criminalisation of the security sector.	The EU arms embargo (and the EU's support for the UN embargo) militarily disadvantaged the state (Bosniaks, to the greatest extent) and unintentionally contributed to the criminalisation of the security sector. It also helped prevent the escalation of violence and reach a diplomatic solution to the Bosnian war.

	The ECMM created a real and symbolic link between the EU and Croatia and provided the former with a unique perspective on the security situation in the country. It was unable, however, to change this situation.	Sanctions against the FRY contributed to the isolation of the Milosevic regime and consolidated the anti-EU sentiment in the country.	The ECMM created a real and symbolic link between the EU and BiH, while providing the former with a unique perspective on the security situation in the country. Nonetheless, the instrument was not capable of changing the situation from war to peace.
Organisational level	n/a	n/a	The EU contributed to police reform in the country by deploying the WEUPOL in Mostar. The mission achieved results of predominantly technical character due to the lack of experience in crisis management, limited financial resources, lack of military power and overly ambitious goals.

ANNEX II 383

	1995-1999		
Political level	The EU embargo on arms, munitions and military equipment contributed to arms control and confidence-building measures, coordinated by the OSCE under the Dayton Agreement.	The EU embargo contributed to arms control and confidence-building measures, coordinated by the OSCE under the DPA. With the start of the Kosovo conflict, the strengthening of the ban against the FRY led to the exacerbation of the anti-EU sentiment among Serbian authorities and security elites.	The EU arms embargo contributed to arms control and confidence-building measures, coordinated by the OSCE under the Dayton Agreement.
		Travel restrictions and oil embargo made the EU even more unpopular. On the other hand, these measures weakened the Milosevic regime and isolated Serbia even from its FRY partner, Montenegro.	
	The ECMM contributed to the stabilisation of the country by monitoring the implementation of the Erdut Agreement and the DPA.		The ECMM contributed to the stabilisation of the country by monitoring the implementation of the DPA.

	The Regional Approach (RA) demanded the state developed a system of democratic governance. It set requirements for depoliticization of the police and army and insisted on the introduction of democratic civilian control over the security sector. It emphasised separation of powers.	The RA demanded the state developed a system of democratic governance. It emphasised separation of powers.	The Regional Approach demanded the state developed a system of democratic governance. It called on BiH to remove political influence over the police and army. It also set conditions for establishing common institutions and state consolidation, before emphasising the importance of separation of powers and good governance.
	The RA promoted the transformation of Croatia into a functional state.	The RA promoted the transformation of the FRY into a functional state.	The RA promoted the transformation of BiH into a functional state.
	Cooperation with the ICTY was identified as a priority, but the EU was not ready to use coercion to improve it.	Cooperation with the ICTY was identified as a priority, but the EU was not ready to use coercion to improve it.	Cooperation with the ICTY was identified as a priority, but the EU was not ready to use coercion to improve it.
	The implementation of the RA was obstructed by the semi-authoritarian regime of Tudjman, who feared it would lead to a new Yugoslavia.	The implementation of the RA was obstructed by the semi-authoritarian regime of Milosevic that harboured strong anti-EU sentiment over the bloc's sanctions.	The RA was sidelined by other efforts of the international community building peace in BiH under the DPA framework.

ANNEX II 385

		The EU was forced to use the RA as a monitoring, and not transformative tool.	The EU was forced to use the RA as a monitoring, and not transformative tool.	The EU was forced to use the RA as a monitoring, and not transformative tool.
Defence		Support for mine clearance action and research on de-mining.	n/a	Support for mine clearance action and research on de-mining. The EU also contributed to the development of the strategic documents on the mine threat.
Police		The RA reports focused on professionalisation of the services and introduction of democratic policing.	The EU used the RA reports to monitor the practices of the Serbian police and criticise them for unprofessionalism and disregard for human rights.	The RA reports focused on professionalisation of the services and introduction of democratic policing.
		The EU recognised the leadership of the UN and OSCE in the reform.		The EU recognised the leadership of the UN in the reform.
				The WEUPOL that finished work in 1996 improved professionalism of the police of West and East Mostar and established the Unified Police Force, active only in the central zone of the town. The mission's achievements, like in the previous period, were mainly technical.

Border services	The reform was framed as a step towards regional reconciliation.	The reform was framed as a step towards regional reconciliation.	The reform was framed as a step towards regional reconciliation.
	Advice on restoration of border controls and introduction of international standards into the work of border services.		Advice on establishing border controls in compliance with international standards.
	Support for the development of customs services as part of border management.		Support for the development of customs services as part of border management.
1999-2013			
Political level	The oversight of the security sector was promoted through support for and advice on establishing parliamentary, civilian and public control measures.	The oversight of the security sector was promoted through support for and advice on establishing parliamentary, civilian and public control measures, as well as demands for state consolidation. To achieve the latter, the FRY/ SCG was asked to ensure separation of powers between the federal/ State Union and republican levels and harmonise security practices between Serbia and Montenegro.	The oversight of the security sector was promoted through support for and advice on establishing parliamentary, civilian and public control measures, as well as demands for state consolidation. To strengthen the state, BiH was required to develop common state institutions and establish effective coordination between different levels of government.

	Good security governance is seen as an element of democratisation and Europeanisation of the state apparatus.	After 2006, the EU's focus shifted to good security governance as an element of democratisation and Europeanisation of the state apparatus. The Kosovo issue kept the salience of the state-consolidation agenda.	Throughout the period the EU continued prioritising state consolidation in BiH. It also highlighted the importance of good security governance for Europeanisation of the state.
	Cooperation with the ICTY was promoted to raise professionalisation of the country's security sector, achieve full civilian control over it and restore trust and peace in the region.	Cooperation with the ICTY was promoted to raise professionalisation of the country's security sector, achieve full civilian control over it and restore trust and peace in the region.	Cooperation with the ICTY was promoted to raise professionalisation of the country's security sector, achieve full civilian control over it and restore trust and peace in the region.
	Regional cooperation was facilitated in policing, border security and to deal with the legacy of war.	Regional cooperation was facilitated in policing, border security, to deal with the legacy of war and over the issue of Kosovo.	Regional cooperation was mostly facilitated in policing, border security and to deal with the legacy of war.

Defence	The EU supported defence reform in the country from the point of its own security infrastructure (e.g. CSDP and Battlegroups), while NATO led the reform strategically.	Engagement in defence reform was delayed until at least 2006, when the SCG peacefully dissolved. The reform mainly focused on preparing Serbia for demands of the EU membership., however in the absence of NATO's pull, the EU was forced to guide the reform strategically at initial stages of the country's independence.	With the help of EUFOR, the EU became the leader of the operational side of the reform, introducing BiH to the CSDP infrastructure and promoting self-sustainability of the army. NATO continued to lead the reform on the strategic level.
	The reform was promoted through policy advice, training, technical assistance and post-conflict support.	The reform was promoted through policy advice, training, technical assistance and post-conflict support. Due to Serbia's involvement in four regional conflicts, post-conflict support was more limited than in Croatia and BiH.	The reform was promoted through policy advice, training, technical assistance and post-conflict support.
	Technical assistance and post-conflict reconstruction had a regional dimension.	Technical assistance and post-conflict reconstruction had a regional dimension.	Technical assistance and post-conflict reconstruction had a regional dimension.

Police	A priority area under Justice and Home Affairs.	A priority area under Justice and Home Affairs.	A priority area under Justice and Home Affairs.
	The reform was promoted through policy advice, training, technical assistance and post-conflict support.	The reform was promoted through policy advice, training, technical assistance and post-conflict support.	The reform was promoted through policy advice, training, technical assistance and post-conflict support.
	Fight against organised crime provided an overarching theme for the reform.	Fight against organised crime provided an overarching theme for the reform.	Fight against organised crime provided an overarching theme for the reform.
	Regional cooperation was placed high among the reform priorities.	Regional cooperation was placed high among the reform priorities.	Regional cooperation was placed high among the reform priorities.
	Having struggled to coordinate its activities with other external actors at the start of the period, the EU adopted more harmonised approached towards the end.	Cooperation with the external actors improved towards the end of the period.	Cooperation with the external actors improved towards the end of the period.

	The EU applied a project-based approach to the reform. It still progressed fast thanks to the achievements of domestic and external actors in the area by 1999, strength of Croatia's statehood and emergence of strong support for membership in the EU.	Having applied a project-based approach at the start, the EU switched to a more strategic approach in 2011-2012, as Serbia was getting closer to the membership in the bloc. The project-based approach was less successful than in Croatia due to the fractured political scene, poor exposure to externally-led programmes in the immediate post-Milosevic period and continuing challenges to Serbia's statehood.	The EU combined a project-based approach with a long-term structural reform. Police reform was identified as one of the key conditions for the membership negotiations. In the conditions of strong opposition to the reform in the RS, which were partly inspired by fears to lose the autonomy of the entity, the EU agreed to postpone its finalisation until BiH implements a constitutional reform. Police reform is therefore going to stay unfinished until BiH removes uncertainty surrounding its statehood.
Border services	A priority area under Justice and Home Affairs.	A priority area under Justice and Home Affairs.	A priority area under Justice and Home Affairs.
	Approached in a more comprehensive way, compared to defence and police reforms.	Approached in a more comprehensive way, compared to defence and police reforms.	Approached in a more comprehensive way, compared to defence and police reforms.

	Framework for the reform was provided by the Integrated Border Management for the Western Balkans, integrated into the Ohrid Process.	Framework for the reform was provided by the Integrated Border Management for the Western Balkans, integrated into the Ohrid Process.	Framework for the reform was provided by the Integrated Border Management for the Western Balkans, integrated into the Ohrid Process.
	The reform was promoted through the areas of legal approximation, training, technical assistance and post-conflict support.	The reform was promoted through the areas of legal approximation, training, technical assistance and post-conflict support.	The reform was promoted through the areas of legal approximation, training, technical assistance and post-conflict support.
	The country emerged as a regional leader in the reform since its borders were never militarised and remained intact since 1998.	The IBM took off only in 2006, when Belgrade gained full control over border issues that previously had to be coordinated with Podgorica. Kosovo's unilateral declaration of independence in 2008 imposed further constrains on the reform.	For a long time, BiH struggled with the IBM as it had no experience in managing external borders until 1995, lacked a state-level border agency until 2000 and its borders sustained the biggest damage during the regional violence of the 1990s. With the help of the European Commission's projects, the EUPM and even EUFOR, it established a working border management system.

	As the only Western Balkan country that was not placed on the negative visa list, Croatia did not have to go through a visa liberalisation process. It harmonised its visa, migration and asylum policies with EU practices within membership talks.	The visa liberalisation process dominated the country's reform in 2008-2009.	The visa liberalisation process dominated the country's reform in 2008-2010.
	Improved regional cooperation was among the priorities of the reform.	Improved regional cooperation was among the priorities of the reform.	Improved regional cooperation was among the priorities of the reform.
	As the EU's IBM strategy for the Western Balkans was integrated in a broader regional initiative, the Ohrid Border Process, the reform benefited from other external actors' contributions.	As the EU's IBM strategy for the Western Balkans was integrated in a broader regional initiative, the Ohrid Border Process, the reform benefited from other external actors' contributions.	As the EU's IBM strategy for the Western Balkans was integrated in a broader regional initiative, the Ohrid Border Process, the reform benefited from other external actors' contributions.

Notes

The publication of the book is supported by the GCRF-COMPASS (ES/P010849/1): Capacity-building in Eastern Neighbourhood and Central Asia: research integration, impact governance and sustainable communities.

Index

ABiH 233, 234, 238
AFBiH 243, 262, 270, 271, 272
Albania 21, 42, 43, 44, 45, 46, 47, 50, 51, 52, 54, 57, 65, 69, 70, 73, 91, 92, 93, 94, 102, 142, 164, 184, 185, 202, 217, 226, 266, 329, 339, 342, 343, 346, 356, 367
Annex 1A *also see* DPA 55, 237, 243
Annex 1B *also see* DPA 54, 184, 237
Arbitration Commission *also see* Badinter Commission 119, 120, 122, 123, 160, 180, 182, 223, 248, 252, 298, 339, 369, 381
arms embargo 51, 115, 119, 120, 124, 125, 126, 160, 180, 181, 182, 183, 186, 187, 188, 190, 226, 248, 250, 252, 253, 257, 298, 300, 326, 381, 383
army of the FRY *also see* VJ 19, 170
Ashdown, Paddy 242, 243, 245, 274, 276, 294, 338
Badinter Commission 122, 123, 125, 183, 226, 248, 249, 298
BCP 128, 155, 172, 185, 214-218, 221, 286-288
Bobetko, Janko 138, 140, 164
Bonn powers 239, 265, 275
border reform
    in Croatia 118, 128, 129, 152-160, 303, 311-313
    in Serbia 172, 178, 214-221, 311-313
    in Bosnia 235, 241, 256-257, 282-288, 311-313
Brcko 239, 240, 262, 263, 275, 277, 280, 281, 283, 311, 363
CARDS 15, 60, 73, 96, 101, 102, 133, 141, 144, 148, 150, 151, 153, 154, 192, 196, 201, 209, 210, 211, 216, 218, 219, 221, 260, 262, 264, 273, 277, 279, 282, 285, 286, 287, 294, 309, 329, 339, 340, 343, 344, 345, 347, 366, 369
centralisation 232, 245, 274, 276, 280, 281, 289, 290, 291, 292, 294, 311
CFSP 15, 21, 81, 91, 95, 120, 122, 130, 181, 187, 188, 191, 228, 251, 255, 258, 324, 336, 337, 338, 341
Common Security and Defence Policy *also see* CSDP 15, 21, 64, 81, 341
complex security governance 24, 25, 26, 37, 40, 79, 114, 122, 125, 297, 318, 325, 326
complex systems 23, 25, 40, 106, 314, 323, 326
complexity thinking 22, 23, 24, 27, 28, 34, 40, 70
Contact Group 68, 74, 108, 187, 293, 319, 370
Croatian Armed Forces 15, 52, 118, 134, 141, 144, 331

395

Croatian Defence Council *also see* HVO 16, 234
Croatian Democratic Union *also see* HDZ and HDZ BiH 16, 50, 113, 234, 238
Croatian mine action centre 15, 127
CSDP 15, 21, 64, 74, 81, 84, 95, 96, 105, 131, 132, 135, 144, 145, 146, 151, 163, 181, 195, 204, 205, 206, 207, 208, 225, 228, 252, 258, 260, 278, 308, 309, 324, 326, 361, 388
Dayton Peace Agreement *also see* DPA 15, 40, 91, 126, 184
Defence reform
   in Bosnia 236-238, 242-244, 253, 268-274, 307, 308
   in Croatia 118, 119, 126-128, 143-147, 302, 307, 308
   in Serbia 170, 171, 175, 176, 188, 204-208, 301-303, 308
demilitarisation 117, 154, 177, 178, 209, 215, 252, 310
de-mining 92, 126, 127, 128, 144, 145, 147, 162, 206, 253, 254, 255, 257, 260, 270, 273, 291, 302, 308, 326, 346, 385
Democratic Party 15, 18, 137, 168, 169, 234, 238
depoliticization 177, 244, 384
Deutsch, Karl 62, 72, 99, 109, 223, 247, 322, 340
Djindjic, Zoran 175, 177, 191, 199, 227
DOS 15, 168, 175, 198, 204
DPA 15, 37, 46, 54, 55, 73, 91, 92, 129, 159, 164, 175, 184, 231, 232, 236, 238, 239, 241, 243, 246, 253, 254, 256, 257, 261, 269, 272, 281, 292, 293, 301, 304, 317, 383, 384
DPS 15, 169, 225, 226
ECMM 15, 120, 121, 122, 125, 126, 160, 164, 186, 228, 248, 251, 252, 253, 254, 257, 259, 298, 299, 300, 301, 359, 361, 382, 383
embargo 51, 124, 125, 173, 180, 182, 186, 187, 188, 189, 190, 226, 242, 250, 251, 253, 298, 300, 303, 368, 381, 383
EU conditionality 100, 136, 199, 259, 263, 264, 276, 282, 311, 315, 353
EUAM 16, 248, 251, 252, 253, 254, 293, 299, 339
EUFOR Althea 64, 111, 146, 243, 258, 269, 270, 289, 307, 359, 369
EULEX 64, 111, 151, 202, 213, 221, 309
EUPM 16, 111, 151, 244, 246, 251, 258, 259, 260, 263, 264, 265, 274, 277, 278, 279, 280, 281, 282, 283, 285, 286, 288, 289, 290, 291, 292, 294, 295, 309, 310, 312, 332, 341, 361, 372, 392
European RSC 37, 41, 44, 46, 49, 52, 64, 66, 69
European Union Police Mission *also see* EUPM 16, 244, 338, 341
Europol 104, 131, 151, 152, 213, 284
EUSR 16, 245, 259, 260, 268, 275, 276, 278, 279, 288, 290, 293, 307

Federal Republic of Yugoslavia 16, 50, 167, 208, 335, 336, 337, 338, 343, 350, 354, 363, 374
Federation of Bosnia and Herzegovina 16, 69, 164, 232, 236
good governance 76, 77, 80, 81, 82, 87, 94, 96, 107, 108, 131, 142, 268, 301, 319, 320, 323, 384
good neighbourliness 55, 71, 108, 152, 174, 222, 317, 377
Hadzic, Goran 191, 200, 350, 353, 359
HDZ *also see* Croatian Democratic Union 16, 50, 113, 114, 115, 117, 129, 139, 140, 234, 238
HDZ BiH 16, 50, 234, 238
Herceg-Bosna 94, 114, 129, 234
HR/EUSR 245, 259, 262, 265, 268, 274, 275, 276, 281
HVO 16, 234, 238
ICTY 16, 74, 93, 104, 108, 117, 119, 127, 129, 131, 133, 137, 138, 139, 140, 141, 142, 143, 147, 162, 163, 164, 167, 175, 185, 189, 190, 191, 192, 193, 196, 197, 198, 199, 200, 204, 223, 224, 227, 228, 239, 243, 257, 261, 264, 265, 268, 270, 274, 281, 291, 294, 302, 304, 306, 307, 313, 320, 331, 340, 353, 355, 357, 358, 365, 372, 375, 378, 384, 388
IFOR 16, 69, 73, 232, 236, 238, 270
Implementation Force *also see* IFOR 16, 69, 232

Instrument for Pre-Accession 16, 60, 96, 104, 133, 260, 347, 349
Instrument for Pre-Accession Assistance 96, 133, 260, 347, 349
Integrated Border Management 101, 153, 154, 178, 215, 217, 219, 246, 282, 303, 311, 338, 340, 346, 354, 360, 363, 391
IPTF 16, 239, 240, 241, 244, 256, 258, 274, 277, 279, 281, 282, 289, 292
JHA *also see* Justice and Home Affairs 16, 98, 99, 102, 103, 104, 105, 132, 147, 152, 192, 201, 260
JNA *also see* Yugoslav People's Army 16, 50, 114, 121, 169, 172, 180, 183, 215, 233, 234, 235, 250, 298
Justice and Home Affairs *also see* JHA 16, 103, 147, 202, 208, 309, 373, 389, 391
Kosovo conflict 32, 53, 56, 71, 109, 173, 174, 181, 187, 204, 206, 226, 301, 303, 304, 317, 321, 383
Kosovo Liberation Army 16, 50, 74, 185, 367
Kostunica, Vojislav 175, 198, 200
local ownership 78, 233, 246, 271, 274, 281, 285, 286
local policing area 17, 245
MARRI 17, 98, 267, 361
member state-building 23, 35, 62, 100, 107, 131, 147, 152, 163, 224, 291, 315, 318, 321, 323

Membership Action Plan 17, 60, 143, 243, 269
Milosevic, Slobodan 58, 74, 113, 167, 168, 169, 170, 171, 172, 173, 174, 175, 179, 181, 182, 183, 184, 187, 188, 189, 190, 195, 197, 199, 210, 211, 222, 223, 224, 226, 227, 266, 299, 301, 302, 303, 304, 310, 312, 338, 354, 366, 367, 369, 382, 383, 384, 390
Mladic, Ratko 168, 175, 191, 199, 200, 243, 265, 268, 355
modernisation 96, 118, 133, 147, 159, 176, 209, 271, 278, 288, 310, 311, 320, 322
Montenegro 21, 42, 44, 46, 50, 65, 72, 102, 142, 158, 163, 164, 168, 172, 174, 178, 180, 182, 183, 184, 185, 186, 189, 190, 191, 198, 202, 205, 216, 217, 220, 224, 225, 226, 266, 267, 276, 284, 287, 295, 299, 301, 304, 305, 325, 329, 332, 338, 340, 341, 344, 346, 364, 373, 383, 387
Mostar 16, 18, 84, 94, 240, 245, 248, 251, 252, 253, 254, 277, 293, 299, 300, 303, 339, 354, 376, 382, 386
Mostar Declaration 245, 277
Multi-Ethnic Police Element 17, 178
NATO 17, 28, 32, 35, 38, 44, 45, 48, 54, 56, 57, 58, 60, 61, 63, 64, 65, 66, 67, 68, 69, 70, 71, 72, 73, 74, 81, 83, 85, 91, 94, 95, 98, 101, 105, 106, 108, 117, 118, 119, 122, 124, 127, 132, 136, 138, 140, 143, 145, 146, 147, 161, 163, 173, 174, 176, 182, 189, 201, 203, 204, 207, 214, 222, 223, 224, 225, 227, 232, 236, 237, 242, 243, 248, 250, 258, 263, 265, 268, 269, 270, 274, 289, 290, 292, 293, 294, 301, 307, 308, 315, 317, 319, 325, 331, 333, 334, 364, 365, 376, 388
Neum 159, 287
Office of the High Representative *also see* OHR 72, 73, 353, 365, 366
OHR 232, 237, 239, 240, 241, 242, 245, 246, 257, 269, 274, 277, 279, 280, 281, 282, 293, 295, 315, 365, 366
Ohrid Process 101, 154, 160, 178, 215, 246, 311, 316, 391
organised crime 51, 57, 59, 70, 73, 94, 98, 102, 103, 104, 108, 124, 125, 142, 148, 150, 151, 162, 171, 177, 181, 182, 201, 209, 211, 213, 214, 218, 228, 239, 241, 246, 247, 256, 264, 266, 270, 278, 280, 285, 287, 291, 295, 303, 309, 311, 317, 320, 326, 389
OSCE 17, 35, 38, 55, 58, 59, 63, 67, 68, 70, 73, 85, 101, 117, 121, 124, 128, 129, 147, 178, 180, 181, 188, 208, 209, 212, 214, 227, 228, 232, 237, 240, 242, 250, 254, 262, 272, 300, 303, 309, 316, 321, 329, 334, 341, 363, 366, 369, 374, 383, 385
oversight 77, 78, 79, 80, 82, 88, 100, 115, 116, 119, 133, 134, 135, 136, 143, 156, 178, 186, 193, 194, 196, 227, 246, 259,

261, 263, 264, 268, 289, 292, 304, 305, 322, 387

Partnership for Peace Programme *also see* PfP 17, 60

PfP 17, 60, 65, 119, 143, 163, 175, 176, 204, 207, 227, 242, 243, 247, 268, 269, 289, 331, 362, 368, 376

Ploce 129, 159, 288

Police reform
    in Bosnia 252, 254, 255, 274-281, 301-303, 309-311
    in Croatia 116-118, 128, 303, 309, 310
    in Serbia 171, 173, 177, 178, 208-214, 301-303, 309, 310

PRC 17, 245, 275, 276, 277

professionalisation 117, 118, 147, 177, 303, 306, 311, 320, 322, 385, 388

Racan, Ivica 137, 138

RCF *also see* regional conflict formation 17, 37, 47, 49, 71, 73, 80, 89, 108, 114, 234, 235, 297, 317

Regional Approach 17, 21, 37, 46, 54, 55, 64, 71, 92, 93, 94, 108, 126, 127, 130, 161, 163, 174, 184, 186, 189, 253, 256, 257, 300, 301, 317, 319, 343, 384

regional conflict formation *also see* RCF 7, 17, 30, 32, 37, 40, 43, 47, 52, 53, 56, 63, 70, 72, 89, 90, 108, 113, 114, 116, 124, 172, 182, 222, 225, 233, 236, 297, 317

regional cooperation 53, 55, 58, 59, 60, 62, 66, 71, 93, 98, 99, 100, 101, 103, 105, 106, 108, 119, 130, 132, 133, 141, 151, 161, 174, 184, 192, 193, 201, 203, 222, 246, 261, 266, 272, 300, 304, 307, 309, 312, 313, 317, 393

regional security complex 17, 26, 29, 37, 41, 70, 316

Regional Security Complex Theory *also see* RSCT 17, 26, 37, 297

Republika Srpska 18, 164, 170, 184, 232, 236, 311, 325

resilience 11, 14, 35, 324, 326

RSCT *also see* Regional Security Complex Theory 7, 17, 26, 27, 28, 29, 32, 33, 34, 35, 37, 38, 39, 40, 41, 42, 68, 69, 72, 297, 314

Russia 27, 38, 39, 49, 54, 58, 63, 67, 68, 74, 187, 204, 207, 208, 234, 325, 351, 365

SAA *also see* Stabilisation and Association Agreement 17, 60, 100, 131, 132, 138, 140, 191, 192, 198, 199, 200, 245, 248, 258, 260, 262, 265, 274, 275, 276, 293, 311, 370

SALW *also see* small arms and light weapons 17, 145, 146, 205, 206, 269, 272, 273, 339, 353, 364, 370, 371

sanctions 51, 54, 70, 119, 124, 172, 173, 174, 180, 181, 182, 183, 184, 186, 187, 188, 190, 222, 223, 226, 234, 293, 298, 299, 300, 330, 354, 384

SCG *also see* State Union of Serbia and Montenegro 18, 167, 176, 183, 186, 191, 193, 198, 199, 201, 204, 214, 223,

228, 305, 308, 310, 344, 387, 388
security community 7, 21, 29, 30, 32, 37, 41, 44, 46, 56, 58, 59, 60, 61, 62, 64, 67, 71, 74, 75, 83, 89, 98, 99, 100, 106, 109, 113, 131, 141, 162, 174, 179, 223, 247, 291, 297, 315, 318, 322, 323, 357
security dynamics 7, 23, 28, 29, 31, 32, 34, 35, 37, 38, 39, 40, 41, 43, 44, 45, 46, 47, 52, 56, 63, 72, 80, 83, 89, 324
security governance 9, 11, 22, 24, 25, 29, 30, 31, 34, 99, 137, 194, 197, 201, 203, 224, 232, 267, 305, 316, 322, 324, 325, 326, 387
security regime 7, 29, 30, 37, 40, 46, 47, 53, 54, 55, 63, 71, 72, 89, 94, 108, 113, 118, 130, 174, 184, 222, 237, 254, 258, 297, 300, 317, 319
security sector reform (SSR) 7, 8, 9, 13, 18, 21, 22, 26, 27, 28, 29, 31, 32, 33, 34, 35, 39, 51, 61, 62, 63, 70, 72, 74, 75, 76, 77, 78, 79, 80, 81, 82, 83, 84, 85, 86, 87, 88, 89, 90, 91, 92, 93, 94, 95, 96, 97, 99, 100, 103, 104, 105, 106, 107, 108, 109, 110, 113, 114, 116, 118, 119, 120, 121, 122, 123, 124, 125, 126, 127, 130, 131, 132, 133, 137, 141, 142, 143, 147, 156, 160, 161, 162, 163, 164, 165, 167, 168, 169, 170, 171, 172, 173, 174, 176, 179, 184, 185, 186, 189, 190, 192, 193, 197, 198, 201, 203, 208, 219, 221, 222, 223, 224, 225, 227, 231, 232, 233, 236, 241, 242, 247, 248, 251, 253, 255, 256, 257, 258, 259, 260, 261, 264, 265, 266, 267, 268, 271, 282, 283, 284, 289, 290, 291, 293, 295, 297, 299, 300, 301, 302, 303, 304, 305, 306, 307, 311, 313, 314, 315, 316, 318, 319, 320, 321, 322, 323, 324, 325, 326, 327, 338, 339, 349, 352, 356, 361, 377, 378, 379, 381
SEESAC 18, 105, 146, 165, 205, 206, 228, 272, 334, 370, 371
Serbian Armed Forces 8, 17, 18, 57, 74, 123, 167, 168, 169, 171, 172, 173, 174, 176, 179, 182, 188, 190, 192, 194, 195, 196, 197, 199, 200, 202, 204, 206, 207, 208, 209, 210, 212, 213, 214, 215, 216, 218, 220, 222, 223, 224, 225, 226, 227, 233, 238, 249, 292, 298, 301, 307, 330, 333, 342, 352, 355, 362, 366, 372, 381, 383, 385
Serbianisation 169, 222
SFRY 18, 72, 73, 114, 119, 123, 163, 167, 169, 180, 183, 206, 222, 225, 298, 305
Silajdzic, Haris 233, 245
small arms and light weapons *also see* SALW 17, 145, 165, 205
Socialist Federal Republic of Yugoslavia *also see* SFRY 18, 46, 72, 114, 336, 371
Stabilisation and Association Agreement *also see* SAA 17, 60, 100, 131, 190, 343, 344, 370
Stabilisation and Association Process 17, 21, 32, 37, 45,

60, 64, 86, 95, 130, 190, 304, 321, 343, 367
Stability Pact 18, 21, 35, 37, 58, 59, 64, 68, 72, 73, 74, 92, 97, 98, 99, 101, 105, 153, 178, 214, 240, 304, 317, 334, 340, 375
State Union of Serbia and Montenegro *also see* SCG 18, 19, 167, 174, 227, 305, 344
statehood 61, 71, 100, 123, 167, 179, 193, 203, 215, 222, 233, 248, 249, 250, 252, 256, 261, 289, 291, 304, 305, 310, 311, 314, 316, 318, 390
Sub-Regional Arms Control Agreement 54, 55, 174, 184, 188, 333, 366
temporality 25, 34, 37, 40, 71
The Hague 137, 138, 140, 164, 167, 175, 180, 185, 191, 198, 199, 200, 224, 264, 265, 294, 302, 307, 360
the High Representative (HR) 191, 213, 232, 239, 242, 244, 245, 258, 259, 262, 265, 268, 274, 275, 276, 281, 282, 290, 292, 293, 307, 347, 363
Tudjman, Franjo 52, 58, 113, 114, 115, 117, 118, 125, 128, 130, 131, 133, 134, 137, 143, 148, 149, 160, 163, 174, 266, 303, 304, 310, 384
Turkey 27, 38, 42, 43, 44, 45, 55, 59, 63, 67, 68, 69, 73, 74, 103, 347
Ukraine 74, 81, 110, 234, 325
UN Security Council 126, 181, 187

uncertainty 11, 22, 23, 24, 25, 58, 79, 167, 193, 203, 204, 222, 261, 293, 308, 311, 312, 314, 323, 326, 390
unintended consequences 125, 137, 326
United Nations 18, 38, 48, 51, 54, 63, 64, 67, 68, 69, 70, 73, 74, 76, 91, 115, 116, 117, 121, 122, 124, 125, 126, 128, 137, 145, 146, 147, 173, 174, 180, 181, 182, 183, 184, 187, 222, 223, 226, 231, 232, 234, 239, 242, 244, 248, 250, 253, 255, 269, 282, 289, 290, 292, 298, 300, 302, 309, 314, 316, 330, 334, 338, 339, 366, 370, 373, 374, 381, 385
visa liberalisation 101, 157, 217, 219, 283, 313, 392
VJ *also see* Army of the FRY 19, 170, 173, 189, 215, 222, 225, 228
VRS 18, 170, 234, 235, 238, 243, 268
VUCA-world 11, 22, 326
war crimes 104, 127, 137, 138, 141, 142, 168, 175, 197, 198, 199, 200, 201, 202, 203, 209, 215, 222, 223, 227, 228, 231, 240, 243, 244, 265, 266, 267, 274, 281, 306, 378
Washington Agreement 235, 251, 293
Western European Union Demining Mission 19, 127
WEU 19, 84, 91, 92, 110, 124, 127, 181, 226, 240, 251, 255, 257, 299, 302, 352, 370, 375
Yugoslav People's Army *also see* JNA 50, 169

BALKAN POLITICS AND SOCIETY

Edited by Jelena Dzankic and Soeren Keil

1 *Valery Perry (ed.)*
 Extremism and Violent Extremism in Serbia
 21st Century Manifestations of an Historical Challenge
 ISBN 978-3-8382-1260-9

2 *James Riding*
 The Geopolitics of Memory
 A Journey to Bosnia
 ISBN 978-3-8382-1311-8

3 *Ian Bancroft*
 Dragon's Teeth
 Tales from North Kosovo
 ISBN 978-3-8382-1364-4

4 *Viktoria Potapkina*
 Nation Building in Contested States
 Comparative Insights from Kosovo, Transnistria, and Northern Cyprus
 ISBN 978-3-8382-1381-1

5 *Soeren Keil, Bernhard Stahl (eds.)*
 A New Eastern Question?
 Great Powers and the Post-Yugoslav States
 ISBN 978-3-8382-1375-0

6 *Senada Zatagic*
 A Neglected Right
 Prospects for the Protection of the Right to Be Elected in Bosnia and Herzegovina
 ISBN 978-3-8382-1521-1

7 *Aarif Abraham*
 A Constitution of the People and How to Achieve It
 What Bosnia and Britain Can Learn From Each Other
 ISBN 978-3-8382-1516-7

8   *Giustina Selvelli*
     The Alphabet of Discord
     The Ideologization of Writing Systems on the Balkans since the
     Breakup of Multiethnic Empires
     ISBN 978-3-8382-1537-2

9   *Anastasiia Kudlenko*
     Security Governance in Times of Complexity
     The EU and Security Sector Reform in the Western Balkans,
     1991–2013
     ISBN 978-3-8382-1720-8

ibidem.eu